International Bank Management

International Bank Management

Dileep Mehta and Hung-Gay Fung

Blackwell
Publishing

350 Main Street, Malden, MA 02148-5020, USA
108 Cowley Road, Oxford OX4 1JF, UK
550 Swanston Street, Carlton, Victoria 3053, Australia

First published 2004 by Blackwell Publishing Ltd

Library of Congress Cataloging-in-Publication Data

Mehta, Dileep R., 1939–
   International bank management/Dileep Mehta and Hung-Gay Fung.
      p. cm.
Includes bibliographical references and index.
   ISBN 1-4051-1128-3 (hardcover: alk. paper)
1. Banks and banking, International–Management. 2. Bank management.
I. Fung, Hung-Gay. II. Title.
   HG3881.M422 2004
   332.1'5'068–dc21

                                                    2003006953

A catalogue record for this title is available from the British Library.
Set in 10/12½ Bembo
by Newgen Imaging Systems (P) Ltd, Chennai, India
Printed and bound in the United Kingdom
by TJ International, Padstow, Cornwall

For further information on
Blackwell Publishing, visit our website:
http://www.blackwellpublishing.com

Contents

List of Figures

List of Tables

Preface

In the past two decades, few enterprises have undergone as radical a change as the banking organization. Globalization of financial markets has been one of several major forces responsible for changing the character of the banking industry. As interrelated agents of change, advances in information technology and a shift in regulatory stance have affected not only the mode of conducting business in the banking arena but also its scope. If the goal of business education is to prepare students for a flourishing career in a business, which happens to be banking here, a focus on primarily domestic aspects of banking will hardly suffice. Educating students for the challenges facing the banking industry in the coming decade is made more difficult by the ever-increasing pace of change, making yesterday's management practices obsolete today.

Existing textbooks in the market place have adopted a variety of approaches to discuss the international dimensions of banking: a focus on domestic bank management with ancillary material pertaining to international banking; an exclusive focus on international banking through case method that highlights the complexity of international bank management with suitable abstraction of reality for expository convenience; and a macroeconomic perspective that focuses on issues related to international monetary economics and foreign exchange.

Our textbook rests on the foundation that integrates the following triad:

- risk-return tradeoff;
- unique or special barriers encountered in conducting cross-border business; and
- unique features of banking business.

Based on the premises of this triad, our endeavor aims at providing "under one roof" an up-to-date and integrated coverage of many important topics in international bank management ranging from foreign exchange markets, derivatives, country risk analysis, and asset-liability management to banking strategies. Analytical frameworks for many of these topics have been devised to accommodate vital ingredients of the decision-making process, and their applicability is illustrated with appropriate examples.

A course utilizing this textbook as its core will require a student to have a basic grounding in financial management and acquaintance with bank management in the "domestic" environment through either the classroom or workplace. Familiarity with elementary statistics will be helpful in understanding the material related to, say, derivatives; however, the textbook does not require a background in advanced mathematics or statistics.

Such a course will be appropriate for Master of Science (MS) or undergraduate students majoring in finance as well as practicing bankers keen on obtaining generalized insights in their profession. In addition, this textbook can also be used as a supplementary text in an MBA or undergraduate course in bank management when offering a stand-alone course is not feasible. Finally, selected material can also be fruitfully assigned to students taking international business courses.

During the process of developing this text, we have benefited from helpful comments and insights of bankers as well as our colleagues and students at several institutions. We would like to thank them, and especially Charles Guez (University of Houston), and Chip Ruscher (University of Arizona), who reviewed the manuscript for Blackwell Publishing. Obviously they are not responsible for remaining errors and omissions. We would also like to thank Seth Ditchik and Elizabeth Wald of Blackwell Publishing for expediting this project.

Last, but not least, we would like to dedicate our book to Marty and Linda for their unstinting support, understanding, and patience during all the years we have been working on this project.

PART I

Overview

CHAPTER 1

Basic Premises

LEARNING OBJECTIVES

- To obtain a bird's eye view of benchmark financial theories
- To learn why financial institutions are relevant
- To discern the role of various market hurdles in the market hierarchy
- To grasp the unique characteristics of banks

1.1 Introduction

The global environment in which financial institutions function has undergone rapid changes over the last two decades. Some of these changes could have been anticipated: consolidation in the banking industry or broadening of the scope of activities undertaken by banks is not surprising to observers of the industry. At the same time, other changes, such as the pace at which the banking business has embraced technology, have been vastly underrated both within the industry and outside. Further, these changes are still unfolding at such a rapid pace that a manager/observer cannot confidently predict what the banking business would look like in the foreseeable future. It is then virtually impossible for the manager to devise an ideal strategy. The best that the manager can hope is to develop the ability to discern and respond to changes in a timely and appropriate fashion. An understanding of fundamental forces that have molded the finance discipline in general and the financial institutions in particular is vital in this endeavor.

This chapter provides a broad brush picture of the major contributions to the finance discipline over the last four decades that have shaped not only our understanding of the finance function but also the practice of managing financial affairs. This description, in turn, facilitates comprehending description and analysis of the changing role of financial institutions such as banks in today's global economy.

1.2   Risk-Return Tradeoffs

The bedrock of finance theory is the nature of the relationship between return on an investment and the risk it entails. Risk is inversely related to the degree of certainty about obtaining the return: the higher the certainty, the lower the risk. Investing in a bank savings account involves little risk especially when the deposits are insured, whereas uncertain future prospects tend to make investing in a fledgling corporation a highly risky proposition. Although there is a consensus that investors demand a higher return for assuming higher risk, the precise nature of the tradeoff has been the focal point of the inquiry in the finance discipline. Four cornerstone theories in the second half of the twentieth century have enhanced our understanding of this tradeoff and in the process transformed the role played by important participants, such as banks, in the financial markets. These four theories are:

- the **Modigliani–Miller (MM) theory** of capital structure;
- the Markowitz–Sharpe–Lintner **capital asset pricing model (CAPM)**;
- the Black–Scholes **option pricing theory (OPT)**; and
- the Jensen–Meckling **agency theory**.

A brief description of the contributions of these theories will set the stage for understanding the role played by banks in the economy throughout the book.

1.2.1   MM theory of capital structure

The MM theory (see Modigliani and Miller 1958) examines the impact of changing the debt proportion in a firm's **capital structure** on its resource allocation process as well as its value. In the ideal impediment-free world where securities market participants obtain relevant information instantaneously without incurring significant uneven cost and process this information correctly (i.e. markets are *informationally efficient*); and can enter or exit the securities market without encountering hurdles such as transaction costs and taxes (i.e. markets are *perfect*), the firm's resource allocation process (hence its value) does not depend on how these resources are procured or how the firm devises its financial structure. The firm thus will decide on the acquisition of a real asset on its own merits and not on the way it is financed. One important implication of this theory is that a firm hedging its financial risk exposure will not increase its shareholders' wealth. This, in turn, implies that reliance on debt, a cheaper source of financing than equity, increases risk for the stockholder. Indeed, the risk premium demanded by stockholders is directly related to the debt-equity proportion in the firm's capital structure.

Of course, securities markets are not ideal; but the critical question is whether imperfections or inefficiencies (either by themselves or jointly) are *long-lasting* and at the same time capable of instigating *unambiguous, material* market distortions that in turn will make the resource allocation and financing processes interdependent. If distortions cannot be characterized in this way, how investments are financed (and thus the firm's capital structure) becomes a superfluous issue for inquiry.

Since banks and other financial institutions play a critical role in the firm's financing activities, validation (or its absence) of the MM theory has a significant bearing on the scope of bank activities.

1.2.2 Capital asset pricing model

So far, we have not defined risk in any precise sense. Any *unexpected* change in the return weighed with the likelihood of its occurrence is the foundation for measuring risk. The statistical measure representing risk is the variance, or its square root, the **standard deviation**. When an investor considers investing in more than one asset, that is, wants to create a port-folio of investments, Markowitz (1952) pointed out that the risk of the portfolio *cannot* be measured by the simple sum of the weighted risks of its components. A portfolio of unrelated investments, for instance, allows the investor to reduce some risk of individual invest-ments. As long as the trends in the returns are not closely correlated, the gains of some investments will compensate for the losses of others. The net effect is that the portfolio risk is less than the sum of risk of individual investments. The reduction in risk depends on the extent to which volatility in returns of individual investments move together: the smaller the comovement, the greater the reduction in risk of the portfolio. In finance literature, this phenomenon is described as *diversification*. Sharpe (1964) and Lintner (1965) extended the notion of the portfolio to the "market" portfolio – consisting of all risky securities ("assets") that are traded in the market – and devised the CAPM framework. They demon-strated that the risk for an individual security in an informationally efficient market is measured by its *contribution to the risk of the **market portfolio*** and not by the standard devia-tion of its returns (since the standard deviation measures the total risk). The total risk of an asset or investment is thus decomposed in two parts: systematic risk that the investor will assume, and the unsystematic risk that will be diversified away when the portfolio includes other assets. The systematic risk is typically measured in terms of an index widely known as "beta." The investor gets compensated for assuming only the systematic risk. Hence, the expected return on a security is given by the *sum* of the return on a risk-free asset (such as a government obligation), and the risk premium on the security is defined by the product of its beta and the market risk premium.

Because the MM theory and the CAPM share the common basis of efficient markets, their compatibility implies that a change in the capital structure (reflected in its debt–equity ratio) of a firm will induce a commensurate change in the beta of its stock.

Notice that investors are compensated for assuming only the systematic risk component of any security trading in the market place. If investors were to invest in fewer securities than those represented in the market portfolio, they would be unable to diversify risk to the extent that the market portfolio would; hence the compensation for risk would not be com-mensurate with risk assumption. A financial institution, such as a mutual fund or a bank, allows an investor to circumvent this return reduction when, say, resource limitations prevent an investor from actually holding a portfolio that resembles the market.

Further, the CAPM requires that market participants allocate their funds in only two investments, risk-free security and the market portfolio, depending on how much risk they want to assume: if they do not want to assume any risk, they should invest exclusively in the risk-free security; otherwise they should invest at least a portion of their capital endowment in the market portfolio.[1] Thus, they do not exercise a choice in excluding some securities trading in the market, nor in investing in larger or smaller proportion in a given security (the proportions are dictated by the market portfolio). Finally, the CAPM does not distinguish between "good" risk and "bad," although any unexpectedly high return (a "good" risk) is certainly liked by the investor.

1.2.3 Option pricing theory

Black and Scholes (1973) showed through the OPT that an individual investor can manage the risk by selling ("writing") or buying **derivatives** that are based on securities. Thus individuals do not necessarily have to hold all securities represented in the market portfolio. Two basic forms of derivatives are **futures** and **options**. In turn, options are divided into **puts** and **calls**. When individuals *sell* a put option, they assume the downside ("bad") risk and receive appropriate compensation for that. If they *buy* the call option, they enjoy the "good" risk, that is, "unexpectedly high" returns without assuming the downside risk; of course, they have to pay the premium to the seller of the call option. For the firm, the OPT has the advantage of risk management, that is, altering the firm's risk profile, without tinkering with its asset or capital structure. Organized markets dealing in derivatives have been striving to satisfy customer needs for risk management products by offering innovative products; however, these markets by their very nature lag behind in meeting customer needs. Banks have been playing an important complementary role by offering customized derivative products that help their customers in fine-tuning risk management.

1.2.4 Agency theory

Like MM and the CAPM, the OPT is founded on the premise of an informationally efficient market where arbitrage action is effective in instantaneously removing any distortions in the pricing of a security. As a result, prices will fully and correctly reflect all the available information. By contrast, the agency theory's basic assumption is that there is asymmetric information in the principal–agent relationship (see Jensen and Meckling 1976). Thus, the principal who has delegated a task to the agent does not have perfect knowledge of the agent's plans or activities. As a result, the principal has to incur monitoring efforts to ensure that the agent does not act against the principal's interest. Suppose there is a highly risky project that has a small systematic risk component and attractive returns. Although the project may be highly desirable from the owner-principals' perspective, manager-agents may choose *not* to undertake it. This is because such investment may entail a failure, tarnishing management reputation and thereby its wealth. The agency theory thus complements the classical theories based on informationally efficient markets and enriches the finance discipline. As we shall see below, inefficient financial markets have been the major justification for the existence of financial institutions, as banks play a major role in reducing agency cost in such markets.

Efficient markets also presume that owners armed with perfect knowledge *control* a firm's allocation of resources. Absence of such presumption along with the agency cost problem raises an important issue: which party – owner-principal or management-agent – ultimately controls the firm's resources? When the management-agent exploits owner ignorance in the resource allocation process that is not in the best interest of owners, banks play an important monitoring role in mitigating the agency problem by holding management accountable through holding equity or extending loans in the firm.

Inefficient markets raise an important problem of **moral hazard** with respect to *bank* management. Moral hazard occurs, for instance, when creditors, who would not have provided additional funding to a bank, loan the money because of their strong belief that the government would bail out the bank in distress. This implicit guarantee by the government thus encourages the bank to pursue unsound management practices. If the government has the right information at the right time, and has the desire as well as the means to prevent the bank from undertaking crisis-prone decisions, moral hazard would be prevented. This is the major argument of advocates for strong regulatory frameworks, who also believe that the market discipline is inadequate because, among other things, the market does not have the right information on a timely basis. The ensuing complementarity of the regulatory frameworks and the market discipline requires reassessment with the globalization of financial markets. Although these macro-aspects are fascinating, a rigorous, systematic investigation is outside the scope of this textbook, given our focus on bank management at the micro level.

1.3 Why Financial Institutions Are Necessary

Financial institutions in an economy pool the savings of investors and invest them in enterprises or assets that generate uncertain returns. In this section, we consider the pivotal role of financial institutions in an economy. In a basic sense, the existence of financial institutions is justifiable only if they can improve the risk-return tradeoff for participants in the financial markets.

1.3.1 Actuarial risk

The CAPM theory described above assumes that an asset is infinitely divisible; hence, an investor having a small endowment can still construct a portfolio that mirrors the market portfolio. In reality, such a possibility does not exist. This divergence underscores the critical relevance of the notion of actuarial risk and the pivotal role played by financial institutions in making it achievable by investors. Suppose an investor has $1,000 to invest and she seeks to invest it in a company whose shares are selling at $1,000 apiece and this company faces a 10 percent chance of failure. If a failure occurs, the investor will lose all her money. Thus the likelihood of 10 percent is meaningless for our investor. Now suppose there are 100 investors each with $1,000 of investment funds and there are 100 investments each with a chance of failure of 10 percent. If investors pool their funds and form a financial institution – a bank – the bank would have $100,000 to loan to these companies. If the bank loans $1,000 to each of the 100 investments with a 10 percent probability of failure, the combined loss would be $10,000. As a result, each investor would face a loss of $100 ($10,000/100).

Though actuarial risk may look similar to portfolio risk because they both involve some risk reduction, there is a fine distinction between the two. Consider the investor in the above example: if these investments were unrelated (uncorrelated or independent in a statistical sense) and if our investor were allowed to evenly distribute her $1,000 in each of the investments, the impact would have been the same for actuarial and portfolio risk considerations. Thus, whenever one of the two conditions, uncorrelated investments and a perfectly divisible allocable amount, is not met, the two notions of risk diverge but still remain complementary. Whereas the portfolio risk focuses on a group of investments from the perspective of an investor, the actuarial risk considers an investment from the viewpoint of a *group* of investors. In the process, the actuarial risk embodies the risk component that is not accommodated in the portfolio risk consideration.

1.3.2 Informational efficiency

As noted above, the major theories in finance (with the exception of the agency theory) assume that information can be obtained and correctly processed by an investor with minimal cost. When this cost contains a significant amount of fixed cost, it distorts the return–risk relationship and creates an important roadblock for entering or exiting the marketplace for some investors. A financial institution like a bank enables these investors to minimize the adverse impact of the roadblock. Along with creating a pool of investors for risk sharing, a bank also creates economy of scale in carrying out financial transactions that may increase the return and/or reduce the risk for these investors. Because of its financial resources, a financial institution such as an investment bank has better access to relevant information than the individual investor. Furthermore, the investment bank uses a staff of skilled analysts to research investment opportunities. With a thorough analysis of the investment information, the investment bank can reduce risk and increase return. The information gathering and processing skills of a bank far exceed those of most individual investors, especially those with limited investment funds. By paying the bank commissions and transaction fees, individual investors can receive the benefits of compiling and analyzing the information at a fraction of the cost they would have individually incurred.

In brief, financial institutions play a pivotal role in an economy in two areas: they facilitate attaining actuarial risk through risk pooling, and they enable investors to achieve informational efficiency.[2]

1.4 Competitive Markets and Impediments

A financial market often functions in an environment containing forces that impede its effectiveness. We have seen above the impediment created by costly information search. But impediments come in a variety of forms. We will classify them in two broad categories: government-induced and structure-based impediments. Governments intervene in the marketplace through actions such as

- *taxes* on gains;
- *tariffs* on transactions;
- *quotas* on the size or number of transactions;
- *laws* that limit market activities; and
- *regulations* that require, say, additional administrative work.

These interventions function to protect or enhance the net welfare of one segment of society and result in net additional costs for other segments.

In addition to government-induced impediments, financial markets also face impediments associated with the very nature of markets themselves. The *market structure* creates conventions that often prevent financial institutions from discarding or enhancing their established roles. For instance, a commercial bank embarking on offering a brokerage service for securities trading to its customers may have difficulty attracting customers to this service when this service is not perceived germane to the bank's primary function. Further, it may have to over-come customer resistance due to loyalty to institutions that currently provide these services; so much so that even if the commercial bank offers the lowest cost and fastest brokerage serv-ice, it may still be unable to lure new customers who have already established a comfortable relationship with traditional brokerage houses. Habits, past experience, desire for conformity or differentiation, preconceived notions, prejudices, lethargy, trepidation, and ignorance are some of the societal forces whose impact is difficult to modify or eliminate.

Impediments create a *challenge* for financial institutions by superimposing additional costs for their services. Suppose enactment of a new tax law imposes a surcharge on the passive income of interest on deposits with a financial institution. Effective enforcement of the law may require financial institutions to report the names and earnings of depositors to tax authorities. The resultant reporting cost reduces the expected return for depositors or own-ers of the financial institutions. Financial institutions may offset this reduction for depositors by offering higher returns on some types of deposits and shifting costs to other products or services they sell, or to the stockholders. (Often, financial institutions maintain returns at their pre-impediment standards by assuming additional risk. This new tax law then results in lower returns and/or increased risk for stockholders.) Thus the challenge faced by the financial institutions is how to minimize the adverse impact of the new tax law.

While impediments may hinder financial markets, they also present *opportunities* for enhanc-ing a financial institution's profitability. It may, for instance, engineer new products to circumvent impediments and their associated costs. In turn, these instruments improve the return-risk profile by increasing return and/or decreasing risk for its clients. This profitability may even be sustained over a relatively long period through ensuring that new products (a) fall outside the realm of current regulations and are not subjected to new regulations, and (b) have innovat-ive features which inhibit competitors from duplicating them in the short term.

It should be noted that when taxes, regulations and laws have a *universally uniform* impact on related − competitive or complementary − activities, they cease to have any impact on choice of an alternative course of action, and they will neither represent an opportunity nor a challenge. In other words, impediments that matter must have a materially differentiable impact on alternative courses of actions. For instance, if all nations adopt and enforce the **bank capital adequacy** requirement in identical fashion, the regulation pertaining to capital adequacy ceases to have any impact on a bank's choice of domicile.

1.5   Market Hierarchies

Markets provide a forum or mechanism for exchange. Markets can be classified in three categories: goods, financial, and foreign exchange. The goods market is the basis of all markets. Initially, goods were bartered in exchange for other goods. This system of exchange became a cumbersome method of matching buyers and sellers with the goods they desired. Emergence of currency as a medium of exchange has allowed market participants to overcome the handicaps of the barter system. Currency not only facilitates a transaction at a given time, but also serves as a store of value (i.e. facilitating transactions that are at different points in time).

With the advent of currency, the **financial market** was born. Rather than exchanging goods for goods, currency was exchanged for goods. A currency is typically issued by a government in order to insure its value (i.e. its ability to purchase goods) in the sovereign state. A critical characteristic of the financial products including money is that they do not have any intrinsic value and their worth is derived directly from the goods market.[3] Thus, the goods market could exist without the financial market but the financial market is entirely dependent upon the goods market.

Because different sovereign governments issue different currencies, one currency may prove useless in another country. To overcome the national barrier, **foreign exchange markets** emerged for exchanging one country's currency for another's. Thus, the existence of a foreign exchange market depends upon the existence of a financial market; however, the financial market can exist even in the absence of the foreign exchange market.

This asymmetric relationship among the three markets has one noteworthy implication. If the goods markets are impediment-free – that is, competitive – financial (and, therefore, foreign exchange) markets will also be competitive. In this case, if a government tries to superimpose controls, say, solely on currency trading, financial market participants may circumvent these controls and render them ineffectual through arbitraging in securities denominated in two different currencies. At the same time, competitiveness of financial or foreign exchange markets does not rest on a competitive goods market. By the same token, competitive foreign exchange markets do not necessarily require competitive financial markets.

A list of some of the impediments associated with the three markets is provided in Table 1.1.

1.6   Uniqueness of a Bank

The commercial bank plays *three* primary roles in the financial market:

- information processing;
- risk sharing; and
- money creation.

Table 1.1 Market hierarchy and related impediments

Market	Impediment	Risk/Opportunities
Goods market	Tariffs and quotas	• Protection for domestic producers against foreign competition • Losses for importers
Financial market	Taxes Laws Regulations (registration of securities, reporting standards, etc.)	• Increase in transaction cost • Creation of new products and markets
Foreign exchange market	Dual rate Fixed rate	• Creation of lopsided payoffs to some traders through differential exchange rates • Cheaper imports • Reduced competitiveness of exports

First, the bank collects and processes information. The bank collects information on both its depositors who provide funds and borrowers who represent investment opportunities for the deposit funds. The bank allows the depositors and the prospective borrowers to avoid the *search cost* of directly finding each other. Further, the bank's specialized resources for screening loan candidates reduce the likelihood of default faced by the depositors on their own. Since the bank undertakes investments in specialized resources on its own account, depositors are able to share the **default risk** not only with one another but also with the shareholders of the bank. As a result, depositors are only concerned with the viability of the bank, and not of individual borrowing entities. Through this process, the bank fulfills its second role of risk sharing. Finally, a bank loan to a business reduces the information asymmetry for other investors through a signal regarding credit worthiness of this entity. Resale of loans with recourse and securitization (explained in detail in Chapter 4) reduce the asymmetry in a more explicit fashion.

In order to sharpen the focus on the role played by a commercial bank, it is useful to consider two other **financial intermediaries**, investment banks and insurance companies. The investment bank engineers specific financial products that are tailored to suit the needs of their customers. To accomplish this task, it focuses on gathering and analyzing information pertaining to its customers' needs. Because the prototype investment bank does not undertake investment activities on its own account, its customers bear the risk of investments on their own. Thus, the investment bank supplies its customers the information, but does not offer them an actuarial risk sharing function.

An insurance company, on the other hand, specializes in risk sharing. Unlike the investment bank, an insurance company (another major financial intermediary) does not gather information on customers' investment needs; instead, it attracts a large number of customers who fund each other in the eventuality of a specific adversity such as a fire or a death. By collectively sharing each other's risk, the insurance company's customers minimize their individual loss in the event that the insured risk materializes.

The commercial bank has basically straddled a position between the investment bank, which specializes in information, and the insurance company, which specializes in risk sharing. (Although a mutual fund offers the advantages of information compiling-processing and achieving risk reduction, its inability to assume risk as an independent entity – intermediary – makes it resemble an investment bank rather than a commercial bank.) With the advances in information technology and the trend toward integration of global financial markets, the lines of demarcation among these financial entities are getting blurred. *Still, it is the third role that preserves the uniqueness of the bank among all other financial intermediaries: the bank serving as a critical link in the money creation process.*

Suppose a depositor deposits $100 with a bank, and the bank determines that only $25 will be withdrawn from that account in the foreseeable future. As a result, the bank loans out $75. To the extent that the borrower does not withdraw the loan in cash but instead writes checks on the bank, the bank has created $75 worth of an additional asset or money. Sovereign governments have traditionally conferred this role exclusively on commercial banks for at least the following two reasons:

- It facilitates the task of controlling or manipulating the money supply for the government's socio-political-economic agenda.
- Every society faces the "social hazard" of thefts by some entities (e.g. tax evasion or illicit transactions) that superimpose cost on other entities in the society. Since these thefts can be potentially eliminated only at prohibitive costs, the government aims at keeping them below some tolerable level (Millon-Cornett 1988). One way of accomplishing this is to appoint banks as exclusive agents for monitoring or exposing thefts that involve monetary transactions. Banks can thus serve a vital role in keeping thefts at a tolerable level.[4]

1.7   Risk Dimensions of the Banking Business

When a bank accepts deposit, it incurs explicit or implicit cost. The bank invests a portion of this deposit to provide its owners with an adequate return in excess of the cost of deposit. The portion invested (or kept in non-earning, liquid form) will depend, among other things, on the contract with the depositors. When the bank accepts a deposit for a known or fixed period of time, and loans out a predetermined portion of funds for the same maturity with complete assurance of repayment on time, there is no risk involved for the bank. Mismatched funds, in terms of the differing magnitude of inflows and outflows at a given point in time, are then a source of risk for the bank. We consider two basic situations below.

When the bank, after making the loan with a given deposit, receives payment before the maturity of the deposit, it faces the task of reinvesting these funds. If the reinvestment rate has decreased, the bank faces the prospects of receiving a smaller profit upon maturity. This is *reinvestment risk*, one component of *interest rate risk*.

Similarly, when the depositor faces low or no cost for premature withdrawal and chooses to withdraw funds earlier than expected by the bank, the bank has to raise funds from another depositor, or sell the loan or another asset. Since the value of an asset generating future benefits will decline with an increase in the interest rate, either of these two actions will mean a reduction in profitability for the bank, if the interest rates have gone up. This is *liquidity risk*, arising from inadequate liquidity, that is, the other component of interest rate risk.

Liquidity risk arises even when interest rates do not change. If the resale market is distorted by government-induced or market structure-related impediments, premature liquidation of an asset will not fetch its intrinsic value, and the bank will face **liquidation** risk. Liquidity risk is particularly important for long-life assets. As a result, capital market securities are often distinguished from **money market** instruments on the basis of the liquidity risk dimension.

Financial assets derive their value from discounting net future benefits with the appropriate interest rate. A change in the interest rate then leads to a change in the asset value. Since an interest rate may contain a risk premium reflecting market attitude toward risk, a change in this attitude may make a financial asset more or less attractive than before. Often, such a change is attributed to *market risk*, just another dimension of interest rate risk.

When a loan is not repaid on time (*delinquency risk*) or will not be paid ever (*default risk*, the extreme form of delinquency), even efficient resale markets or ex ante matched maturities do not help the bank in avoiding liquidity risk. This gives rise to *credit risk*, comprised of delinquency risk and default risk. In a purely domestic context, when a **counterparty** fails to deliver on its part of the contractual obligation, the bank faces *settlement risk*. It should be obvious that settlement risk here is just another form of credit risk. Thus, the basic risks faced by a bank stem from interest rate movements, inefficient resale markets, and inability or unwillingness of the borrower or counterparty to meet in a timely fashion its obligations arising from its contract with the bank.

One consequence of these risks should be noted. When depositors perceive, rightly or wrongly, that the bank investments are too risky for the safety of their deposits, they may en masse attempt to withdraw deposits as quickly as possible, threatening the bank's very existence. Given the interrelationships among banks in a system, when depositors panic and create a "bank run," the banking system faces a crisis. This eventuality is the *systemic risk* that monetary authorities want to avoid because of the vital role played by banks in the money creation process.

Authorities can exercise a combination of alternatives such as (a) suspension of deposit withdrawals through devices like declaring bank holidays; (b) deposit insurance; (c) being a lender of last resort; and (d) preventive regulations and supervision that would inspire confidence in the system's viability. The first measure is drastic and may be too strong a medicine in a given situation. The next two alternatives could present a potential for "moral hazard." For instance, when bank deposits are insured, bank owners who have relatively little capital invested in the bank will be tempted to gamble with the insured funds in order to increase the return on equity: if risky investments perform well, the bank owners will get a high return; if investments turn sour, the burden of these losses will be primarily borne by the insuring agency. As a result, the last alternative, whereby regulations pertaining to reserve and capital requirements are imposed on banks, is employed.

When a bank conducts business across borders, it faces the risk of changes in the foreign currency's value, that is, *foreign exchange risk*. Further, assessment of credit risk acquires an additional dimension not encountered in the purely domestic situation: *country risk*. Because the bank now faces differentiated legal, regulatory, and fiscal hurdles along with the new and distinct culture for conducting business, the bank faces additional challenges. When the international dimension is introduced, the nature of the risk encountered by the bank has not changed, only its *magnitude*.

1.8 Conclusion

This chapter first briefly discussed the theories that provide insights in return–risk tradeoff in financial activities. It then examined the basic role of financial intermediaries in general and the commercial bank in particular as they function in the financial market. This role revolves around improving the risk–return tradeoffs for investors through (a) placing their funds in suitable investment opportunities, and (b) where that compatibility between investors and investments does not exist, transforming either the time or the risk dimension. Time dimension transformation requires the intermediary to assume the risk of mismatched maturities (or the interest rate and the liquidity risks). The commercial bank, as an intermediary, also allows depositors to avoid or minimize default or credit risk through personally assuming the risk. The overall risks are reduced through portfolio construction or through risk sharing achieved by bringing together a large number of investors and investments. Although the commercial bank shares (or is precluded from playing) the above roles with other financial institutions, it plays the exclusive role of serving as a critical link in the money creation process.

The risk–return tradeoffs that still remain are shaped by impediments in the market place, whether it is the goods or the financial market. In turn, impediments either stem from the very structure of the market or arise from government intervention in the market place through taxes, tariffs, quotas, regulations, and laws. Because of its unique role in the money creation process, the bank is subjected to special regulations and laws. When the international dimension is introduced, the onus or advantage of these regulations and laws undergoes further transformation, in addition to creating foreign-exchange risk for market participants. In the rest of the book, challenges and opportunities arising from introduction of the international dimension on bank management will be explored.

DISCUSSION QUESTIONS

1 Explain why financial institutions are necessary in an economy.

2 Suppose 30 securities are traded in a market. Joseph has invested in 3 of the securities, whereas Maria has invested in all 30 securities in proportion of their market values. Both Joseph and Maria expect to earn 12 percent on their investments.

    a Is it possible to say whose portfolio is more desirable (in terms of less risk) – Joseph's or Maria's?

    b What additional information would you need to rank the two portfolios?

3 Mr Jones, a neighbor and friend of Ms Shaw, knows that Gamut National Bank headed by Ms Shaw pays 1 percent less on comparable deposits than other banks in the area. He still maintains his checking account with Gamut National Bank, although he does not obtain – nor does he anticipate obtaining – any special services from the bank. How would you reconcile Mr Jones' maintaining the account with Gamut National in the framework of efficient financial markets?

4 Absentee owners of a closely held firm have told the managers that the firm is too risky for their liking: the returns on assets are very volatile, and the volatility in the return on equity is further aggravated by the firm's excessive financial leverage. Managers face a dilemma. They can liquidate some risky business activities and pay off some of the debt. But that would entail huge liquidation costs, as well as prepayment penalties on loan reduction. What alternatives would you recommend the managers to explore?

5 What are market impediments in the financial markets and how do they affect the financial institutions?

6 Several small countries in a region decided to form a union. Their goal has been that goods, services, capital, and people should move freely within the union, that is, without being hampered by any taxes, tariffs, or quotas. They have also felt that a single currency would be ultimately desirable. Their action plan calls for first abolishing all the intra-union border tariffs; then harmonizing income and sales taxes; and in the interim creating a framework that would allow mutual conversion of member countries' currencies at fixed rates that would facilitate (a) the task of creating the single currency, and (b) promote the intra-union trade by reducing the risk of currency conversion. Evaluate this course of action in light of the market hierarchy notion.

7 Of the several roles that financial institutions play, which one(s) is (are) unique to the commercial bank? Why?

8 What risks does a bank incur?

9 A typical US bank earns a rate of return around 1 percent.

   a Do you think that this return is adequate for investors holding bank securities in their portfolios? Why?
   b How would your answer in (a) change, if the US regulatory authorities were to abolish both the reserve requirements and deposit insurance?

10 In the USA, regulations in the past prevented commercial banks, investment banks and insurance companies from encroaching on each other's territory. What likely consequences emerge now that these regulations are phased out?

11 Under the perfect market assumption of MM, there is no major role for banks. In recent years, it is suggested that **financial innovations** and deregulation have propelled the financial market toward perfection. Hence, some observers predict that banks would become as extinct as dinosaurs. Do you agree? Why?

NOTES

1   When investors want to assume more risk than the market portfolio, they borrow (or negatively invest) in the risk-free security.

2   Several studies provide more detailed analyses of these imperfections (e.g. Benston and Smith 1976 focus on scale economies in information production).

3   While financial assets do not have any intrinsic value in themselves, they are critical in reshaping consumption over time. But that requires that investors in financial assets should have "faith" in the investments when they acquire them: when financial markets are not competitive, the government needs to step in and insure that investors pay (obtain) "fair value" upon their acquisition (disposal). This is then one rationale for regulation of the financial markets.

   In so far as *money* is concerned, the government is directly involved in preserving its value, since it has the monopoly for issuing money – or granting such rights to its agents. In turn, the value of money is inversely related to the value of goods and services in general. Hence, economic or political agenda may nudge the government toward *regulating* the financial markets and the agents entrusted with issuing money or its substitutes.

4   Consider, for instance, the regulation that requires the US banks to report to authorities any single transaction in excess of $10,000. Although its effectiveness may be questionable, it does complicate the life of a drug trafficker in moving the cash around.

PART II

Foundation

CHAPTER 2

Globalization of Commercial Banking

LEARNING OBJECTIVES

- To analyze different organizational forms of international banking
- To describe major international banking activities
- To highlight important characteristics of a global financial market

2.1 Historical Background

Banking activities across national borders have exhibited several notable patterns in the post-World War II era. Near the end of World War II, various nations met at Bretton Woods, New Hampshire and agreed that the Great Depression of the 1930s was unnecessarily prolonged by widely adopted economic measures, such as unilateral **devaluations**,[1] tariffs, export subsidies, and import quotas. The "Rules of the Game" instituted by the **Bretton Woods Agreement** meant that individual member countries would, among other things, commit to the fixed exchange rate system[2] and undertake a currency devaluation only as a last resort to correct chronic economic conditions. The **International Monetary Fund (IMF)**, a multilateral agency, was created to work with member countries facing crises: it would help a member country (a) assess whether the crisis was sufficiently serious to warrant devaluation; (b) determine the size of devaluation that would avert the crisis; and (c) help arrange financing to maintain the **exchange rate** when the crisis would not warrant devaluation.

The Bretton Woods Agreement dominated the international monetary scene until 1973. The banks' role during this era (1945–73) can be characterized as follows.

- Typically, changes in the exchange rates were infrequent; however, any such changes were of large magnitude. Foreign exchange activities of banks, as a result, were primarily confined to the **transaction motive**, and the **hedging** or **speculative motive**[3] received the spotlight only when an exchange rate change was considered imminent.

- Foreign direct private investment flows significantly increased, primarily to circumvent tariffs, quotas, taxes, and regulatory roadblocks hampering cross-border trade in goods, services, and currencies. Prior to 1973, multinational firms were typically "multi-domestic" in that their foreign subsidiaries were self-contained and inter-subsidiary business remained peripheral. Banks' foreign units helped foreign subsidiaries of the multinational firms in obtaining local intelligence, raising funds in local currencies, and facilitating funds transfer activities with the parent organization. Trade financing remained perhaps the most dominant international banking activity.
- Initial post-World War II reconstruction efforts and development activities involved multilateral agencies like the **World Bank**, or direct government initiatives such as the Marshall Plan for the Western European economies. Private bank involvement in providing any medium- or long-term funding to governments was virtually non-existent.
- Regulations on foreign direct private investment and inconvertibility of some, but not all, currencies did encourage banks to develop "Eurocurrencies" and offshore markets (to be discussed in Chapter 4). Banks increasingly became instrumental in satisfying the huge appetite for funds by multinational firms, especially since offshore markets remained the domain of banks.

Two major events in the early 1970s dramatically changed the above patterns: the demise of the Bretton Woods system, and the oil crisis. By the late 1960s, currencies belonging to the members of the Bretton Woods system were hopelessly misaligned. For instance, European economies had smartly recovered from the ravages of World War II by 1960. Still, they were loath to revalue their currencies because that would reflect their economic strength. On the other hand, escalated war effort by the USA in Vietnam coupled with the Great Society program initiated by the Johnson administration in the latter half of the 1960s unleashed inflationary forces that only managed to distort further the misaligned Bretton Woods system. In 1971, the Bretton Woods fixed exchange rate system was a terminal case, and its official demise occurred in 1973. Major currencies since then have embraced the floating rate system, especially vis-à-vis the US dollar.

The Oil Producing and Exporting Countries (OPEC) decided to cope with the inflationary spiral of the late 1960s by tripling the crude oil prices in 1973. Oil importing countries, both industrialized and developing, felt the shock of the oil price increase in the escalating deficits in their current account balances, since they could not immediately cut back on their energy consumption nor increase overnight their exports that would pay the higher energy bills. OPEC members, experiencing surpluses in their current account balances, were reluctant or unable to finance deficits of oil importing countries, and chose instead to deposit funds on a short-term basis with US banks. During the 1970s, US banking activities in the international sphere, as a result, underwent two major changes.

- Given the inability of multilateral agencies to finance nations' deficits, the task fell on the commercial banks to perform the classical function of intermediation through funding medium-to-long-term needs of oil importing countries with short-term deposits of

OPEC members. The twist, however, was that the borrowers were sovereign governments rather than private entities. Ironically, oil price increases that resulted from inflationary pressures ended up emasculating economic measures aimed at subduing inflation in the USA and elsewhere.

- At the same time, increased energy cost required reallocation of resources, a process that reached its peak in the USA in the early 1980s. The magnitude and net impact of inflationary forces all throughout the 1970s remained uncertain, and this uncertainty led to increased volatility in both interest and exchange rates. As the 1970s progressed, bank loans to governments shifted from industrialized nations to developing or emerging economies, both oil exporting and importing countries.

In 1979, oil prices were again raised by the OPEC group. In 1982, inability to sustain oil revenues because of a dramatic drop in oil demand forced Mexico and Venezuela (two major OPEC members) to declare a debt service moratorium. As their floating-rate based loans were denominated in the US dollar, the cost of these loans – both private and governmental – skyrocketed in the wake of the climbing US interest rates and soaring dollar value in the early 1980s. A reduction in revenues and increases in debt service adversely affected their ability to service debt. Internal factors such as diverting currency reserves from genuine development needs to domestic political expediencies as well as capital flight only worsened the crisis. The crisis spread to other countries, and by the end of 1985, 15 countries had $9.6 billion interest arrears on their long-term obligations (Kim 1993). Bank behavior during the 1980s exhibited the following pattern.

- The debt crisis of the 1980s caught banks by surprise and largely unprepared. Further, banks had not faced such a crisis in the recent past. As a result, they handled the crisis in a tactical, ad hoc fashion. Help by the US government under the Baker and Brady plans (discussed in Chapter 8) helped banks to some extent, although these initiatives did not resolve the crisis.
- In light of the above experience with the emerging economies,
  - banks switched to extending loans to sovereigns in the *industrialized* nations often at a razor-thin margin; and
  - banks also started to focus on catering to the private sector's need for containing risks in goods, financial, and currency markets as well as funds for mergers and acquisitions.

In 1994–5, Mexico faced another currency crisis. Abolition of controls in the goods and financial markets over the previous decade led to a rapid increase in imports. High interest rates, combined with the fixed exchange rate, made returns on Mexican investments attractive to foreign banks and their customers, and induced significant capital inflow from abroad. This inflow in turn encouraged imports and allowed the Mexican government to postpone implementation of unpalatable corrective measures.

Mexican banks' short-term borrowing from foreign sources increased either because of their own volition or due to foreign lenders' preference for keeping their funds in interest-bearing bank deposits.[4] In either case, increased liquidity encouraged Mexican banks to aggressively finance both household consumption and working capital needs of domestic businesses. In turn, such aggressive financing meant an increasing proportion of marginal or non-performing loans. Macroeconomic indices, however, remained positive in terms of low inflation rate and fiscal budget surplus.

A bailout by the IMF called for restructuring of the Mexican banking sector in return for a loan package. At the same time, Mexico responded to the currency crisis by removing the impediment of the fixed exchange rate, that is, it allowed the exchange rate to float. The destabilizing impact of the currency crisis was contained within a relatively short time period.[5]

The South-East Asian currency crisis surfaced and become a worldwide event in mid-1997. Countries affected were Thailand, South Korea, Malaysia, Indonesia, and the Philippines. There is widespread agreement that export-orientation of these countries deepened the impact of the crisis in terms of both the unemployment rate and inflation rate. Given the strong economic fundamentals of these countries, however, the crisis and its depth took observers, market participants, and policy makers by surprise. So much so that extensive analysis of the crisis has failed to forge an agreement on the causes responsible for it as well as its implications, as discussed in detail in Chapter 8. Attempts to resolve the crisis constituted a combination of (a) overall financial commitments to the tune of about $50 billion by various multilateral agencies that parceled out the funds to individual countries by attaching varying conditions for financial reforms (especially the banking sector), and (b) unilateral, ad hoc actions by individual governments. The latter actions were often antithetical to the financial reforms desired by the multilateral agencies; a noteworthy example was Malaysia, which imposed stringent currency controls.

In August 1998, Russia not only suspended debt service on its treasury bills but also withdrew its support from the ruble. Economic liberalization policies had failed to quell foreign investors' anxieties regarding ineffectual tax collections, a vulnerable banking system and a paralyzed but corrupt political system in the face of rising unemployment. In the aftermath of the Russian crisis in August 1998, investor attention turned to Brazil whose economy was suffering from excessive fiscal deficit and an overvalued, **pegged currency**. An aid package arranged by IMF for $42 billion in exchange for Brazil's promise to reduce the fiscal deficit helped abate the potential crisis that would have spread to other non-industrialized nations.

The crisis, however, flared again in January 1999 when one of the Brazilian states defaulted on its dollar-denominated obligations. The Brazilian government had failed to make any progress on containing the fiscal deficit. An initial devaluation of 8 percent was hardly adequate, and was followed by Brazil's decision to let float its currency, subsiding the crisis at least temporarily.

Currency crises were not just confined to emerging or developing economies. In the early 1990s, Sweden, Finland, and the UK suffered from heavy reserve losses due to their pegged, overvalued currencies. France also faced an attack on its currency in 1993, and the crisis was barely averted by the major modification in the Exchange Rate Mechanism (ERM), a form of fixed exchange rate system adopted by the members of the European Union (EU).[6]

During the 1980s and 1990s, many countries (industrialized as well as emerging economies) suffered from currency crises. These crises were instigated, sustained, or abetted by distortions (impediments) in the foreign exchange market. Further, the universal vogue of market-based economies since the mid-1980s has spawned two developments: a virtual end of central planning and privatization. These developments, along with the increasing integration of financial markets across nations, have managed not only to spread crises across national borders (the arguable impact of the Russian crisis on Brazil, for instance) but also to change the scope of bank activities.[7]

This historical backdrop, admittedly broad brush, allows us to explore factors that have transformed the banking industry worldwide in the last two decades of the twentieth century. This chapter first discusses the organizational structure of a bank pursuing international banking activities. Section 2.3 briefly explains the scope of international banking activities. Section 2.4 discusses various factors that have influenced the increasing globalization of financial markets. The final section provides the summary of the chapter.

2.2 Structure of an International Banking Organization

The appropriate organizational form is intricately related to the scope of international activities that a bank wants to pursue. Further, a bank may adopt several forms in a country, since these forms are not necessarily mutually exclusive. Typical forms provide a range: correspondent banking relationships, representative offices, agencies, foreign branches, foreign subsidiaries and affiliates. In the USA, commercial banks can participate in the offshore banking activities through **international banking facilities** (IBFs) and **Edge Act corporations**.

The presence of foreign banks in the USA has been increasing, probably reflecting the potential size and profit opportunity of the US market.[8] On the other hand, the shrinking physical presence of US banks overseas may partially reflect fading attractiveness of foreign operations in the aftermath of large losses from loans to **less developed countries** (LDCs), especially for regional banks. However, a larger force at work is very likely the restructuring of priorities and strategies because of the perceived need for greater efficiency in the fiercely competitive global banking environment.

2.2.1 Conventional form of international banking

Correspondent banking

A correspondent bank is a bank that provides services, typically as an agent, to anther bank located elsewhere.[9] A correspondent bank is the most common conduit for participating in international banking activities. It also has the minimum cost (on both time and money dimensions) for a bank in terms of not only initiating the process but also reversing that choice. This agency relationship obviates the need for a physical presence in another country. Thus, US banks without a physical presence abroad can rely on their correspondent banks to provide to their clients services such as local intelligence reports, foreign exchange conversions, letters of credit, or loans. Reciprocity of services, maintenance of balances, and fees charged to customers for services are some forms of compensation provided to a correspondent bank.

Another advantage of correspondence banking is that it is a stepping-stone for a more involved relationship with the **correspondent bank**. Regional banks, for example, have often relied on their past experience to join loan syndicates formed by foreign correspondent banks.

Against these advantages, the bank has to consider disadvantages of the correspondent banking relationships. Disadvantages are basically related to the *agency problem*, mentioned in Chapter 1. That is, the agent's interests do not necessarily coincide with the principal's, and the agent does not necessarily act in the best interest of the principal. First, a correspondent bank may assign a low priority to the needs of the principal bank or its customers. Second, a correspondent bank may not be willing to provide credit on a regular and timely basis. Third, and in contrast to the first two problems, a typical agency problem faced by the principal bank may be the agent taking away its lucrative customer business. Fourth, when reciprocity of services is the major element of the correspondent banking agreement, the bank may find itself providing a disproportionately large share of services. Finally, a favorable experience with a correspondent bank may prompt a bank into deeper (and ex post regrettable) involvement that a sound analysis would have recommended against in the absence of precautionary safeguards.

Representative office

A **representative office** solicits customer business locally, and provides advisory services to bank customers located elsewhere. It also provides some services previously rendered by the correspondent banks and thereby prevents the latter from getting overburdened. Representative offices do *not* book loans nor accept deposits. However, in a large country or region, a loan booking facility along with several representative offices allows a foreign bank to expedite the loan business through the groundwork – of customer contact and devising suitable forms of loan agreements – being done by the representative offices, and signing of the contracts done at the loan booking facility.

Physical presence allows a representative office to obtain firsthand economic and political intelligence on the host country as well as the local financial market. It also enables the bank to interact with other local institutions overseas (especially when time differences are crucial). It also makes sense to set up a representative office overseas if the business volume abroad is small, since a representative office involves a relatively low overhead.

One chief drawback for setting up a representative office is the difficulty of attracting qualified personnel, especially since they are not involved in a decision-making capacity. In such instances, explicit or implicit agreements regarding promotions are vital in attracting and retaining competent personnel. Even in that case, the ensuing mobility of personnel may defeat the purposes of cultivating clientele and obtaining accurate as well as timely local intelligence.

The disadvantage of the representative agency discussed above is linked to the difficulty in overcoming the **structural impediments** in foreign markets. When these hurdles are high, the cost of resources required to overcome them may be too high in relation to potential benefits of available banking business.

Table 2.1   Foreign banks in the USA

Year	No. of foreign bank offices in the USA	Assets ($ billion)
1980	441	252.2
1985	621	485.8
1990	700	822.4
1991	726	910.3
1992	686	946.1
1993	660	933.1
1994	652	951.0

Source: Aguilar (1995).

Agency

An **agency** is like a full-fledged bank except that it does not handle retail deposits. Thus, it is still a restricted form of bank entry in the foreign market. An agency is primarily used to book loans; as such, legal and tax environments, in addition to the size of the client base, are vital considerations in selecting an agency site. The desirable "critical mass" of the potential business is much larger for the agency than a representative office. As a result, the personnel problem faced by a representative office is attenuated for the agency; still, it does not avoid the problem completely.

Branch

A **branch** is a direct extension of the parent bank in the overseas market, and thus requires equity contribution from the parent bank. It enables the parent to gain access to both retail and wholesale markets locally by accepting deposits and placing surplus funds.

Branching is a common approach used for enhancing physical presence overseas. This physical presence allows a bank to expedite services to its home-based clients in foreign countries and attract local customers who plan to undertake activities in the bank's home country. To the extent that (a) economies do not move in consonance, and (b) demand for bank services moves with the business cycle, foreign branches help augment the bank earnings as well as reduce its overall earnings volatility through diversification. The accelerated trend of global market integration, however, has reduced the potency of the diversification advantage; and increased competition has whittled the profit potential of overseas branches. Finally, rapid advances in communications technology has significantly reduced the lure of physical presence of a branch overseas, especially given the large fixed overhead for operating a branch. As a result, the number of branches has decreased in the 1990s, although their total assets have increased, as shown in Table 2.1.

Apart from direct considerations of risk and return for operating a branch, the bank has also to analyze carefully one additional matter: a branch is subject to two sets of regulatory and tax authorities (two sets of **market impediments**). Thus, the home authorities may not permit a bank branch to undertake activities that are routinely allowed by the foreign regulators to banks under their jurisdiction. Similarly, double taxation in the absence of tax treaties may significantly erode the profit potential. Naturally, the other side of the coin is the enhanced profit potential in the absence of non-uniform regulatory and tax environment. For instance, during the 1970s, European branches of the US banks were able to participate in some investment banking activities that were not permitted in the USA. Similarly, US banks exploited the UK provision to write off transportation equipments in one year by booking their leases to the US airlines through their branches in the UK.

Subsidiary

A foreign **subsidiary** of a bank is a locally *incorporated* bank that has its own capital and charter. Even when it is *wholly owned* (and consolidated with the parent for financial reporting purposes), its legal entity is distinct from its parent and thus subject to only local regulations – the same way as a domestic bank – in contrast to the branch. Similarly, the parent is normally liable for the wholly owned subsidiary's earnings only when they are repatriated in the form of dividends.

When a bank has only a *partial ownership* in a subsidiary, it enjoys advantages that stem from partners' strengths such as greater name recognition, greater familiarity with the territory, and ability to share losses. On the other hand, if the ownership interest of a US bank in a foreign country is less than 10 percent, it would not be able to obtain credit from the US government for foreign income tax payments. More significantly, incompatible management style or culture among partners can quickly unravel the best laid-out plans. A more serious set of problems can be governance or control (who will have, for instance, decision-making authority in a given arena) that may stem from agency or asymmetric information, where too detailed specifications of procedures avoid such problems only by negating any potential advantages (such as maneuvering flexibility) of such a joint venture. Banks from different nations have frequently formed consortia in the post-World War II period, but their success has not been conspicuous. In recent years, banks have also initiated reciprocal equity ownership agreements (such as 5 percent ownership of each other's equity) to test the water before jumping into a relationship. It is, however, not clear what unique advantages such agreements entail. Setting up a subsidiary abroad magnifies the agency problem (locally recruited personnel do not necessarily act in the interest of the parent bank), especially information asymmetry (the parent does not have full information or ability to react swiftly in response to the changing environment in foreign market) outlined in Chapter 1.

One environmental factor has an overarching influence on the effectiveness of a bank's physical presence abroad. We now turn to discussion of this factor.

2.2.2   Management typology for foreign presence

Countries may be broadly classified as either *relationship-* or *transaction-oriented*.[10] *Civil law* based economic systems are conducive to relationship orientation. France, Spain, and Italy have the civil law tradition. Contracts in a civil law oriented economy are not easily enforceable in case of default, since contractual terms are only one consideration in determining redress for default. Swift contract enforcement then calls for a stronger remedy than a court of law – say, societal pressure. Protracted contractual enforcement also suggests that modifications in law are required in the civil law economy before securities markets can flourish. Underdevelopment of securities markets is also reinforced by the privileged nature of information that cannot be reasonably inferred in a given situation. As a result, banks play a crucial role in this economy. Indispensability, in turn, allows a bank in a relationship-oriented economy to undertake an unprofitable transaction with a customer set by generating benefits from other transactions with the same customer set. This latitude also suggests that the bank has a vested interest in preserving the status quo, especially in regards to thwarting competition.

The reverse will be true in countries that are transactions-oriented, that is, where the legal system is based on the Anglo-Saxon *common law* tradition such as in the UK and the USA. Legal enforcement is strictly based on the terms of agreement; only when these terms are not explicit or legally unacceptable that enforcement would rely on a broader framework than the contract itself. Thus, expeditious legal enforcement necessitates that transactions should be transparent. This transparency not only allows development of securities markets but also fosters innovation of new products. Banks, as a result, would lose their market share unless they are competitive. They also have less room for errors, and low pricing leading to inadequate returns is unlikely to be defensible on the basis of getting compensation elsewhere or in other transactions with the customer in future.[11]

Effectiveness of a bank in a foreign country depends on strong leadership in the organizational form chosen by the bank. Among the leadership attributes, two traits are:

- *P-type* or people-skill of the manager;
- *Q-type* or quantitative and technical (or analytical) skill of the manager.

The above description of the *relationship society* suggests that people skills are more pertinent in a leader/manager than his or her possession of technical or quantitative skills requisite for devising optimal contracts. The former type will also enable the bank to preserve and amplify its market share. In contrast, in the *transactions-oriented* society, the technically competent manager will be more effective in enhancing the bank's profitability. A mismatch, on the other hand, is likely to harm long-term prospects for survival for a foreign bank.

Naturally, a bank cannot presume that the status quo will continue forever. The bank has also to consider a prospective change in the orientation and the resultant change in its strategies, especially in regard to the managerial selection process. For instance, during the last decade France has made tremendous strides in modifying civil law oriented business laws to permit introduction of innovative financial products. These modifications have nudged France toward transaction orientation more than ever before. A US bank cannot count on continued effectiveness of a well-connected manager just because of his impressive past record.

In sum, as we progress from correspondent banking, representative offices, and agencies to branches and subsidiaries (whatever may be their form), the increased scope of activities also brings in its wake added complexity and cost – especially the cost of reversing the decision. Hence, a bank should take a careful look at (a) its objectives and envisioned scope for international involvement, (b) the costs involved by different forms discussed above, and (c) whether the least cost alternative is acceptable in the first place, before jumping into the fray. When a joint venture for a branch or subsidiary form is deemed desirable, special precaution should be taken to ensure "cultural" compatibility among partners along the dimension of management typology.

2.2.3   Specific forms for US-based banks

Edge Act Corporation

An **Edge Act corporation**, or "edgie," is a specialized banking organization in international trade-related transactions or investments open to US domestic banks since 1919 and to foreign banks since 1978. Edge Act corporations are restricted to handle foreign customers and to handle the international business activities of domestic customers. These activities include trade-financing arrangements, deposit taking from outside the USA, lending money to international businesses and making equity investments in foreign operations.

An edgie allows a bank to undertake the above-mentioned activities especially in a port city, which may be in a different state from the state of the bank's domicile. Thus it enables a bank to circumvent prohibition of interstate operations, a feature that was much more appealing prior to 1978 when the deregulation movement started.[12] By its very nature, the edgie undertakes activities peripheral to the mainstream business; hence competent employees have not been enthusiastic about assignment to the edgie business, unless it is understood as interim.

US international banking facilities

Since 1981, US banks have been allowed by the Federal Reserve System to establish IBFs as adjunct operations to conduct international banking activities that are exempt from certain regulations and taxes. Thus IBFs are not subject to domestic banking regulations, such as a reserve requirement and interest rate ceilings, as well as various local and state tax assessments. As a result, this form of organizational structure enables the bank to escape or minimize the burden imposed by some government-induced impediments (regulations and taxes).

An IBF can accept deposits only from non-US residents with a minimum amount of $100,000; thus these deposits are not insured. Further, for practical purposes, it involves wholesale banking. As a result, it does not call for physical facilities typically needed for retail banking operations. Often, a nameplate acknowledging the IBF existence is all that is required in addition to maintaining separate financial transactions books. One interesting consequence of IBF formation has been that initially Italian and Japanese banks with US operations took far greater advantage of this form than even the US banks, because they did not have to obtain permission from their home country authorities for an IBF. A comparable offshore facility in a tax haven country, on the other hand, would have required an approval from their home country authorities.

2.3   International Banking Activities

Foreign trade financing is one major activity pursued by banks, small and large. Various forms of *guarantees*, including the letter of credit, facilitate foreign trade for enabling exporters to minimize the risk of payment and importers to minimize the risk of performance. Although financing is not a necessary condition for providing these guarantees, financing is usually a part of the package.

In addition to trade financing, banks also *provide or convert foreign exchange* for trade participants. Participants may also require arrangements for "local" borrowing or hedging the currency exposure of the trade transactions. Firms with foreign operations would require these services on an ongoing basis and on a larger scale.

The term "local" here connotes not only the foreign location where the participant has the business interest and is subject to government regulations but also the unregulated, offshore markets. Offshore markets are commonly called "Euro"-markets. One segment of the Euro markets is the Eurocurrencies market where spot currency transactions as well as trading in short- and medium-term funds and instruments are undertaken. The "interbank" market, where banks conduct business among themselves, significantly overlaps the Euro markets; hence, the term "interbank" is often used interchangeably with "Euro-" or "Eurocurrencies" markets.[13] Eurocurrencies markets are notable in two respects: (a) over 80 percent of foreign exchange trading takes place in these markets; and (b) given their informational and cost efficiencies, these markets greatly facilitate banks' asset-liability management to attain targets of liquidity and interest rate exposures.

It is only since 1990 that banks in the USA are permitted to allow customers to hold their deposits in foreign currencies. US banks accommodated businesses desiring to maintain their accounts in foreign currencies by opening foreign branches or subsidiaries. Even the relaxed policy does not improve US-based banks' competitive position, since Regulation Q prohibits banks in the USA to pay interest on demand deposits,[14] irrespective of whether they are held in dollars or foreign currencies. Foreign countries, on the other hand, routinely allow demand deposits to earn interest.

The third major area of international activities comprises *investment banking*. Investment banking activities include securities underwriting, corporate finance (e.g., analysis or arrangement for mergers and divestitures for clients), secondary market trading in securities, and portfolio management. Financial management has become an integral part of these activities: design of financial products and derivatives tailored to suit clients' needs, especially related to risk or exposure management of various kinds. Typically, large commercial banks extensively participate in the investment banking field.

It is worth noting that US commercial banks do *not* have a significant market share of the commercial banking business in Europe because of structural impediments in various European countries. Their market share has hovered around 3 percent in recent years. At the same time, US commercial banks have been important players in the investment banking arena in spite of the fact that they were prohibited to participate routinely in the investment banking activities in the USA up until very recently because of the regulatory constraints imposed by the erstwhile **Glass–Steagall Act**.[15]

2.4 Globalization of Financial Markets

Basically **globalization** of markets connotes absence of segmentation of markets on a global scale. Segmentation occurs because of impediments. Impediments, in turn, modify or distort the impact of market forces. Hence, the process of globalization requires removal, harmonization, or minimization of impediments. Suppose there are two countries in the world, A and B. **Quotas**, regulations, or laws barring banks from undertaking certain financial activities in country A (but not in B) are impediments that need to be removed in country A for true globalization. Taxes or transaction costs, required in both countries but of different magnitudes, should be made uniform, or harmonized. When practical circumstances prevent uniformity, the differences should be minimized for the purpose of globalization. Thus, removal, harmonization, and minimization of impediments are progressively weaker conditions for globalization.

We discuss below the transformation of government-induced impediments in light of technological innovations since 1980. The interrelationships of these two forces (government-induced impediments and technological innovations) with foreign exchange rates and interest rates, the two salient indicators of the financial markets, are highlighted in this discussion to underscore the distinct character of the emerging global financial market.

2.4.1 Changing role of government

While international transactions in the aftermath of World War II entailed rather complicated and inflexible bureaucratic procedures (imposed by governments and financial institutions), participants today conduct their financial transactions with relative ease. A major force responsible for this phenomenon has been the development of the offshore markets that have flourished because of taxes as well as transaction costs arising from government regulations. Although these markets have allowed participants to circumvent or minimize the regulatory or tax burden and thereby limit the influence of individual governments, they have also been useful to these governments for raising a reasonable amount of financial resources without giving up their control over domestic economic policies, as highlighted by the oil crises of the 1970s.

Second, governments have come to realize that financial institutions protected by regulations have little incentive to manage their resources efficiently, and the resultant inefficiencies of these institutions entail difficult-to-justify costs for their economies. Public ownership of banks is an extreme case of regulatory protection. Irrespective of the public ownership of banks, governments have painfully grasped that as economies open up, domestic banks overburdened by regulations are unable to compete effectively against their foreign counterparts.

In the mid-1970s, because Japanese banks were proscribed from participating in offshore markets, they were unable to participate in the sovereign lending business created by the oil price increase. This was one reason why the Japanese government later lifted the sanctions against offshore market participation.[16]

Finally, governments have come under pressure from other governments or multilateral agencies to scrap or modify regulatory barriers[17] that keep foreign competition out. Reforms in the Japanese capital markets were in no small measure due to pressure by the US government. Similarly, the **reciprocity principle** is one measure that has come under pressure. Suppose Germany allows banks to undertake brokerage activities, but the USA does not. Under the reciprocity principle, Germany would not permit US banks operating within its border to transact brokerage business, even when the USA proscribes all banks irrespective of their national origin from the brokerage business. A more liberal stance is the **national**

treatment under which Germany would not discriminate against US banks so long as the USA does not unfavorably discriminate against German banks operating in the USA.

Finally, the counter pressure for re-regulations should be noted. Financial market integration suggests that in case of a contagious crisis, a country is hapless when financial forces are unleashed elsewhere. Recent crises in South-East Asia as well as Brazil demonstrated that measures by a particular country that would have historically contained the crisis might not be adequate today. The recent case of LTCM (Long Term Capital Management – an investment fund)[18] also suggests that a single firm is capable of globally inflicting substantial damage on financial institutions, and the result may resemble the "worst case scenario" under systemic risk measurement. Whether, as a result, there is a rationale for regulation is not pertinent here: even *perception* of systemic risk is capable of generating political pressure for adoption of stronger regulations.

2.4.2   Innovations in communication technology

Advances in information processing and transmission technologies have greatly improved efficiency in international trade and finance. Due to satellite links, one obtains virtually instantaneous access to unfolding developments elsewhere in the world. Furthermore, the dramatically decreasing data transmission costs coupled with improved features of online services have provided a strong boost to the demand for these services. Even a foreign tourist with access to an ATM (automatic teller machine) is today able to obtain local currency at virtually wholesale rates that would have been unthinkable ten years ago.

With the removal of impediments long associated with nation-state boundaries and the improved access to information, the international financial market has moved closer to becoming a more perfect market. In addition to cheaper access to information, the rapid advances in computing power at a cheaper price allow today even small banks to undertake complex information processing undreamed of two decades ago. Nevertheless the exposure to a massive number of computer-generated reports poses a danger of information overload for the recipient, especially when the underlying analysis and its implications are not clearly understood. Banks are not immune to this danger. Typically, commercial banks devote their computer resources for information *access* rather than *analysis*. Often, neither employees are properly trained nor the useful information is made available to them in a form amenable for more efficient or profitable customer service. Further, banks fail to utilize internally available information for monitoring effectiveness of their employees or services on a timely basis. As a result, banks overlook a valuable tool for reducing risk. Indeed, unbridled decision-making authority coupled with an easy access to an array of financial products can be disastrous, as illustrated by the collapse of Barings Bank in February 1995 (Stoneham 1996).

2.4.3   Increased volatility in interest and foreign exchange rates

As we move toward a global economy, a lack of coordination among leading countries with regard to their economic priorities and policies creates volatility in real interest and foreign exchange rates, as suggested above. Furthermore, any unanticipated action on the part of one country may very likely be immediately, but not necessarily in a commensurate fashion, reflected in the changes in the relevant interest and foreign exchange rates. When the Federal Reserve raised the short-term interest rates in 1994 to forestall inflationary forces, the financial market reactions were negative (ex post underestimation of inflationary forces) rather than positive (ex ante inflationary forces would be kept at bay by the cautious and vigilant Fed). The impact was more severe in Singapore than in Europe.

Given the complex linkages among currencies, the impact of the change is just not confined to the obvious relationships.

> The Mexican peso crisis in 1995, partially emanating from the 1994 Fed action described above, spilled over in securities markets in many emerging economies even when their relationship with Mexico can be best described as tenuous.

Three aspects of this volatility in the financial indicators are noteworthy. *First*, events in the last 20 years have cast doubt on two popular assertions that (a) the floating rate system would allow a government to pursue its fiscal and monetary policies without any regard to the policies of other governments, and (b) any government intervention in the currency markets is not only unnecessary but also counterproductive.

> The US government in the early 1980s, and the German government a decade later, followed first the tight money policies. Later, even when these governments reversed the course of direction of their monetary policies, their respective currencies kept on appreciating. In the case of the USA, the record government deficits accompanied by mushrooming current account deficits did not dampen the trend of the appreciating dollar. Finally, the "bubble" burst and the dollar reversed the direction only after major governments undertook intervention on a concerted basis in late 1986. Thus, foreign exchange rates do not behave as the theory would suggest they should as a result of a change in the economic policy of a government, either in terms of magnitude or even in terms of direction.

If a government undertakes intervention, and (a) its domestic economic policies in themselves are inconsistent; (b) its interventions are fundamentally inconsistent with domestic policies (which in themselves may be consistent); (c) its interventions are pursued half-heartedly (or are perceived that way); *or* (d) its actions convey signals through the intervention measures but the government does not follow up with requisite economic policy changes, intervention measures will be ineffective, and are likely to contribute needlessly to exchange rate volatility.

Coordination among major players with respect to their economic policies thus remains desirable even under the floating exchange rate system. In the absence of such coordination, governments have come to appreciate, when faced with a crisis, either the need for a concerted intervention action or graciously bowing to (and nudging) the market forces to contain the excessive volatility.

> The Bank of England was unable to defend the parity of the pound sterling in 1992, because the concerted intervention was not decisive. When, in 1993, the French franc faced a similar onslaught in the currency market, the ERM of the EU widened the parity range to ± 15 percent to cool the speculative fever while indirectly admitting supremacy of market forces.

These events also underscore enormous difficulties in implementing economic policy coordination even when coordination is clearly defined (e.g. with respect to government debt burden, budget deficits, and interest rate policies) and formally endorsed as the Maastricht Treaty demonstrated. The inescapable conclusion then is that volatility in the financial benchmarks is going to stay with us at least in the foreseeable future.

Second, this volatility has created a huge appetite for risk management services and products by non-financial entities. Computer technology has allowed financial institutions to offer a variety of products unheard of some 15 years ago. Because the forces behind the volatility are ever changing, demand for these products is constantly shifting, thus shortening economic life of the products. Competition – both among commercial banks and between commercial banks and investment banks – has further accentuated the trend of a shortened **product life cycle**.

Third, just as these volatilities provide banks with profitable opportunities, they also present challenges. Unless risk management products' risk is shifted to entities – especially non-banks – able and willing to bear the risk, the aggregated risk has the potential of undermining the viability of the banking system. Recognizing these dangers, industrialized nations set up the Basel Committee on Banking Supervision in 1988. Its major mission has been to fortify banks' capital base so as to withstand, among other things, unfavorable or undesirable consequences of interest and exchange rate volatilities. This mission has led to regulations (in the USA and elsewhere) that attempt to fortify banking capital adequacy framework (they are discussed in more detail in Chapter 10).

2.5 Conclusion

This chapter first provided a bird's eye view of historical developments or crises that provided impetus for transforming the banking industry in the last two decades. Next, different forms of organization for undertaking cross-border activities were described. The scope of various banking activities in the international sphere was then identified in light of their distinctive character. Finally, the process of globalization of financial markets was examined in light of forces responsible for and emanating from the process: a shift in the government stance toward regulating or controlling economic activities, advances in information technology, and increased volatility in the financial benchmarks of interest and foreign exchange rates. This discussion will allow us to examine in detail special aspects of each of these activities and its management in subsequent chapters.

DISCUSSION QUESTIONS

1 What were the notable banking activities in the post-World War II period and what forces in the early 1970s led to changes?

2 The fixed exchange rate system under the Bretton Woods Agreement was widely held responsible for volatility in currency markets during the early 1970s. Why did major currency crises occur during the 1990s when an ever-increasing number of countries embraced the floating rate system?

3 What are different organizational forms for cross-border banking? Discuss why some forms are more appropriate than others for each one of the following activities:

   a import trade financing;
   b advisory activity for a domestic client;
   c providing banking services to a potential client abroad;
   d payment services for a foreign subsidiary of a domestic client;
   e selling risk management products related to foreign exchange.

4 Why have Japanese and Italian banks used the form of IBFs?

5 Suppose a US bank is considering opening a branch in a sub-Saharan African nation with civil law orientation. The bank is considering several candidates for the managerial position. A professor at the local university has recommended for that position an MBA candidate who has been a native of that country but had spent several years in the USA during his childhood and early youth. Discuss various considerations for and against selecting this candidate for the position vis-à-vis other candidates, if their educational records and prior work experience are comparable.

6 Advances in computer technology and in communications industry have been identified as a critical force in accelerating globalization of financial markets in the last two decades. Why should a bank desiring to be a global player maintain *physical* presence in foreign countries?

APPENDIX A: FOREIGN EXCHANGE RATE SYSTEMS

A government issuing a currency faces three broad alternatives with respect to conversion of its currency in foreign currencies: conversion determined by the market forces of demand and supply; official proclamation of its currency's value in terms of a foreign currency or precious metal; and an alternative representing the mix of the first two alternatives.

Free-float System

Under the freely floating exchange rate system, each country's exchange rate is determined by market forces — supply, demand, and expectations. The government does not have to maintain reserves of foreign currencies. Theoretically at least, the government is free to pursue any monetary and fiscal policies it chooses. The currency market is unimpeded and it values the currency in terms of what it can buy vis-à-vis the other currencies. Given the large number of market participants, the market is likely to be informationally efficient. As relevant new information continually arrives and the market response is immediately incorporated in currency prices, the exchange rate or the currency value will fluctuate. Movement of the exchange rate is thus similar to those in the efficient financial securities markets.

Fixed Exchange Rate System

A country may peg its currency to a benchmark foreign currency like the US dollar or German mark. The typical benchmark currency is **convertible** in that it is demanded by market participants outside the issuing country. The peg or the stated value of a country's currency in terms of the benchmark currency is also known as the **par value**. The government's credibility is assessed in the markets by its ability to defend the par value, that is, its readiness to supply the benchmark currency upon demand.

Under the fixed exchange rate system, currency value remains stable — to a point. The par value defense is unlikely to be a major problem, when economic policies of the country issuing the pegged currency and the country of the benchmark currency are consistent and well coordinated. When that is not the case, distortions surface in the financial and goods markets. If the parity rate for a currency is way above its intrinsic value, that is, the currency is overvalued, the country of that currency faces loss of foreign markets for its goods due to overpriced exports as well as flooding of domestic markets with "cheap" imports. This results in balance-of-payments deficits and a decline in foreign currency reserves with which the government is able to maintain the parity value. Barring devaluation that tries to restore consistency between the parity rate and the intrinsic value, the government resorts to various policy measures pertaining to the currency, financial and goods markets in order to alleviate the pressure on the parity rate.

In the foreign exchange markets,

1   it creates dual or multiple parity rates: more desirable uses are accorded more favorable parity rates;
2   it restricts foreign exchange for non-essential purposes;
3   it prohibits foreign exchange for short- and long-term investment.

In the financial markets,

1   it raises domestic interest rates to attract foreign capital and/or to halt capital flight;
2   it introduces or raises withholding taxes on dividends and interest income paid to foreign sources of capital to discourage such outflows; at other times, it lowers these taxes to encourage new capital flows;
3   it stiffens regulations and laws prohibiting capital flight including capital repatriation and dividends by foreign enterprises, which have domestic operations.

In the goods markets,

1 it introduces or increases tariffs and quotas on imports;
2 it provides direct or indirect subsidies to exports.

Although the above list is not comprehensive, it clearly highlights the impact of distortions in the foreign exchange markets that engender impediments in the financial and goods markets. In the absence of such measures, the arbitrage processes we referred to in Chapter 1 would set in motion in these latter markets, and would exhaust foreign exchange (government) reserves and force devaluation.

Typically, revisions in the par value are infrequent and deliberate. However, a government may make the process "automatic" by linking the par value to a set of specified indicators. For instance, when an economy experiences persistently high inflation rate, the government may adopt the policy of quarterly, monthly or even weekly revision of its currency's par value in light of the current domestic inflation rate vis-à-vis the counterpart inflation rate in the benchmark currency. The government is thus adopting a **crawling peg** system. That is, the currency is allowed to depreciate periodically by a widely accepted amount or percentage. Brazil used such a system historically.

Benchmark of a Basket of Currencies

Usually, a country adopting a fixed exchange rate system has a significant trade relationship with the country of the benchmark currency. Some West African countries, for instance, have strong historical and economic ties with France; hence they have pegged their currencies to the French franc. Similarly, strong trade relationships with the USA have led many Latin American countries to peg their currencies to the US dollar. When a country has important trade relationships with several strong currency countries, it may peg its currency to a **basket** of these strong currencies.

Gold Standard

A variant of the fixed exchange rate system is the **gold standard**. In this case, the issuing country states its currency value in terms of gold. It maintains gold reserves instead of the benchmark currency, although it may hold reserves of a currency pegged to the gold standard. (Prior to World War I, the pound sterling was linked to gold, and countries around the world held reserves in pound sterling because of Great Britain's economic supremacy.) The "Rules of the Game" for the monetary system under the gold standard are to maintain (1) a constant value of the currency, and (2) a non-discretionary monetary policy linked to the country's gold reserve (that is, expansion of money supply when reserves rise and contraction of money supply when reserves fall). As a result, the government has no room for discretion for measures aimed at promoting growth or reducing unemployment. Under the conventional fixed exchange rate system, a decoupling of a country's reserves and its monetary policy is possible.

Currency Board System

Another variant of the fixed exchange rate system is the **currency board system**. Under a currency board system, a government establishes a fixed exchange rate between the domestic currency and an external currency. Further, and more significantly, it makes a commitment to link its monetary policy to its reserves of the benchmark currency. Thus changes in its reserves are mirrored in the changes in its monetary policy. As a result, its monetary policy under the currency board system is as constrained as under the gold standard, and the government is unable to pursue a monetary policy to correct maladies such as a mild recession.

Various countries have adopted the currency board system across the globe in recent times. Hong Kong pegged its currency to the US dollar in 1983. Similarly, Argentina (1991) and Lithuania (1994) have linked their currencies to the US dollar, and Estonia (1992) and Bulgaria (1997) to the German mark.

Managed Float

The central bank will smooth out exchange rate fluctuations under the **managed float** system, although the currency value is by and large determined in the market place. The managed float system appears in a variety of forms. At one extreme, the central bank buys or sells foreign currencies against its own currency in order to smooth out (a) undesirable daily fluctuations in the exchange rate, or (b) a transition from one rate to another because of a change in the business cycle phase. At the other extreme, the government tries to peg its exchange rate without officially proclaiming such a policy. Among the industrialized nations, Japan followed most conspicuously the managed float policy in the aftermath of the Bretton Woods system.

DISCUSSION QUESTIONS

1   Discuss the strengths and limitations of different exchange rate systems.
2   Explain what roles the banks play under different exchange rate systems in the context of financial market globalization.

APPENDIX B: EUROPEAN UNION

In 1957, six European countries signed the Treaty of Rome, ushering in the existence of the European Economic Community (EEC) or Common Market. Its goals were to reduce or eliminate customs duties among the member countries and pursue a Common Agricultural Policy (CAP). In 1985, the EEC published the White Paper on "completing the internal market" with a goal of freedom of movement of goods, services, capital, and people within the Community. In 1987, the Single European Act was implemented by 12 member countries to modify the Treaty of Rome and it set the date of January 1, 1993 for completion of the single market. The 1992 **Maastricht Treaty**, signed by foreign ministers of member countries and implemented later by individual member countries, replaced the EEC or European Community by instituting the European Union (EU). It also endorsed the notion of Economic and Monetary Union (EMU), embodying a true integration of monetary and economic policies of member countries by having one currency in place of the existing currencies. Thus the concept of EMU that went beyond the true integration of the economic (and political) systems was to be achieved in three phases of the transition, from the irrevocable fixing of exchange rates leading to the progressive introduction of a single currency, the euro. During the first two phases, the original Exchange Rate Mechanism (ERM), which was a fixed-exchange rate system where member countries agreed to defend parity values of each other's currency, still remained in force. The 1995 Madrid Summit laid down details, especially for the final phase of the transition that earmarked the actual beginning of the monetary union. In particular, it defined the following *convergence criteria* that a member country must fulfill before it can become a part of the EMU:

1   Inflation rates, observed over a period of one year, must not be more than 1.50 percent above the average of the three best-performing members.
2   Long-term interest rates observed over a period of one year must not be above 2.00 percent of the average of the best three member states in terms of price stability.

3   Budget deficits (including central, regional and local government) should not exceed 3 percent of **gross domestic product** (GDP).

4   Public debt ratio should not exceed 60 percent of GDP.

Price stability and budgetary discipline have been the primary objectives for the convergence criteria.

The EU is now a union of 15 independent states (Austria, Belgium, Denmark, Finland, France, Germany, Greece, Ireland, Italy, Luxemburg, the Netherlands, Portugal, Spain, Sweden and the UK) pursuing political, economic, and social cooperation. Poland, Hungary, the Czech Republic, Estonia, Slovenia, and Cyprus have been in accession talks with the EU since 1997. The European Commission has proposed talks with seven countries (Latvia, Lithuania, Romania, Bulgaria, Slovakia, Malta, and Turkey), and possibly Egypt, to join the EU.

In January 1999, at the Madrid Summit, there was the irrevocable fixing of the conversion rates of the 11 countries that qualified[19] for the EMU. The European Central Bank now initiates a single monetary policy and a foreign exchange rate policy conducted in euro. New tradable public debt will be from now onward issued in euro. On January 1, 2002, the new euro notes and coins were introduced, and by July 1, 2002 national currencies had been completely replaced and ceased to be legal tender.

During the second half of the twentieth century, the EU has made tremendous strides toward regional integration through overcoming national political, economic, social, and cultural differences. Challenges on all these fronts still remain, especially in light of the fact that more countries – notably from the former Soviet block – are to join the EU. Limitations on public borrowing and pursuing discretionary and politically expedient monetary policies will not be palatable to "local" parties in power. At a more basic level, the EU vested with overriding economic and political powers represents further surrender of "national" sovereignty. But these challenges should not be overemphasized. Many member countries have already given up voluntarily a great deal of policy freedom, and in return obtained for their institutions, both private and public, a greater sphere of influence over a wider area than ever before. An area of particular interest for us is the forging of the new legal and regulatory framework in the Union. We examine that in some details below.

European Financial Regulation

Some critics complain that too much attention has been levied on the use of a single currency, and not enough on the architecture of the single financial market, especially a regulator along the lines of the US Securities and Exchange Commission (SEC). Still, they concede that banking enjoys an EU-wide regulatory framework, even if the application of the rules varies. In particular, the 1989 Directive

- sets out the principle that a bank with a license from its own government is a citizen of Europe at large and thus can set up branches anywhere else in the EU;
- puts *home*-country supervisors in charge of prudential oversight while *host*-country regulators are to ensure that local bank branches, wherever their headquarters, observe local rules;
- favors the "national treatment" rule over the "reciprocity principle"; thus, if the British rule for a "Chinese wall" between investment and commercial banking units of a firm is applicable to all banks irrespective of their national origins, the German regulators allowing complete integration of all financial services to its banks cannot deny it to the British banks operating under its jurisdiction simply because German banks are not permitted such a privilege in the UK.

The securities and insurance industries, however, lack coherent supervision. Several problems exist including:

- Retail investors still face a bureaucratic battle and high fees if they want to invest in foreign shares, which are typically listed on a foreign stock exchange but cleared and settled under local rules.
- Some member countries still use bearer share certificates rather than using the registration process. This difference, in turn, has ramifications for shareholder rights and taxes.
- Companies are subject to different rules on accounting, information disclosure, and the treatment of minority shareholders.
- A firm listed in one market does not have an easy access to markets in other countries; it still has to go through the "local" listing requirements.

As some of the factors listed above fail to encourage investors from participating in EU equity markets, they may also hamper potential equity issues by new enterprises seeking capital for growth. Nevertheless progress is being made on modifications or removal of the barriers on several fronts.

- National regulators have already set up links with each other and many have agreements covering the sharing of information across borders.
- Securities regulators in Europe established a Forum of European Securities Commissions (FESCO) at the end of 1997. FESCO is working on improvements in the EU directive on **prospectus** issues.
- London and Frankfurt stock exchanges have managed to persuade six other exchanges to join them.
- The European Commission has started to draw up a new set of ground rules to govern a single wholesale capital market, and more open retail markets.
- Other Commission directives, designed to encourage the development of open and secure retail markets, would cover the cross-border marketing of mutual funds.

One of the top priorities of the EU Commission is a directive on takeover bids, which is designed to honor the fair treatment of minority shareholders across Europe. An attempt to set up a single European company statute was vetoed by Spain. The takeover directive faces a similar fate. In the end, although attempts to set up a securities committee under the Commission to assist in the drafting of European securities regulations have run into roadblocks of national sovereignty, securities trading on the Internet may render moot any issues related to physical trading on various exchanges.[20]

DISCUSSION QUESTIONS

1 Why did the EU introduce a phased approach to adopt a single currency? Why did some countries refuse to join the EMU?

2 Discuss the potential gains and challenges that the EU faces as it includes additional members.

3 Do you think that regional blocks like the EU are stepping stones for ultimate globalization, or do they create a wall to keep out the rest of the world?

APPENDIX C: BALANCE OF PAYMENT

The **balance of payment** (BOP) of a country records all transactions between residents of that country with the rest of the world during a given time period, say, a year. The BOP statement is similar to the sources-and-uses statement of a firm. To record the international transaction, it is either a "source" or a "use" in the BOP document; and every "source" must be "used" elsewhere. The source is assigned a "+" sign while the use is assigned a "−" sign. Although total sources are by definition equal to total uses, the net balances in subcategories of the BOP may be positive ("surplus") or negative ("deficit"). But, just as a sources-and-uses statement for a firm gives insights regarding a firm's financial health, a BOP statement helps one understand demand and supply forces behind a country's currency.

There are three major subcategories in a BOP statement: **current account** (CA); **capital account** (KA); and the **official reserves account** (OR).

Current Account

The CA includes the **merchandise account**, which is a record of exports and imports in *goods*. The net balance in the merchandise account is known as the **trade balance**. In addition, the current account includes

- **trade in services** such as transportation, consulting, insurance, and banking. The net balance in services is also known as the **invisible (trade) balance**.
- **unilateral transfers**, which are non-contractual payments or receipts, such as donations, development aid, gifts, and wages repatriated by foreign workers.
- **factor income**, which consists largely of interest and dividend payments and receipts.

Capital Account

The KA is a record of the financial inflows and outflows connoting investment, loans, and amortization. Although foreign *investments* by the country's residents increase the claims they have on foreigners, these investments connote *funds outflow* currently. As a result, these outflows create or contribute to a *deficit* in the capital account. Similarly, foreigners' investments in the country − capital inflow − contribute to a capital account *surplus*.

KA transactions are classified as follows:

- *Direct investment*: transactions through which investors from one country have a controlling interest in (or participate in the management of) operations undertaken in the other country.
- *Portfolio investment*: transactions in which foreign securities are bought or sold for financial investment, but not for management.
- *Short-term capital*: transactions including bank deposits, purchase, or sale of money market instruments, and trade credit. These transactions, which can be regarded as part of the portfolio investment, are sensitive to changes in relative interest rates between countries.

Official Reserve Account

The **official reserves** of a country include a *change* in the stock held by the official government agency (e.g. the Federal Reserve) of

- gold;
- government holdings of foreign currencies and other liquid claims in the form of, say, foreign treasury bills;

- balances held with the IMF; and
- allocations of **special drawing rights** (SDRs) by the IMF (any allocations in a given period is a positive entry).

A *negative* sign connotes an *official reserve surplus*. It results from (a) a net surplus in CA and/or KA, or (b) sale of the domestic currency (increase in supply) to foreigners leading to an *increase* in the stock of gold, foreign currencies, etc. Similarly, a *positive* sign suggests an *official reserve deficit*, which may result from a purchase of domestic currency through the use of (*decrease* in the Government held stock of) gold, foreign currencies, and so on.

Statistical Discrepancy

This number reflects errors and omissions in collecting data on international transactions. A credit (+) in this account reflects an inflow of funds while a debit (−) amount reflects an outflow. Essentially, this is a balancing item that preserves the identity of sources with uses.

PROJECT

Detailed data on the BOP for the USA can be found at the website: http://www.bea.doc.gov/bea/di1.htm.

1 Prepare the balance of payment for the USA for the two most current years in the same format as the one used in Table C.1.

2 Analyze the ramifications of the BOP statements you have prepared.

APPENDIX D: US REGULATION FOR FOREIGN BANKS

The number of foreign banks in the USA has grown substantially since the 1980s. Foreign banks operating in the US market typically concentrate on the wholesale market. Often, but not always, these banks have acquired control of US firms to expedite their foothold in the US market; for instance, Credit Suisse acquired First Boston.[21] The size of the foreign banking assets ranges from 20 to 25 percent of the total US banking assets, and the majority of the foreign banks are Japanese banks.

Two major regulations are applicable to foreign banks doing business in the USA. The first is the International Banking Act (IBA) of 1978. This Act primarily sets up a *national treatment* (as opposed to *reciprocity principle* – see p. xx) for all foreign banks, that is, it provides a level playing field for both domestic and foreign banks. Thus foreign banks are (a) expected to meet reserve requirements, and (b) subject to Federal Reserve (Fed) Examination.

The second important regulation for foreign banks is the Foreign Bank Supervision Enhancement Act (FBSEA) of 1991. This Act establishes five major features. First, entry by foreign banks requires the approval of the Fed to set up any organizational form. Second, the Fed can close down a foreign bank if its home country supervision is inadequate, if it violates US laws, or if it engages in unsound and unsafe banking practices. Third, the Fed can examine each office of the foreign bank. Fourth, deposits of foreign banks are qualified for FDIC (Federal Deposit Insurance Corporation – a US bank regulator) insurance. Finally, the state-licensed branch or agency of foreign banks cannot engage in any activity not allowed to a federal bank branch.

Table C.1 Illustration of a US balance of payment (in $ million) in 1994

		Credits (+)			Debits (−)
Current account					
Exports			**868041**		
Merchandise		502398			
Service	199675				
Factor Income	165968				
Imports					**950529**
Merchandise				668590	
Service			131878		
Factor Income			150061		
Net unilateral transfer					**39192**
Private transfer				19658	
Official transfer				19534	
Balance on current account					**121680**
(Sum of export, imports and transfer)					
Capital account					
Direct investment					**33259**
US investment abroad				80697	
Foreign investment in USA		47438			
Portfolio investment			**119050**		
US investment abroad				101235★	
Foreign investment		220285			
Other capital account					**469**
Balance on capital account			**85322**		
Official reserve account					
US official reserve assets			**5346**		
Foreign official reserve assets			**39583**		
Balance on reserve transactions			**44929**		
Statistical discrepancy					**8571**

★ Includes US government assets abroad ($390 million).

Source: Data provided at: http://www.bea.doc.gov/bea/di1.htm

APPENDIX E: DEREGULATION, GLOBALIZATION AND JAPANESE BANKING

Japanese commercial banking industry has undergone several radical changes in the twentieth century. Before 1930, the Japanese banks operated without government intervention. For example, there was no minimum capital requirement for banks. In the aftermath of the banking crisis of 1930, the Japanese government changed its attitude toward regulating banks. Regulation of banks underwent transformation during the US occupation of Japan when Article 65, modeled after the US Glass–Steagall Act, was implemented to restrict the joint undertaking of investment and commercial banking activities – albeit

Table E.1   Ratio of bank debt to assets for Japanese firms

	All industries	
	Large firms	Small firms
1978	0.3786	0.3332
1983	0.3513	0.3600
1988	0.3202	0.4161
1993	0.2934	0.4342
1998	0.2761	0.4257

Note: Large firms have a book value of equity greater than ¥1 billion.
Source: Hoshi and Kashyap (1999).

not so restrictive as in the USA, as a concession to the Japanese keiretsu system that had the corporate conglomerate structure of cross-holding of shares in Japan.

In recent years, Japan has mounted a major effort for deregulation that has considerably weakened, among other things, historical barriers between investment and commercial banking activities. Under the 1992 Comprehensive Financial Reform Law, for instance, banks are allowed to establish subsidiaries that engage in a wide range of securities activities. To protect small brokers, the law does not permit banks to engage in retail equities brokerage, an activity allowed to banks in the USA.

Similarly, the reforms from April 1998 onward – collectively known as the "Japanese Big Bang" have led to significant liberalization of the Japanese financial market including

- a removal of interest ceilings on time deposits;
- opening up of the domestic **commercial paper** and bond markets;
- globalization of the Japanese markets; and
- facilitating start-up firms to raise capital on the over-the-counter (OTC) market.

As a result of changes in the financial market, several important activities related to commercial banks' investment and funding source have been affected.

- Big corporations have substantially reduced their financial dependency on commercial banks because of their increased access to other financing channels (e.g. initial public offerings (IPOs), bond markets, and commercial papers).
- Banks have strategically shifted their focus to loans to small firms so as to make up for the loss of the big corporation clientele.

Table E.1 on the debt/asset ratio for the Japanese firms presents evidence in support of the above two observations.

- Banks have increased the proportion of real estate activities in their loan portfolio. In 1970, the proportion of loans to the real estate industry was about 4 percent as compared to 12 percent in 1996.
- Direct bank loans for real estate as well as bank loans based on the collateral of the real estate and shares led to a dramatic increase in soured loans in 1990s in the aftermath of collapse of real estate and stock markets in the late 1980s. Bad debt is estimated to be about 7 percent of GDP.

Historically, Japanese households have held the dominant part of their financial assets in banks. Table E.2 shows a comparison of the deposits-to-GDP ratio for major industrialized countries.

Table E.2 Ratio of deposit to GDP

	Canada	France	Germany	Italy	Japan	UK	USA
1983	0.63	0.61	0.50	0.67	1.58	0.35	0.57
1996	0.79	0.65	0.60	0.52	2.06	1.06	0.42

Source: Hoshi and Kashyap (1999).

Table E.3 ROA and adjusted ROA for Japanese banks

	ROA	Adjusted ROA
1977	0.0013	0.0028
1980	0.0007	0.0013
1985	0.0023	0.0051
1990	0.0027	0.0009
1995	−0.0002	−0.0045
1996	−0.0042	−0.0077
1997	−0.0001	−0.0024

Source: Hoshi and Kashyap (1999).

These data suggest that the Japanese ratio of deposits-to-GDP is the highest among the industrialized countries. It is conceivable that the size of bank deposits in Japan reflects (a) a limited direct access to investment alternatives, and/or (b) substantial transaction costs in channeling funds to other investments. However, deregulation of the brokerage industry after October 1, 1999 is likely to lead to a dramatic reduction in transaction costs for buying and selling securities. In turn, this may result in a shift of funds from bank deposits to security investment.

In the past, the large deposit base of the banking sector enabled the Japanese banks to be important players in the global financial market. For instance, six of the 10 largest banks in the 1980s were Japanese. Shrinkage in the deposit base, however, is unlikely to hold back the large Japanese banks. Deregulation will allow them to issue straight bonds[22] (currently they are allowed to issue only convertible bonds). Thus they are set to raise a significant amount of money by issuing straight bonds; for instance, the three big banks (Sanwa Bank, Sakura Bank, and Sumitomo Bank) are to issue up to $61 billion over the next five years.

- The profitability performance of the Japanese banking industry over the past 10 years can be best characterized as disappointing since its profitability has been low or even negative in recent years. The poor performance is due to a number of factors.
- The Japanese banks have been suffering from the overhang of non-performing loans and bad debts.
- The Japanese banks' cautiousness, if not timidity, coupled with crippling government restrictions on their ability to undertake fee-based activities have not helped the situation. In recent years, many Japanese banks have retrenched from the global banking business.
- That the Japanese banks' capital base is below the minimum 8 percent designated by the **Bank for International Settlements** (BIS) only enhances the challenge for the Japanese banks in improving their profitability.

Table E.3 reports the return on assets (ROA) and adjusted ROA (where income is adjusted for gains or loss of trading securities) for the Japanese banks.

On the brighter side, although the banking sector has been struggling under a mountain of bad loans and poor investments, it recently received a welcome injection of ¥7.4 trillion of public funds in its capital base. Further, any sustained improvement in the domestic stock market will help reduce, or eliminate, valuation losses on security portfolios. The sector's access to funds has also improved, thanks to a reduction in the "Japan premium" – the extra interest charged to Japanese banks for borrowing money. Similarly, in spite of the Japanese banks grappling with a maturity mismatch between their assets and liabilities, or between their short-term deposits and long-term loans to corporate borrowers, their plans to increase reliance on long-term debt should reduce the maturity mismatch. Finally, the consolidation trend in the global banking industry is also surfacing among the Japanese banks. For example,

- Three large banks (the Industrial Bank of Japan, Fuji Bank, and Daiichi Kangyo Bank) announced in August 1999 that they would be merging over the next couple of years to create Japan's largest bank.
- Sakura Bank, a leading Japanese bank, and Nippon Life, one of the world's largest life insurance companies, are forming a personal loan joint venture. It is the first time that Nippon Life has teamed up with a large Japanese city bank.
- In a separate venture, Nippon Life is also moving into online banking by taking a 10 percent stake in Japan's first pure internet bank, set up by Sakura Bank and Fujitsu, the largest computer manufacturer.
- Sumitomo and Sakura, two of Japan's largest banks have announced plans for a merger in 2002 to create the world's second largest banking group, with assets of US$927 billion.

These moves provide a striking sign of the consolidation sweeping Japan's financial sector, as competition in domestic and overseas financial markets intensifies. The resultant increase in the size from consolidation has a potential for improving the global competitive position of the Japanese banks.

NOTES

1. A country devalues its own currency in terms of foreign currencies in order to make its exports competitive in foreign markets and foreign goods more expensive – hence, less competitive in the domestic market.
2. See Appendix A for a description of various exchange rate systems.
3. Hedging activity aims at reducing losses from foreign exchange exposure, whereas speculation is undertaken to profit from anticipated currency value changes through changing exposure in that currency.
4. Foreigners' expectations that the IMF will bail out banks during troubled times renders banks an attractive conduit for foreigners' investment.
5. The decrease in revenue due to oil price decline in 1998 did not have the same impact on Mexico in 1998 as it did in 1982 because of the diversified nature of Mexican exports. Oil exports, for instance, represented only 5.9 percent of the total exports in 1998 as compared to 29 percent in 1986 and 70 percent in 1982. Further, the floating exchange rate adopted by Mexico in 1995 managed to avoid the exacerbated impact of the fixed exchange rate that prevailed earlier.
6. See Appendix B for a brief discussion on the European Union.
7. The change in the nature of crises has also affected the mode of analyzing the crises, and especially the reliance on tools such as the balance of payments (BOP) document. Appendix C briefly describes the composition and structure of the BOP document for a country.
8. A brief discussion on the US regulation of foreign banks is provided in Appendix D.
9. Communications between correspondent banks are largely through the Society of Worldwide International Funds Transfer (SWIFT); and settlement between banks is through the Clearing House Interbank Payments Systems (CHIPS).

10 See Rajan and Zingales (1998). This is a broad characterization in that situations rarely correspond to the two extremes discussed here.

11 Are opaqueness and civil law tradition solely responsible for relationship orientation? In the USA until the mid-1970s, and in the UK until the mid-1980s, relationship orientation prevailed even among investment banks. When deregulation of the securities market took place, competitive forces were unleashed and the same investment banks had to quickly shift their orientation from the "relationship" to the "transaction." Regulations of the securities market were thus responsible for the relationship orientation and not the legal system. It is then conceivable that the civil law system may further nudge toward the relationship orientation; but it is not a necessary condition for such an orientation.

12 Now that the interstate banking prohibition is no longer in force, the edgie should be even less relevant than before.

13 To compound the confusion further, the term "euro" has now been adopted by the EU to designate the common currency to replace currencies (e.g. German mark and French franc) of several member countries of the Union.

14 Although individuals may circumvent this regulation by opening NOW (negotiable order of withdrawals), for-profit businesses are not permitted to open NOW accounts. US-based banks have managed to avoid this restriction for US dollar-denominated deposits by sweeping end-of-day demand deposit balances in overnight interest-bearing instruments that revert back to demand deposits the next day. This practice, however, is not practicable for foreign currencies in significantly different time zones (Zagorski and McPartland 1999).

15 Although regulations related to underwriting debt securities were lifted earlier, the repeal of the Glass–Steagall Act took place in 1999.

16 The development of the Japanese banking industry under the changing regulatory regime is presented in Appendix E.

17 Deregulation, implying a net reduction in regulation is often a misnomer in characterizing the ongoing process of globalization, since introduction of a new set may further constrain a bank's activities. It is the unevenness of regulations that is being replaced by their uniformity across countries. Capital adequacy guidelines under the Basel agreement are a pertinent example of the harmonization process.

18 See Chapter 8 for further details.

19 Greece was unable to meet the convergence criteria; however, in May 2000, it was certified to have met the criteria, thus paving the way to allow her to join the Union in 2001. The UK, Denmark and Sweden have so far "opted out" from joining the EMU.

20 Even the LIFFE (London International Financial Futures and Options Exchange) persisted in expensive "open outcry pit trading" long after its business migrated to screen trading and trading through the so-called Electronic Communications Networks (ECNs). Of course, as a result, its busiest contracts fled to Eurex, its cheaper, Frankfurt-based rival that resulted from a merger between the Deutsche Terminboerse or DTB and Soffex, the Swiss futures exchange.

21 Credit Suisse and First Boston first formed a joint venture in 1978. In 1988, Credit Suisse acquired First Boston when the latter suffered a large cash shortage resulting from the market crash of 1987.

22 Relaxation of the Glass–Steagall Act, even before its repeal in1999, allowed US banks to garner a significant market share of new bond issues, especially low-rated.

CHAPTER 3

Foreign Exchange Market Participation

LEARNING OBJECTIVES

- To envisage the institutional background of a foreign exchange market
- To learn the mechanics of spot and forward foreign exchange rate quotes
- To learn how arbitrage and speculation work in the foreign exchange markets
- To learn about swap transactions in the spot, forward, and money markets
- To understand forces that affect currency values and interrelate goods, financial, and currency markets

3.1 Introduction

Foreign exchange markets facilitate currency trading among entities using different base currencies. They can be classified in two categories: the *wholesale market* and the *retail market*. Commercial and investment banks dominate the wholesale market, also known as the interbank market. The volume of transactions on the wholesale market roughly exceeds four times that in the retail market. Transactions in the retail market arise from activities related to international trade (imports and exports), **foreign direct investment** (transfer of goods and services; infusion of funds through debt or equity financing; and dividends as well as capital repatriation), foreign portfolio investment (securities purchases and sales), tourism, and unilateral transfers or gifts.

The most widely traded currency in the foreign exchange markets today is the US dollar (US$), followed by the euro (€), and the Japanese yen (¥). Because of their truly global nature, foreign exchange markets are the most active among financial markets – including even those for securities such as equities and bonds. The *daily* volume of trading on the foreign exchange markets exceeds US$1.5 trillion. In addition, foreign exchange markets play a critical role for multinational banks because currency markets provide them opportunities not only for generating large profits but also for improved risk management. Thus, a study of the international dimension of the banking industry requires a reasonable familiarity with operations in foreign exchange markets.

This chapter discusses the mechanics of the foreign exchange market, the relationships of the foreign exchange market with goods as well as other parts of financial markets, and related issues.

3.2   Institutional Background

There are two sets of transactions in foreign exchange: spot and forward. A **spot** transaction involves exchange of two currencies immediately (normally the transaction is settled two business days after the agreement is reached). The **forward** transaction requires exchange of one currency for another at a specified future date (e.g., one month or two months from today) at a mutually agreed upon rate.

Transactions among banks, channeled through the interbank or wholesale market, are mostly swaps. A **swap** transaction is a combination of two transactions of different maturities, one for buying and the other for selling a given currency. When the near-term maturity of a swap transaction is today, it is called a **spot-forward** swap; when both transactions of a swap are to be executed in the **forward market**, it is a **forward–forward** swap. A swap transaction is similar to the **repurchase agreement** (which allows a bank to trade cash for riskless securities today and simultaneously agree to trade securities for cash at a future date, or vice versa). The underlying motivation for both sets of transactions is also similar, as we shall see later in this chapter.

Major participants in the foreign exchange market are commercial and investment banks, foreign exchange brokers (who obtain commissions through matching buyers and sellers of currencies), central banks of different countries, multinational corporations, commercial customers, and other financial institutions such as mutual funds.

Commercial banks are typical **market makers** in given currencies. Thus a bank makes a market not only by actively buying and selling in a specific currency on its own account but also through serving as a counterparty for other market participants who want to buy or sell that currency. As a result of its market-making activities, the market-making bank creates liquidity in currency markets and provides continuous price quotes for other market participants. As a market maker, the bank faces substantial risks by quoting bid/ask prices (i.e. buying and selling prices announced by the bank for other currencies in terms of a given currency) because at any moment the bank may find, for instance, that the number of times it is "hit" on the ask side is much larger than on the bid side, that is, there are more buyers than sellers for a given currency. As a result, the bank reduces its **long position** (depletes its stock) and may even find itself facing a **short position** in that currency. Essentially, the two types of *price-related* risks faced by the market maker are:

- the opportunity loss due to premature disposal of the currency (selling the currency earlier at a lower price); and

- the storage cost due to failure of timely disposal of the currency (selling the currency later without adequate compensation for investment in the currency).

When a bank is an active participant (irrespective of whether it is a market maker) in the foreign exchange market, it internally controls its *transaction-based risk* exposure by requiring individual traders to observe preset ceilings not only per transaction but also on a cumulative basis throughout the day. Since it is not unusual to find a currency gaining or losing 2–5 percent of its value in a day, a large trading limit for a single trader can put the bank at great risk. Such ceiling requirements can be set aside only by higher-level management. Thus ceilings are raised for traders with proven track records; for example, in 1987 one trader at Bankers Trust had a trading limit of $700 million, an amount equivalent to almost one-quarter of the bank's capital, and he managed to trade at times for a single transaction of about $2 billion.[1]

Another risk facing the bank is the **settlement**. Suppose that a US bank agreed to sell Canadian dollars for euros to a foreign bank, and this transaction was to channel through the **Society for Worldwide Interbank Financial Telecommunications (SWIFT)**, an international network for settlement of transactions. Suppose further that the US bank fulfilled its commitment by delivering Canadian dollars; the SWIFT network would provisionally credit the bank's account for euros upon delivery of Canadian dollars. If, for whatever reason, the foreign bank failed to deliver euros, the US bank's account for euros would be debited, and it would have to obtain the requisite euros very likely at another rate. If timing was of essence in obtaining the delivery of euros, the US bank might have faced an additional loss.

Typically, wholesale transactions between two parties are first agreed upon via telephone and later confirmed in writing. Can a counterparty refuse to acknowledge the agreement because of a subsequent adverse movement in the currency market? Because banks maintain transcripts of all telephone conversations on audiotape for a month or so, the potential for such occurrence is small; still, it does exist, and remains a source of risk.

3.3 Mechanics of Currency Quotes and Trading

3.3.1 Spot market

In the spot market, a bank gives a quote for buying or selling a foreign currency to another party. The **bid** price is the amount a *quoting* bank is willing to pay for *purchase* of a unit of foreign currency. The **ask** price is the amount the bank would like to obtain for *sale* of a unit of foreign currency. To make a profit in the exchange of a foreign currency, the selling price (ask) must be higher than the buying price (bid). The *spread* between the bid and ask prices is the compensation for the bank carrying the inventory (and associated risks) of the foreign currency.

The following aspects or implications of the foreign exchange quotes are noteworthy.

Denominating versus "commodity" currency

Example 3.1

Suppose in the spot market, a market-making bank gives a bid-ask quote of

$$US\$/CHF\ 0.5921\text{--}0.5934$$

In this case, the "US$" preceding the quote connotes that the US dollar is the medium of exchange, the *base currency, currency of quote*, or the *denominating currency*. The symbol "CHF" representing the Swiss franc, is in the denominator for which the quote is being provided; hence, it is a "commodity." Thus, the quote is for one unit of this "commodity." The quote may also be written as

$$US\$0.5921\text{--}0.5934/CHF$$

or

$$US\$0.5921/CHF\text{--}US\$0.5934/CHF$$

For currencies having small values in the US$ terms, the quotes are for 100 or 1000 units. For example, the Japanese yen is quoted for 100 units.

This quote states that the *quoting* bank is willing to *buy* one CHF from the customer for 59.21 cents (i.e. US$0.5921) and willing to *sell* one CHF at a price of US$0.5934. As this example shows, the ask price is higher than the bid price. Thus, for each CHF that the quoting bank can buy at US$0.5921 and then sell at US$0.5934, it will earn profit of US$0.0013.

Direct versus indirect quote

A bid-ask price of CHF/US$ 1.6852–1.6889 indicates that the quoting bank is willing to buy US dollars – now the commodity – at CHF 1.6852 and to sell US dollars at CHF 1.6889. The bid price of 1.6852 in this case is the reciprocal of 0.5934 (the ask price in Example 3.1), while the ask price of 1.6889 is the reciprocal of 0.5921 (the bid price in Example 3.1).

As can be seen from the above examples, a bank may provide bid-ask quotations for a currency in two formats. If a bank offers a quote in terms of the domestic currency (dollars in the US case), the bank has offered a **direct** quote or an *American* quote to a US resident. In the first case above,

$$US\$/CHF\ 0.5921\text{--}0.5934$$

is a direct quote because it indicates the cost of exchange in terms of dollars for one CHF. Similarly, if a bank provides a quote in terms of a foreign currency (CHF in our example), the bank has offered an **indirect** quote or a *European* quote to a US resident. In the second case,

$$\text{CHF/US\$ } 1.6852–1.6889$$

is an indirect quote because it provides the costs for selling or buying one dollar in terms of CHF. Note that in our examples, the direct quote for a US resident is an indirect quote for the Swiss resident, and the indirect quote for a US resident is a direct quote for the Swiss resident.

In brief,

$$\text{Direct bid} = 1/\text{Indirect ask} \quad \text{Direct ask} = 1/\text{Indirect bid}$$

Size of the bid–ask spread

The size of the bid-ask spread (the difference between bid and ask rates for a currency) indicates risks faced by the quoting or market-making bank and thus depends on the breadth and depth of its market reflected in indicators such as volume of transactions, number of dealers in the market, liquidity, and volatility of the market for that currency. This spread is usually expressed in terms of a percentage of the *ask* price[2] and is calculated as:

$$\text{Percentage spread} = (\text{Ask price} - \text{Bid price})/\text{Ask price}$$

In the first case of the direct quote, the percentage spread is

$$(0.5934 - 0.5921)/0.5934 = 0.0022 \text{ or } 0.22\%$$

Suppose a customer has agreed to buy CHF 1,000 from a bank in the spot market at the above quotation. Soon after the agreement is struck, she changes her mind and decides to sell the CHF back to the bank. In this case, initially she spends US\$593.40 (=US\$0.5934/CHF × CHF 1,000) to obtain CHF 1,000. Later she receives US\$592.10 (=CHF 1,000 × US\$0.5921/CHF) from the CHF sale. Thus, she manages to lose US\$1.30 (=US\$593.40 − US\$592.10) or 0.22 percent. This cost to the customer is the transaction cost, and it also represents the bank's profit.

For widely traded currencies the spread ranges from 0.1 percent to 0.5 percent. However, for less actively traded currencies, the spread may exceed the upper limit of the range, because the bank may have to carry the inventory of these currencies longer than for widely traded currencies. In the process, the bank faces a larger carrying cost and a higher risk of loss in value of these currencies.

In the wholesale market, traders typically quote only the last two digits. For instance, when the quote is

$$\text{US\$/£}1.4789–1.4797$$

(the bid price for the British currency – £ or BP – in terms of the US dollar is 1.4789 and the corresponding ask price is 1.4797), the dealer quotes

$$89-97$$

to the other trader. Note that each transaction is for US$3 million or more; consequently, the quotes carry *4 to 5 digits after decimals*. If the quote were rounded up to a fewer digits, it would be uncompetitive and thus unacceptable to one or the other party.

For a £10 million transaction, the above quote represents US$8,000 of profit [= £10 million (US$1.4797 − US$1.4789)] for the quoting dealer. A rounding up to three digits will mean US$10,000 of profit, which may be unacceptable to the customer bank. Finally, if the quote were for two digits after the decimal, the dealer providing the quote would not have any compensation!

Change in currency value

A change over time in the value of a currency is connoted as appreciation-upvaluation or depreciation-devaluation.

Example 3.2

Suppose last year, we had the quote

$$CHF\ 1.56/US\$$$

And today, we have

$$CHF\ 1.90/US\$$$

In this case, the "commodity" currency, the US$, has increased in value or *appreciated*[3] in terms of the base currency by

$$(1.90 - 1.56)/1.56,\ or\ +21.79\%$$

These quotes can also be restated as

$$US\$0.6410/CHF\ last\ year\ and\ US\$0.5263/CHF\ today$$

And, as a result, the CHF has decreased or *depreciated* by

$$(0.5263 - 0.6410)/0.6410,\ or\ -17.89\%$$

Thus the same change in the relationship between two currencies does not translate into the identical percentage change of appreciation (+21.79% for US$) or depreciation (−17.9% for CHF).

3.3.2 Forward market

When a commercial bank agrees to deliver one currency (say, CHF) to another party at a future date in terms of a specified amount of another currency (US$), this agreement is called a **forward contract**. For example, an importer, who needs to pay in Japanese yen (JY or ¥) one month from now, enters into a 30-day forward contract with a bank to buy JY. At the end of the month, the exchange will take place at the rate specified in the contract and this rate may differ from the actual – spot – exchange rate prevailing on the thirtieth day. Similarly, an American exporter anticipating payment in euros two months from now signs a forward contract with a bank to sell euros to get US$. In both cases, the exchange rates are specified in the contract before the exchange actually occurs.

From the perspective of importers and exporters, forward contracts function as a **hedge** against uncertain exchange rate movements because the forward contract locks in the rate at which the foreign currency is to be bought or sold at the designated time in future. Once a bank commits to the price of the forward contract, it assumes the risk of currency rate fluctuation. To offset its exposed foreign position, the bank may engage in other exchange transactions such as swaps (as defined above) or wait for another customer who will need an offsetting transaction.

Forward contracts are usually denominated in one-month, two-month, three-month, six-month and twelve-month maturities. However, other maturities are also available but must be negotiated with a bank. These contracts are also negotiated for the precise amount desired by the customer. Because of this tailor-made feature with respect to both timing and amount, forward contracts are very popular among non-financial entities, especially those with only occasional need for buying or selling foreign exchange. At the same time, the customized nature of a forward contract prevents it from having a secondary market, because its pricing is unlikely to be transparent to a potential buyer of the contract. As a result, a forward contract needs to be held till maturity. Further, it is executed upon maturity even if in the interim the revised circumstances make it unnecessary or even undesirable for the customer to carry out the obligation of the forward contract.[4]

Forward rates can be expressed in three ways:

1 outright quote;
2 swap rate method; and
3 forward premiums or discounts.

The **outright quote** is the actual price of the forward contract. This quote is usually employed for commercial customers. A **swap (rate) quote** connotes the difference between the outright forward quote and the corresponding spot rate. The swap rate quote is commonly used in interbank transactions.

Example 3.3

Suppose the following quotes are obtained for the spot, one-month, and two-month CHF:

	Bid-ask spot	One-month	Two-month
US$/CHF	0.5921−0.5934	4−6	9−7

For the one-month forward contract, the **swap quote** of "4–6" means *adding* "4" points to the last digit of the (spot) *bid* price and "6" points to the last digit of the (spot) *ask* price, in order to obtain the corresponding outright forward quotes. Thus the one-month swap quote provided above translates in the corresponding *outright* forward bid price of

$$US\$/CHF\ 0.5925\ (= 0.5921 + 0.0004)$$

And the ask price of

$$US\$/CHF\ 0.5940$$

When the first number of the swap quote is *larger* than the second number, as in the "9–7" quote for the two-month forward contract, these numbers are *subtracted* from the spot bid and ask prices respectively to obtain the outright quotes. Thus, the outright prices of the two-month forward contract are obtained by subtracting "9" points from the last digit of the bid price and 7 points from the last digit of the ask price. As a result, the two-month outright forward contract quote is

$$US\$/CHF\ 0.5912 – 0.5927$$

This example illustrates that the one-month forward contract is selling at a *premium* (i.e. the forward rate is above the spot rate) while the two-month forward contract is selling at a *discount* (i.e. the forward rate is below the spot rate). The third method presents the quote in terms of a ratio representing *(annualized) premium or discount (rate)*. This forward premium or discount rate can be expressed as:

Forward premium (discount) rate

$$= \frac{\text{Forward rate} - \text{Spot rate}}{\text{Spot rate}} \times \frac{12\ \text{months (or 360 days)}}{\text{Forward contract maturity in months (or in days)}}$$

or

$$= \frac{\text{Swap rate}}{\text{Spot rate}} \times \frac{12\ \text{months}}{\text{Forward contract maturity in months}}$$

where the negative quantity is the *discount* rate, and the positive, the *premium* rate. It is obvious from the expression above that a positive (negative) swap rate implies a forward premium (discount) rate.

Example 3.4

The annualized one-month forward bid rate for the CHF in Example 3.3 is

$$0.008\ \text{or}\ 0.8\%\ [= \{(0.5925 - 0.5921)/0.5921\} \times 12 \times 100]$$

Similarly, the corresponding two-month **forward discount** rate for bid is

$$0.912\% \: [= \{(0.5912 - 5921)/0.5921\} \times (12/2) \times 100]$$

Just as in the case of the spot rate where appreciation for one currency does not equal depreciation for the other currency, a premium for one currency does not necessarily imply the discount of the same magnitude for the other currency. In the above example, the spot and the one-month forward *bid* rates for the US dollar are

$$1/0.5934 = 1.6852 \quad \text{and} \quad 1/0.5940 = 1.6835$$

respectively. As a result, the one-month forward discount rate on the US dollar is

$$-1.21\% \: [= \{(1.6835 - 1.6852)/1.6852\} \times 12 \times 100]$$

Thus the discount rate for the US dollar does not have the same magnitude as the corresponding premium on the CHF.

3.3.3   Settlement date

Spot or forward contracts are settled on the date of delivery of the funds promised in the contract. Spot contracts are usually settled two business days (or less) after the agreement is reached. The settlement day for the spot contract is also called the **value date**. For example, the spot contract is entered into on July 7, 20xx. The value date for the spot contract is July 9, 20xx. (If July 9 is a holiday, then the next business day is the value date.)

When currencies of countries sharing the same time zone are traded in the spot market, such as the US$ and the Mexican peso, the value date is usually one business day after the agreement is reached.

The value date of the forward contract is similar to that of the spot contract except that the length of the maturity is added to the spot value date. Thus, for a one-month or 30-day forward contract, 30 days are added to the contract's appropriate spot value date (one- or two-day). But, there are special cases to be considered as illustrated in the following two examples.

Example 3.5

Suppose a one-month forward contract is entered into on July 7 (Wednesday). Since the spot value date, which is two business days after the contract, is July 9, the settlement day for the forward contract will be August 9. For two-month forward contracts, the settlement day will be September 9.

Example 3.6

Suppose on July 28, a one-month forward contract is traded; and the spot value date is July 30. Then the settlement date will be August 30. If August 30 is a holiday, then August 31 will be the settlement day. If August 31 is also a holiday, then the following day as the settlement day would go beyond August into September, a different calendar month. As the settlement date would have been shifted to a new month, the actual settlement date will be moved *back* to August 29, the last trading day in August, for delivery.

3.4 Locational Arbitrage

3.4.1 Two-location arbitrage

Arbitrage opportunities arise from discrepancies in quoted exchange rates in different locations or countries. Because two locations may happen to have two different market rates for a given currency, the bank can extract a profit from this discrepancy. The *locational arbitrage* takes place when a bank buys a currency in one location and simultaneously sells it at a higher rate in another location. Hence,

> An arbitrage is possible when a *bid* quote for a currency in one location is *lower* than an *ask* quote for the same currency in another location.

Notice also that the arbitrage transaction is based on the premise of *knowledge* of discrepancies, and not *expectation* of such discrepancies. Since expectation entails uncertainty, ruling out expectations also means that an arbitrage transaction rules out assuming any risk. Hence, the arbitrage profit is riskless.

3.4.2 Triangular arbitrage

An extension of the locational arbitrage is the **triangular arbitrage**, which arises from misalignment of exchange rates in three different locations or currencies.

   An important element in the triangular arbitrage transaction is the existence of discrepancy in the actual rate vis-à-vis the implied **cross rate**, the exchange rate between two currencies, A and B, calculated from exchange rates given for each of these two currencies in terms of a third currency, C. If the quoted rate between A and B differs from the corresponding implicit cross rate, there is an arbitrage opportunity.

   Suppose, ignoring the bid-ask price differences, the Frankfurt quote for CHF in terms of US$ is

$$US\$/CHF \ 0.2510,$$

while the New York quote for the pound sterling (£) is

$$US\$/£ \ 2.810$$

Further, the London quote for CHF is

$$CHF/£ \ 11.17^5$$

In this example, from the US investor's perspective, the *actual* cross-rate between the Swiss franc and pound sterling is CHF/£ 11.17 and the *implied* cross-rate is

$$CHF/£\ 11.1952$$

as given by the chain:

$$
\begin{aligned}
CHF/£ &= (CHF/US\$) \times (US\$/£) \\
&= [1/(US\$/CHF)] \times (US\$/£) \\
&= (CHF1/US\$\ 0.251) \times (US\$2.810/£) \\
&= CHF/£\ 11.195
\end{aligned}
$$

Because the actual cross-rate is lower than the corresponding implied cross-rate, an arbitrage opportunity exists (buy low and sell high): buy £ in London with CHF11.17; sell £ for US$ 2.810 in New York; and convert US$2.810 in CHF 11.1952 in Frankfurt.

Note that the implied cross-rate uses the *chain rule* where the actual quotes of two currencies in a third currency are combined so as to eliminate the third currency and one currency now is quoted in terms of the second currency. The following example illustrates in greater detail the chain rule as well as the nature of the triangular arbitrage and corresponding profits.

Example 3.7

New York:	US$/CHF	= 0.4875
	US$/MP	= 0.1555
Zurich:	CHF/US$	= 2.0513
	CHF/MP	= 0.3245
Madrid:	MP/CHF	= 3.0510
	MP/US$	= 5.4515

These currency quotes at three different locations are not necessarily consistent. We need to find out first which quotes are inconsistent, that is, which quotes are not in equilibrium.

In New York, the implied indirect rate for CHF (the price of US$ in terms of CHF) is

$$CHF\ 2.0513/US\$\ (= 1/[US\$0.4875/CHF])$$

which is the same as the price quoted for $ in Zurich, that is CHF 2.0513/$. Thus, the exchange rates for the dollar and the CHF are in equilibrium.

In New York, the implied indirect rate for MP (Mexican peso) is

$$MP/US\$\ 6.4309$$

a quote higher than the quote in Zurich, MP 5.4515/US$. Alternatively, in Madrid, the price for MP in terms of US$ is

$$US\$/MP\ 0.1834$$

which is higher than the New York quote of US$/MP 0.1555. Thus, the exchange rate between US$ and MP is not in equilibrium. Hence, MP should be bought in New York, and sold in Madrid against US$.

In Zurich, the price of CHF in terms of MP is

$$MP\ 3.0817/CHF$$

which again is different from the quote in Madrid, MP 3.0510/CHF. Thus, the CHF is less expensive in terms of MP in Madrid than in Zurich, or the MP goes much further in Madrid than in Zurich for buying the CHF.

Step 1   If we initiate arbitrage transactions with US$1 in New York, we first convert it to MP 6.4309 in New York (and not Madrid) because sale of the US$ brings in more MP in New York than in Madrid.

Step 2   Given that we now have MP 6.4309, we must decide whether we should convert them in CHF in Madrid or Zurich. We should convert MP into CHF in Madrid because it obtains

$$CHF\ 2.1080 = MP\ 6.4309 \times CHF\ 0.3278/MP$$

Step 3   We convert CHF2.1080 in US$1.0276 in Zurich (or in New York, for that matter) by the conversion rate CHF 2.0513.

The result is that all these transactions yield a profit of

$$US\$.0276\ per\ US\$\ or\ 2.76\%$$

By starting US$ (NY) → MP (Madrid) → CHF (Zurich or NY) → $

The profit of 2.76 percent is a free lunch to the trader because these transactions do not require any initial investment.

This example shows that $ and CHF are consistent, but MP is out of sync. In a chain, except for the beginning and the end (since we start and end in the same currency), no currency should appear twice; otherwise the transaction will overstate the profit.

In brief, the principle of triangular arbitrage is to examine which pair(s) of exchange rates is not in equilibrium. Once we know these misaligned pairs of exchange rates, we select the appropriate quotes and locations that give the positive returns. It should be noted that

• It does not matter in which currency one starts. One condition is that one should begin and end in the same currency. The *percentage profit* will be exactly the same for any starting point. Thus for a starting point in CHF, the chain of activities will be

$$CHF\ (Zurich) \to \$\ (NY) \to MP\ (Madrid) \to CHF$$
$$CHF\ 1\ (Zurich) \to \$0.4875\ (NY) \to MP\ 3.1350\ (Madrid) \to CHF\ 1.0275$$

which is the same percentage profit as when we started with $ (except for the rounding error).

- Once one has selected the beginning (and ending) currency, the other two currencies in a triangular arbitrage can appear only once in the chain.[6]

When bid and ask prices are provided, the above procedure still holds, with one caveat: the inverse of a direct bid is the indirect ask price, and vice versa, as we noted earlier. Thus

$$\text{CHF}/\pounds \text{ BID} = (\text{CHF/US\$ BID}) \times (\text{US\$}/\pounds \text{ BID})$$
$$= [1/(\text{US\$/CHF ASK})] \times (\text{US\$}/\pounds \text{ BID})$$

Care should be exercised in determining which currency is being bought or sold and where. It should be noted that time is of essence especially in a well-functioning currency market, because the arbitrage action resulting from disequilibrium very quickly removes any discrepancies in the market place.

The example above illustrates the process of locational arbitrage. Another type of arbitrage activity is related to the interest rate parity, and the activity is known as the **covered interest arbitrage**. Interest rate parity is one of the most important relationships in international finance.

3.5 Theories of the Foreign Exchange Market

3.5.1 Interest rate parity theory (IRPT)

Interest rate parity (IRP) is one of the several *parity* conditions in foreign exchange markets. It establishes the relationship of interest rates in domestic and foreign money markets with the spot and forward currency rates in the foreign exchange market. This parity condition essentially states that in impediment-free financial (money and foreign exchange) markets, returns on two comparable investments in two different currencies will be equal once they are adjusted for exchange rate differences. This condition is illustrated below with an example.

Example 3.8

Suppose a bank, facing the decision of investing excess funds for three months, has obtained the following information.

- The annualized domestic certificate of deposit (CD) rate (r) for three months is 10 percent.
- The comparable UK CD rate ($r^\star$) is 12 percent.
- The spot exchange rate (SR) is US\$1.50/$\pounds$.
- The three-month forward rate (FR) is US\$1.51/$\pounds$.

The bank faces two options. The first option (Option A) is that the bank will invest domestically, that is, in the US CD market. Under the second option (Option B), the bank will

1 Convert the US\$ in $\pounds$,
2 Invest in the UK CD market, and
3 Sell the investment proceeds in $\pounds$ for US\$ in the three-month forward market.

The choice of Option A or B depends on which option gives the bank the higher dollar return.

- Investment value at the end of the three-month period for Option A:

$$\$1(1 + r/4)$$

or

$$\$1\ (1 + 10\%/4) = \$1.025$$

- Investment value at the end of the three-month period for Option B:
  - Convert US$ to £ in the spot market

$$£/US\$\ 0.6667\ (= 1/1.50)$$

  - Invest £ proceed in the UK money market today. Three months from now, this investment will yield

$$£\ 0.6667(1 + 12\%/4) = £0.6867$$

  - Enter today into a three-month forward contract to convert investment proceeds in £ back to US$

$$£\ 0.6867\ (\times\ US\$1.51/£) = US\$1.0369$$

Because the return (expressed in terms of US$) under Option B (the foreign market route) exceeds the return under Option A (the domestic route), the foreign market alternative is preferred. The return under the second alternative is of course immune to fluctuations in the spot rate between £ and US$.

If many US banks or investors were to invest in the UK market, the demand for spot £ and UK CDs, and supply of forward £ will increase. Consequently, any combination of the three things could happen. First, the US CD rate could go up to attract investors. Second, the UK interest rate could go down. Third, the exchange rates (spot rate and/or forward rate) could change.

When changes in financial markets occur, there comes a point when the capital flows from the USA today (reversing in three months) will stop, and the returns in the two currencies would achieve parity. This happens when

$$[(US\$1)/(SR)](1 + r^\star)(FR) = (1 + r)$$

where SR is the spot rate for £ in terms of US$, that is, US$/£; and FR is the forward rate for £ in terms of US$.

The term in the bracket on the left side of the equation above is the amount of foreign currency available for investment abroad upon conversion of US$1. The second term, along with the term in the bracket is the investment proceeds in the foreign currency. The third term converts that investment proceed back into US$. The right side of the equation represents the investment proceed in US$ as a result of the investment of US$1 in the domestic money market.

A rearrangement of terms of the equation above leads to:

$$FR = SR(1 + r)/(1 + r^\star) \qquad (3.1)$$

or

$$(FR - SR)/SR = (r - r\star)/(1 + r\star) \tag{3.1a}$$

Note that the relationship does not have adjustment terms for forward rates for less than a year, since such adjustments are made in the interest rates. For example, when the investment is for a six-month period, the quoted annualized interest rates are modified to reflect the six-month period. One can also use quoted interest rates as they are in the annualized form, and annualize the corresponding forward premium rate. The important matter is that both forward premium and the interest rates should have a consistent time dimension.

Equation 3.1 is called the *interest rate parity condition*. This relationship is critically related to the "covered" interest arbitrage since, as Example 3.8 demonstrated, fluctuations in the spot rates have no bearings on the profit. Indeed, Equation 3.1 contains variables that are observable, and do not require any *expectations*. IRPT is thus an ex post equilibrium relationship. As a result, disequilibrium affords participants an arbitrage opportunity: before the market reaches equilibrium, any investor can make money without any out-of-pocket investment. For the arbitrage process, the following steps are required for riskless profits:

Step 1   Using the data from Example 3.7, we compute FR^c, the *critical* or *intrinsic* forward rate as

$$
\begin{aligned}
FR^c &= SR(1 + r/4)/(1 + r\star/4) \\
&= 1.5(1 + 0.1/4)/(1 + 0.12/4) \\
&= 1.4927
\end{aligned}
$$

Step 2   We compare the intrinsic forward rate, FR^c with the *actual*, market-quoted forward rate, FR (in this example $1.51/£).

1   If $FR > FR^c$, then the actual forward rate is *overvalued*, and £, the overvalued currency, should be sold in the forward market. This transaction also has two additional implications:

- We will have to have £ three months from today to meet our obligation in the forward contract, that is, a long £ position in the money market to offset the short position created through the forward foreign exchange market. Thus mirror positions are created in financial and foreign exchange markets.
- When we sell forward £, we create a long position in US$. Therefore we need to create a short position in US$ three months from now, that is, borrow US$ initially for three months. In other words, a *short* position in currency A in the forward market should be initially accompanied with a *short* position in currency B in the *money* market.

These implications suggest that we should

- borrow US$ today at the domestic interest rate (create a short position in the US$) for three months;

- convert them into £ at the spot rate;
- invest the proceeds in the UK (foreign) money market for three months (have a long position in £); and
- sell £ proceeds in the forward market.

In the above example,

- borrow US$1,000 for three months at the 10 percent annualized interest rate;
- convert US$1,000 in £ at the spot rate of US$1.5/£;
- invest the proceeds in £s at the 12 percent annualized interest rate for three months in the UK market;
- sell investment proceeds in £s in the forward market at US$1.51/ £.

Given the US$1.51/ £ forward rate quote, the dollar proceeds net of debt service (interest and principal) will be:

$$[US\$1000/(US\$1.5/\pounds) \times (1 + 0.12/4) \times US\$1.51/\pounds - US\$1000 \ (1 + 0.1/4)$$
$$= US\$1036.86 - US\$1025$$
$$= US\$11.86$$

The profit of US$11.86 per $1,000 is, as already noted, immune to foreign exchange exposure and thus is a free lunch to the trader.

2 When $FR < FR^c$, it follows that the forward rate is *underpriced*. Hence we need to buy the foreign currency at the quoted market forward rate. This suggests that we need to borrow in the foreign money market now, convert them in US$, and invest the US$ proceeds in the domestic (US) money market for the duration of the forward rate.

A casual look at the quotes provided in the newspapers may indicate arbitrage opportunities along the above lines.[7] However, when transactions cost and taxes are considered, the arbitrage profit ceases to exist. Indeed, these quotes reflect parity conditions in the *Eurocurrency markets* (discussed in detail in Chapter 4) that are free from government-induced impediments such as transaction costs and taxes encountered in the domestic markets. Further, as commercial banks are typical market makers in both foreign exchange and Eurocurrency markets, they are unlikely to provide a free lunch to others at their expense! Nevertheless, the possibility still remains that distortions in the regulated domestic money markets may provide an arbitrage opportunity.

The IRP relationship is not just significant for arbitrage activities; it also has implications for hedging and speculative activities, since it allows one to consider two alternative ways for dealing in currencies: spot-money markets and the forward market. A more detailed discussion of the benefit/cost analysis of the two alternatives is undertaken later in the chapter.

3.5.2 Purchasing power parity theory

Financial analysts heavily rely on the **purchasing power parity** (PPP) theory to predict future changes in exchange rates. PPP views two currencies in terms of the amount of goods that each can purchase and assumes that in reasonably well-functioning markets, a currency's ability to buy a given amount of goods remains the same everywhere. Thus if one dollar is able to buy one orange in the USA, and one pound sterling is able to buy two oranges in the UK, an exchange rate of US$2/£ should prevail under the PPP theory. If the US$ upon conversion in £ at the current foreign exchange rate, for example, is able to buy more goods in the UK (it is overvalued in terms of £ and its value is above its PPP or intrinsic value), a disequilibrium exists and the PPP theory suggests that its value in terms of £ sterling is likely to decline.

Since this result is intuitively appealing, the PPP theory is often used to predict the foreign exchange value of the dollar (Hakkio 1992). Further, the PPP theory has been commonly used by central banks as a guide to setting up new parity values for their currencies under the fixed exchange rate regime. For example, under the **European Monetary System** (EMS), the currency realignments were reportedly based on the PPP values (Cheung et al. 1995).

There are two versions of PPP: *absolute PPP* and *relative PPP*. In the absolute version, PPP states that the exchange rate-adjusted price for any good (or a basket of goods) is the same everywhere. This relationship is defined as follows:

$$eP^\star = P \tag{3.2}$$

where $P^\star$ and P are the foreign price and domestic price of the good, respectively, and e is the current foreign exchange rate (DC/FC, or worth of a unit of foreign currency in terms of the domestic currency)

Notice that SR was used earlier to depict the spot exchange rate: the difference is that, while SR is a *nominal* foreign exchange rate, e is the corresponding *real* or *equilibrium* rate[8] and its future value (e.g. e_1 at time 1) signifies the real foreign exchange rate at the corresponding time.

The *absolute* version of PPP defines the exchange rate, e, by taking the logarithm of Equation 3.2, that is,

$$\log(e) = \log(P) - \log(P^\star)$$

If PPP holds, the exchange rate changes should not deviate significantly from zero, and the foreign exchange rate should remain constant.

A problem with the absolute version of PPP, either for a single good or a bundle of goods, is that, among other things, it does not reflect differences in consumer tastes in two countries. Suppose there is only one type of wine available in the world. Whereas the Japanese consumers may still regard wine as a "commodity" that has a viable substitute in sake, in France wine may be considered a differentiated good – a "necessity" – that cannot be easily substituted by other beverages. The price elasticity of demand for wine in France then is likely to be much less than that in Japan. Even when the general inflation rates are comparable, the French wine distributor may raise prices far more readily in France than the Japanese wine distributor would in Japan. A reverse scenario is likely with respect to sake in Japan. In any case, the distortion in relative prices may not reflect in the foreign exchange rate linking currencies of the two countries.

The *relative* version of PPP, which overcomes biases such as consumer tastes, suggests that the change in the exchange rate *over time* between two countries will reflect relative changes in the price levels (or the difference in the inflation rates) of the two countries.[9] Formally, the relative version of PPP relationship is:

$$e_1/e_0 = (1 + INF)/(1 + INF\star) \qquad (3.3)$$

or

$$(SR_1 - SR_0)/SR_0 = (INF - INF\star)/(1 + INF\star) \qquad (3.3a)$$

where SR_1 and SR_0 are the exchange rates at time 1 and 0 respectively. Further, SR_1 is the *expected* rate one period from today (date $= 0$).[10] *INF* and *INF*$\star$ are the *expected* domestic and foreign inflation rates, respectively, for period 1. The relative PPP is an ex ante relationship that describes the future exchange rate behavior, and underscores a one-to-one relationship between the inflation differential and exchange rate changes.

Empirical tests on PPP have been conducted on both the relative and the absolute versions. As to the *absolute* version, empirical investigations, such as Abuaf and Jorion (1990), Adler and Lehmann (1983), and Roll (1979), report that deviations from PPP-based exchange rates are stable and do not manage to cancel each other out. More recent studies (e.g. Cheung and Lai 1993; Fung and Lo 1992; and Kim 1990) using more refined techniques, such as variance ratio analysis and a cointegration method,[11] tend to reject the hypothesis that deviations from PPP are stable in the long run.

Empirical tests (e.g. Huang 1990) generally do not support the one-to-one relationship postulated by the *relative* version of PPP between exchange rate changes and the inflation differential between countries. Because the relative version calls for expectations of inflation rates, it is believed that exchange rate changes should consider deviations from the expected values (or unexpected changes in the inflation rates) as a result of the existence of a risk premium. These investigations suggest that the existence of a risk premium in the foreign exchange market cannot be ruled out.[12]

When will real or equilibrium exchange rates change? Such changes occur when, for instance, a more efficient production technology is developed or a cheaper source of raw material is found. Because these are exogenous changes, they do not affect the validity of PPP.

Another possibility is when real rates change as a result of feedback from short-term disturbances. Unlike the first situation, if this possibility exists, it would cast doubt on the validity of the relative PPP. In general, goods markets can hardly be described as "well functioning": structural impediments dominate an economy, even if all government-induced distortions are removed. Economists of all persuasions, as a result, admit "sticky prices" in the goods market, and conclude that PPP will not necessarily hold in the short run. But when short-term deviations permanently affect the long-term competitiveness of industries, the real rate will have undergone a change, and the PPP in the long run will be violated. As Gartner (1993: 27) has observed:

> Possibly, the extraordinarily pronounced and long-lasting overvaluation of the dollar between 1981 and 1985 has shattered and reorganized structures in the world markets so deeply that a return of the real exchange rate to its former value is not enough to reestablish original structures. Five years of massive dollar overvaluation gave foreign competitors of American companies

sufficient time and incentives to enter the American market and to drive the American companies out of markets in third countries.[13]

Inconclusive empirical evidence or ambiguous theoretical implications notwithstanding, PPP relationship is valuable for managerial purposes; the questions raised only suggest that predictions solely based on PPP should be viewed with caution.

Example 3.9

Suppose the current spot rate, SR_0, for the USA and Germany is US$0.50/€. The anticipated US inflation rate (INF) is 10 percent, and the German inflation rate ($INF^\star$) is 12 percent. Then, the expected future exchange rate is

$$SR_1 = SR_0(1 + INF)/(1 + INF^\star)$$
$$= US\$0.50 \times (1.1)/(1.12)$$
$$= US\$0.4911/€$$

Because of higher inflation in Germany, we expect euros to depreciate against the US$.

3.5.3 Fisher Open parity

Fisher Open parity attempts to link the money markets to the exchange rate markets. This parity, which assumes *constant*, *real* interest rates (or the difference in real interest rates in countries are constant), can be expressed as:

$$SR_1/SR_0 = (1 + r)/(1 + r^\star) \tag{3.4}$$

or

$$(SR_1 - SR_0)/SR_0 = (r - r^\star)/(1 + r^\star)$$

Fisher Open is an ex ante relationship linking differentials of current nominal interest rates (reflecting inflation expectations) in two countries with the expected change in the exchange rate. If this relationship holds exactly, it implies that there is no unique risk premium in the forward rates quoted in foreign exchange markets.

A comparison of Equation 3.4 with Equation 3.1 – depicting covered interest arbitrage – reveals that the only difference between the two equations is the replacement of FR, the forward rate in Equation 3.1, with SR_1 in Equation 3.4. Because the market participant acting on the basis of Equation 3.4 is exposed to fluctuations in the spot rate, Equation 3.4 is sometimes described as the *uncovered interest parity* condition.

Example 3.10

Suppose the US nominal interest rate is 8 percent while the nominal interest rate in Japan is 12 percent. Given the current exchange rate, SR_0, of US$0.01/¥, the expected exchange rate will be:

$$SR_1 = SR_0(1 + r)/(1 + r^\star)$$
$$= [US\$0.01/¥] (1.08)/(1.12)$$
$$= US\$0.00964/¥$$

Because the Japanese nominal interest rate is higher than the US counterpart, its currency is expected to depreciate. The logic is based on the premise that the increase in the interest rate is inflation driven and the underlying real interest rates in the two economies are constant. In other words, if the increase in the nominal interest rate is not driven by inflation, the Fisher Open may not hold. Further, it rests on the assumption that the spot rate in the near term will remain constant.

Since the nominal interest rate is comprised of real interest rate and inflation (i.e. $r \approx$ real rate + inflation rate), an increase in inflation will lead to a commensurate increase the nominal interest rate. This relationship is commonly called the **Fisher Effect**.

When real shocks (resulting from, say, a change in technology or oil prices) affect the real interest rate, it is likely that the nominal interest rate would reflect this real interest rate change. Given the exogenous nature of the shocks, the real (and thereby the nominal) interest rate change does not affect the validity of the Fisher effect and hence of the Fisher Open. When, however, a change in the real interest rate is *induced* by the nominal interest rate, the Fisher Open becomes suspect and its predictive ability comes under question.

> In 1991–2, Germany's Bundesbank raised the short-term interest rates, which led to downward revision of inflation expectations by investors. In turn, both the increase in the nominal interest rate and the decrease in the expected inflation rate led to higher real interest rate and managed to make German investments more attractive and induce a substantial capital inflow in Germany. As a result, the spot DM (German mark) became more attractive relative to other currencies such as the French franc (FF). Thus higher interest rates changed the spot currency value, presumably in response to a change in the real interest rate, contrary to what the Fisher Open would have implied. This result then clearly contradicted the Fisher Open prediction.

It should be noted that whenever a central bank raises the short-term interest rate, it does not automatically translate into higher real interest rate. If the market had anticipated such an action, and the actual action *falls short* of the market expectation, the market may revise upward the inflation expectation, thus lowering the real rate in face of the increased short-term interest rate. Even when the market has not anticipated the central bank initiative, the impact of such an unanticipated action need not be positive on the real rate.

> In early 1994, the Federal Reserve tightened the monetary policy unexpectedly, the market apparently concluded that the Federal Reserve's action implied that there was inflation potential the market had not considered (or underestimated), and consequently it revised upward the inflation expectation!

The Fisher Open does not allow interest rates to *influence* the current or expected spot rate, since it admits an interest rate change strictly as a result of a change in inflation expectation, and assumes that the real interest rates are both constant and stable across national boundaries. The above examples show that the real rates across countries are not only different but that they remain volatile, unlike what the Fisher Open requires. In turn, the real interest rate volatility also underscores greater influence of capital flows on the exchange rates than that of goods flows.[14]

3.5.4 Unbiased forward market hypothesis

As already noted, IRPT relates interest rate differentials to the forward price while the Fisher Open relates the interest differential to the expected exchange rate.[15] Equating the two equations (3.1 and 3.4) – because their right sides are identical – we obtain:

$$FR = SR_1 \tag{3.5}$$

Equation 3.5 simply suggests that the forward price is an **unbiased predictor** for the future spot price. This is the unbiased forward market hypothesis, or **speculative efficient market (SEM) hypothesis**.

Recent empirical studies have widely shown that the forward rate is a biased predictor of the expected future spot rate. This bias is explained by suggesting that the future spot rate contains a risk premium.[16] Some studies have also asserted that the risk premium is not constant over time; instead, it varies over time (Cheung 1993, and Wolff 1987). (Not that a constant premium over time is a comforting thought in itself!) The Fisher Open linking interest rates to the foreign exchange rate is predicated on perfect investment substitutes in the domestic and the foreign currencies; and an asset that is a perfect substitute for the other cannot have a differential risk premium, that is, perfect substitutes and differential risk premiums are mutually exclusive phenomena. Thus, existence of risk premium, even when it is constant, violates the uncovered interest parity and thereby the (speculative) efficient market hypothesis. Varying risk premiums over time only worsens the picture (see Note 11).

Studies by Bekfaert and Hodrick (1993) and Kaminsky (1993) differ from earlier ones in that they link risk premiums specifically to *changes in monetary policies* or *shifts in regimes*. The basic premise underlying these studies is that investors in the foreign exchange market can be rational, but that does not preclude them from making repeated mistakes (i.e. being slow learners or having a short memory span!), because the true model of exchange rate determination evolves over time, resulting in a forward rate that is not equal to the expected spot rate. One of the issues, raised by these analyses, is of considerable interest to a bank manager involved in currency management: will the forward rate adequately reflect the *size* of the impact on the spot rate due to an impending regime change (e.g. a shift in monetary policy or parity exchange rate)?

The answer is a "qualified yes." The market may be able to estimate accurately the *size* of the impending change; however, it may not be able to correctly forecast the *timing* of the change. Consider, for instance, the "peso problem" analyzed in the finance literature highlighting the devaluation of the Mexican peso in 1976. Prior to the 1976 devaluation, the Mexican peso was routinely sold at a discount in the forward market, an observation consistent with the notion that market participants fairly accurately anticipated the likelihood of sizable peso devaluation. As investors in the foreign exchange market did not know the *timing* – exactly when the devaluation would occur – and the actual devaluations had low frequency but large magnitude, naturally the ex post forward rate consistently underestimated the *expected* spot rate *prior* to devaluation.

The **peso problem** (where the forward rate consistently underestimates the future spot rate prior to the actual devaluation) has also been analyzed in the framework of "bubbles" that are rationally expected to grow in a probabilistic fashion even when their existence or growth cannot be justified by fundamental variables. Although bubble theories' strength is that they do not contradict the foreign exchange market efficiency, they fail to explain why the bubble is formed in the first place. Further,

> [since] a bubble is defined in relation to some … model … empirical work on bubbles always tests a joint hypothesis: that the scrutinized data were not generated by a bubble and that the equilibrium model is correct (Gartner 1993: 223).

What does all this mean to the bank manager? A bias due to the risk premium (even when it is volatile over time) in the expected spot rate does not mean that the corresponding forward rate shows market unawareness of impending regime changes. Market participants fairly accurately anticipate *size* of these changes and build them into the forward rates. However, regime changes are heavily influenced by political considerations, whose nuances are not necessarily accurately captured in the *timing* related to the impending changes. As a result, when the bank manager senses market signals regarding an impending change, he or she should set in motion an investigation process looking into political considerations surrounding such changes.

3.5.5 Foreign exchange rate predictability

Can we predict foreign exchange rates? Is it a worthwhile exercise? The ongoing debate on market efficiency in particular and on stability of the real exchange rates in general has generated a variety of responses. Endorsement of *technical analysis* is one such response: it is based on the premise of usefulness of historical data for predicting the course of the foreign exchange rates. Economic models that highlight "real" factors such as productivity changes and shifts in consumption preferences are still other responses. A third avenue considers complex issues such as differing expectations on the part of participants – not all of them being "rational" in the conventional sense. Finally, model builders have become increasingly sensitive to the influence of political realities on the exchange rate behavior. All these efforts have one important implication for managers: to keep an open mind toward all approaches, especially new models, with checks provided by a healthy dose of skepticism.

3.5.6 Foreign exchange market and market hierarchy

The different parity – and related – theories develop linkages among the three markets: goods market, financial market, and foreign-exchange market.[17]

- PPP theory relates the goods market to the foreign exchange market;
- IRPT links securities or money markets and the foreign exchange market;

- Fisher Open links securities or money markets to the spot exchange rate market; and
- Fisher Effect relates goods markets to the securities or money markets.

As we saw in Chapter 1, the competitive goods market ensures competitive financial and foreign exchange markets; hence, validation of the PPP theory will ensure the other three conditions. However, given the asymmetric relationship between the goods and the financial market, a competitive financial market or, more to the point, an efficient foreign exchange market does not require validation of the PPP theory. In this light, the linkages among the above relationships are not so robust as one could have thought. Nevertheless, they do provide valuable insights in the workings of the markets.

Take, for instance, the relationship between the financial market and the foreign exchange market. If a government intervenes in the financial market that results in distorted interest rates, both spot and forward rates prevailing in a *competitive* foreign exchange market will insure, through covered interest arbitrage, the maintenance of interest rate parity. On the other hand, when financial markets are reasonably competitive, government interferences in the foreign exchange markets (e.g. adopting dual exchange rates or retaining the fixed exchange rate regime) without commensurate measures in the money market (e.g. restrictions on borrowing or holding deposits by foreigners) would allow the arbitrager to circumvent restrictions in the foreign exchange market through actions in the money market.

3.6   Motivations of Participants in the Foreign Exchange Market

The foreign exchange market has three types of activities: arbitrage, hedging, and speculation. Because arbitrage activity has been discussed in a previous section, the following discussion will focus on hedging and speculative activities.

3.6.1   Hedging

Exchange rates among major currencies have been very volatile since the inception of the floating rate regime starting in 1973. This volatility has a potentially serious impact on the profitability of importers, exporters, and multinational corporations with transactions or positions denominated in foreign currencies. **Hedging** allows these businesses to avoid currency exposure, that is, volatility in profits due to exchange rate volatility. Banks, which provide hedging services, assume this risk. Banks may also undertake hedging actions on their own account due to, say, loans to customers in foreign currencies. We consider here the bank's net currency exposure, irrespective of its origin.

Hedging risk: Diversifiable or systematic?

One basic issue related to hedging currency exposure is whether the risk is diversifiable or systematic for the bank. In the absence of regulatory constraints, if a risk were diversifiable, the bank assuming this risk would not see an increase in its equity cost. On the other hand, if it hedges such risk, which entails cost, it will only reduce its profitability and thus adversely affect its share price. By the same token, the bank assumption of systematic risk increases its equity cost, and unless the bank receives adequate compensation for that, its share price would suffer. It is useful to consider three scenarios.

1 *Diversifiable risk for both the customer and the bank.* In this case, it is not worthwhile for either party to hedge. But if the customer wants to hedge, the bank need not take any hedging action on its own account. Suppose a bank provides a forward contract to a large firm, which wants to buy €10 million in the one-month forward market. If another customer has already sold – or is anticipated to sell – exactly the same amount 30 days from now, the bank has managed to diversify the risk, and has earned profit from both sides of the basic transaction without any net increase in the currency exposure.[18] Even in the absence of such eventualities, as suggested above, an increase in the risk that is diversifiable (that does not threaten, for instance, the very existence of the bank) should not automatically trigger the hedging action on the part of the bank.

2 *Systematic for the customer but diversifiable for the bank.* Suppose a privately owned small firm wants to hedge £50,000 in the 90-day forward market, because any unfavorable swing in the currency value can seriously harm its prospects for survival. The bank may be able to assume the risk on its own account without worrying about the exposure. This situation is similar to that faced by an insurance company in dealing with actuarial risk (Chapter 1).

3 *Systematic for both the customer and the bank.* Even when prospects for offsetting the risk are not bright under this scenario, the bank may want to use the interbank market for the offset forward transaction.[19] The bank may also resort to the money market alternative explained below.

Alternatively, the bank may have the potential of playing the role of an insurance company, that is, risk sharing. Although currency risk assumption may have dire consequences for an individual customer, a reasonably large number of similar transactions over time may allow the bank to charge a premium that is reasonable for an individual customer but provides the bank more than adequate compensation for assuming the risk.

When the bank does not anticipate a large number of similar transactions, the bank may want to "reinsure," that is, sell the risk to another bank, which may have greater ability to assume the risk.

In any case, the bank may first want to consider the amount for hedging, since it is possible that the bank may have a smaller offset amount requirement than the customer. We now turn to this issue.

Hedge ratio

The forward market hedge is the forward position to be taken relative to the cash position to be hedged, or the **hedge ratio**. Most studies have assumed the hedge ratio to be one, that is, one unit of exposure in foreign currency is hedged with one unit in the forward market (see Eun and Resnick 1988), while others (Swanson and Caples 1987) suggest that the hedge ratio is less than one. Thus, if a US bank has a liability of €10 million maturing in three months, it may want to commit to purchase €10 million (assuming the unitary hedge ratio, i.e., it is equal to one) or less (assuming that the hedge ratio is less than one) in the forward market. In general, three sets of factors affect the hedge ratio.

- Taxes and transactions costs may call for a larger forward amount than the cash position, that is, the hedge ratio in excess of one. When a country, for instance, disallows losses on foreign exchange positions for tax purposes but subjects gains to taxes, the hedge ratio will exceed one.
- The hedge ratio will be affected by the comovement of the spot and forward rates, that is, the smaller the comovement, the smaller the hedge amount requirement. Fung and Leung (1991), however, have shown that the simple strategy of the unitary hedge ratio is convenient to implement, and yields results similar to costly strategies that require estimating the **covariance** of spot and forward over the variance of the forward rates.
- It is possible that given a bank's position in the money market, it needs to commit to a smaller amount in the forward market.

How can a bank hedge its currency exposure in the money market? Suppose it has a negative exposure of €10 million in three months. The bank will create a *synthetic forward hedge* by (1) borrowing US dollars, (2) converting them to euros at the spot rate, and (3) investing the proceeds for three months. All these transactions are undertaken in the interbank markets, although the corresponding "local" markets may be used to exploit any advantages. The cost of this synthetic forward transaction is compared with the cost of the actual forward transaction in terms of resources commitment to determine the superior alternative. Briefly, if the euro is underpriced in the forward market in Equation 3.1, the forward route is preferable; and the overpriced forward euro leads to the choice of the money market alternative.

Suppose, instead, the bank is expected to *receive*, that is, has a positive exposure of €10 million in three months. The bank can (1) borrow euros in Germany for three months, (2) convert the proceeds in US$ at the spot rate, and then (3) invest the amount in the US money market for three months. These steps enable the bank to achieve the same results as selling the forward contract in three months.

The following example illustrates these procedures.

Example 3.11

Given the following information:

Spot rate:	€ 1.50/US$ or US$0.6667/€
Forward rate:	€ 1.59/US$ or US$0.6289/€
Euro interest rate:	12% per annum
US interest rate:	10% per annum

A payment of €10 million is required in three months.
Which market (forward or money market) should be used for hedging

a   the cost in the forward market in three months

$$US\$ 0.6289/€ \times € 10 \text{ million} = US\$6.289 \text{ million}$$

b the cost in the money market?

We need to follow three steps:

Step 1   Find the present value of the foreign currency at the foreign market rate. Because we invest in the euros money market that will yield €100 in three months, the amount of euros required today is the present value of €100 at 12 percent, i.e.,

$$€10 \text{ million}/(1 + 12\%/4) = €9.709 \text{ million}$$

Step 2   Convert this amount to US$ at the prevailing spot rate to determine the borrowing amount in US$.

$$€9.709 \text{ million} \times US\$0.6667/€ = US\$6.473 \text{ million}$$

Step 3   Determine the future payment in US$ to pay off the loan in the money market at 10 percent.

$$US\$ 6.473 \text{ million} \times (1 + 10\%/4) = US\$6.635 \text{ million}$$

In this example, the outflow in the money market (US$6.635 million) is higher than the outflow in the forward market (US$6.289 million). Hence, the forward market hedge is a preferred strategy.

We can reach the same conclusion by computing FR^c:

$$FR^c = SR_0 \, (1+0.10/4)/(1+0.12/4) = US\$0.6635/€$$

Because the synthetic forward € is overvalued (US$0.6635 > US$0.6289), obtaining the foreign currency through the money market is not desirable.

A reverse conclusion follows, if we expect to receive €10 million in three months. Since we sell the foreign currency in future, it is preferable to sell it in the overpriced money market.

Just because in our example the IRPT does not hold should not necessarily imply that there is an arbitrage opportunity. Here, we have ignored the bid-ask spreads in both the foreign exchange and the money markets. Further, we may not have access to foreign money markets (especially for borrowing) for hedging purposes. Finally, realistic analysis requires consideration of not only taxes but also transaction costs stemming from non-uniform regulations.

3.6.2   Speculation

Pure speculation

Suppose a bank *expects* CHF to appreciate against US$. How can it generate profit from this expectation?

- It can convert some of the bank's US$ in CHF in the spot market and invest the funds in the EuroCHF market, an alternative designated as the *spot* or *money market alternative*.

The expected profit from this transaction is given by

$$E(\$SR_1/\text{CHF}) \times (\text{CHF investment proceeds}) - \text{cost of giving up profitable opportunities in US\$}$$

where E represents expectation.

- Alternatively, it can also enter in a forward transaction whereby it agrees to *buy* forward CHF at a suitable date at the designated rate $\$FR/\text{CHF}$. The expected gain will be

$$E(\$SR_1/\text{CHF}) - \$FR/\text{CHF}$$

When the IRP holds, the bank would be indifferent as to which of these two alternatives it chooses. By the same token, when the IRP does not hold, it would choose the alternative yielding higher expected profit.

Buying (or selling) the forward contract strictly on the expectation of making future profit and without any position in foreign exchange for other purposes at the time of initiating the transaction in the foreign currency is commonly called **speculation**.

When a market participant engages in a transaction strictly in the forward or spot market along the lines suggested above, the transaction is characterized as *pure speculation* in that any change in the foreign exchange rate has a full impact on the realized profit or loss.

Swap transactions

Swap transactions allow speculation with a *moderated* impact on the realizable profit or loss. In the above example on CHF appreciation, suppose the bank is not so sure of its expectation; and when it buys (invests in) the forward CHF (CHF money market), it also sells forward CHF (borrows CHF) for *shorter* maturity for the same amount. The result is a swap transaction that is also known as the **repurchase agreement** in the money market.

To see the impact of the swap, suppose the bank swaps a one-month short forward CHF with a three-month long forward CHF (it agrees to buy CHF in the three-month forward market and at the same time sell CHF in the one-month forward market). This transaction has two effects on the bank's profits.

- Given its round-trip nature, the swap transaction enables a bank to reduce its transaction cost.
- Any movement in the foreign exchange rates before the end of the month will cut the realizable profit (loss) on the three-month forward transaction by a loss (profit) on the one-month forward transaction.

In essence, the swap activity involves moderated speculation on the future movement of the exchange rate or some related financial variable (e.g. interest rate).

Spreading

A transaction involving forward contracts (FC) with two different maturities is also called **spreading**. Two types of strategies characterize the spreading transactions: **bear and bull spread strategies**.[20] These strategies involve three dates: the decision date (0 or today), the near maturity (t, such as one month from today), and the more distant maturity (T, such as three months from today).

These strategies are illustrated below.

1   Bear spreads.

Date 0:   (1) Buy FC forward at a shorter maturity, $FR_{0,t}$
            (2) Sell FC forward at a longer maturity at $FR_{0,T}$
Date t: (1) Sell FC spot at spot rate, SR_t
            (2) Buy FC forward for the period between t and T at $FR_{t,T}$
Date T: Settlement of $FR_{0,T}$ and $FR_{t,T}$ forward contracts.

Profit from the bear spreads strategy will be:

$$\text{Profit (bear)} = (FR_{0,T} - FR_{0,t}) - (FR_{t,T} - SR_t) \tag{3.6}$$

Terms in the first parentheses represent transactions on date 0; those in the second parentheses represent transactions undertaken on date t. Transactions on date 0 underscore the participant's pessimistic or bearish view of the FC. Similarly, the pair of transactions on date t unwinds both the near-term and the far-term positions taken on date 0, reducing the net exposure to 0. This reasoning then implies that

- The change in currency value anticipated by the bearish participant must take place *before* date t.
- The greater the difference between t and T, the larger the profit (or loss) potential. At the one extreme, when $t = T$, there is no speculative profit or loss; at the other extreme, $t = 0$ reflects the pure speculative position with the maximum profit or loss.
- There is no uncertainty by the end of date t about the profit on the FC maturing on date T, although profit has not been realized on date t.

2   Bull spreads.

Date 0:   (1) Sell FC forward at a shorter maturity, $FR_{0,t}$
            (2) Buy FC forward at a longer maturity at $FR_{0,T}$
Date t: (1) Buy FC spot at spot rate, SR_t
            (2) Sell FC forward for the period between t and T at $FR_{t,T}$.
Date T: Settlement of the two forward contracts with $FR_{0,T}$ and $FR_{t,T}$.

Profit from the bull spreads strategy will be:

$$\text{Profit (bull)} = (FR_{0,t} - FR_{0,T}) - (SR_t - FR_{t,T}) \tag{3.7}$$

It can be seen that profit (bear) $= -$profit (bull). The underlying assumption of the bear (pessimistic) spreads is that the longer-term forward rate (expressed in a direct quote) will decline. On the other hand, the bull (optimistic) spreads strategy assumes that the longer-term forward rate will increase.

Given the IRP relationship, any expectation of a change in the forward rate is tantamount to the expectation of change in the interest rate differential (or an independent change in the spot rate). Thus, spreading can also be employed when interest rate changes are anticipated.

Example 3.12

Suppose

$$\text{Spot rate: CHF1} = \$0.4875$$
$$\text{Eurodollar interest rate} = 11\%$$
$$\text{EuroCHF interest rate} = 8\%$$

Assume the forward rate is in equilibrium, that is, the IRPT holds. A bank analyst expects the EuroCHF interest rate to increase by 0.5 percent in one month. Then the following strategy can be implemented. If the EuroCHF interest rate increases as anticipated, the longer-term forward rate (longer than one month) for CHF against the US$ will decrease. Thus, the *bear spreads* strategy should be employed.

Assume that the analyst

- undertakes a set of transactions comprised of buying one-month forward CHF at $FR_{0,1}$, and selling 12-month forward CHF at $FR_{0,12}$; and
- one month later closes his position by selling CHF at spot rate, SR_1, that reverses his original one-month position, and by buying 11-month forward CHF at $FR_{1,12}$ that reverses his original 12-month position.

From the IRP relationship, the forward prices can be computed as follows:

$$FR_{0,1} = \$0.4875 \ (1 + 11\%/12)/(1 + 8\%/12)$$
$$= \$0.4887/\text{CHF}$$
$$FR_{0,12} = \$0.4875(1 + 11\%)/(1 + 8\%)$$
$$= \$0.5010/\text{CHF}$$

Assuming the spot rate remains unchanged, that is, SR_1 is still equal to $0.4875, and if the EuroCHF interest rate increases as anticipated, the forward price for the remaining 11-month on the original 12-month contract will be:

$$FR_{1,12} = \$0.4875(1 + 11\% \times 11/12)/(1 + 8.5\% \times 11/12)$$
$$= \$0.4979/\text{CHF}$$

Then, the profit of the bear spreads strategy will be:

$$= (F_{0,T} - F_{0,t}) - (F_{t,T} - e_t)$$
$$= (\$0.5010/\text{CHF} - \$0.4887/\text{CHF}) - (\$0.4979/\text{CHF} - \$0.4875/\text{CHF})$$
$$= \$0.0019/\text{CHF}$$

In the above analysis, we assumed a constant spot rate. If the spot rate were to appreciate in one month from $0.4875 to $0.49, the corresponding profit will be still $0.0019. If the spot CHF were to depreciate in one month to $0.4850, the corresponding profit will be $0.0020. Thus, as long as the anticipated interest rate increase materializes, the bear spreads strategy always yields profits, albeit of different magnitudes, for the bank regardless of the spot exchange rate movement.

3.7 Risk-Return Tradeoffs in Foreign Exchange Transactions

The discussion so far assumed that the risk faced by a bank stems from fluctuations in the foreign exchange or the interest rates. However, this is only one part of the story. When, for instance, a bank sells a customer foreign currency through a forward contract and covers its short position by entering in another forward contract buying that currency, it seems that the bank has squared its position. But what would happen if either of the counterparty in these forward transactions defaults by the time the contracts mature? It is clear that such a default exposes the bank to the fluctuation in the foreign exchange rate through its obligation to the non-defaulting counterparty. Thus the risk that the bank faces is not just the foreign exchange rate risk but also the credit risk. Several implications are noteworthy.

- It should be obvious why banks insist on a bonafide forward need on the part of their non-financial customers.
- Even a genuine forward contract with a marginal customer may require a bank to take prudent or precautionary measures such as *minimum balance maintenance* that would cover potential loss from fluctuations in the foreign exchange rate in the event of non-performance by its customer.
- Risk of non-performance is not confined to non-financial customers; it can also occur in the interbank transactions even for spot trades.
- Consideration of the above implications also points to a potential gap in the monitoring mechanisms employed by banks. When a bank has several foreign exchange traders, it is well appreciated that relying on the aggregate position of an individual trader in a given currency on a daily basis can mask the dangerous exposure faced by the bank through swap transactions of comparable magnitudes but of uneven maturities, as described above. Consequently, banks require daily reporting for different maturities. As the discussion above suggests, however, unless credit dimension is properly considered, the higher level management may be lulled into a false sense of security. A simple solution in this case may be to establish trade limits for a given category of a non-financial customer or a counter-party bank (and financial intermediary in general).

In brief, a sound monitoring mechanism requires consideration of both the foreign exchange and the credit dimensions, and the latter also needs to reflect counterparties in the interbank transactions.

3.8 Conclusion

This chapter initially discussed the institutional background of the foreign exchange market. Commercial banks' role as market makers in the foreign exchange market was described. Familiarity with the institutional background is necessary for foreign exchange market activities of arbitrage, hedging, and speculation undertaken by banks themselves or by their customers (sometimes at the expense of the banks).

Different theories and parity conditions (PPP, IRP, Fisher Open, and market efficiency) in the foreign exchange market were analyzed. This analysis facilitated explanation of the underpinnings of arbitrage, hedging, and speculation activities. Finally, assumption of credit risk by banks as foreign exchange dealers for these activities was discussed in the context of a critical need for an appropriate mechanism for monitoring lower management activities.

DISCUSSION QUESTIONS

1 Explain the following terms: forward market; spot-forward swap; forward-forward swap; value date; cross-rate; bear and bull spread strategies; and market maker.

2 What does a bid-ask quote for a currency mean?

3 What is the normal range of a percentage spread for a widely trade currencies?

4 Compute the percentage spread given the bid-ask price is $0.5656/CHF−$0.5662/CHF.

5 Discuss different ways in which forward exchange rates are quoted. Why are they quoted in different ways?

6 Given the following quotation for the Swiss franc, compute the one-month and three-month (a) outright forward rates; (b) swap rates; and (c) premium or discount rates.

Bid/ask price	One-month	Three-month
$0.5922−0.5933	5−6	10−7

7 If the spot contract is entered on June 6, 20xx, when will the two-month forward contract be delivered if (a) June 6 is Friday, and (b) June 6 is Tuesday?

8 What is the bid-ask price of Hong Kong dollars in terms of US dollars, given the following quotation: HK$7.73−HK$7.75/US$?

9 The Hong Kong American Bank gives a bid-ask price quote

HK$7.74/US$−HK$7.75/US$; and

JY120/US$−JY125/US$

What bid-ask quote should the bank give for the Japanese yen in terms of the Hong Kong dollar?

10 The quotations for different currencies at different cities are as follows:

Frankfurt:	US$/CHF 0.6252
New York:	US$/£ 1.98
London:	CHF/£ 3.30

Determine whether and where there is any arbitrage opportunity. Compute the arbitrage profits (if any).

11 Discuss the relationships among fundamental economic forces that are interrelated with the currency value. Explain these relationships in terms of the market hierarchy.

12 Suppose the spot rate is US$0.50/CHF, the US interest rate is 6 percent (i.e. the term structure is flat for all maturities), and the Swiss franc interest rate is 10 percent (i.e. flat term structure). Assume the IRPT holds.

   a What are the one-month and 12-month forward rates for the US$ in terms of the CHF?

   b If a bank anticipates that the Fed will increase the short-term US interest rate by 1 percent in one month's time, and interest rates of all maturities will shift upward by 1 percent, what spot-forward swap strategy should the commercial bank adopt? How would it be different for a forward-forward swap if the bank cannot exceed a forward contract for more than a year?

   c Compute the profit under each of the swap strategies in (b), if the spot rate at the end of the month is $0.51/CHF and the US interest rates of all maturities increase by 1 percent. (Assume that the forward-forward swap will be liquidated at the end of the month.)

13 Given the following data:

   The foreign inflation and interest rates are 10 percent and 13 percent.

   The domestic inflation and interest rates are 6 percent and 9 percent.

   The current exchange rate is 7.8 (FC/$),

   a Calculate the future exchange rate using the Fisher Open theory and the PPP theory.

   b Suppose the domestic interest rate all of a sudden increases by 1 percent. What impact would this change have on exchange rates under (i) the Fisher Open theory; and (ii) the Asset Market theory.

14 Suppose the spot exchange rate for the Canadian dollar (CAD) is US 0.6521 − 0.6527, while the three-month forward rate is US$ 0.6550−6558. The three-month CAD interest rate bid-ask quote is 5.2−6 percent while corresponding US$ interest rates are 8.5−8.875 percent. How should the bank quote the three-month CAD forward rate to its clients in order to prevent them from obtaining arbitrage profits at its expense?

15 Tiger Fund, one of the biggest **hedge funds** in the world with US$2 billion in assets at the peak, was liquidated at the end of March 2000 because of its huge losses. From library and internet resources, determine to what extent the Fund's activities in the foreign exchange markets contributed to its ultimate demise.

NOTES

1 See *The Economist*, April 1993, p. 16.

2 A spread is akin to a markup or profit margin in a commodity sale. One major difference should be noted. Whereas the markup is stated in terms of the seller's cost, the spread is related to the seller's sales price (ask price), and not the cost (bid price).

3 Conventionally, a currency "appreciates" or "depreciates" under a floating exchange rate system and it is "revalued (upvalued)" or "devalued" under the fixed exchange rate system.

4 Of course, when a customer has agreed to buy (sell) foreign currency in future through a forward contract, the original contract can be effectively liquidated prior to maturity by entering into another contract maturing on the same day to sell (buy) the same amount of foreign currency.

5 Actually this is a quote for £ sterling in terms of CHF. However, the UK convention employs the indirect quote, and reports this as "a quote for CHF against £ sterling."

6 If there are four currencies instead of three, there will be three intermediate currencies. Thus the arbitrage process will follow the same principle of three intermediary currencies that individually appear only once.

7 The *Financial Times* is an exception in that it provides the forward quotes calculated on the basis of Equation 3.1.

8 The concept of equilibrium is always in connection with a given theory; hence, in the present case, e connotes PPP based on the foreign exchange rate.

9 We should not regard the relative version as a weaker condition of the absolute version of PPP. The Law of One Price – a form of the latter – may hold in a given case; however, the relative version requiring a bundle of goods may not hold because of, say, changes in consumer tastes over time.

10 The underlying assumption is that either there is a floating exchange rate system or that the authorities would instantaneously adjust the currency value under the fixed rate system.

11 The cointegration analysis basically examines the disequilibrium errors (e.g., in our case the errors that are not prescribed by the PPP conditions) to see if they are persistent or not. The error persistency would imply that PPP would not hold. The result is due to the fact that the disequilibrium errors should be random under the PPP condition.

12 Still the ambiguity persists in interpreting these results. The risk premiums may remain constant over time and cancel out; or its size may vary for different currencies, and the difference may be statistically insignificant. Further, the deviations may result from persistent measurement errors. Thus the problem may or may not be due to existence of the risk premium.

13 But a little longer run perspective counters this inference of structural change in favor of non-US firms, as American companies rose to the challenge by the early 1990s, and reasserted their competitive position in the late 1990s.

14 The Asset Market (AM) theory (see, for instance, Frankel 1979) also underscores influence of capital flows on the (current) spot rate. Unlike the Fisher Open that holds constant the real interest rates, the AM theory keeps constant the inflation expectations (and thereby the expected spot rate). Here we regard both sets of assumptions convenient but restrictive.

15 More precisely, changes in both interest differentials and the expected exchange rates stem from changes in the expected inflation differentials.

16 See, for instance, studies by Huang (1989) and Mark (1988) that explain risk premiums in the capital asset pricing framework.

17 This discussion is based on Mahajan and Mehta (1991).

18 The usual caveat of settlement risk and credit risks remains and is assumed away here.

19 The bank may be able to use organized derivative – futures and options – markets discussed in Chapter 5.

20 The two strategies are drawn mainly from Adler (1983).

CHAPTER 4

Eurocurrency Market

LEARNING OBJECTIVES

- To learn about the institutional features of the Eurocurrency market and various centers
- To understand the process of financial activities such as arbitrage in the Eurocurrency markets
- To learn about the Eurocredit market and investment/financing opportunities in the Eurocurrency market

4.1 Introduction

The domestic financial market in a country exists in order to facilitate funds transfer from investors with surplus units to users with a deficit in units. The financial institutions, which are the critical parts of this financial market, provide valuable services of (a) identifying and bringing together the two parties, and (b) creating suitable vehicles – securities – that meet the needs of both investors and users, as described in Chapter 1. Typically, for convenience, the domestic market is partitioned in two parts on the basis of maturities of instruments: money market (with short maturity) and capital market (with long maturity). Although these parts are intertwined, the distinction is justified on the basis of their relationship to interest rate and liquidity. Thus interest rates in the money market are more sensitive to moves by monetary authorities than those in the securities market. Similarly, liquidity is supposed to have greater relevance in the capital market than in the money market. Still, given their close interrelationships with respect to interest rates, we will discuss in this chapter characteristics of salient financial instruments from both money and capital markets.

An international money market known as the **Eurocurrency market** is similar to the domestic money market. The critical distinction between the two markets revolves around the degree of control on participants, or their transactions, exercised by the currency issuing government through regulations, taxes, or laws. Distortions in market forces and phenomena induced by government regulations, taxes, and laws are virtually absent in the Eurocurrency market.

Because the Eurocurrency market involves various currencies of different countries, it is closely linked with the foreign exchange market. Further, this market offers deposit and loan alternatives to the individual national domestic markets. Hence, it forges a link between the domestic and the Eurocurrency interest rates.

In this chapter, we discuss factors contributing to the growth of the Eurocurrency market and its structure. Differences among various Eurocurrency banking centers are highlighted in the process. Linkages between interest rates in the domestic and its counterpart Eurocurrency markets are then discussed. This discussion facilitates analysis of various hedging strategies that integrate the bid-ask prices in the Eurocurrency interest rates with the foreign exchange rates. Finally, we describe and discuss different instruments such as **note issuing facilities** (NIFs), **floating rate notes** (FRNs), and bonds, in the Eurocurrency and Euro-security markets.

4.2 Development of the Eurocurrency Market

4.2.1 Structure

Eurocurrency is a currency, just like the US dollar or any other freely convertible currency, deposited in an interest-bearing account with a bank either outside its country of origin or within its boundary but not subject to its sovereign restrictions. Two factors are then pertinent for creation of a Eurocurrency.

First, currency has to be **convertible**, that is, it should have an effective demand outside its country of origin. Since money does not have intrinsic worth, it is demanded for its ability to facilitate transactions, whether they are contemporaneous or intertemporal. The latter trait suggests money should have storage value. This rules out several currencies from qualifying for Eurocurrency status. In turn, absence of external demand may stem from a variety of factors such as runaway inflation in the country of origin (as was the case with the Argentinean peso in the late 1980s), absence of tradable goods and services desired by foreigners (as has been the case with many sub-Saharan African countries), and instability in the socio-economic-political structure of the currency issuing country. Foreigners often want to hold a long position in a currency, but they do not want to physically keep their long position in the issuing country. Their reluctance stems from concerns related to economic or political factors. Convertibility – demand outside the issuing country – allows them to have a long position without necessarily maintaining their deposits in the issuing country. The erstwhile Soviet Union, for instance, is alleged to be a prime mover in the development of the **Eurodollar** market in the post-World War II era that allowed it to maintain dollar-denominated deposits outside the USA and thus avoid (a) very low interest rates obtainable in the USA at that time, and (b) potential political reprisal by the US government in settling cold war related issues through freezing the Soviet Union deposits in the USA.

Second, the currency issuing government has to acquiesce with the idea of potential dilution of its control over currency by permitting its trade in the Eurocurrency market. Since monetary policy is one important tool in the arsenal of a government to achieve its political goals, *government acquiescence* is sometimes a more binding constraint than convertibility. Thus the reluctance on the part of the Japanese government prevented yen from being a Eurocurrency through the mid-1980s.

But then why would a government allow its currency to trade in the Eurocurrency market and, to that extent, circumscribe its sovereignty through diluting effectiveness of its monetary policy? One answer is that this is not such a one-sided case as one would think because of the relationship between convertibility and the foreign exchange rate behavior. When a currency is convertible and is allowed to be traded in the Eurocurrency market, deposits in this market siphon off inflationary pressures generated by expansionary fiscal or monetary policies pursued by the government to achieve its near-term political goals. This potential is particularly valuable under the fixed exchange rate system. Thus the US government's butter-and-guns policies (the Great Society program and financing of the Vietnam war effort) in the late 1960s with accommodation from the Federal Reserve allowed it to postpone the day of reckoning in terms of dollar devaluation because of the Eurodollar market where participants were willing to hold their deposits.

Another reason for governments permitting their currencies to be Eurocurrencies is that, with the increased global trade, there has been great demand for liquidity that has been satisfied with speed and low cost by the Eurocurrency market. Further, many of these governments have frequently relied on these markets to borrow money expediently. During the oil crisis of the early 1970s, several developed countries saw their current account surplus turn into deficits because of oil imports. The Eurocurrency market allowed them to finance these deficits and thereby avoid resorting to drastic or unpalatable fiscal or monetary alternatives.

The Eurocurrency market has three components:

- the Eurocurrency deposit market is where banks accept deposits from non-bank clients;
- banks accept deposits and make loans among themselves in the interbank market;
- the Eurocurrency credit market enables banks to loan money to non-bank borrowers.

This last component usually takes the form of anywhere from Euro-commercial paper to syndicated loan. Of the three components, the interbank market is the most active one.

Interest rates in the Eurocurrency market are quoted in the bid and ask prices. The bid rate is the *deposit* rate while the ask rate is the *loan* rate. Deposit and loan rates are typically based on a reference rate called the **Interbank Offer Rate (IBOR)**, that is, the rate at which a bank is willing to *lend* to another bank for a given maturity. While the most prominent benchmark interest in the Eurocurrency market is the **London Interbank Offer Rate (LIBOR)**,[1] other frequently used **reference rates** represent different currencies, such as the Euro Interbank Offered Rate (EURIBOR), or locations, such as the Bahrain Interbank Offered Rate (BIBOR), Hong Kong Interbank Offered Rate (HIBOR), and Singapore Interbank Offered (SIBOR). A final group of reference rates include domestic rates such as the US T-bill and prime rates. Domestic reference rates appear in eurocredits because banks sometimes want to place their surplus funds from domestic sources to the Eurocurrency market.

For the Eurodollar market, the deposit rate is typically higher than the US counterpart, while the corresponding loan rate in the Eurodollar market is lower than the US rate. Thus a difference of 25 basis points (bps) between the Eurodollar and the US markets is standard for deposits of comparable maturities.

Why would a US bank accept a lower spread on loans in the Eurodollar market than in the USA? The reasons are as follows.

1 The cost of regulations borne by the bank in the USA is absent in the Eurodollar market. Among other things, Eurodollar deposits do not carry deposit insurance cost, nor do banks face reserve requirements for deposits.

This does not mean that **Eurobanks** loan out the last penny of their deposits, because they do maintain prudent reserves. However, these reserves in the Eurodollar markets have an element of flexibility absent in the domestic arena. Suppose a Eurobank is confronted with an unanticipated but temporary shortfall in the target reserve. The bank does not necessarily have to borrow additional money or liquidate some assets prior to their maturity at a loss. Instead, the bank may choose, at least for the time being, to live with lower reserves than desirable, normal levels.[2]

2 Depositors in the external market face potential risk not present in the domestic market, such as default risk.

In the absence of deposit protection offered by domestic authorities, Eurodeposits carry an additional compensation element that may reflect (a) country risk and affiliated information processing (Grabbe 1991); or (b) the likelihood, however small, that the government of the domicile of the Eurobank will not bail it out in case of a liquidity crunch.

> When Banco Ambrosiano, an Italian bank, failed due to mismanagement of funds abroad during the 1980s, Italian authorities chose to merge domestic operations with another bank and thereby assume obligation of domestic deposits but refused to accept any responsibility for its Euro-deposits.

3 In addition to the above two reasons, facilities in tax havens[3] that accept deposits and book loans as well as fierce competition in the Eurocurrency market have resulted in a narrower spread in the Eurocurrency market than in the domestic market.

The case of the Euroyen is noteworthy with respect to its relationship with counterpart domestic deposit rate: Euroyen bid rates have been typically lower than the comparable domestic Japanese Gensake (repurchase) Certificate of Deposit rates. For the three-month Euroyen data, the bid rates were 17.5 basis points *lower* than the Japanese Gensake rate for the period 1984 through January 1993 (Lo et al. 1995). Such anomalies have also existed for other Eurocurrencies. As Dufey and Giddy (1994: 104) have noted:

> [Germany and Switzerland] at various times during 1970s imposed capital controls on the inflow of foreign funds [limiting depositor arbitrage], promptly causing the external deposit rate to fall below the equivalent domestic deposit rate, which would otherwise represent an effective "floor" for the Euro Swiss franc or Euro German mark rate.

However, the yen case is unusual for the persistence of its "aberration" over a long period when the capital controls were being phased out in Japan. One plausible explanation could be that external yen holders accepted a rate of return lower than the domestic counterpart in expectation of getting compensated by the yen's appreciation over other currencies.

Many major currencies (e.g. US dollar, euro – and its predecessors French franc and German mark – Japanese yen, and British pound) are now represented in the Eurocurrency market. However, the US dollar is the most important one and has a share of over 60 percent of the market. The historical role of the US dollar as the reserve currency since World War II, its status as the major currency of denomination in foreign trade related transactions (e.g. oil prices), and the significant share of the US economy in the global context (around 25 percent of the world output) are some of the reasons for this prominence of the US dollar.

4.2.2   Functions of the Eurocurrency markets

The Eurocurrency market serves several important functions.

- Its very nature allows market forces a fuller play than the counterpart domestic market constrained with regulations and laws. Thus, it gives a more accurate reading of market forces. Indeed, the more opaque the domestic market due to distortions, the more critical the role of the Eurocurrency market as a barometer of market forces. A paradox should be noted here. Since this market owes its existence to impediments in the domestic markets, it stands to reason that any reduction (if not removal) in regulations in the domestic markets in recent years should decrease the relevance of the Eurocurrency market. However, its significance has increased rather than diminished over time. It is likely that taxes and transaction costs have assumed a much more pivotal role than ever before because of pressures on bank profits created by intensified competition.
- The Eurocurrency markets are well connected and efficient. As a result, the market can be used for hedging purposes. Banks can buy and sell foreign currency denominated assets and liabilities of different maturities and amounts for managing their exposure to interest rate and currency risk.
- The Eurocurrency markets are well funded, and thus are convenient sources for funding a bank's domestic and international loans.
- Finally, new products are needed by the bank's clientele to contain exposure resulting from globalization, and such products may have legal, regulatory, or tax implications that make them unsuitable for introduction in the domestic market.

A US multinational firm's deposits abroad, when labeled as a limited-life preferred stock in a tax haven, may allow that firm to reduce its global tax liabilities. Although the interest income from deposits may be identical to the "preferred dividend" income in the tax haven, such dividend income is likely to allow the multinational firm to generate tax credits in the USA that are unavailable on the interest income from abroad. The multinational firm thus lowers the effective tax rate on its income without sacrificing flexibility.

4.2.3   Money supply growth in the Eurocurrency market

The Eurocurrency market handles a large volume of funds. One issue of concern is what impact it has on money supply and whether the impact is inflationary. In order to examine this issue, we look at some market transactions that highlight the funds transfer process in the Eurocurrency market.

Table 4.1   First round – IBM deposits $1 million from US Bank to Eurobank X

Assets	Liabilities
US Bank's account	
N/A	$1 million due to Eurobank X
Eurobank X's account	
$1 million in US bank	$1 million due to IBM
	[$1 million of Euro$ created]

Suppose a US firm, say IBM, shifts $1 million from its US domiciled bank to Eurobank X in order to receive a higher return on its deposits. The US bank now has a liability of $1 million due to Eurobank X because ownership of the liability is shifted from the customer IBM to Eurobank X. At the same time, Eurobank X will recognize the deposits from the US bank with the corresponding liability due to IBM. Table 4.1 records this transaction.

In the second round, when Eurobank X lends $1 million to Eurobank Y,

- the asset side of the Eurobank X will reflect its loan to Eurobank Y; however, its liability structure remains the same;
- for the US bank, its balance sheet essentially remains unchanged; only its liability changes from Eurobank X to Eurobank Y;
- for Eurobank Y, its asset side reflects the deposit of $1 million with the US bank, and its liabilities and equity side recognizes $1 million liability to Eurobank X.

Table 4.2 reports these transactions.

Table 4.2 Second round – Eurobank X Loans $1 million to another Eurobank Y

Assets	Liabilities
US Bank's account	
N/A	$1 million due to Eurobank Y
Eurobank X's account	
$1 million in Eurobank Y	$1 million due to IBM
	[Euro$1million – 1st round]
Eurobank Y's account	
$1 million in US Bank	$1 million due to Eurobank X
	[Euro$1million – 2nd round]

At the end of the second round, the gross size of the Eurodollar market measured by the total deposits in Eurobanks is $2 million ($1 million in Eurobank X and $1 million in Eurobank Y).

If this process continues, that is, the initial $1 million deposit shifts from one Eurobank to another, we may wind up with an infinitely large sum of money supply. In other words, the money multiplier should be infinite or extremely large. In reality, however, the multiplier has been estimated between 1.0 and 2.0 suggesting that there are significant leakages in the growth process.[4]

- When a Eurobank loans out the money to a non-bank borrower, this borrower's payment to a US resident stops the growth process.
- If the original depositor (IBM in our case) withdraws the deposit, the growth process also stops.
- Although Eurobanks are not required to maintain reserves, they do maintain prudent reserves (often in excess of mandatory reserves!).
- Even in the absence of the constraints just cited, the growth process stops because each round requires the spread for the lending bank, and the cumulative spread soon makes the market uncompetitive.
- Since any potential abuse or destabilizing activity is likely to generate a swift punishing response from regulatory agencies, Eurobanks are unlikely to test the limit.

During 1968, the Federal Reserve followed the tight money policy to no avail, because US banks facing interest ceilings of Regulation Q shifted their clients' domestic deposits to the high-interest bearing Euro-deposits, and recycled them for loans to their domestic customers at still higher interest rates. This process stopped only when the regulatory authorities threatened banks with drastic actions such as reserve requirements on the deposits held by foreign branches of US banks.

The Eurocurrency interbank markets are well integrated. Thus, the issue of potential contagion effect arises, whereby one bank's failure causes other banks in the Eurocurrency market to fail. This potential stems from (a) imperfect information signals generated in the market, and (b) the intricate networks of participants readily facilitating the quick transmission of bank runs to other banks.

4.3 Eurocurrency Centers

A Eurocurrency or international banking center is a place where a number of banks are concentrated to conduct transactions related to deposits and loans denominated in various Eurocurrencies. Although Eurocurrency markets are global in nature, the deposit and loan rates in each location are somewhat different, reflecting the local risk and impediments.

- Different time zones thrust different locations into the limelight during a typical day.
- Differing regulatory (e.g., disclosure or report filing) or tax (e.g., annual registration fees) requirements may lead to development of new locations.
- Locations that meet the infrastructure needs (e.g., communications network and availability of skilled personnel) have always been a major drawing card for well-established centers, such as London and New York.

There are five major Eurocurrency centers: Western Europe (represented by London as the headquarters), the Caribbean and Central America, the Middle East, Asia, and the USA.

London is the oldest and foremost Eurocurrency center. Its prominent position is the result of its history of financial expertise and lack of government regulations for Eurocurrencies. The Bank of England does not have reserve requirements on Eurocurrency deposits or capital requirements for the branches of foreign banks. During the 1980s, Japanese and US banks dominated the London market. Now banks from other European countries have a respectable representation.

In the Caribbean and Central American currency center, the Cayman Island is one of the most attractive locations for setting up "shell" branches for US banks where transactions are booked or routed to for a variety of reasons such as lenient disclosure requirements and low or no profit taxes. It is not difficult for a large multinational bank to open a branch in the Cayman Islands. The minimum capital requirement can be met by using the capital of the parent bank. Furthermore, there are no reserve requirements for Eurocurrency operations.

Bahrain is the center of the Middle East market in terms of the foreign exchange and Eurocurrency trading. Its close proximity to Saudi Arabia and Kuwait is important for currency trading and lending activities in the region.

Tokyo, Singapore, and Hong Kong are three major Asian currency centers. The Japanese government has been widely known to have a stronghold on its financial markets. Because of intense pressure from the USA and other governments, the Japanese government has gradually deregulated its financial markets. In late 1986, the Japanese government set up the Japan Offshore Market (JOM) in Tokyo for booking accounts exclusively for non-resident transactions (including transactions of foreign subsidiaries of Japanese corporations). Transactions in JOM are exempt from reserve requirements, withholding tax, and interest rate controls that apply to domestic banking. The major beneficiaries of JOM are Japanese regional banks that do not have overseas branches.

Although Japan was attracting more attention through the 1980s in the Asian currency market because of liberalization of the Japanese financial market and the prominent position of the Japanese banks globally, several recessions in the 1990s coupled with political indecision has at least temporarily removed the bloom of the JOM.

Two major reasons for the existence of Singapore and Hong Kong are (a) the abundance of the US dollar circulating among Far Eastern residents during the Vietnam War; and (b) the differences in time zones vis-à-vis the USA and Europe that create inconvenience for conducting business transactions dealing in the US dollar. Thus, the combination of the Asian dollar market, European centers, and the US market provides 24-hour service to customers all over the world.

Singapore is now the headquarters for the "Asian" dollar market. The Singapore government, in an attempt to compete with Hong Kong for leadership in the Asian dollar market, eliminated its 40 percent withholding tax on interest income earned by non-residents in 1968, and reduced its tax on bank profits on offshore loans in 1973. In addition, other taxes have also been reduced or eliminated while the **exchange control** measures for promoting growth in the Asian dollar market have been liberalized.

A special feature of the offshore New York market is the IBF, mentioned in Chapter 2. Since December 1981, the Federal Reserve System has permitted US banks and branches of foreign banks in the USA to establish IBFs, which are exempt from reserve requirements, federal taxes, and deposit insurance. The intent of setting up IBFs was to attract offshore banking business to the USA. Many "shell" bank branches in places like the Cayman Islands or the Bahamas really amounted to nothing more than a small office and a telephone for booking loans and deposits. The location of IBFs reflects the location of banking activity in general. Thus it is not surprising that over 75 percent of the IBF deposits are in New York State.

IBFs do not require physically separate banking entities, as they are just the booking facilities located in the USA and sharing basic characteristics of Eurobanks outside the country. IBFs can do business with only non-bank foreign residents; thus IBFs cannot lend to or accept deposits from US residents. Although borrowing from a US bank is allowed, it is subject to reserve requirements. At the same time, IBFs are not allowed to issue negotiable instruments such as CDs. Because of these restrictions, IBFs are not a perfect substitute for offshore deposit facilities. Still, to make them more competitive with offshore banking, the minimum deposit maturity is overnight for interbank IBFs and two business days for non-bank foreign residents. The minimum size of deposits is in excess of $100,000; hence they are not subject to deposit insurance.

4.4 Eurocurrency Interest Rates

Three aspects of the Eurocurrency interest rates need examination: the term structure of the Eurocurrency interest rates; the potential for bank runs; and the causal relationship between the Eurocurrency (offshore) interest rate and their domestic (onshore) counterparts.

4.4.1 Term structure of interest rates

Profitability of lending and borrowing across maturities for an individual bank depends on the spreads between the bid and ask rates in the interbank market, and the premium added to the reference rate for (a) the credit risk of the borrowers and (b) the interest rate risk due to mismatched maturities of loans and deposits. We will discuss credit risk in Chapters 7 and 8. The mismatch of maturities of loans and deposits depends to a great extent on the values of interest rates for different maturities – or, the term structure of interest rates. We discuss in some detail now the concept of the term structure, as it plays a significant role in understanding instruments such as the forward rate agreement (FRA) discussed in Section 4.5 below.

The **term structure** refers to the relationship of the **spot interest rate** with the maturity. An upward (downward)-sloping term structure connotes the interest rate increasing (decreasing) with the maturity term. For a flat term structure, the interest rate is constant across the maturity dimension. The spot interest rate refers to a loan that pays both the principal and accumulated interest charges only at the maturity. It is also known as the pure discount rate.

Suppose a bank is considering two alternatives. The first option is to lend the money for two months; the second option is to loan its money *initially* for one month and then re-lend the proceeds from the first month's investment for an additional month. If the two-month spot interest rate is $i_{0,2}$ and the current one-month spot interest rate is $i_{0,1}$, the bank can compute the implied forward interest rate for the second month as:

$$(1 + i_{0,2})^{2/12} = (1 + i_{0,1})^{1/12}(1 + f_{1,1})^{1/12}$$

where $f_{1,1}$ is the one-month (implied) forward interest rate starting one month from now.

Example 4.1

Suppose the two-month annualized interest rate, $i_{0,2}$, is 10 percent and the one-month annualized interest rate, $i_{0,1}$, is 8 percent, then the one-month forward rate $f_{1,1}$ is given by

$$(1 + 0.10)^{2/12} = (1 + 0.08)^{1/12}(1 + f_{1,1})^{1/12}$$
$$f_{1,1} = [(1.10)^{2/12} / (1.08)^{1/12}]^{12} - 1$$
$$= (1.0160119/1.006434)^{12} - 1$$
$$= 12.04\%$$

If the (*spot* interest rate) term structure is rising (upward-sloping), the term structure of the *forward* (interest) rate is also rising and is above the spot interest rate term structure as shown in Figure 4.1. By the same token, if the term structure is downward sloping, the implied forward interest rate term structure will also be downward sloping, and lies below it as shown in Figure 4.2.

If the two alternative courses of actions (Figures 4.1 and 4.2) give the bank identical payoffs, then the bank will be indifferent between the two alternatives.[5] In Example 4.1, if the

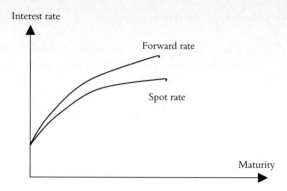

Figure 4.1 Rising term structure of spot and forward rates

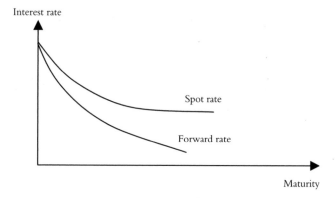

Figure 4.2 Declining term structure of spot and forward rates

bank borrows for two months at the two-month interest rate at 10 percent and loans the funds out for one month at 8 percent and then for another month at 12.4 percent, the bank will break even. This example suggests that if the bank borrows long term and loans in the short term, the bank will break even, if the actual rate for the second month is equal to the implied forward interest rate. Alternatively, the bank will also break even if it loans long term but borrows short term and refinances at the implied forward interest rate.

When the bank's expectations are different from the implied forward interest rate, the bank can anticipate to make some money by lending and borrowing for mismatched maturities. As the swap transaction discussion in Chapter 3 suggested, when the bank loans for long maturity and funds it initially with shorter maturity, the bank is betting that by the time funds are needed to cover the loan, it will be able to obtain them at a lower rate, that is, the actual future borrowing rate is expected to be below the implied forward interest rate.

4.4.2 Potential bank runs

In a single economy with a large number of banks, if one bank fails, other healthy banks are also likely to be adversely affected by such failure. In the first place, the failing bank might have obligations to other banks that become worthless, thus affecting the value of other healthy banks' assets as well as their net worth. When depositors perceive this danger and start withdrawing their deposits, other banks' liquidity as well as net worth (through untimely liquidation of assets) plummet. A high degree of financial leverage exacerbates the situation. This is the essence of the contagion effect resulting in bank runs.

When economies are not integrated, the impact of a bank run in one economy will not be fully transmitted to other economies. Eurocurrency markets change the situation, however. Since Eurocurrency markets in different currencies are closely interrelated – as the discussion on IRPT and the uncovered interest rate parity (Fisher Open) in Chapter 3 suggested – a bank run in one currency would be quickly transmitted to other currencies. If monetary authorities do not act in a timely fashion, the viability of the financial markets on a global scale would be endangered. Thus Eurocurrency markets amplify the potential for bank runs. At the same time, participants in Eurocurrency markets may be better informed than monetary authorities on a bank's failing health and thus better prepared to mitigate the danger of bank runs on a global scale.

On April 18, 1984, the Continental Illinois bank announced an increase of $400 million in its problem loan portfolio. This announcement did not seem to have any noticeable effect on the market. Still, on May 10, 1984, the comptroller of the Currency publicly denied rumors that Continental Illinois was in a serious financial problem. The market apparently did not put much stock in this announcement, and it continued to shorten the maturity of funds sought by the Continental Illinois: the bank's purchased funds (such as longer term CDs) decreased by 7 percent; however, its demand deposits increased by similar amounts (Saunders 1988).

In any case, the bank run did not materialize.

If the market attitude displayed in the Continental Illinois case is typical, the contagion effect requiring, among other things, a critical element of surprise does not appear to be a serious problem. Nevertheless, just because it did not occur in the past does not guarantee its absence in the future.

4.4.3 Causal relationship between offshore and domestic interest rates

The causality linkage between interest rates in the offshore and domestic markets has two alternate plausible explanations. The first one traces the impact from domestic to the offshore market by relying on evidence pointing to (a) greater volatility in the offshore interest rates, and (b) relative immunity of the domestic market from volatile offshore forces (e.g. Levin 1974; Kwack 1971; and Hendershott 1967). That the central bank influences the short-term rates domestically lends credence to the assertion that the transmission process originates domestically.

The alternate explanation contends that interest rates in the domestic markets are constrained by regulatory and other roadblocks and thus are unable to respond to the market forces as quickly and fully as the offshore market; hence, volatility in itself does not establish the causality (Giddy et al. 1979).

More recent studies (Fung and Isberg 1992; Swanson 1988; and Hartman 1984) provide evidence that shocks in domestic interest rates lead interest rates in offshore Eurodollar markets, and observe weaker feedback from Eurodollar to domestic markets.

Does this relationship always hold? Note that the interest rate relationship may be changing over time as the financial markets become more mature or integrated. Thus, we may observe some elements of market segmentation in earlier periods that may disappear over time. A recent study by Fung et al. (1997) investigates the Eurodollar and domestic interest rate relationship in terms of both the mean and volatility of the interest rate movements. The results show that the contemporaneous feedback from the domestic market to the offshore market in both the mean and volatility is stronger than that from the offshore to the domestic market.

The studies cited above focused exclusively on the US dollar. Does this relationship also hold for other Eurocurrencies? A study by Lo et al. (1995) on the Euroyen and domestic yen interest rate markets suggests that in the earlier period causality is strongest from the Euroyen market to the domestic yen interest rates. However, strong feedback effects are observed in both directions in more recent years.

In brief, the dominance of the US domestic market and the prominent role of the US dollar in the Eurocurrency market to date have allowed the transmission of influence from domestic to offshore markets. On the other hand, for relative latecomers like the Japanese yen, the offshore interest rates have strongly affected the domestic interest rates, as the alternative hypothesis suggests. However, in both instances, as time progresses, the strong causality is weakened as the domestic and offshore markets become more integrated.

The discussion so far has ignored the issue of the process of integration (of the domestic and offshore markets) and the activities of arbitrage, hedging, and speculation (pure or in the modified form of swaps) described in Chapter 3. We examine this issue below.

4.5 Activities in the Eurocurrency Market

Comparable interest rates for a given currency in the Eurocurrency and the counterpart "domestic" markets can differ only to the extent that no participant is able to arbitrage away remaining distortions in the domestic markets induced by taxes, regulations, and laws. Suppose the only distortion present is that the domestic income is subject to a 20 percent flat tax rate, and the offshore income is tax-free. Then before-tax domestic loan rates should not exceed the offshore rates by 25 percent, or in general,

$$[(1 - \text{tax rate}) \times \mathit{Int} \ (\text{dom})] \leq \mathit{Int} \ (\text{offshore})$$

(The inequality here reflects the consideration that any participant who is tax-exempt or is not subject to taxes in a given year will reduce further the tax-induced differential.)

Because of the Eurocurrency market's unregulated nature and intense competition among participants, the covered interest rate parity or the IRPT typically holds through arbitrage activities. As a result, comparable interest rates in any two Eurocurrencies will hold in equilibrium with the spot-forward foreign exchange rates for the two currencies.

With respect to the (interest rate) term structure relationships between a Eurocurrency and its domestic counterpart or another Eurocurrency, introduction of a new instrument called the **forward** or **future rate** agreement (FRA) has greatly facilitated establishing the equilibrium. The FRA specifies the *reference* interest rate for a designated amount for a future period between a buyer-borrower (who wants protection from an *increase* in the future interest rate) and the seller-lender (who wants protection against a *decrease* in the future interest rate). The parties in the agreement do not actually enter into a loan transaction at the designated time in the future. If at that time, the actual interest rate is higher than the corresponding reference rate, the seller compensates the buyer for the difference; and if the actual interest rate is lower than the reference rate, the buyer pays the seller for the difference.

Suppose Bank A needs to borrow six months from now $10 million for three months. Bank A approaches Bank B for an FRA at the interest rate, say, 8 percent, six months from now with a reference interest rate of a three-month LIBOR for $10 million. Then Bank A is the buyer and Bank B is the seller in the FRA. If six months from now, the six-month LIBOR happens to be 7 percent, Bank A will compensate Bank B; and were it 9 percent, Bank B will pay Bank A to compensate for the increase in the interest rate over 8 percent. Specifically, in the first case of LIBOR of 7 percent, Bank A will pay Bank B:

$$\frac{[\text{Contract interest rate} - \text{LIBOR}] \times \text{Amount} \times \text{Annualized time period}}{[1 + \text{LIBOR} \times \text{Annualized time period}]}$$

or

$$\frac{[8\% - 7\%] \times \$10\text{million} \times 3/12}{[1 + 7\% \times 3/12]}$$

i.e. $24,570.

The numerator above represents the interest amount due at the end of the three-month period (or, nine months from today); the denominator is the present value factor. Thus the amount $24,570 would be payable at the *beginning* of the forward period, that is, six months from today.

The core concept behind the FRA is the relationship between the spot interest rate, $Int(0,n)$, and the forward rates, $Int(1,2)\ldots Int(n-1,n)$ embedded in the expectations theory of interest rate term structure discussed above. Any time for a given segment $(t - i)$ to (t), if the offshore and domestic markets are out of kilter, an arbitrageur can profit by combining a money market swap with an FRA and thereby restore the equilibrium in the market, as the following example demonstrates.

Example 4.2

A bank can obtain $10 million through a one-year CD for funding a two-year loan at the going market rate. Describe how it can hedge, given the following data:

- Currently, one-year and two-year *spot* rates in the USA are 10 percent and 11 percent respectively.
- The corresponding one-year and two-year spot rates in the Eurodollar market are 9.875 percent and 10.625 percent.
- Currently, one-year Eurodollar FRA, one year from now is available at 11.375 percent against LIBOR for $10 million.

The implicit one-year forward rates are

$$(1.11)^2/(1.10) - 1 = 12.01 \text{ percent in the domestic market}$$
$$(1.10625)^2/(1.09875) - 1 = 11.375 \text{ percent in the Eurodollar market}$$

The Eurodollar FRA rate, while consistent with the implicit one-year Eurodollar forward interest rate, is inconsistent with the domestic implicit forward interest rate.

Hence, the bank should

- loan $10 million in the USA for two years at 11 percent;
- raise $10 million in the USA for one year at 10 percent;
- purchase one-year Eurodollar 10 million FRA for one year at 11.375 percent.

If the bank manages to raise $10 million for one year by the end of the first year at the LIBOR of 11.375 percent, the bank will clear by the end of two years

$$\text{Revenue } (1.11)(1.11) = 1.2321$$
$$\text{less: Cost } (1.10)(1.11375) = (1.2265)$$
$$\text{Profit} = 0.0056 \text{ or slightly above 0.5 percent on \$10 million.}$$

Because the FRA has allowed the bank to lock in the one-year forward LIBOR for one year, the actual one-year LIBOR prevailing at the end of the current year does not matter; if it is higher than the contract rate of 11.375 percent, the counterparty would pay compensation that would offset the increased cost for the bank; and if it is lower, the bank would pay the counterparty just enough to raise the overall cost of funding for the second year to 11.375 percent.

Of course, in the above case, directly going to the Eurodollar market for a two-year loan would have increased profits even more; however, policy or other constraints may prevent a bank from accessing the Eurocurrency market for maturity exceeding a given period. In any case, actions by several participants along the lines suggested would reduce the one-year forward differential to, say, 0.25 percent between the domestic and the Eurodollar markets.

In a similar vein, the spot-forward interest rate relationship embedded in the FRA can be linked to more than one currency via the IRPT. As a result, it brings together the three components described above, viz., interest rates over time, interest rates in different currencies, and interest rates in the Eurocurrency market with those in the counterpart domestic markets.

Example 4.3

The FRA values, interest rates and forward rates provided below are not properly aligned.

6-month EuroSF FRA one year from now	5.50%–5.625%
6-month Eurodollar FRA one year from now	4.25%–4.3750%
1-year forward exchange rate today	$0.4995–0.5000/SF
18-month forward exchange rate today	$0.4975–0.4980/SF

a   Suggest how one can make arbitrage profit.
b   Indicate what consequences are likely as a result of such arbitrage activity.

The structure of this problem requires consideration of two alternatives:

1   one year from now, we arrange to borrow $1 for six months (Euro$ FRA offer rate); convert (12-month $/SF offer rate) and invest in SF immediately for six months (EuroSF FRA bid rate); and sell SF in 18-month forward market from today (18-month $/SF bid rate); *or*

2   one year from today, we arrange to borrow SF for six months (EuroSF FRA offer rate); immediately convert and invest in $ for six months one year from now (Euro$ FRA bid rate); and buy SF in 18-month forward market from today (18-month $/SF ask rate).

Thus, for alternative (1) we have:

•   Between 12 months from now and 18 months, the annualized forward discount rate for SF (against US$) 12 months from now is:

[(18-month bid rate − 12-month offer rate)/(12-month offer rate)]
    × annualization factor, or

[($0.4975 − $0.50)/$0.50] × (12 months/6 months)   = − 1%

- And the corresponding interest differential is

$$(1 + \text{6-month Euro\$ FRA offer rate})/(1 + \text{6-month EuroSF FRA bid rate}) - 1.0, \text{ or}$$
$$(1.04375)/(1.055) - 1.0 = -1.07\%$$

Thus the forward SF is selling in the 12-month market for an 18-month maturity at a smaller discount rate than the corresponding FRA interest differential would suggest, that is, the forward SF is overpriced in the foreign exchange market. Hence, the arbitrager should sell the SF in the 18-month forward market and buy it in the 12-month forward market. At the same time, the arbitrager should sell today a 6-month EuroSF FRA one year from now and buy the corresponding Eurodollar FRA in order to lock in the deposit (SF) and the loan (\$) rates.

The set of transactions will be

Step Description
1 Borrow through FRA 12 months from now \$1 for 6 months at 4.3750%
2 Convert the loan proceed of \$1 through the forward market in SF at \$0.50, i.e., obtain SF 2.0
3 Invest SF 2 through FRA at an interest rate of 5.5%
4 Six months later (18 months from now), sell the proceeds in the forward market in SF for \$ at \$0.4975/SF.
5 Profit will be

$$\underset{\text{step 2}}{\uparrow} \text{SF2} \times \underset{\text{step 3}}{\uparrow} (1 + 0.055/2) \times \underset{\text{step 4}}{\uparrow} \$0.4975/\text{SF} - \underset{\text{step 1}}{\uparrow} \$1 \times (1 + 0.0475/2) = \underset{\text{step 5}}{\uparrow} \$0.00049$$

The arbitrage activity along the above lines will result in

a Raising the six-month borrowing cost for Eurodollar in the 12-month market;
b Lowering the corresponding offer rate in the Euro SF market;
c Raising the six-month discount rate for SF in the one-year forward foreign exchange market; or
d any combination of the above.

It should be noted that no new concept has been introduced in the arbitrage activity in Example 4.3. It has only used the IRP relationship with one additional twist: instead of using the spot foreign exchange market and borrowing or lending currencies today, it employed the forward markets and shifted the time scale for one year.

The above illustration helps us understand how a change in the US monetary policy, for example, will transmit its impact on other economies. Suppose the Fed unexpectedly raises the domestic discount rate by 0.5 percent. This action will change the shape of the domestic term structure, depending on the market's interpretation of the Fed action. The term structure in the Eurodollar market will take its cue, and in turn will transmit the impact to other segments of the Eurocurrency market. Finally, the arbitrage potential will ensure that domestic counterparts of the other Eurocurrencies are adjusted.

Although our discussion focused on hedging or arbitrage activity, it can be easily extended to opportunities for speculation. For a case of speculation, suppose a dealer thinks that the market has not reflected some imminent changes in the foreign exchange or interest rates. Then she can resort to FRAs. If a dealer in Example 4.3 thinks that the term structure of Euro SF interest rates is likely to shift downward in a year, she would offer six-month FRA one year from now to the arbitrager in the example.

A comparison of FRA with forward contract

A comparison of the FRA with the forward contract is instructive. While the forward contract locks in the forward foreign exchange rate, the FRA locks in the *forward* interest rate. The settlement of the forward contract is for the designated amounts (of the two currencies) and it takes place upon maturity of the contract. In contrast, the FRA only requires settlement for the designated amount in terms of the differential of the contract interest rate over the reference rate, and this settlement occurs at the beginning of the contract period.

4.6 Eurocredits and Investments

Eurocurrency markets have different instruments with a wide range of maturities. We briefly discuss a few of them now.

4.6.1 Notes issuance facility (NIF)

Sovereign debt crisis in the 1980s gave incentives to banks to look for alternatives to generate income. One such alternative was the development of the NIF arrangement. Under this arrangement, the bank makes a medium-term (1–15 years) *underwriting commitment* to a borrower who can issue within a predefined period of, say, 2–5 years

- a short-term (anywhere from one month to nine months) note at a time;
- for up to a specified amount of the facility;
- at a defined spread over LIBOR or other such reference rate.

Typically, the first tier of a NIF arrangement is a syndicate of banks *underwriting* such a facility by committing to purchase the unsold portion of a note. Upon maturity, the note may be repaid or rolled over at the borrower's discretion. The arranging or **lead bank** receives one-time underwriting fees for the services, which it splits with other members belonging to the first tier of the syndicate.

The second tier of a NIF arrangement is the *tender panel*, which consists of a group of member banks that only *promise* to participate in the auction of the notes. A member bank is able to bid on a note up to a designated amount at its discretion. Participating banks with the lowest bid rates in the auction will get the notes. The benefit of being a tender panel member is a priority in purchasing the notes.

In this hierarchy, the risk-return set is the highest for the lead bank, and the smallest for the tender panel member bank. Typically, the range of compensation or the risk borne is not wide, nor is the tender panel membership mutually exclusive of membership in the under-writing syndicate.

Banks value NIFs because they provide an opportunity to generate income while avoiding holding assets. Further, although their commitment to a borrower may run for a multi-year period, they are able to limit their credit exposure (a) by reducing the actual maturity term of exposure, and (b) by drafting the agreement that renders the facility null and void when and if there is a material deterioration in the borrower's creditworthiness. Very often, the borrower wants to have the facility as a buffer, and doesn't intend to use it under normal circumstances. In such a case, the credit exposure becomes relevant only when the facility is utilized.

Intense competition among banks have led to **multi-option facilities** (MOFs), a variant of the NIF. A MOF gives the borrower an option to raise funds in different currencies and for a variety of maturities, typically involving flexibility of instruments, such as **Euro-commercial paper** (Euro-CP) and **Euronotes**, also known as **floating rate notes** (FRNs) (these instruments are explained below). Banks writing this option incur risk that requires adequate compensation. It is uncertain whether banks properly assess the underlying risk, and in case of proper assessment, whether they require adequate compensation. In either case, inadequacy of compensation is conveniently justified in terms of intense competitive pressures!

For borrowers, the NIFs (even more so the MOFs) allow them to borrow short-term funds at a lower cost than the syndicated loans. Businesses facing unanticipated but short-term liquidity crises find the buffer of NIFs very attractive; so would a firm considering acquisition prospects.

4.6.2 Euro-commercial paper issue

Another competitive source of raising short-term funds by a business firm is through Euro-CP. Traditionally, a Euro-CP, like the domestic commercial paper, is an *unsecured* promissory note for maturity not exceeding nine months. Today, however, it is not uncommon to find *collateralized* Euro-CP issued in conjunction with securitization (discussed in Section 4.6.4 below).

A Euro-CP is quoted on a discount basis, similar to the US market. For example, the interest rate is quoted as "actual/360," which means that the price is equal to 100 less the discount interest rate times the actual number of days to maturity divided by 360. For example, an issue of "60/360" with a 6 percent yield rate will have the price of $100 - 6\% (60/360) = \$99$ for a $100 par issue.

A Euro-CP may be issued on a stand-alone basis or in conjunction with a NIF. As a stand-alone instrument, it tends to cost less than a NIF arrangement because it requires impeccable credit, or guarantee by a firm with sound credit credentials. A bank active in this market derives income from the spread between buying and selling prices, which is usually small. If it has sufficiently high creditworthiness, it may provide a borrower with less-than-impeccable-credit a *standby letter of credit*, which allows the borrower to issue a Euro-CP on the strength of the bank's creditworthiness. In this case, the bank stands ready to pay the paper holders upon maturity in case of the borrower's default. Again, the contingent nature of credit exposure for a limited time may appeal to a bank in light of the compensation it will receive.

In the Euro-CP market, investors represent the spectrum from central banks of different countries to multinational corporations and financial institutions including banks. A Euro-CP has an active secondary market, while the US commercial paper has a relatively illiquid market as investors usually hold them until maturity. The Euro-CP rate is typically higher than that on the US counterpart because a Euro-CP is not necessarily rated by agencies such as Moody's or Standard & Poor's that is essential for placing the US counterpart.

4.6.3 Floating rate notes

The FRN is a medium-term (3–8 years) financial instrument whose **coupon** rate floats with the reference interest rate. The reference rate typically used is the LIBOR rate. The coupon rate is reset every three or six months to a new level based on the prevailing reference LIBOR at that time. The coupon rate consists of the reference rate and a "spread" – or quoted margin – that reflects the quality of the borrower. Many issues carry a call feature that allows the borrower to redeem the FRN prior to maturity. Typically the early redemption by the borrower occurs in the wake of improvement in the borrower's quality that would allow him to borrow at a smaller spread than one built into the FRN.

In comparing two FRNs in terms of return, the standard approach is to consider the size of spread over the LIBOR (or other benchmark rate) for each FRN. The *discount margin* is a measure of the effective spread relative to LIBOR assuming the FRN will be held to maturity.

Figure 4.3 illustrates the procedure to compute the discount margin.

- L_q is the *quoted* current LIBOR rate applicable to the FRN for the period between the last coupon payment date $(-\varepsilon)$ to the next coupon payment date $(+\varepsilon)$.
- L_e is the *expected* LIBOR rate for the remaining life of the FRN after the next (forthcoming) coupon payment date.
- QM is the quoted margin on the FRN.
- N is the number of periods after the next coupon payment date.

In Figure 4.3, the discount margin is obtained (iteratively) by equating the following variables assuming quarterly coupon payment periods and $100 par value of the bond.

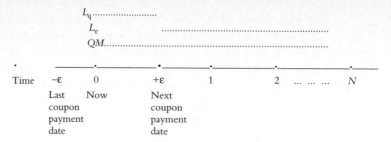

Figure 4.3 Computing the discount margin

$P + A$ = present value of coupon received at the next coupon payment date
+ present value of the remaining coupons for periods 1 through
N evaluated at the next coupon payment date

$$= [0.25(L_q + QM)]/[1 + (L + DM)\ D/360]$$
$$+ \{1/[1 + (L + DM)D/360]\}\{\Sigma_{t=1,N}\ [0.25(L_e + QM)]/$$
$$[(1 + (L_e + DM)/4]^t] + 100/[(1 + (L_e + DM)/4]^N\}$$

where P is the price of the FRN at time 0; A is the accrued interest since the last coupon payment up to date now; DM is the discount margin (percent); L is the prevailing LIBOR rate (percent) between "now" and the "next coupon payment date"; and D is the number of days remaining before the next coupon date from today (now).

The first issue of FRN was floated in 1970. During the 1970s when the inflation rate and its volatility were high, long-term investors found FRNs more attractive than fixed-coupon Eurobonds (discussed in Section 4.6.6 below).[6] When inflationary forces abated in the 1980s, popularity of FRNs decreased. As a result, a feature such as the "cap floater" – putting a ceiling on the borrower's cost (or "floor" guaranteeing a minimum for the investors') – was added to enhance FRN acceptance in the market place. Another feature to boost the sagging popularity of FRN issues was to give the holder an option to receive payments in currency other than the original currency in which the FRN was issued.

4.6.4   Asset-backed commercial paper and notes

A bank or its customer can raise financing in the forms of commercial paper and medium-term notes by providing collaterals of a variety of assets such as credit card receivables, leases, auto loans, commercial loans and real estate mortgages. Normally such collaterals are not very attractive to investors when these assets cannot be readily disposed of because of the absence of secondary markets. However, when securities are issued against ownership in these assets exclusively, these securities can be traded in the secondary market. In turn, trading provides liquidity to investors in these securities and they are likely to settle for a smaller yield than the rate they would demand for a direct claim against the underlying illiquid asset.

Typically the entity interested in obtaining financing sets up a **special purpose vehicle (SPV)** to which the interested borrower sells assets without recourse. These assets have one common characteristic: their aggregated cash flow is highly predictable (the notion of actuarial risk obtained through the law of large number). The SPV, in turn, issues securities such as commercial paper, medium-term notes (floating or fixed-rate), bonds, and even "equity" against the assets acquired from the original entity. At times, only a single form of "pass-through" claims is issued. At other times, several tranches or classes of "pay-through" claims are created; the hierarchy of these claims is based on maturity and seniority.

Essentially, this type of financing is securitization. It involves arbitrage along dimensions such as transactions cost, regulation, taxes, and "habitat." For instance,

- Transactions costs are lowered, since the prospective lenders do not have to investigate the originator of assets; instead, they need to consider the quality of its "divested" assets only.
- When a financial institution, for example, an insurance company, invests in the claims issued by the SPV, it requires less capital requirement than had it loaned funds directly to the originator, since the divested assets have a much higher rating. Similarly, a bank selling its loan portfolio, say of $100 million to the SPV and retaining interest worth $5 million requires capital adequacy only for the residual interest of $5 million, and not for the entire amount of $100 million.
- The SPV can have tranches of both commercial paper and preferred stock; the latter not only provides the corporate investor advantage of exemption of 70 percent of dividend income, but also serves as an equity cushion for commercial paper holders that lowers the cost of commercial paper.
- At times, some segments of the financial markets enjoy greater popularity than others ("preferred habitat"). For instance, during times of heightened interest rate or inflation uncertainty, commercial paper segment may enjoy sufficient popularity to lead to a very tight bid-ask spread. The SPV is able to exploit such opportunities leading to lower cost of financing for the original owner.

Similarly, pay-through collateralized mortgage obligations (CMOs) create preferred habitats of "fast pay" and "slow pay" tranches. Early redemption of mortgages (the underlying asset) is first used to liquidate claims of "fast pay" holders, whereas "slow pay" holders will be the last ones to face premature liquidation. "Fast pay" claims are generally preferred by banks, as the more probable call feature enables them to earn higher income and they do not mind premature redemption. On the other hand, pension funds like "slow pay" with slightly lower interest income because they reduce the expected transaction costs of reinvesting proceeds of premature redemption.

It should be noted that if a bank arranging or funding a customer's SPV also loans to the customer directly, it should keep in mind one adverse side effect: if the customer's most liquid or the top grade assets are sold to the SPV, the remainder of the assets will have, by definition, less liquidity or lower grade; hence the collateral value of the firm's residual assets for its loans will decline.

4.6.5 Syndicated loans

A syndicated loan involves a lead bank along with a number of other participating banks in providing relatively large credit to a single borrower. A syndication offers advantages to both the borrower and the lenders. The borrower can raise a larger sum of money than any single bank would be willing (or, at times, able) to lend and incurs a lower negotiation cost than when a loan is arranged with multiple independent sources. The lenders on the other hand can (1) diversify their asset portfolios, (2) reduce default risk because of enhanced penalties of a group that can prevent the borrower's access to financial markets, and (3) have the opportunity to communicate with other banks and thus have access to additional information and expertise.

In the early 1960s, the accepting houses in London served as the lead banks in the syndication process. In recent years, commercial banks in the USA, Canada, Japan, and Germany have become lead banks. These commercial banks have greater resources because of their large size and thus can make a firm commitment to the syndication loan as compared to the best efforts commitment made by the accepting houses.

Borrowers usually select a particular bank as the lead manager on the basis of an ongoing relationship with that bank. Upon obtaining the request for the loan in a statement from the borrower called the *mandate*, the lead bank may begin to (1) assemble a number of banks for this purpose, and (2) negotiate with the potential borrower and draw up a proposal to indicate terms of loans (pricing and fees) and whether the syndication will be fully committed, partially committed or best efforts. For a fully committed syndicated loan, the lead bank will provide the full amount of the loan in any event (other than those that constitute violation of the agreement; for example, unacceptable credit deterioration of the borrower).

When there is preliminary agreement on details, the lead manager will prepare a *placement memorandum*, a printed brochure giving more detailed information on (1) the borrower, (2) the detailed terms and conditions of the loan, and (3) the proposed loan agreement. The lead bank will then invite other banks to participate in the loan. Prospective participating banks are usually invited by fax or telex along with the placement memorandum.

There are several parts to a banking syndicate. First, the *lead bank* is responsible for setting up the terms of the loans and arranging for other banks to participate. Other banks participating in the syndication loan are called the *participating* banks. *Co-managing* banks are participating banks that have a greater share in the loan and may advise the lead bank. If there are several co-managers in the syndication process, one of them will be appointed to oversee the loan. This bank is then called the *agent* bank and is now responsible for collecting payments due and disbursing these payments to the other banks.

Compensation received by the loan syndicate has the following components.

- *Front-end fees*. The syndicate upon signing the loan receives these fees. Effectively it is a discount on the loan, reducing the loan amount.
- *Spread*. This represents the spread over the reference rate. In risky loans, the spread may decrease when some phases are successfully completed.
- *Management fees*. A designated bank acts as a conduit between the borrower and the syndicate members. In this capacity, it handles routine operations such as payment

distribution as well as more substantive tasks such as monitoring covenant observance by the borrower.

• *Commitment fees.* When the borrower does not draw the full amount of the loan upfront, but wants to utilize the full amount by some later date, the syndicate charges the commitment fees on the balance amount still not drawn by the borrower.

The syndicate generally determines the "all-in-one-spread" in the same way as the yield to maturity. When a borrower insists on a lower spread, the syndicate may accommodate the borrower by charging additional front-end fees or a balloon payment at maturity so that the desired "all-in-one" spread is preserved. The borrower, in this case, may want lower nominal spread, because the front-end fees being proprietary information may give an advantage in future negotiations with unrelated lenders.

Although the idea of an all-in-one-spread is basically sound, the altered timing of cash flows suggests that liquidity – and perhaps the credit – exposure of the participating banks does not remain invariant. Further, unless the borrower's insistence can be ascertained to stem from motives such as its image in the community,[7] such insistence conveys the borrower's preference for transaction motive over relationship desire we alluded to in Chapter 2; hence, undertaking the current transaction at a lower profitability to be compensated by future transactions may require closer scrutiny.

Straight syndicated loans of the yesteryear have been replaced by the **leveraged loans** since 1985. Although initially they were tied to leveraged buyout transactions with equity not exceeding 15 percent, recent transactions have encompassed many strategic transactions, such as plant construction and commercialization of technological breakthroughs where the borrower's equity is between 20 and 30 percent. Leveraged loans exhibit several distinct characteristics vis-à-vis straight syndicated loans of the past.

• Leveraged loans have been a major profit contributor[8] to banks in recent years and continue to offer an attractive alternative to low-priced investment-grade loans. Although highly leveraged transactions are riskier than traditional bank loans, these risks have been rendered manageable through
    – Careful analysis of the business risk and protection against it through various measures and covenants; for example, insistence on a long-term contract from a high-volume buyer, and insurance for (a) key management personnel, or (b) contingent legal liabilities related to consumer safety or pollution;
    – The borrower's track record, reputation, as well as a sound, carefully conceived business plan are critically evaluated against greater risk, say, of longer loan maturity, longer grace period for amortization, or poorer credit rating.

A typical syndicated leveraged loan
    – is collateralized,
    – is tied with a securitization vehicle,
    – requires rating, or
    – has a combination of these measures.

There is now an active secondary market for leveraged loans.

- Typically, syndicated loans through the 1980s did not provide lenders – mainly banks – adequate compensation for the risk. In contrast, institutional lenders during the 1990s brought a portfolio-management approach to the leveraged lending segment.[9]
- Broader participation, especially by financial institutions beside banks, has brought liquidity, allowing investors to assume higher credit risk. This is especially true of large loans.

4.6.6 Eurobond market

A **Eurobond** is a bond issued outside the country in whose currency it is denominated. The following characteristics of the Eurobond are noteworthy.

- It is not subject to regulatory requirements of the country in whose currency it is denominated. For instance, Eurodollar bonds avoid the Security and Exchange Commission (SEC) requirements of registration and prospectus issuance.
- It is subject to minimal regulatory requirements of the country in which it is physically issued.[10] These two requirements distinguish it from a "foreign" bond issued by a foreign business in a country in whose currency it is denominated; as such, the foreign bond has to meet the regulatory requirements of the country where it is placed.
- Typically it is issued in several countries simultaneously.
- The Eurobond markets are self-regulating.
- For a foreign, private-sector entity desiring dollar-denominated obligation, a Eurobond issue also means that the issuer bypasses the requirements imposed by the Financial Accounting Statement Board (FASB) standards that would have necessitated time-consuming restatement of its financial statements. Such restatement would also have meant unpalatable disclosure of perceived proprietary information.
- Avoidance of the regulatory requirements enables the borrower to cut the lead time (between the decision to issue and receiving funds from the issue placement) for an issue to a matter of days. In contrast, the lead time in the USA can stretch to several months.
- It is a bearer bond; hence, it does not have an ownership record with the issuing firm.
- Investors often forsake the protection afforded by regulations (e.g., veracity of information) because bearer bonds allow them to avoid or evade taxes on interest income.
- It carries a fixed-rate coupon. Thus even when it is privately placed, it is different from a securitized loan that carries a floating rate coupon.
- Its bearer characteristic allows it to avoid interest withholding taxes.
- Its unregistered form also prevents the issuer from exercising the call feature even if it existed. Hence these bonds have an effective maturity equivalent to the stated maturity.
- Prior to the 1980s when the secondary markets for the Eurobonds were not well developed, and the bearer form carried the danger of fraud, investors insisted on the quality of the issuer and the maturity of the issues were shorter than the counterpart domestic issues; for instance, dollar-denominated Eurobonds had maturity less than 15 years vis-à-vis 15–25 years for a domestic bond.

- Development of the secondary markets in the late 1980s and demand for funds for mergers and **leveraged buy-outs** (LBOs) shifted the emphasis from insistence on quality to adequate compensation for risk assumption and even shorter maturities.

The dollar-denominated Eurobond is still the largest segment of the Eurobond market, followed by the pound sterling and the Japanese yen. The Euro-denominated Eurobonds are likely to receive more and more importance as it now encompasses major world currencies such as the German mark and the French franc.

Two important roadblocks initially stimulated the growth of the dollar-based Eurobond market: the 1963 US **Interest Equalization Tax** (IET) on foreign securities issued in the USA for raising funds; and the 1965 voluntary (later mandatory) control of foreign direct investment by the US multinational firms. The introduction of the IET led to a shift of location of financial activities from New York to London, transforming foreign bonds (in this case, the "Yankee" bonds issued by foreigners in the USA) into dollar-denominated Eurobonds. The foreign direct investment constraint further abetted the shift to London by driving US multinationals to finance their foreign subsidiaries abroad.

Over the years, increased trading in the secondary markets has improved liquidity of the Eurobond markets. At the same time, FRNs and medium-term notes have provided competition to the conventional Eurobonds especially by allowing the issuers to convert their obligations into desirable currencies and from floating rates to fixed rate interest payments through swap activities, to be discussed in Chapter 6. Of course, swaps have also favorably affected the Eurobond market by allowing issuers to take advantage of softness in a currency by denominating the issue in that currency and converting the proceeds and debt service in desirable currencies through swaps.

In the mid-1980s, foreign investors were not allowed to invest in the Japanese bond markets. Domestic yen bonds were subject to 15 percent withholding taxes. At the same time, Japanese firms were not allowed to issue yen-denominated Eurobonds; however, they were allowed to issue Eurobonds in other currencies.

Two recent developments in the USA have affected the nature of the dollar-denominated Eurobond markets not only for initial placement but also for secondary market trading.

- The SEC introduced **shelf registration**, which permits an issuer the flexibility to place an issue any time within two years of its registration, to qualified issuers. This feature reduces the attraction of the Eurobond issues by cutting the lead time between the decision to issue and receipt of funds from issue placement.
- The SEC also approved **Rule 144a** that allows qualified investors to buy and sell privately placed securities (that have bypassed the initial registration process[11]) without meeting the restriction of the two-year holding period.

The Eurocurrency market has considerably broadened the scope of banking activities beyond pure foreign lending activities of the not-too-distant past, reflecting a more aggressive attitude of banks. Banks have thus been playing an active, if not the primary, role in not just the Euro-CPs and FRNs at the relatively short-term end of maturity but also syndicated loans and privately placed Eurobonds. With the repeal of the Glass–Steagall Act, banks will participate more aggressively in the publicly placed Eurobonds either directly or indirectly through acquisition of investment banking firms.

Increased competition and the increased demand for new financial products have shifted the bank focus to (a) fees related to placing – rather than acquiring – an income-generating asset; and (b) concomitantly, contingent liability that obviates the need for raising funds through straightforward debt, as was the case in the past. The driving force behind both these changes is the critical change in the bank attitude, replacing passivity of the yesteryear with aggressiveness in serving its clientele – a change that often reflects dissatisfaction with status quo, ambition, and insecurity.

4.7 Conclusion

This chapter discussed various issues related to the Eurocurrency market. Specifically, it explained development as well as the structure of the Eurocurrency market. The growth of the Eurocurrency results from government-induced impediments and it requires sustenance from "benign indifference" on the part of the government issuing the currency. Institutional setting of various geographic centers such as the Asian currency centers, Japan offshore market and international banking facilities was described to highlight the requisite ingredients for development of such centers.

The traits of interest rates were discussed with respect to time (term structure), space (other currencies), and impediments (domestic versus offshore). Interrelationships among the three were brought out through arbitrage activities facilitated by new tools, such as FRAs based on conventional concepts of term structure and interest parity theories. Finally, the role of the Eurocurrency market in the development of new products was discussed with illustrations of NIFs, Euro-CP, asset securitization, and Eurobonds. It was suggested that it is not the far-reaching novelty of these products that is important, but what they symbolize: a change in the bank attitude that marks a break with the past.

DISCUSSION QUESTIONS

1 What is Eurocurrency and what factors are responsible for the creation of a Eurocurrency? Why are the Eurocurrency deposits time deposits but not demand deposits?

2 How are bid-ask prices in the Eurocurrency market related to "domestic" deposit and loan rates? Why? Is this relationship universally observed?

3 It is suggested that "domestic" regulations have been responsible for development of the Eurocurrency market. What will be the role of these markets as financial markets increasingly become globally integrated?

4   In this era of instantaneous communications through telephone and elec-
    tronic mail, why should we be concerned with physical locations of
    Eurocurrency centers in the world?

5   If New York is a major Eurocurrency center, why did the Fed promulgate
    rules for establishing IBFs by US banks?

6   Discuss the causal relationship between domestic and offshore US interest
    rates.

7   What is an FRA? How is it connected to interest term structures and
    forward contracts in currencies?

8   Compute the amount of money that a seller of an FRA needs to pay to or
    receive from the buyer if the market interest rate is 8 percent, when the
    reference LIBOR is 7 percent. Assume the FRA is for six months duration
    and has a face value of $10 million.

9   Given that:
    a   one-year and two-year interest rates in the USA are 11 percent and
        12 percent, respectively, and
    b   one-year Euro $FRA one year from now is 13.5 percent

    what would you propose to do in order to make arbitrage profit?

10 Given the:
    a   bid-ask price for the six-month DM FRA one year from now is
        5–5.25 percent;
    b   bid-ask rate for the six-month dollar FRA one year from now is
        4–4.3 percent;
    c   one-year forward rate today is $0.5/DM--$0.505/DM;
    d   18-month forward rate today is $0.4985/DM--$0.4990/DM

    what is the arbitrage profit (if any) for the above quotes?

11 Suppose that the spot bid-ask price of £ sterling is $0.4429–0.4439, while
    the one-month forward rate is $0.4451–0.4461. The one-month euro-pound
    sterling deposit and loan rates are 5.875 percent and 6 percent,
    respectively. At the same time, the one-month Eurodollar rates are
    10.6875 percent and 10.8125 percent. What should be the bank's hedging
    strategy if the bank has debt of £10 million due one month from now? What
    course of action should the bank take to minimize cost if the £10 million
    debt is due today, if the bank has access to both Euro–US$ and Euro–£ ster-
    ling to pay the debt today and will have sufficient US$ a month from now?

12 What is a Euronote issuance facility? Why should a firm desiring to issue
    Euro-CP go through the trouble of establishing such a facility? What would
    be the likely impact of announcement of the facility on a firm's stock?

13 What are the potential consequences for a bank that encourages its cus-
    tomer to resort to Euro-commercial paper? Would your answer be different
    if the customer is already employing domestic commercial paper?

14 The current money market rates and FRA rates in US$ are as follows:

	Money market rate (%)			FRA (%)	
	Bid	Ask		Bid	Ask
3 months	10.50	10.52	3 against 6	10.54	10.64
6 months	10.52	10.63			

A customer approaches an international bank and deposits US$50 million for a six-month maturity. However, the bank desires to shorten the maturity of the deposits in order to maintain its optimal mix of asset and liability and liquidity. The bank likes to change the maturity of the deposit from six months to three months. What alternative courses of actions are available to the bank? What course of action should the bank take to achieve the desired asset-liability mix at the minimum cost?

15 The current LIBOR rate for US$ is 9.5 percent. FRNs without credit risk are typically priced at par, which is equal to $100 at the pre-set repricing dates. As a banker, you helped place three FRNs by firms that were an impeccable credit risk last year (as a result, these issues did not carry a spread over LIBOR). The coupons on these three FRNs are linked directly to the prevailing LIBOR on the pre-set repricing dates. Today, the remaining maturities of the three FRNs are 5 years, 10 years and perpetual.

You find the credit risks of these three FRNs have changed since last year. After some analysis, you have concluded that each of these three FRNs has a similar revision in credit risk, which would entail a spread of 50 basis points above the current LIBOR rates. Coincidentally, a new client interested in issuing two new FRNs with a maturity of 5 years and 10 years respectively has approached you. The two new FRNs appear to have similar credit risk characteristics as the three existing FRNs.

a What should be the price of the three existing FRNs today? Discuss the relationship between pricing and maturity of the FRNs.

b What should be the price of the two new FRNs? Is there any difference in pricing the old and new FRNs? Explain.

NOTES

1 This rate is determined by averaging the loan rates of 12 major banks randomly selected from a pool of 20 participating banks in the London Eurodollar market. The two highest and two lowest of the 12 quotes are deleted. The arithmetic mean of the remaining eight quotes is the LIBOR.

2 Euromarkets are self-regulating. Their information network is supposed to be far more efficient than that of a government. As a result, if the market perceives that a bank's sudden liquidity problems are chronic, it would rather shut out the bank from the market than temporarily accommodate it. Thus a Eurobank should not expect a great deal of flexibility in maneuvering through a liquidity crisis. See in Section 4.4.2 the example of Continental Illinois Bank in 1984.

3 Tax havens have typically minimal regulatory requirements on banks for conducting their business, broad interpretation of proprietary information, and minimum or no taxes on income.

There are more than three dozen tax havens around the world; e.g., Bahamas, Virgin Island, Channel Islands, and Republic of Panama.

4 See Swoboda (1982: 337–8). In the USA, overnight Eurodollar deposits are counted in the M2 definition of the money supply while longer-term Eurodollar deposits are counted in the M3 definition of the money supply. Note, however, US banks' obligations to non-residents do not change with the expansion of Eurodeposits.

5 Under the *pure expectations theory* of the interest rate term structure, the anticipated interest rate prevailing in the second period will be the same as the implied forward interest rate. Thus, when equilibrium prevails under the pure expectations theory, there is no profit potential in the loan extension of different maturities.

6 Unlike many other instruments, FRNs enjoyed far greater popularity in the Eurocurrency market than in the USA. One reason for this peculiarity was little enthusiasm for the "uncertain" floating rate among both investors and borrowers in the USA. This aversion was also reinforced by the Fed policy to maintain stable interest rates in the post-World War II period through the end of 1970s.

7 During the 1970s, many state governments reportedly insisted on low spread conveying strong credit image in the financial as well as political world.

8 It is not unusual to find a leveraged loan to a speculative-grade rated borrower to carry the interest rate of LIBOR + 250 bps.

9 The volatility factor has been small on levered loans because of the floating interest rate and absence of prepayment penalty. The latter factor, along with trading on the secondary market, has led the lender to unload holdings when market conditions turn favorable for the borrower (since, otherwise, the borrower would take advantage of the situation and refund the loan through new borrowing at a lower interest rate); such lender behavior keeps the market price much less volatile. Still, lenders typically require compensation for the prepayment risk they bear.

10 A local government may impose guidelines of settling up underwriting syndicates, types of issues that can be placed, and timing of the issues.

11 As Marr (1995: 75) has noted, other SEC rules, however, prevent a foreign issuer from escaping this requirement.

CHAPTER 5

Futures and Options in Currency and Interest Rate Markets

LEARNING OBJECTIVES

- To compare and contrast the forward and futures markets
- To discern the basic characteristics and pricing of currency and interest rate futures contracts
- To comprehend the basic characteristics and pricing of call and put contracts as well as the put-call parity relationship
- To apprehend the option feature and determine its impact on forward/futures contracts

5.1   Introduction

Commercial banks are involved in futures, options, and other derivative instruments in two important ways. First, they design or price these derivative instruments for their clients. Second, they also use derivative instruments in managing interest rate and currency risks specifically and asset-liabilities in general. Introduction of the international dimension to bank management transforms various risk facets and their management. For instance, domestic interest rate risk of a bank may be mitigated or magnified in the presence of the currency risk it faces. Further, the economics of benefit-cost analysis regarding risk management on behalf of the bank's clients as well as on its own account significantly changes in the presence of a bewildering array of derivative instruments available on international dimension (swaps, to be discussed in the next chapter, belong to this category). Thus, an understanding of these instruments is vital for managing operations of multinational banks.

   This chapter focuses primarily on currency and interest rates related derivative instruments because they are widely used by multinational banks. First, differences and similarities between forward and futures contracts are discussed. Then, salient characteristics of both currency and interest rate futures contracts are described. Options and options on futures are finally explained. One major purpose of this chapter is to highlight linkages among futures, options, and their underlying assets. This discussion serves as a foundation for discussion of some intricate derivative instruments such as interest rate and currency swaps, interest rate caps and range forward contracts in the following chapter, where these complex instruments will be shown as a combination of the basic (option and futures) instruments.

5.2 Forward and Futures Contracts

A **futures contract** is a standardized agreement between an individual entity and a clearing house of an organized exchange pertaining to future exchange of a good (commodity, currency, or a financial asset) at an agreed price. Basically both forward and futures contracts represent commitment to be executed in future at an agreed price. Several important features such as the existence of organized exchange, standardized contracts, the role of a clearing house, and settlement practice distinguish the futures contracts from the forward contracts. Each of these features is discussed below.

5.2.1 Organized exchange

Futures contracts are traded on an organized exchange, a voluntary, non-profit association of its members. For example, several currency futures are traded on the International Money Market (IMM) of the Chicago Mercantile Exchange (CME). Physical trading in futures contracts takes place only during official trading hours in a designated area called a *pit*. Electronic trading of futures contracts has become increasingly important in recent years. This development may have substantial impact on the US and global derivative markets.

Traders in the pit use an unofficial system of hand signals to express buy and sell orders. Officially, all offers to buy or sell must be made through open outcry in the pit in contrast to the specialist system used in stock exchange trading.

As we saw in Chapter 3, forward markets are loosely organized and have no physical location devoted to trading. Participants such as multinational banks, brokers, and large corporations through electronic communications networks conduct transactions related to forward market in currencies.

5.2.2 Standardized contract

Futures contracts always have standardized contract terms while forward contracts are tailor-made to the customers. In general, the futures contract specifies (1) the quantity of the currency to be delivered, (2) the delivery date and method for closing the contract, and (3) permissible minimum and maximum price fluctuations in daily trading.

For example, the unit contract size of futures contracts traded in the IMM of the CME for the British pound futures contract is BP 62,500, for the Japanese yen is JY12,500,000 and the Swiss franc is SF125,000. Expiration dates for all currency futures traded in the IMM are the third Wednesday of March, June, September, and December.

Standardized contracts serve one important purpose. They are a necessary condition for transparency in transactions. In turn, transparency reduces transaction cost barriers for potential market participants. Greater participation in turn promotes greater competition in the market place that, among other things, is likely to prevent price manipulation by some participants at the expense of the rest of the market.

5.2.3 Clearing house

The **clearing house**, which is a separate corporation or part of the futures exchange, guarantees the integrity of all trades. The clearing house is the buyer for every seller and the seller for every buyer; hence, every trader in the futures markets has obligations only to the clearing house. As a result, trading parties on the two sides of a transaction do not need to trust or even know each other. They have to be concerned with the reliability of only the clearing house. Given the well-capitalized clearing house, the risk of a future default by the clearing house is small.

The clearing house provides a cost effective means to reduce the impact of credit risk. A bank, for example, faces credit risk of the forward contract when a client does not honor the forward contract. In case of default, the bank has to take costly legal actions to enforce the contract in order to reduce losses.

In the futures market, the number of contracts bought must equal the number of contracts sold. Thus, if all outstanding long and short futures market positions are considered, the total always equals zero.

5.2.4 Margin requirement and marked-to-market

The prospective investor must deposit funds with a broker for acquiring a futures contract. This deposit is called the **initial margin**, whose purpose is to provide a financial safeguard for contract obligations. The amount of this margin varies from contract to contract and may vary with different brokers. The initial margin approximately equals the maximum daily price fluctuation permitted on the contract. The margin may be posted with cash, a bank letter of credit or Treasury bills. The trader retains title to these funds.

After the initial agreement, if the daily price moves against the buyer (i.e., the price goes down) or against the seller (i.e., the price goes up), the resulting loss will be charged to the margin account. When the balance in the broker's account drops to a specified level called the **maintenance margin**, the broker will ask the trader to furnish additional funds to replenish the broker's account up to the initial margin. The maintenance margin is generally about 75 percent of the amount of the initial margin. The additional amount the trader must provide when the deposit with the broker is less than the maintenance margin is called the **variation margin**.

At the end of the trading day, there is a settlement of the contract, and the futures contract is **marked-to-market**. It is *as if* the old futures contract is closed out and a new contract is written in its place. As a result, the trader will have the obligation to sell or buy at the new price for the remaining time of the futures contract. Example 5.1 explains the daily settlement procedure for futures transactions.

Example 5.1

Suppose a currency trader in a bank wants a long position in a SF futures contract maturing in three days. The margin requirements for the contract are as follows:

Initial margin	US$1,755
Maintenance margin	US$1,300
One SF futures contract	SF125,000

Time	Event-action	Investor's cash flow
Monday morning	Investor buys one SF futures contract maturing in three days. Price is US$0.65/SF	(a) US$1,755 (initial margin)
Monday close	Futures price drops to US$0.649. Position is marked-to-market.	(b) Investor pays: $125,000 \times (0.65 - 0.649)$ = US$125. (c) Margin a/c balance $1,755 - $125 = $1,630
Tuesday close	Futures price drops to US$0.645/SF. Position is marked-to-market.	(a) Investor pays: $125,000 \times (0.649 - 0.645)$ = US$500 (b) Margin a/c balance US$1,630 − US$500 = US$1,130 (*below* maintenance margin of US$1,300). (c) Investor supplies variation margin of US$625 to make up to US$1,755.
Wednesday close	Futures price rises to US$0.646/SF. Contract is closed out.	(a) Investor receives $125,000 \times (\$0.646 - \$0.645)$ = US$125 (b) Margin a/c balance: US$1,755 + US$125 = US$1,880. (c) Investor pays $125,000 \times US\$0.646/SF$ = US$80,750 (to close out the futures contract)

In Example 5.1, the **net cost** to the investor will be:

Closing cost (US$80,750) − Fund amount returned (US$1,880) + Variation margin paid (US$625) + Initial Margin paid (US$1,755) = US$81,250.

The **unit price** paid by the investor for one Swiss Franc is:

US$81,250/SF 125,000 = US$0.65/SF (which is the same price as the initial contract price).

As this example shows, the daily settlement does not change the basic idea that the futures contract offers a fixed price like the forward contract. In Example 5.1, the buyer puts up US$625 earlier during the three-day life of the contract, rather than putting up the entire amount at the end of the contract as in a forward contract (i.e., no cash flow is exchanged during the life of a forward contract).[1] If time value of money is ignored for the early capital outlay, the futures contract is exactly the same as the forward contract. Ignorance of time value is not an entirely unreasonable assumption, since (a) the contract's maturity is typically less than a year, and (b) any favorable price movement also allows the trader to withdraw gains earlier or cover subsequent losses.

When a trader whose account falls to the maintenance margin fails to meet the variation margin requirement, the contract is immediately closed out. Thus the daily settlement mechanism insures the integrity of the futures contract and prevents payment default by the trader. Since the daily settlement does away with the credit investigation or collection cost for the futures contract, it is likely to be priced in an economically efficient fashion.

5.3 Functions of Futures Contracts

In 1974, Congress established the Commodity Futures Trading Commission (CFTC) to monitor and regulate the futures markets. The CFTC examined two issues. The first issue related to the use of futures contracts for price discovery and hedging purposes. The **price discovery function** is the ability of the futures price to predict underlying future spot price movements. Under the *speculative efficiency hypothesis* (SEH) (Bilson 1981), the futures price is an unbiased predictor of the future spot price.

SEH ignores the daily settlement feature of the futures contracts. If we incorporate the daily settlement of the futures contracts, the futures price will be a biased predictor for the expected spot price (see Appendix F):

$$f_{0,T} = E(S_T) + COV(R, S_T)/(1 + r_{0,T})^T \qquad (5.1)$$

where $f_{0,T}$ is the settlement price at time T, agreed upon by the two parties at time 0; E is the expectation operator; S_T is the spot price at time T; $r_{0,T}$ is the interest rate at time 0 for the period ending at T; $R = (1 + r_{0,1})(1 + r_{1,2}) \ldots (1 + r_{T-1,T})$, where $r_{i,i+1}$ is the 1-period interest rate starting at the period i; and COV is the covariance term.

If there is a *positive* **correlation** between the interest rate (R) and the future spot price (S_T), the futures price will be *higher* than the corresponding expected price. Similarly, a negative relationship between R and S_T implies that the futures price will be below the expected spot price.

Futures contracts offer an attractive alternative to banks for risk management. As we saw in Chapter 3, since interest rates and currency values are closely interlinked, futures contracts enable banks to manage the combined risks in an efficient way. The process of interest and currency risks management is more closely examined below.

The second issue considered by the CFTC was *cornering*. This practice describes manipulation of futures contracts deriving illegal profits. One strategy followed by traders is to stockpile the underlying good and at the same time buy (or long) the futures contracts that enable them to buy more of the underlying good at a predetermined price. This strategy is greatly facilitated when there is misalignment between spot price and futures price. In this way, the traders manage to acquire a long position at reasonably low prices. Further, they manage to create an artificial supply shortage near the time of maturity of futures contracts, and force the price of the underlying good to catapult. The net result is handsome profit.

In order to mitigate the potential corner problem, CFTC has allowed acceptability of multiple grades (for agricultural commodities) or different instruments for delivery purposes on the expiration date. For example, in the Treasury bond (T-bond) futures contracts, different types of T-bonds with different coupons can be delivered as long as they meet requirements, such as a minimum of 15 years to maturity at the time of delivery, and an average coupon rate of 8 percent.

Furthermore, the cornering problem is unlikely to occur, if there is a large number of participants in the futures market. A large number of participants is likely to entail an arbitrage free relationship between the futures price and its underlying spot price. That is, if there is a misalignment between the futures price and its underlying spot price, the arbitrage process generating riskless profit will set into motion and it will self-extinguish as those opportunities vanish. Absence of misalignment, in turn, would discourage cornering by reducing its profit potential.

5.3.1   Currency futures

Pricing

The model to price currency futures is the same as the currency forward price, that is, via the Interest Rate Parity Theory (IRPT). In the futures literature, it is also called the *carrying cost model*.[2] If there is a sizable difference between currency forward and futures prices, arbitrage opportunities may exist. Example 5.2 illustrates an arbitrage scenario.

Example 5.2

Suppose the interbank forward bid for September 17, 19xx on the SF is US$0.65/SF while the SF futures price at IMM is US$0.648/SF. Thus, the dealer may simultaneously buy a German futures contract at US$0.648 for US$81,000 (i.e., SF125,000 × US$0.648/SF) and sell the SF in the interbank market for the equivalent amount at

US$0.65 for US$81,250 (i.e., SF125,000 × US$0.65/SF). The profit for the trader will be US$250 for SF125,000. As a result, the futures price will go up or the forward bid will come down until approximate equality is restored so as to stop the forward-futures arbitrage process. One caveat in the above example is that the daily settlement characteristic is ignored in the pricing analysis.

In light of Equation 5.1, as forward price does not require daily adjustment of cash flows, it should be equal to the expected future spot price only under (a) risk neutral conditions, or (b) when the interest rate and the future spot price are uncorrelated. A priori it is difficult to ascertain that either of the two conditions prevails. Alternatively, it can be argued that

- if $COV(R, S_T)$ is *positive*, the futures price will be *higher* than the forward price.
- if COV is negative, the futures price will be lower than the forward price.
- Finally, if COV is zero, the futures price should be the same as the forward price.

Empirical investigations of the currency forward/futures under different phases of the interest rate cycle show that the difference between currency futures and forward price is small. In other words, there is no significant difference between futures and forward prices.

Risk management

Futures contracts are commonly used as tools for risk management because the futures price movements are similar to the spot price movements. Suppose on February 2, a bank anticipates an outflow of SF1,250,000 on February 16. The spot price on February 2 is US$0.65/SF when the bank buys 10 contracts of SF futures contracts (each contract is for SF125,000) to hedge the currency risk. The SF futures price is US$0.66. The transaction is shown as follows:

	Cash market	Futures market
February 2	Spot rate = US$0.65/SF	Long (buy) 10 contracts of SF March futures at US$0.66/SF
February 16	Buy SF1,250,000 in the spot market at the spot rate = US$0.68/SF	Reverse March SF futures transactions by shorting (selling) 10 SF futures at US$0.69/SF
Gain (loss)	− US$0.03	+ US$0.03

In the above example, the gain in the futures market will offset the loss in the cash − spot − market. Thus, we achieve a net zero gain (loss) position, a major goal in hedging. The above illustration is based on the assumption that the movement of the futures price is in exact tandem with the spot price. That is, the differential of cash price and the futures price, which is called the *basis point*, remains unchanged (US$0.01 for February 2 and February 16). Based on this assumption, the bank should buy the same amount of the futures contract (i.e., SF 1,250,000) as the exposure in the cash market. In our present case, we have a one-to-one hedge (the futures position is equal to the cash position).

If the basis point is not constant, then we need to estimate the required futures position to cover the spot position. That is, we need to estimate the **hedge ratio** (the futures position to the cash position). The hedge ratio, b, in the futures contracts is obtained by minimizing the variance of cash price variability and futures price variability (see Appendix G for details):

$$b = COV(\Delta S, \Delta f)/VAR(\Delta f) \tag{5.2}$$

where COV is the covariance between ΔS and Δf; VAR is the variance of Δf; ΔS is the difference in the cash price, that is, $S_1 - S_0$; and Δf is the difference in the futures price, that is, $f_1 - f_0$.

The hedge ratio for any other futures contract is similarly defined. Thus, the relationship defined in Equation 5.2 is general and can be easily computed. Nevertheless, the hedge ratio is rarely computed by directly measuring COV and VAR in the relationship (Equation 5.2). Instead, a regression analysis is used to obtain the hedge ratio.

Consider the equation

$$y = a + bx$$

where y, the dependent variable (which is now ΔS), is regressed on x, the independent variable, which is denoted by Δf. In the regression result, we obtain the intercept, a, and the coefficient b. The coefficient b, by definition, is equal to $COV(\Delta S, \Delta f)/VAR(\Delta f)$, the hedge ratio.

Example 5.3

Data on historic biweekly spot price (S) and futures price (f) for the British pound ($£$) in terms of the US dollar are as follows.

Date	S(Spot)	ΔS	f(Futures)	Δf
$t - 10$	1.57		1.62	
$t - 9$	1.58	0.01	1.61	-0.01
$t - 8$	1.55	-0.03	1.59	-0.02
$t - 7$	1.54	-0.01	1.57	-0.02
$t - 6$	1.56	0.02	1.58	0.01
$t - 5$	1.53	-0.03	1.56	-0.02
$t - 4$	1.58	0.05	1.57	0.01
$t - 3$	1.59	0.01	1.59	0.02
$t - 2$	1.62	0.03	1.62	0.03
$t - 1$	1.59	-0.03	1.60	-0.02
t(now)	1.58	-0.01	1.63	0.03

Regressing ΔS (as the dependent variable) on Δf (as the independent variable) yields the following results with their standard errors below the estimates.

$$\Delta S = 0.0002 + 0.829\, \Delta f$$
$$(0.007)\ (0.353)$$
$$R^2 = 0.40$$

(R^2 is the coefficient of determination in regression analysis and it measures the degree of hedging effectiveness in the hedging literature. A higher R^2 indicates a better hedging effectiveness.)

In this case, the value of the hedge ratio, b, is 0.829. The *amount* of futures contracts needed for the hedge is given by:

$$\text{Spot position} \times \text{hedge ratio}$$

If the exposure in the cash market is £5 million, the position in the futures will be for the amount:

$$= £5,000,000 \times 0.829$$
$$= £4,145,000$$

As a result, the *number* of futures contracts needed for the hedge, given the standardized contract size (i.e., £62,500) in the exchange, is:

$$£4,145,000/£62,500$$
$$= 66.32 \text{ contracts or 67 contracts (by rounding up)}$$

In this example, the hedging horizon is two weeks, so we used bi-weekly data in the analysis. If the hedging horizon is one-week or one month, we should use one-week and one-month data, respectively, for running the regression.[3]

5.3.2 Interest rate futures

We discuss below three categories of interest rate futures: Treasury bill (T-bill) futures, Eurodollar futures and Treasury bond futures. These three categories represent a large portion of the interest rate futures market. We discuss below two US interest rate instruments because (a) they may be an ideal vehicle for hedging, arbitraging, or speculating in international transactions, and (b) they help us understand complications involved in pricing as well as the use of interest rate futures in general.

Treasury bill futures

The Treasury bill futures, traded at the IMM, allow delivery of a 90-, 91- or 92-day T-bills. Thus, the days to maturity (DTM) of the T-bills to be delivered can vary accordingly. However, the futures price quotation is based on a 90-day bill. The T-bill futures contract calls for the delivery of T-bills (on March, June, September, and December) with a face value of US$1 million. As a result, the pricing of 91- or 92-day T-bill futures needs to be adjusted for the difference in days to maturity.

The price of the T-bill futures is based on a **discount yield** (DY) method on the IMM Index. Discount yield is not the same as the **yield to maturity** as will be shown later in the section.

Example 5.4

Suppose on October 3, 20xx, the discount yield (DY) (in percentage) of the T-bill futures is 4.25 for the December contract. Then the IMM *quoted* price is

$$100 - DY = 100 - 4.25 \text{ or } 95.75$$

The 95.75 price is called the IMM Index, which is not the actual price. The *actual* price, f, is given by the following equation:

$$f = \text{US\$1,000,000} - DY(\text{US\$1,000,000}) \ DTM/360$$

Thus, for the 90-day T-bill futures, its futures price will be:

$$
\begin{aligned}
f &= \text{US\$1,000,000} - 0.0425(\text{US\$1,000,000})90/360 \\
&= \text{US\$1,000,000} - \text{US\$10,625} \\
&= \text{US\$989,375}
\end{aligned}
$$

If the discount yield increases to 4.26, the future price will drop to US\$989,350, reflecting a decrease of US\$25 for a basis point (i.e., 0.01% = 0.0426 − 0.0425).

The above example shows that the quoted price or the IMM Index, in contrast to the actual price, deducts the discount as if the holding period is annual.

Eurodollar futures

The Eurodollar futures, which are highly liquid short-term interest rate contracts, are very popular contracts. While T-bill futures track default-free short-term US government securities, Eurodollar futures track the three- month LIBOR. The size of the Eurodollar futures is US\$1 million, similar to the T-bill futures.

The pricing of the Eurodollar futures is similar to the T-bill futures using the IMM Index method. For example, given the discount yield of 5 percent, the IMM Index will be 95, and thus the price of the Eurodollar futures will be:

$$
\begin{aligned}
f &= \text{US\$1,000,000} - DY(\text{US\$1,000,000})90/360 \\
&= \text{US\$1,000,000} - 0.05(\text{US\$1,000,000})90/360 \\
&= \text{US\$1,000,000} - \text{US\$12,500} \\
&= \text{US\$987,500}
\end{aligned}
$$

Treasury bond futures

T-bond futures contracts are traded in the Chicago Board of Trade (CBOT). The T-bond futures allow the short-seller the option to deliver a variety of T-bonds each one with a minimum of 15 years of maturity or first permissible call date.

This *delivery option* (or *quality option*) is not so simple as it sounds. Indeed, the delivery at the expiration date has several features that contribute some confusion to the delivery process. The short-seller will deliver the cheapest instruments among the permissible set that either maximizes the highest net cash flow – or minimizes the cash outflow – after considering the **invoice price** (the *adjusted* futures price that the short-seller will receive upon delivery), which is defined as:

$$\text{Invoice price} = \text{Futures price} \times \text{Conversion factor} + \text{Accrued interest} \qquad (5.3)$$

Each T-bond instrument has a different conversion factor depending on the maturity and coupon payments. The conversion factor is similar to an entry in the time value of money table.

The futures price quoted for the T-bond is based on the underlying T-bond price with 8 percent coupon and 20-year maturity. This is the reason we have to adjust the invoice price via Equation 5.3 to reflect the pricing differential when delivering different T-bonds that have different coupons and maturity. Accrued interest is the interest accrued from the last coupon payment to the delivery date.

Example 5.5

Suppose the quoted T-bond futures price is 72 – 31. There are two deliverable T-bonds, A and B, whose prices are 71 – 16 and 73 – 12, respectively. The conversion factors (CF) for A and B are 0.9641 and 0.9878, respectively. Assume the accrued interest for both bonds is zero. Which bond, A or B, should be delivered?

- Determine the *quoted* price for the T-bonds to be delivered, that is, the payment to be received for delivering a particular bond. The bond price is quoted on 1/32 basis and is based on US$1,000 par value. Thus for T-bond A, it is 71 – 16 where

$$71 \text{ corresponds to US}\$71,000$$
$$16 \text{ corresponds to US}\$1,000 \ (16/32) = \text{US}\$500$$

Thus the quoted price for T-bond A is US$71,000 + US$500 = US$71,500. Similarly, for T-bond B the quote 73 – 12 translates into US$73,375.

- The futures price for the T-bond is quoted just like the T-bond price. Hence, for bond A, the futures price is 72 and 31, where

$$72 \text{ corresponds to US}\$72,000$$
$$31/32 \text{ equals to US}\$968.75.$$
$$\text{The } \textit{quoted} \text{ futures price is US}\$72,968.75$$

- Compute the net cash flow for the short position, which is equal to the invoice price less the price of the delivered T-bond.

$$\text{Bond A: Net Cash flow} = \text{Invoice Price} - \text{Price of Bond A}$$
$$= \text{US}\$72,968.75 \times 0.9641 - \text{US}\$71,500$$
$$= \text{US}\$ - 1,150.83$$

$$\text{Bond B: Net Cash flow} = \text{Invoice Price} - \text{Price of Bond B}$$
$$= \text{US\$72,968.75} \times 0.9878 - \text{US\$73,375}$$
$$= \text{US\$} - 1,296.47$$

Because the short position receives negative cash flow, bond A should be delivered to minimize the cost of the transaction. Thus, the cheaper instrument to deliver is bond A.

Besides the delivery option, there is also another option called the **wild-card option** embedded in the T-bond futures. This embedded option enables the short trader to notify the clearing house of his/her intention to deliver until 8.00 p.m. Eastern time. The T-bond futures ceases trading at 2.00 p.m. Chicago time (3.00 p.m. Eastern time), while T-bonds are traded until 4.00 p.m. Chicago time (5.00 p.m. Eastern time). If there is adverse information that depresses the bond prices after the close of the bond trading, the short-trader of the T-bond futures can notify the clearing house to deliver at the 2.00 p.m. settlement price. Thus the invoice price will be higher at 2.00 p.m. than later, and the short-trader can buy the T-bond at a cheaper price the following day. This way, the trader can enhance her profit or reduce her losses.

5.3.3 Use of interest rate futures

Interest rate contracts can be used for a variety of purposes.

- *Arbitrage.* Interest rate futures can also be used to eliminate any mispricing in the underlying interest rate instruments through the arbitrage process.
- *Price discovery.* The interest rate embedded in the futures contract can be used to predict the future interest rate movement. This is closely related to the speculative efficiency market hypothesis discussed earlier.
- *Hedging.* From the bank's perspective, interest rate futures instruments are primarily useful for hedging purposes. Although a regression format (discussed in the previous section) can be used to estimate the hedge ratio, and thus the number of futures contracts to be used, the most common hedging method used in the interest rate scenarios is the **price sensitivity hedge ratio** (PSHR).

Extensive use of this hedging method is probably due to its simplicity and the readily available data. PSHR gives N_f, the *number* of contracts in interest rate futures (such as T-bill or T-bond futures) necessary to hedge the anticipated interest rate risk (see Appendix H):

$$N_f = -\frac{D_s S/(1 + r_s)}{D_f f/(1 + r_f)} \tag{5.4}$$

where D_s is the **duration** of the spot interest rate instrument to be hedged; D_f is the duration of the underlying interest rate instrument for the corresponding futures contract; S denotes the spot price and f is the futures price; r_s and r_f are the yield to maturity for the spot and futures interest rate instruments.

The negative signs means if the hedger is short (long) in the spot instrument, he should take a long (short) position in the interest rate futures contracts.

Example 5.6

On January 5, a commercial bank *anticipates* to issue on February 10, US$10 million CDs with a maturity of 180 days. Suppose the interest rate (or discount yield) on the current 180-day CD rate is 10.87 percent. Then, the value of the CD (proceeds of the CD issue) will be equal to:

$$\text{US\$10M} - 0.1087 \times (180/360) \times \text{US\$10M}$$
$$= \text{US\$9,456,500}$$

The annualized interest cost to the bank for issuing the CD today will be equal to:

$$(\text{US\$10m}/9.4565)^{365/180} - 1 = 12\%$$

On February 10, the bank will be willing (able) to borrow money at 12 percent only if the interest rate does not change between now (January 5) and February 10.

Now, consider the bank wants to use the Eurodollar futures traded at the IMM to hedge the CD interest rate risk. At the IMM, the March Eurodollar IMM Index is 88.40, which suggests the discount yield of the Eurodollar futures is 11.60 percent (i.e., $100 - 88.40$). Thus, the price of the Eurodollar futures per US$100 is:

$$100 - \text{discount yield} \times (90/360) = 100 - 11.60 \times$$
$$90/360 = 97.1$$

As a result, the price of the Eurodollar futures per contract (US$1 million) is US$971,000. In addition, the implied yield computed by using the compounding method is $(100/97.1)^{365/90} - 1 = 12.68\%$.

Given the above information, the bank can now figure out the number of Eurodollar futures contracts to hedge the CD issue using the PSHR formula:

$$N_f = \frac{-D_s S/(1 + r_s)}{D_f f/(1 + r_f)}$$

The duration of the spot CD is 6 months because of its 180-day maturity; duration of the Eurodollar futures is 3 months because the Eurodollar futures contract is based on the 90-day (3-month) maturity of the underlying CD. The yield to maturity for the spot, r_s, is 12 percent and for the futures contract, r_f, is 12.68 percent. The price of the futures contract is US$971,000, as derived above. Thus we have

$$N_f = -\frac{(1/2)\ \text{US\$9,456,500}/(1 + 0.12)}{(1/4)\ \text{US\$971,000}/(1 + 0.1268)}$$

$$= -19.6 \text{ (contracts)}$$

As a result, the bank sells 20 contracts (rounded for 19.6) of the Eurodollar futures. On February 10, suppose the discount yield on the 180-day CD in the cash market is now 11.3 percent, and the Eurodollar IMM Index is now 88.

The 11.3 percent discount yield on CD suggests that the bank will receive proceeds from the CD issue equal to:

$$US\$10M - 0.113 \times (180/360) \times US\$1M = US\$9,435,000$$

The IMM Index of 88 implies the Eurodollar futures price is:

$$US\$1M - 0.12 \times (90/360) \times US\$1M = US\$970,000$$

The banker should reverse its futures contracts by buying back 20 contracts Eurodollar futures at a price of US$970,000/contract.

The gain from the futures contract is

$$20 \times (US\$971,000 - US\$970,000) = US\$20,000$$

The opportunity cost in issuing the CD due to delay is $US\$10,000,000 \times (11.3\% - 10.87\%)/2 = US\$21,500$.

The net cost will be

$$US\$20,000 - US\$21,500 = -US\$1,500.$$

Thus the cost of US$1,500 is considerably less than the unhedged cost of US$21,500 (summarized in the following table).

	Cash market	Futures market
January 5	US$10M CD to be issued DY = 10.87% Proceeds (if issued): US$9,456,500.	Short 20 Eurodollar futures contracts at IMM = 88.4, i.e., price = US$971,000.
February 10	Issue US$10 million CD DY = 11.3% Proceeds = US$9,435,000	Long 20 contracts of Eurodollar futures at IMM = 88, i.e., price = US$970,000
Profit	−US$21,500 i.e. (US$971,000 − 970,000) × 20	+US$20,000

It should be noted that, for the sake of thoroughness, the bank should compare the results of the analysis above with those obtained through the alternative of FRA in Chapter 4, whereby the bank would purchase six-month FRA 36 days (January 6–February 10) from now.

5.4 Option Markets

5.4.1 Call and put

High volatility in both interest and foreign exchange rates have kindled interest (no pun intended) in an instrument that allows the user to protect its business against adverse movements in a financial variable while taking advantage of its favorable movements. This flexibility distinguishes the option from the forward or futures contract. Of course, this flexibility comes at a price, and whether paying this price is worthwhile is an issue worth exploration, but first we discuss below some institutional and conceptual aspects of options.

There are two basic options: call and put options. A **call option** is the right (not obligation) to buy a fixed number of underlying securities (instruments) at a specified price, called the *strike price*, for a specified period of time. A **put option** is the right to sell a fixed number of underlying securities at a specified price (also called the strike price) for a period of time.

For every buyer, there is a seller, and the seller in an option contract is also known as the *writer*, who initially receives the premium income from the buyer and, in turn, allows the buyer the flexibility to exercise the contractual rights.

The right embedded in a call or a put option has a cost. The cost of buying the right is called the *premium*. Since the right is not exercised when there is an adverse movement in the price of the instrument, the maximum loss for the call buyer is the premium paid; however, what about the gain? The *positive* difference between the *prevailing* spot price and the **exercise price** is defined as the gain, and this gain is commonly referred to as the *intrinsic value* of the option. When the difference is not positive, the intrinsic value is zero.

Now for the call buyer, the upside potential gain is unlimited. Prior to maturity, even when the intrinsic value is zero, the option trades at a positive value reflecting the worth of unexpired time to maturity. At maturity, the value of the call option, c, is the maximum of zero and spot price, S, of the instrument net of the exercise price, E, that is, $c = \max(0, S - E)$.

To illustrate, if the **call premium** of an option for buying one unit of SF is US$0.01 and the exercise price is US$0.65 per SF, the payoff diagram for the call option is shown in Figure 5.1 as follows.

Example 5.7

A bank buys a call option to hedge SF12.5 million in payables. The premium is US$0.025/SF. The exercise price is US$0.56. At maturity of the option, the spot exchange rate is US$0.58. Should the bank exercise the option? How much does the bank have to pay for the transaction after the premium is paid?

Since the spot price exceeds the exercise price at the option's maturity, the bank should exercise the option. The total cost including the premium is:

$$(\text{US}\$0.56/\text{SF} \times \text{SF12,500,000}) + (\text{US}\$0.025/\text{SF} \times \text{SF12,500,000})$$
$$= \text{US}\$7,3125,500$$

The payoff for writing (shorting) a call will be the mirror image of the payoff for buying the call, that is, the long call. The gain on the long position will be the loss for the short

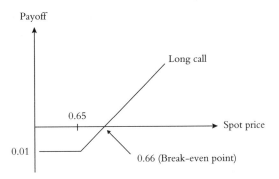

Figure 5.1   Call option

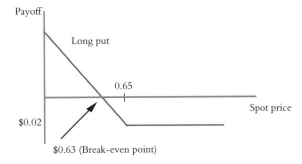

Figure 5.2   Put option

position, and the sum of the long and short position will be zero. Thus, the payoff for an option is sometimes called a zero-sum game.

Similarly, the loss for the put (p) buyer is restricted to the premium, but the gain is defined by the difference between the exercise price, E, and prevailing spot price, S. At maturity, the value of the put option, p, is at the minimum zero, and the maximum this difference, or $p = \max (0, E - S)$. Since the spot price cannot be negative, the maximum gain for the put buyer is the exercise price net of the initial premium payment.

Of course, the writer of an option has the maximum profit potential of the premium income, when the buyer walks away from the option. The maximum potential loss, on the other hand, is equal to the exercise price net of premium revenue for the put writer and infinite for the call writer.

Suppose the put premium is US$0.02 per SF, the payoff diagram of the put at its maturity date is shown in Figure 5.2.

Suppose further the current spot exchange rate is US$0.62/SF; then the put option is **in-the-money** because the exercise price is greater than the spot price. Similarly, if the exercise price is equal to (less than) the spot price, the put option is **at-the-money (out-of-the-money)**.

For the *call* option, if the strike price is equal to, above, or below the spot price, we call the call option at-the-money, out-of-the-money, and in-the-money option, respectively. So, in this regard, the label for the call option is opposite to the put option because of the nature of the right (one is to buy while the other is to sell).

The payoff for writing (shorting) a call will be the mirror image of the payoff for buying the call, that is, the long call. The gain on the long position will be the loss for the short position, and the sum of the long and short position will be zero. Thus, the payoff for an option is sometimes called a zero–sum game.

Similarly, the loss for the put (p) buyer is restricted to the premium, but the gain is defined by the difference between the exercise price, E, and prevailing spot price, S. At maturity, the value of the put option, p, is at the minimum zero, and the maximum this difference, or $p = \max(0, E - S)$. Since the spot price cannot be negative, the maximum gain for the put buyer is the exercise price net of the initial premium payment.

Of course, the writer of an option has the maximum profit potential of the premium income, when the buyer walks away from the option. The maximum potential loss, on the other hand, is equal to the exercise price net of premium revenue for the put writer and infinite for the call writer.

Example 5.8

The bank wrote a put option with a premium of US$0.02, and with an exercise price of US$0.65 for one SF. On maturity, if the spot price is US$0.61/SF, what is the gain or loss on this transaction?

Because the spot price is less than the exercise price, the put option buyer will exercise the option. As a result, the bank will suffer loss due to the difference in the spot and exercise price, and this difference will be reduced by the premium received upfront for each SF:

$$
\begin{aligned}
\text{Loss} &= (US\$0.65/SF - US\$0.61/SF) - US\$0.02/SF \\
&= US\$0.02/SF
\end{aligned}
$$

If the option can be exercised any time before its maturity (i.e., within the specified period of time in the contract), the option is called an **American option**. However, if the option can be exercised only at maturity, the option is called a **European option**. Since prior to maturity, the value of an option is larger than the intrinsic value (reflecting positive value of unexpired time), an option should be sold before maturity and should not be exercised. Hence the distinction between American and European options is not critical, except for a potentially larger gain on sale of the American option before maturity.

There are both American and European style, exchange-traded put and call options. These exchange-traded options are standardized with respect to size, exercise prices, standard maturities (one, three, six, nine, and twelve months) and fixed-day maturity (such as specific days in March, September, June, and December). The Philadelphia Stock Exchange (PHLX) offers both American and European foreign currency options on several currencies.

5.4.2   Exchange-traded and over-the-counter option markets

Currency options are available in both the organized exchanges and the **over-the-counter** (OTC) market. The OTC activity is concentrated in London and New York, the world financial centers. Options traded on the OTC markets are customized with respect to both the amount and the maturity. They are also available for more currencies than the limited number of currency exchange-traded options. Because the OTC options are tailor-made for the customers, there is not an active secondary market.

The OTC currency options market consists of two sectors. The first is a *retail market* composed of non-bank customers who purchase from banks what amounts to customized insurance against adverse exchange rate movements. These customers prefer the OTC market to the organized exchanges because of their ability to obtain terms that fit their needs. The second is a *wholesale market* among commercial banks, investment banks, and specialized trading firms. This market has options that are larger in contract size than elsewhere, and typically European-style.

In general, the OTC options differ from the exchange based options in the following respects:

1   OTC options are customized options unlike the standardized exchange-traded options with respect to both amount and maturity. Thus, the exchanges can be viewed as the discount stores (or "one-size-fits all" stores) of different instruments in the industry. On the other hand, the international banks are boutiques offering tailor-made products to customers.

2   Premiums on OTC options are higher than the comparable exchange-traded options. This difference primarily reflects the customized nature of the OTC options.[4]

3   OTC options are typically European style, and thus they do not have the flexibility of the exchange-traded American options. Because there is no secondary market, the distinction between the American-style and the European-style is significant.[5]

4   A desired maturity less than the standard maturity for an exchange-traded American option can be easily accommodated, although the transaction cost on such a contract may not be justifiable.[6]

5   Exchanges require margins for writers of the options. The term margin in an option transaction refers to the collateral the broker receives from the option writer in order to ensure fulfillment of obligations in the event of exercise of the option. In most exchanges, options buyers have to pay the premium up front. LIFFE does not require upfront premium on options; option buyers have to set up a margin account based on the delta factor;[7] and they receive profits on a daily basis without any need for liquidating the position. LIFFE also allows automatic offset of margins on a combination of options. This feature is also common in the US option exchange for trading different option strategies.

The collateral requirements on OTC options cannot be generalized, but they primarily depend on the customer's creditworthiness, perceived value of its business by the bank, and the exposure created by the option position of the bank, among other things.

6 Exchange-traded contracts have the backing of the clearing house unavailable in the OTC options. Consequently credit risk analysis of the counterparty becomes critical in an OTC option.

In 1987, County Natwest suffered estimated losses in excess of US$10 million in the aftermath of the stock market crash, when writers of put options (on equities) bought by County Natwest traders were unable to meet their commitments. County Natwest management was widely chastised in the press for their inadequate control mechanism, which did not detect its traders' unauthorized transactions of excessive size *with individuals*.

This criticism of County Natwest missed one significant point: creditworthiness of the counterparty, irrespective of whether it is an individual or a financial institution, dictates whether the transaction is worthwhile.

The example of County Natwest (an investment banking subsidiary) points to a larger issue for commercial banks that very often ignores or downplays the challenge of entering the field of OTC derivatives. Such derivatives are typically the prerogatives of the capital market group which is not well-coordinated with the credit or Commercial & Industrial (C&I) group; and the higher level management to whom these groups report does not insist on obtaining the *aggregated* bank exposure to a party in terms of products offered to it by different groups.

As OTC options are customized trade transactions, settlement risks are clearly not the same everywhere. For example, for a counterparty (which may be another bank), risk of funds inadequacy faced by a bank due to temporary illiquidity is one thing, while similar risk stemming from losses inflicted by bank traders on a bank on the verge of bankruptcy (prior to the option maturity) is another. Further, as regulators closely scrutinize a bank that deals with derivatives, the regulatory endorsement of bank capital adequacy conveys a positive signal to the counterparty. For instance, the Bank of England has deemed a bank as adequately hedged when it uses options for the amount defined by delta to cover the underlying foreign exchange and interest rate exposures. Such measures convey to the market that banks are credible to deal with options in the OTC market. Still, the regulatory examinations cannot catch the problems in time. Hence, caution is urged in extensively relying on a relatively unknown bank writing an option contract.

5.4.3 Relationship between futures and options: put-call parity

As call and put options are derived from the same underlying assets, such as the DM exchange rate, their prices should be related in some way. We explore one such relationship through the following illustration, where we use two different strategies focusing on an option on Japanese yen, and compare their payoffs in a one-period world.

Table 5.1 Results of the hedging activity

Actions	Cash flow		
	Time 0	At maturity	
		$SR_1 > E$	$SR_1 < E$
First strategy			
(1) Lend PV (¥ 1)	$-SR_0/(1 + r^\star)$	SR_1	SR_1
(2) Buy a yen put option	$-p$	0	$E - SR_1$
(3) Borrow PV of US$E	$+E/(1 + r)$	$-E$	$-E$
Net cash flow	$-SR_0/(1 + r^\star) - p + E/(1 + r)$	$SR_1 - E$	0
Second strategy			
Buy a yen call	$-c$	$SR_1 - E$	0

Under the first strategy, we take three actions.

- Lend the present value (PV) of JY1.0 due at the end of one period in Japan, that is, invest $1/(1 + r^\star)$ today, where $r^\star$ is the foreign (Japanese) interest rate. Equivalently, the present value in dollar terms will be $SR_0/(1 + r^\star)$, where SR_0 is the spot exchange rate for JY in terms of US$. At the end of the period (i.e., time 1), this investment will amount to US$ SR_1, where SR_1 is the spot exchange rate (US$/JY) at time 1.
- Buy a Japanese yen put option for 1 Japanese yen with a strike price of E (US$/JY) for premium US$p$.
- Borrow the present value of US$E (i.e., US$E/(1 + r)$ where r is the US interest rate for a period).

Under the second strategy, we simply buy a Japanese call option.

The above two strategies have been summarized in Table 5.1.

Because the two strategies yield the same payoffs at maturity, the value of both strategies at time 0 should be the same so as to prevent risk-free arbitrage. Thus, the dollar price of the call option (c) must equal the dollar value of the Japanese investment which is converted at the current exchange rate (USSR_0) *plus* the price of the put option purchase (USp) *less* the borrowed amount equal to the exercise price of the put (USE). That is,

$$c = SR_0/(1 + r^\star) + p - E/(1 + r) \tag{5.5}$$

Equation 5.5 is called the put–call parity for currency options, and can be arranged in any way one wants because it is only an algebraic relationship.[8]

As seen in Chapter 3, the interest rate parity relates the interest rate difference to the forward rate as:

$$FR/(1 + r) = SR_0/(1 + r^\star)$$

Substituting the above equation into Equation 5.5, we obtain the following **put-call-forward parity**:

$$c = p + \frac{FR - E}{(1 + r)} \tag{5.6}$$

Example 5.9

A bank's customer, who is going to receive SF three months from now, has approached the bank to provide it a put option with a maturity of three months and an exercise price of US$0.72/SF. In this case, the bank has to write a put option for one of its customers. The put option is not quoted on the exchange, although a call option with the same exercise price and maturity is being traded on the exchange at the latest quote of US$0.03/SF. The three-month forward rate and US interest rate are US$0.74/SF and 10 percent (annualized), respectively.

What premium should the bank charge to the customer?

The put price can be computed using the put-call-forward parity (Equation 5.6) as:

$$
\begin{aligned}
p &= c - (FR - E)/(1 + r) \\
&= \text{US\$0.03} - (0.74 - 0.72)/(1 + 10\%/4) \\
&= \text{US\$0.0105/SF}
\end{aligned}
$$

As a result, the bank should charge US$0.0105/SF plus a fee to its client.

In brief, the put-call-forward parity condition allows a bank to create a *synthetic* put if it were to long the call and short the forward contract. Similarly, a synthetic call can be created if it were to long both the put and the forward contract.

5.4.4 Option valuation

Valuation of an option on a common stock was initially derived by Black and Scholes (1973) with the following assumptions:

- the stock price, S, follows a Geometric Brownian Motion;
- absence of transaction costs and taxes;
- the interest rate is constant; and
- the stock does not pay dividends.

The value of the European call option in the Black and Scholes framework is:

$$c = (S)[N(d_1)] - (E)\,(e^{rT})[N(d_2)] \tag{5.7}$$

where S and E are spot and exercise prices, respectively; $d_1 = [\ln(S/E) + (r + \sigma^2/2)T\sigma\sqrt{T}$; $d_2 = d_1 - \sigma\sqrt{T}$; σ is the standard deviation of the stock price return; r is the domestic (US) interest rate; E is the exercise price of the option; $N(.)$ is the cumulative normal density function; and T is the time to maturity of the option.

If the assumption that a stock pays constant dividend yield holds, then the Black and Scholes option model can be modified to incorporate the dividend yield (Merton 1973). In simple terms, the stock price should be decreased to reflect the dividend payment. As a result, S in Equation 5.7 should be replaced by S less the present value of dividend (i.e., $S - PV(\text{dividend})$) or by $Se^{-\alpha T}$, where α is the dividend yield.

Similarly, the put option price for a non-dividend paying stock can be derived as:

$$p = (E)\,(e^{-rT})[N(-d_2)] - (S)\,[N(-d_1)] \qquad (5.8)$$

Currency option

The Black and Scholes option model serves as the foundation of all option pricing models. To derive the option model for currency, we can view the foreign currency as a stock that pays "dividend" of $r^\star$, the foreign interest rate, during the period equal to the maturity of the option, T. Thus, the currency option model, similar to the stock paying dividend option model, will be:

$$c = (S)(e^{-r^\star T})\,[N(d_1)] - (E)(e^{-rT})\,[N(d_2)] \qquad (5.9)$$

where $d_1 = [\ln(S/E) + (r - r^\star + \sigma^2/2)T]/\sigma\sqrt{T}$; $d_2 = d_1 - \sigma\sqrt{T}$; c is the premium of the call option expressed as dollar (US\$) per foreign currency (FC); S is the current exchange rate (US\$$/FC$); E is the exercise exchange rate (US\$/FC); σ is the volatility (standard deviation) of the exchange rate; and the other variables are defined as before.

Similarly, by invoking the put call parity, we can derive the put option, p, for a currency. First, we have to convert the put-call parity from the discrete term to continuous compounding (because the option pricing is commonly expressed as continuous compounding) as:

$$c = p + Se^{-r^\star T} - Ee^{-rT} \qquad (5.10)$$

Use of Equation 5.9 leads to the following value of the put option:

$$p = (E)\,(e^{-rT})[N(-d_2)] - (S)\,(e^{-r^\star T})\,[N(-d_1)] \qquad (5.11)$$

Example 5.10

Given S (current exchange rate) = US\$1.73/£; E = US\$1.725/£; T = 0.25 (90-days); σ = 0.115; r = 0.07; $r^\star$ = 0.09, compute the call option using Equation 5.9.

First, we compute d_1 and d_2 as:

$$d_1 = \frac{\ln(1.73/1.725) + (0.07 - 0.09 + 0.115^2/2)0.25}{0.115[\sqrt{0.25}]}$$

$$= -0.007869$$

$$d_2 = -0.007869 - 0.115[\sqrt{0.25}]$$

$$= -0.065369.$$

From any standard cumulative normal table, we find that

$$N(-0.007869) = 0.4969, \text{ and } N(-0.065) = 0.4739$$

After substituting these numbers in Equation 5.9, we have:

$$c = 1.73e^{-0.09(0.25)}(0.4969) - 1.725e^{-0.07(0.25)}(0.4739)$$
$$= 0.8405 - 1.725(0.98265)(0.4739)$$
$$= US\$0.037$$

As a result, the European currency call option has a price of US\$0.037/£.

Equations 5.9 and 5.10 are European currency option pricing models. There are also American option pricing models, such as the binomial pricing model and Whaley–Barone type. Because these pricing models do not have a closed form solution, it is difficult to provide a simple formula. Besides, for a short-term option (i.e., its maturity is less than a year), price differential derived from the European and American option pricing models is small.

Options on debt instruments

An interest rate call (put) option is the right to buy (sell) an interest-rate-bearing debt instrument at the exercise price on or before the time to maturity. They include options on T-bills, options on Eurodollar deposits, and options on Treasury bonds. Options on debt instruments are less popular as compared to interest rate futures options (i.e., options on the interest rate futures contracts) because of liquidity and flexibility in the latter contracts. We discuss here only T-bill options and illustrate their use to be followed by a discussion of the interest rate futures options in the next section.

T-bill options contracts are traded on the American Stock Exchange (AMEX) on the underlying T-bill with a face value of US\$1 million and a maturity of 90 days. The exercise price of the T-bill option is quoted in terms of an index price, I, and I defines the annualized discount yield, d, say, 8 (percent). The index, I, similar to the IMM index, equals 100 minus the quoted discount yield, that is, $92 = 100 - 8$. The exercise price of the option, E, is then computed as:

$$E = \frac{[100 - d(90/360)]}{100} \times US\$1,000,000$$
$$= US\$980,000$$

As a result, the exercise price at $d = 8$ (percent) will be US\$980,000. Note that the exercise price is based on a 90-day maturity and a 360-day year assumption. On the other hand, the premium of the option is quoted in terms of the *annualized basis point* (ABP), say, 0.95. In this case, the actual premium is:

$$\text{Premium} = (\text{ABP}/100)(90/360)US\$1,000,000$$

$$= (0.95/100)(90/360) \text{ US\$1,000,000}$$
$$= \text{US\$2,375}$$

The call and put options on the debt instruments can be used as a hedging instrument. Example 5.11 illustrates how the call on the T-bill can be used to hedge the interest rate risk.

Example 5.11

Suppose a bank anticipates some cash inflow next month which it intends to invest in 90-day T-bills. The bank wants to hedge the interest rate risk, as it is afraid that the interest rate may decline in the interim. The bank does not wish to fix its rate of return by using an FRA or a futures contract in order to retain flexibility that guarantees the floor rate and allows it to participate in any upside potential. The bank, therefore, intends to buy an at-the-money call option on the T-bill.

The exercise price of the call option at the current discount yield of 8 (percent) is:

$$E = \frac{[100 - d(90/360)]}{100} \times \text{US\$1,000,000}$$
$$= \text{US\$980,000}$$

The price of the cash T-bill is:

$$\frac{[100 - d(90/360)]}{100} \times \text{US\$1,000,000} = \text{US\$980,000}$$

The annualized yield to maturity (YTM) on the spot T-bill is equal to

$$(1,000,000/980,000)^{365/90} - 1, \text{ or } 8.54\%.$$

The bank anticipates that the interest rate will fall below the current yield, 8.54%.

The bank buys the call option at the quoted (annualized) basis point of 0.9. The call option costs the bank US\$2,250 (i.e., $(0.9/100)(90/360)1,000,000$).

- If the discount rate rises to 9 percent, that is, $d = 9$, the T-bill price is US\$977,500. The bank will not exercise the call option, and will lose US\$2,250 (premium payment). As a result, the net cost to the bank in buying the T-bill will be US\$979,750 (T-bill price + premium = US\$977,500 + US\$2,250). The corresponding YTM is $(1,000,000/979,750)^{365/90} - 1 = 8.65$ percent.
- If the discount yield decreases from 8 percent to 7 percent, then the T-bill price will be US\$982,500. The bank will exercise the call option and earn profit of US\$250 (i.e., US\$2,500 less the premium paid, US\$2,250). The cost of buying the option and T-bill will be US\$979,750 (i.e., T-bill cost + profit = $980,000 - 250$). The effective YTM will then be 8.65 percent.
- In situations where the interest rate sinks very low, the bank will not suffer any loss in interest income. In that case, the bank will exercise the option and pay US\$980,000 for the exercise price along with premium, US\$2,250 which is paid upfront. The YTM in

this case will be 7.53 percent [i.e., $(1,000,000/982,250)^{365/90} - 1$], which is the lowest interest rate that the bank can earn by hedging with the call option.

5.5 Option on Futures/Forward Contracts

The option on the forward/futures is particularly useful to bank clients with customized needs for hedging currency risk. Suppose a client will know 30 days from now whether it will be awarded a contract. If it is awarded the contract, it will need to buy an option to cover foreign exchange payments seven months from now. The client approaches the bank for help. The issue is how the bank can provide an option satisfying the client's need. Basically, in this scenario, the bank needs to provide to the client an option that enables him/her to buy the currency forward contracts.

The valuation for call and put options on futures/forwards contracts can be derived in a straightforward manner (see Black 1976). By making use of the fact that the futures/forward price is the future value of the current spot price, that is, $f = Se^{rT}$, we substitute the futures/forward price, f, for S in the Black and Scholes option pricing model:

$$c = fe^{-rT}N(d_1) - Ee^{-rT}N(d_2)$$
$$\text{or, } c = e^{-rt}[fN(d_1) - EN(d_2)] \tag{5.12}$$

where $d_1 = [\ln(f/E) + 0.5\sigma^2 T]/\sigma\sqrt{T}$; $d_2 = d_1 - \sigma\sqrt{T}$; and the other variables are defined as previously.

The put option can be derived similarly as:

$$p = e^{-rt}[EN(d_2) - fN(d_1)] \tag{5.13}$$

Example 5.12

A bank's client XYZ wants to bid on a contract that requires it to purchase £ sterling-denominated materials and services. The successful bid will be announced at the end of three months. If the bid is successful, XYZ will buy the £ sterling proceeds at the end of another six months. If the bid is unsuccessful, XYZ will walk away. Essentially XYZ needs a three-month option on a six-month long £ sterling forward contract (i.e., the option expires earlier than its underlying instrument).

Relevant information is as follows:

$$f = \text{US\$1.64/£}$$
$$E = \text{US\$1.60/£}$$
$$T = 3 \text{ months}$$
$$\sigma = 0.2$$
$$r = 10\%$$

From Equation 5.12, we have:

$$d_1 = \frac{\ln(1.64/1.6) + 0.2^2(0.25)/2}{0.2\sqrt{0.25}}$$
$$= 0.2969$$
$$\text{and, } d_2 = 0.297 - 0.2\sqrt{0.25}$$
$$= 0.1969$$

From the normal distribution table, we get:

$$N(d_1) = N(0.297) = 0.6167$$
$$N(d_2) = N(0.197) = 0.5780.$$

After substituting the above values into Equation 5.12, we obtain:

$$c = e^{-0.1(0.25)}[1.64(0.6167) - 1.6(0.5780)]$$
$$= \text{US\$0.0845}/\pounds$$

Hence, the client needs to adjust the bid by 8.45¢ per £ sterling (and should convert the £ sterling-based cost into US$ at the rate $f = \text{US\$1.64}/\pounds$).

This illustration assumes that the value of f (futures or forward price) is available. When it is not available, it can be obtained, for instance, in the following way. Suppose the bank has data on the six-month FRA rates that will be delivered in three months. Then the bank is able to find the *implied* six-month forward rate *three months* from now by using the IRPT formula. The implied forward rate (*IFR*) is given by

$$IFR = SR_3(1 + FRA/2)/(1 + FRA^\star/2)$$

where $FRA^\star$ is the forward rate agreement rate (annualized) for the £ sterling. SR_3 is the spot rate prevailing three months from now. An additional step removes the uncertainty embedded in this future spot rate, SR_3, by viewing it as a three-month forward rate,

$$SR_3 = FR_3 = SR_0(1 + r)/(1 + r^\star),$$

where r and $r^\star$ are the three-month domestic and foreign interest rates, respectively (see Chapter 3 for details). Thus

$$IFR = [SR_0(1 + r)(1 + FRA/2)]/[(1 + FRA^\star/2)(1 + r^\star)]$$

This *IFR* is the currency rate that XYZ will lock in today to buy foreign currency nine months (6 months + 3 months) from now. It can now be used in place of f in Equation 5.12 to obtain the premium[9] for the option desired by XYZ.

If the bank writes a three–month call option on the six–month forward contract, the bank can minimize the risk of writing such a contract by the following steps.

1 Initially the bank determines the amount it needs to borrow in US$ by discounting the £ sterling amount (needed nine months from now) with the three-month interest rate $r^\star$; *and* the embedded six-month $FRA^\star$ rate. It borrows this US$ amount today for three months.

   a If XYZ exercises the option to have the six-month forward contract, the bank will roll over its debt for another six months. (In this case, XYZ will deliver the US$ amount that will enable the bank to extinguish its liability in US$ nine months from now.)

   b If XYZ chooses not to exercise the option, the bank will pay back the loan in US$.

2 It converts this US$ amount in £ sterling at the current spot rate, SR_0, and invests the proceeds for three months.

   a If XYZ exercises the option to have the six-month forward contract, the bank will reinvest the £ sterling proceeds for another six months.

   b If XYZ chooses not to exercise the option, the bank will use the proceeds to convert it in US$ to extinguish the loan in (1b).

3 It will buy today US$-based $FRA^\star$ and sell £ sterling-based $FRA^\star$. (This step will enable the bank to lock in the rollover borrowing rate in US$, and reinvestment rate in £ sterling at the end of three months, in case XYZ exercises the six-month forward option at the end of the third month).

The bank has here hedged against the exposure created by the XYZ exercise of the option. However, if XYZ does not exercise the option, the bank faces the risk of loss due to £ sterling moving against it, that is, decreasing in value against the US$ in steps 1b and 2b. One way to avoid this contingent loss is for the bank to buy a three-month put option in £ sterling. If the call premium is smaller than the premium calculated through formula 5.12, the bank needs to adjust it upward.

5.6 Conclusion

In this chapter, the basic features of both futures and options contracts were analyzed. In addition, pricing of these instruments and their linkage through put-call parity and IRPT were discussed and illustrated with particular emphasis on interest rate and currency risk management. This analysis is useful in itself since it facilitates risk management by banks either on their own account or for their customers in face of the increased volatility in both foreign exchange and interest rates. Further, it also provides building blocks for discussion of more complex derivative instruments to be discussed in the following chapter.

DISCUSSION QUESTIONS

1   Compare and contrast foreign exchange futures and forward markets.

2   The following are the closing prices of the futures pound sterling contract at the IMM of the CME.

	Date	Prices
May	2	1.52
	3	1.54
	4	1.56
	5	1.53

If you short the £ sterling on the morning of May 2, at the price of 1.53, trace the daily change in the account with your broker. Assume that

a   the futures contract is worth £62,500; and

b   your initial margin requirement is US$ 1,500.00.

3   What are the important functions of the futures markets?

4   Suppose that the weekly hedge ratio for the pound sterling currency futures is 0.85. What is the number of currency futures contracts needed if the anticipated receipt in one week is £20 million (one futures contract is worth £62,500)?

5   Given the discount yield of the T-bill contract at 8 percent, what is the price of the T-bill futures contract for the long position?

6   How is the Eurodollar futures price determined in the settlement process?

7   If the T-bond futures price is 75–25, and there are two bonds that qualify for delivery for the T-bond futures contracts that are priced at 74–12 and 75–24, which of the two bonds should be delivered if these two bonds have conversion factors equal to 0.965 and 0.99, respectively. Ignore the accrued interest payment in the calculation.

8   The chief financial officer (CFO) of a corporation plans to sell 180-day commercial paper with a face value of US$10 million in a month. The current yield on the CD is 10.4 percent.

a   If the CFO wants to hedge for the CD issue, what is the number of contracts she should sell in the Eurodollar futures today, given the IMM Index for the Eurodollar futures at 88?

b   When should she use the FRA agreement instead of resorting to the futures market?

9   What is a call option or put option? Under what condition do people sell these options?

10 A multinational firm buys a put option in anticipation of receiving SF1 million one period from now. Today, the one-period put is quoted US$0.01 per SF for an exercise price of US$0.60 (a contract is worth SF62,500).

    a If the spot price at maturity is US$0.585/SF, should the firm exercise the option?

    b What is the net US dollar receipt for the firm one period from now?

    c As a banker to the firm, what alternative courses of hedging actions would you initially suggest to the firm?

    d Under what circumstances is a course of action likely to be (i) the cheapest for the firm and (ii) also most profitable for your bank?

11 A trader buys a call option at the price of US$0.01/£ for the exercise price of US$1.50/£. On maturity date, the spot price of the pound sterling is US$1.53/£. Compute the profit for the trader per pound sterling.

12 What are the differences between OTC and exchange-traded foreign exchange options?

13 A client approaches a bank to buy a Swiss franc call option with an exercise price of US$0.565/SF one month from today. Given: the spot rate is US$0.565/SF; the US interest rate is 12 percent; the forward rate is US$0.568/SF; and the IMM quotes for the one-month put option is US$0.01/SF, what should be the price of the call option?

14 Given the following information on the Japanese yen, compute its call option premium. Spot price for the Japanese yen is JY143.5/US$, the exercise price of the option is JY145/US$, the foreign and domestic interest rates are 9.5 percent and 5.3 percent, respectively. Volatility (σ) is 15 percent. Time to maturity remaining for the option is 0.132 of a year.

15 Traditionally, the most important activity in bank management has been management of loans and deposits. Why should bank managers learn about derivatives, such as futures and options?

16 The spot rate is US$1.55/£; the one-month sterling interest rate is 10 percent; and the corresponding US interest rate is 8.5 percent. The volatility (annualized standard deviation) of the pound sterling is 17 percent. How much is the cost of the one-month sterling call option if the strike price is US$1.75?

17 On June 15, the yen put option maturing on September 15 is 0.0514 cents per yen at the strike price of 0.077 cents. The forward rate for September 15 is 0.787 cents per yen while the three-month US interest rate is 8 percent. What should be the call premium for a similar maturity of the same currency?

18 On May 3, the computer system of the Metro Bank was down. A client comes by and requests a quote to buy Swiss francs in 45 days (mid June) from the bank. The client is interested to know how much one has to pay now for buying SF500,000 at US$0.65 in 45 days and secondly, how much

the call option of the Swiss franc would cost (assuming the option can only be exercised at the end of the 45 days).

At that time, the only current information available to the banker working for that client is the *Wall Street Journal* for the day and other printed materials. Several pieces of information are found:

The US T-bill rates data are:

Date	Bid	Ask	Change	Yield
June 1	7.8	7.78	−0.02	7.82
June 18	7.81	7.79	−0.01	7.84
July b4	7.90	7.85	−0.03	7.93

Among other currency futures contracts, the futures price of the Swiss francs from the *Wall Street Journal* are shown as follows:

Swiss franc (CME) 125,000 francs; US$ franc

	Open	High	Low	Settle	Change	Life Time High	Low	Open Interest
June	0.674	0.676	0.672	0.675	0.002	0.701	0.655	57,177
Sept	0.676	0.678	0.673	0.677	0.002	0.702	0.663	6,969
Dec	0.675	0.680	0.676	0.679	0.002	0.704	0.677	422

The option prices traded on the Philadelphia Option Exchange are:

	Strike price	Call-Last June	Sept	Dec	Put-Last June	Sept	Dec
62,500 Swiss francs – cents per unit							
Sfranc							
66.54	65	r	2.3	2.5	0.82	1.4	2.5
66.54	67	1.9	r	3.2	r	2.3	r

a   What price should the bank charge to its client for the forward contract?
b   What is the price of the call option?
c   What other information or caveat should be considered in using the available information to price the option?

APPENDIX F: DERIVATION OF THE FUTURES PRICE UNDER RISK NEUTRALITY

This appendix explains the pricing of futures contracts that are settled daily.

At the beginning of the trading at time 0, a trader can undertake two actions. First, the trader buys a futures contract unit that yields $(1 + r_{0,1})$, where $r_{0,1}$ is the one-day interest rate at time 0 for time

1 (i.e., one-day later). There is no initial investment for the futures contract. At the end of the day, the value of the futures contract maturing at time T will equal

$$(f_{1,T} - f_{0,T})(1 + r_{0,1})$$

where $f_{1,T}$ is the futures price at the end of day 1, and this price is unknown at the beginning of the day.

Second, the trader buys a one-day bond with an amount equal to the current futures price $f_{0,T}$. The initial investment for the bond is $-f_{0,T}$ (the negative sign reflecting the cash outflow). The value of the bond will be $f_{0,T}(1 + r_{0,1})$ at the end of the day.

In the above transactions, the cash flows for these two contracts can be summarized as:

		Cash flow
First Day (Time 0)	Today	One day later
Buy futures	0	$(f_{1,T} - f_{0,T})(1 + r_{0,1})$
Buy one-day bond	$-f_{0,T}$	$f_{0,T}(1 + r_{0,1})$
	$-f_{0,T}$	$f_{1,T}(1 + r_{0,1})$

The arbitrage activities in futures trading require the following two transactions:

- investing the entire proceeds from day 1 activities (i.e., the sum of the two alternatives of cash flows) in *bonds* again, and
- buying *additional* futures with an amount equal to $(1 + r_{1,2})(1 + r_{0,1})$, where $r_{1,2}$ is the interest rate for one-day bonds starting at time 1. Thus, $r_{1,2}$ is unknown at time 0.

On the beginning of the second day of trading, the net cash flow will be zero due to the first transaction of bond investment. However, at the end of the second day, the cash flow from the futures contract will be:

$$(1 + r_{0,1})(1 + r_{1,2})(f_{2,T} - f_{1,T}) \tag{F.1}$$

At the same time, the bond investment proceeds will be:

$$(1 + r_{0,1})(1 + r_{1,2})(f_{1,T}) \tag{F.2}$$

Addition of Equations F.1 and F.2 yields the net cash flow for the second day investment as:

$$(1 + r_{0,1})(1 + r_{1,2})(f_{2,T}) \tag{F.3}$$

If we continue this process daily, the price of the futures contract price, $f_{T,T}$, at maturity should equal the prevailing spot price, S_T, at that time. The proceeds from the investment will be:

$$[(1 + r_{0,1})(1 + r_{1,2})...(1 + r_{T-1,T})]S_T \tag{F.4}$$

We invest an amount $f_{0,T}$ and receive an amount shown in Equation F.4. It must be true that the present value of Equation F.4 should equal $f_{0,T}$. If the trader is risk neutral, we can use the current rate, $r_{0,T}$, for the entire T period as the discount rate. As a result, we obtain:

$$f_{0,T} = E\{[(1 + r_{0,1})(1 + r_{1,1})...(1 + r_{T-1,T})]S_T\}/(1 + r_{0,T})^T \tag{F.5}$$

where E is the expectation operator. If we define $R = (1 + r_{0,1})(1 + r_{1,1})...(1 + r_{T-1,T})$, Equation F.5 can be expressed as:

$$f_{0,T} = E(R \star S_T)/(1 + r_{1,T})^T \tag{F.6}$$

By definition, $E(R \star S_T) = E(R) \times E(S_T) + \text{cov}(R, S_T)$. In addition, using the pure expectation theory in term structure, we have $E(R) = (1 + r_{0,T})^T$. As a result, Equation F.6 can be simplified as:

$$f_{0,T} = E(S_T) + \text{COV}(R, S_T)/(1 + r_{1,T})^T \tag{F.7}$$

The above expression simply says that under risk neutral conditions and the pure expectation theory, the futures price today is equal to the expected future spot price plus a present value of the covariance term, which reflects the interaction of interest rate due to the daily settlement and the expected spot price.

APPENDIX G: DERIVATION OF THE OPTIMAL HEDGE RATIO

If we expect to sell one unit of an asset (say, one unit of foreign currency) at time 1 and hedge the risk of the price movement at time 0 (now) by shorting b units of its futures contracts – b is the hedge ratio, that is, the number of futures position for every unit of the cash position – the change in wealth (W) for this investor will be the net result of a change in the cash price (S or the spot rate) and the change in the futures price (f), and is denoted as:

$$W = (S_1 - S_0) - (f_1 - f_0)b \tag{G.1}$$
$$W = \Delta S - b\Delta f$$

or

where $\Delta S = S_1 - S_0; \Delta f = f_1 - f_0$.
The variance (VAR) of Equation G.1 can be found as:

$$VAR(W) = VAR(\Delta S) + b^2 VAR(\Delta f) - 2b COV(\Delta S, \Delta f) \tag{G.2}$$

where COV is the covariance.
Minimization and simplification of Equation G.2 with respect to b yields:

$$b = COV(\Delta S, \Delta f)/VAR(\Delta f) \tag{G.3}$$

APPENDIX H: DERIVATION OF THE PRICE SENSITIVITY RATIO

The value of the futures and spot position, V, can be specified as

$$V = S + fN_f \tag{H.1}$$

where f is the price of the futures contract; S is the value of the spot price of the interest rate instrument; and N_f is the number of futures contract required for hedging.

Differentiating Equation H.1 with respect to interest rate r, and setting the result to zero yields:

$$\partial V/\partial r = \partial S/\partial r + (\partial f/\partial r)N_f$$
$$= (\partial S/\partial r_s)(\partial r_s/\partial r) + (\partial f/\partial r_f)(\partial r_f/\partial r)N_f$$
$$= \partial S/\partial r_s + (\partial f/\partial r_f)N_f = 0 \tag{H.2}$$

In Equation H.2, we assume there is a parallel shift of interest rate so that $\partial r_s/\partial r = 1$ and $\partial r_f/\partial r = 1$. Since S and f are the present value of cash flows at the respective interest rate r_s, and r_f, we obtain:

$$\partial S/\partial r_s = D_s S/(1 + r_s) \tag{H.3}$$
$$\partial f/\partial r_f = D_f f/(1 + r_f) \tag{H.4}$$

After substituting Equations H.3 and H.4 into Equation H.2 and solving for N_f, we obtain the following expression:

$$N_f = \frac{-D_s S/(1 + r_s)}{D_f f/(1 + r_f)} \tag{H.5}$$

NOTES

1 Even if a futures contract is closed out before the expiry date – as is the usual case – the acquisition cost in a long contract is still the same. The closing out only represents the net payoff: revenue from the short position for the remainder of the life of the original contract less the cost of acquisition in the original contract.

2 The major difference in pricing financial futures and the commodity futures lies in the computation of the carrying cost in these contracts.

3 The use of the regression analysis for estimation purposes not only entails convenience of implementation, but also facilitates adjustment for problems such as autocorrelation and heteroscedasticity in the variables, which cannot be handled easily under the direct method of computing the hedge ratio. A recent approach to estimate the hedge ratio assumes that the variance of the futures and spot price and their covariance is time-varying. It employs a **Generalized AutoRegressive Conditional Heteroscedasticity** (GARCH) approach. Since it appears to outperform the conventional regression approach, it may be used instead to estimate the hedge ratio (Kroner and Sultan 1993).

4 Retail customers, who are the major users of the customized options, pay the higher price, because (a) they do not know how to replicate a customized option, or (b) incur too high a transaction cost to make worthwhile replication of the option.

5 Theoretically it is possible for, say, an American call buyer to write a similar option for the unexpired maturity. The time and effort involved may not be insignificant especially since reasonableness of the synthetic sale price cannot be easily ascertained in the absence of a secondary market.

6 Mismatched maturity and amount of an exchange-traded option can be complemented by futures contracts and Eurocurrency market operations via the put-call-forward parity to obtain a customized option, as discussed below and in Chapter 6.

7 Delta factor refers to the sensitivity that the option moves with its underlying asset (described in detail below).

8 Equation 5.5 is similar to the put-call parity in the context of a common stock (share), with the only difference that the first term on the right-hand side represents the value of a common stock, S, i.e., $c = S + p - E/(1 + r)$.

9 This premium is the cost for the bank. Hence the bank will have to add a markup for its profit in the transaction.

PART III

Applications

CHAPTER 6

Swaps and Other Derivative Instruments

LEARNING OBJECTIVES

- To acquire a basic understanding of the swap markets
- To comprehend the pricing and risk management of currency and interest rate swaps
- To get acquainted with different types of interest rate and currency derivatives such as caps, floors, range forward contract, knockout, and basket options.
- To learn more about the credit derivatives and their pricing issues.

6.1 Introduction

Although the exchange-traded futures and options have very appealing properties, they are inflexible, expensive, or just not available to meet a specific need of a bank or its customer. For instance, a futures contract having only four standardized maturities for one year will not meet the need of a bank that wants to lock in interest or currency rate on a series of payments or receipts over three years. Similarly, option contracts to hedge four quarterly obligations for the coming year may entail substantial premium cost. As a result, additional derivative instruments have been developed to satisfy needs that could not be met – or have high price tags – by conventional basic exchange-traded derivative instruments.

Very often these new instruments are essentially a combination of the basic instruments described in Chapter 5. At other times, the new instruments are just instances of intermediation by financial institutions like banks. In the international arena, an access to or presence in offshore and other national markets provide banks special opportunities for developing derivative products that (a) have attractive spreads, or (b) can reduce banks' interest or foreign exchange exposure. Finally, new instruments come into existence simply because there is a need for them, and they are neither the combinations of basic instruments nor do they reflect any unique advantage of the financial intermediaries. This chapter builds on the material developed in the previous chapter and explains additional derivative instruments that have become very popular in recent years. Specifically, it deals with interest rate and currency swaps; swaptions; interest rate caps, floors, collars; range forward contracts; indexed currency option notes; basket options; knockout options; and credit derivatives.

6.2   Swap Market

6.2.1   Background

The swap market originated in the late 1970s when **parallel loan** transactions, precursors of currency swaps, were introduced to get around currency controls. A parallel loan involved two multinational firms each from a different country. Each parent would agree to extend a loan denominated in one's own currency to the other's subsidiary domiciled in one's own country. The amount was equivalent in both cases when translated at the spot rate prevailing at the time of concluding the agreement, and the interest rates prevailing in each country dictated the loan rate.

The parallel loan required two separate agreements, but it was cumbersome since it did not have a standard format or set of covenants. A variant of the parallel loan was the **back-to-back loan,** whereby the two parent firms would forge a single agreement between themselves to extend loans to each other's subsidiary in one's home currency. Although this variant reduced the transaction cost, it still did not overcome the problem of one party's obligation for its subsidiary's default in the other country.

Development of the simple **currency swap** agreement managed to overcome the problems of the parallel and the back-to-back loans by expediting both formulation and execution of the agreement: currencies would be exchanged between two parties, either directly or through an intermediary, for a number of periods at designated currency rate(s). This expediency enabled swaps to retain their popularity in the post-Bretton Woods era of volatile foreign exchange rates even when exchange controls on major currencies were phased out. A major currency swap transaction between the World Bank and IBM added to the luster of currency swaps in 1981. IBM wanted to convert its DM- and CHF-denominated debt service obligations into US$. The World Bank with a bulk of its scheduled loans denominated in DM and SF (thus was to receive future payments in these currencies) wanted to tap the Eurodollar market for funding these loans.[1] Salomon Brothers arranged the deal whereby IBM agreed to service US$-denominated borrowing of the World Bank, and the World Bank agreed to service a designated amount of IBM's loans in DM and SF.

In addition to the currency swap, the other basic transaction is the **interest swap** where one party agrees to assume the other party's fixed interest obligation in exchange of other party's assumption of its floating interest-based obligation.

These two basic forms of swaps have spawned off a variety of swap transactions over the years, allowing an individual entity to tap the most expedient form of financing without exposing itself to excessive costs or risk, given its cash flow characteristics. The swap market

Table 6.1 Notional value of swap transactions (US$ billion)

	1991	1992	1993	1994	1995	1996
Interest rate swaps						
All counterparties	3,065.1	3,850.8	6,177.3	8,815.6	12,810.7	19,170.9
Interbank member	1,342.3	1,880.8	2,967.9	4,533.9	7,100.6	10,250.7
Other end-user	1,722.8	1,970.1	3,209.4	4,281.7	5,710.1	8,920.2
Currency swaps						
All counterparties	1,614.3	1,720.7	1,799.2	1,829.7	2,394.8	3,119.3
Interbank member	449.8	477.7	437.0	422.5	619.9	850.0
Other end-user	1,164.6	1,243.1	1,362.2	1,407.2	1,774.9	2,269.3

Source: Bank for International Settlements, International Banking and Financial Market Development (various issues) and International Swaps and Derivatives Association (ISDA).

has grown tremendously over the past decade since 1987. In 1991, the outstanding balance in the swap market, as shown in Table 6.1, was over US$4 trillion, with about 80 percent of the swaps being interest rate swaps and the remaining 20 percent being currency swaps. In the currency swap market, dollar-denominated swaps have been the largest and, consequently, the most dominant component of swap transactions; however, the dollar market in new swaps has been declining.

A swap agreement typically encompasses a series of future transactions. Thus it is comparable to the forward and futures agreements. Swaps offer several advantages over the financial futures or forward transactions.

- Swaps are tailor-made to meet the customer needs. Thus, swap agreements are more likely to meet specific needs of the participants than exchange-traded instruments.
- Forward and futures agreements have a short lifespan, whereas swap agreements can be easily devised for the long term, say, 10 years. Even when the conventional forward contracts were available for longer duration for some currencies, their being confined to a single transaction meant executing several agreements to accomplish what a swap agreement can do with a single contract.
- Swap documentation is standardized, and participating firms can negotiate master agreements with partners to enhance development of long-term business relationships.
- Swaps are administratively cheaper because they require less government monitoring.
- One of the most significant advantages offered by the swap transaction has been the offset clause whereby a party to the agreement is absolved from its obligation if a counterparty fails to fulfill its obligation. For instance, if a party goes bankrupt, the counterparty may have to fulfill its part of the obligation and then be an unsecured creditor in the absence of an offset clause. (Other related contracts have by now adopted this feature of the swap contracts.)

The swap agreement has some inherent limitations.
- In order to consummate a swap transaction, one must find a counterparty that is willing to take the opposite side of the transaction. A firm desiring a swap for specifically structured cash flows may find it extremely difficult, if not impossible, to find a counterparty.

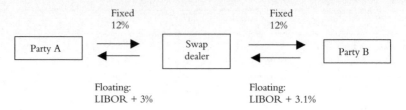

Figure 6.1 Plain-vanilla interest rate swap

- Swap transactions cannot be altered or terminated without mutual consent.
- In spite of the offset clause, the default risk in a swap contract is more than that in an exchange-traded futures contract. As we saw in Chapter 5, the daily settlement and the margin requirement enables a counterparty to avoid the default risk. In a swap contract, if a party defaults, the counterparty may get stuck with much higher cost for replicating the balance of the swap contract due to unfavorable external circumstances.

International commercial banks are involved in the swap markets in three ways. They can be the end-users, swap brokers and swap dealers. As an *end-user* of the swap transactions, a bank's primary purpose is to manage the interest rate risk due to the mismatching of the assets and liabilities. Consider Bank A, a US money center bank, which has raised funds by issuing US$-denominated medium-term notes with a 10 percent fixed interest rate obligation. In this scenario, this fixed rate obligation will appear on the liability side of Bank A's balance sheet. On the asset side, the bank makes adjustable-rate, $-denominated loans indexed to LIBOR or other benchmark rates (such as the federal funds rate). Because of its floating-rate loans on the asset side and its fixed-rate liabilities, bank A faces a negative duration gap (i.e., the duration of the asset is shorter than the duration of the liability). Bank A can hedge the interest rate exposure by decreasing the duration of the liabilities by swapping them into floating rate liabilities.

In swap transactions, a commercial bank may serve as a *swap broker*. The bank does not bear financial risk but merely assists two parties (buyer and seller of the swaps) in completing the swap transaction. Potential participants of the swaps can approach the swap dealer for advice and assistance in finding a counterparty. Once the swap broker finds the suitable counterparty, the broker brings the two parties together and helps negotiate and complete the swap contract. The swap broker receives a fee from each of the counterparties.

A commercial bank can also serve as a *swap dealer* in the swap markets. A swap dealer fulfills all the functions of a swap broker. In addition, a swap dealer takes a risk position in the swap transaction by becoming an actual party to the transaction, shown in Figure 6.1.

In Figure 6.1, Party A of the swap transaction pays fixed rate interest to and receives floating rate interest from the swap dealer. Party A has a *long* position in the swap transaction. At the same time, Party B (another firm) receives fixed payments from and pays floating rate interest payments to the swap dealer. Party B has a *short* position in the swap transaction. In Figure 6.1, Party A is depicted as owning floating rate assets. Hence the swap transaction allows it to match its cash flows.

Table 6.2 Indication pricing for interest rate swaps

Maturity	Bank pays fixed rate	Bank receives fixed rate	Current TN rate (%)
2 years	2 yr TN sa + 20 bps	2 yr TN sa + 45 bps	8.55
3 years	3 yr TN sa + 25 bps	3 yr TN sa + 52 bps	8.72
4 years	4 yr TN sa + 28 bps	4 yr TN sa + 58 bps	8.85
5 years	5 yr TN sa + 34 bps	5 yr TN sa + 60 bps	8.92
6 years	6 yr TN sa + 38 bps	6 yr TN sa + 66 bps	8.96
7 years	7 yr TN sa + 40 bps	7 yr TN sa + 70 bps	9.00
10 years	10 yr TN sa + 50 bps	10 yr TN sa + 84 bps	9.08

Note: TN = Treasury note rate; sa = semi-annual.

6.2.2 Pricing schedule

Swap banks regularly prepare indication-pricing schedules for use by their capital market personnel for firms interested in the interest rate swaps. An **indication-pricing schedule** provides the swap dealer with guidelines for pricing swaps. Prices take the form of interest rates and are stated in terms of basis points (bps). Table 6.2 illustrates the pricing of an interest swaps schedule.

Suppose a bank is a swap dealer negotiating with two counterparties: A, which wants a long position (wants to pay at a fixed rate and receive at a floating rate) and B, desiring a short position in a five-year swap. The indication schedule in Table 6.2 displays that the bank should *receive* from A the fixed rate set or the Treasury note rate must be multiplied by 360/365.

6.2.3 Rationale for swap transactions

The finance literature suggests that at least two factors are responsible for swap transactions. The first one relates to *imperfections in the financial markets* while the second one is linked to the *need for risk management* pertaining to interest rates and currency fluctuations.

Market imperfections: Comparative cost advantage

In many situations, one firm may have better access to certain parts of the capital market than another firm. For example, a US firm may be able to borrow easily in the USA, but it might not have such favorable access to the capital market in Germany. Similarly, a German firm may have good borrowing opportunities domestically but poor opportunities in the USA. Other market imperfections – such as foreign exchange controls imposed by various governments, differences in tax treatments of interest in different countries, and government loan guarantees – also distort pricing in the marketplace and may translate into higher fixed or variable transaction costs for some market participants. By the same token, these imperfections may generate profitable opportunities for other participants.

Table 6.3 Interest rate scenarios before swap

	Firm A Aa	Firm B Bb	Difference (%)
Fixed rate	7.75%	8.75%	1.00
Floating rate	LIBOR + 0.35%	LIBOR + 0.55%	0.20

Table 6.4 Interest rate scenario after swap

	Swap	Original	Net (%)
Firm A	+8.25%	−7.75%	+0.50
Firm B	+ LIBOR + 0.30%	−(LIBOR + 0.55%)	−0.25

To further illustrate the use of comparative advantage of the interest rate swap, assume that Firm A, which is rated as Aa, can borrow funds at the fixed rate of 7.75 percent and at the floating rate of LIBOR + 0.35 percent. On the other hand, Firm B, which is rated as Bb, can borrow funds at the fixed rate of 8.75 percent and at the floating rate of LIBOR + 0.55 percent. Both firms in this case can benefit from an interest rate swap. Table 6.3 illustrates the situation.

The difference in the fixed rate market between Firm A and B is 1.0 percent while it is 0.2 percent in the variable rate market. Firm B appears to have a *relative* advantage in the variable rate market and Firm A has a comparative advantage in the fixed rate market. Note that a value of 0.8 percent interest differential (i.e., the difference between 1.0 percent in the fixed-rate market and 0.2 percent in the fixed-rate market) motivates the interest rate swap transaction.

Suppose that Firm A borrows in the fixed rate market at 7.75 percent and agrees to pay Firm B LIBOR + 0.30 percent for the swap, while Firm B borrows in the floating rate market at LIBOR + 0.55 percent and agrees to pay a fixed rate of 8.25 percent to Firm A. The net effect of the swap for Firms A and B is shown in Table 6.4.

For Firm A, the net interest rate payments is

$$LIBOR - 0.20\% \text{ (i.e., LIBOR} + 0.30\% - 8.25\% + 7.75\%)$$

Thus, a gain of 0.55 percent is generated over direct borrowing in the floating rate market. Similarly, Firm B will gain as well. Its net interest payment will be

$$8.50\% \text{ (i.e., } 8.25\% + LIBOR + 0.55\% - [LIBOR + 0.30\%])$$

Thus, the gain for Firm B will be 0.25 percent as compared to the direct borrowing in the fixed-rate market.

The total gain for Firms A and B is 0.8 percent (i.e., 0.55 percent for Firm A + 0.25 percent for Firm B). This 0.8 percent is exactly equal to the interest rate differential shown in

Table 6.5   Borrowing rates (%) for two firms in two currencies

	US ($)	UK (£)	Differential
US firm	9.0	7.0	2.0
UK firm	11.0	7.5	3.5

Table 6.3. If there is a financial intermediary in the swap transaction, three parties (a bank, Firm A and Firm B) will share the 0.8 percent interest differential.

The currency swaps, like the interest rate swaps, can be motivated by comparative advantages as well as by the need for hedging exchange and interest rate risks. First, we use an example to explain how the currency swaps are motivated by comparative advantage. Suppose that a US firm and a UK firm are offered fixed interest rates in US dollars and sterling, shown in Table 6.5.

This table shows that US interest rates are higher than UK interest rates.[2] The US firm is clearly more creditworthy than the UK firm since it obtains more favorable interest rates in both currencies. However, the differences between the rates offered to the US firm and the UK firm in the two markets are not the same. The UK firm pays 2.0 percent more than the US firm in the US$ market and only 0.50 percent more than the US firm in the £ sterling market. It is clear that the UK firm has a comparative borrowing advantage in the sterling market and the US firm has a comparative borrowing advantage in the US dollar market. This might be because the UK firm is better known to UK investors, while the US firm is better known to US investors.

Suppose the US firm wants to borrow £ sterling while the UK firm wants to borrow US$. This creates a perfect situation for a currency swap. The US firm and the UK firm each borrow in the market where one has a comparative advantage; that is, the US firm borrows US$ while the UK firm borrows £ sterling. They then use a currency swap to transform the US firm's loan into a £ sterling loan and the UK firm's loan into a US$ loan.

As already mentioned, the difference between the dollar interest rates is 2.0 percent while the difference between the sterling interest rates is 0.5 percent. By analogy with the interest rate swaps case, we can expect the total gain to all parties to be 2.0−0.50 percent = 1.50 percent per annum.

Need for risk management

The second motivation for swaps is associated with normal business operations. Financial institutions manage their assets and liabilities through a process known as **gap management** by restructuring the mix of floating and fixed rate debt in the loan portfolios and deposit structure. For instance, for a commercial bank that has a positive gap (i.e., asset values are more susceptible than liability values to interest rate fluctuations), an interest rate swap can help to bridge the gap between their rate-sensitive assets and liabilities by swapping their floating rate-linked income stream for a fixed rate asset stream. Similarly, many thrift and savings and loan associations have a negative gap in that the value of their liabilities (money market deposit accounts and variable rate certificates of deposit) is more prone to changes in interest rates as compared to their assets (mortgage and consumer installment loans). An interest rate swap can change the debt mix from floating rate to more of a fixed rate debt without actually retiring the debt.

In currency swaps, exchange rate and interest rate risk management are important considerations. Consider:

1 A US bank is holding mostly floating-rate, short-term US$-denominated assets that are partly financed with a four-year £50 million note carrying fixed 10 percent annual coupons; and

2 A UK bank with mostly long-term, fixed-rate assets denominated in £ sterling has partly financed its asset portfolio with $100 million short-term, US$-denominated EuroCDs with interest rate of one-year LIBOR + 2.00 percent.

Here the US bank is faced with both interest rate and foreign exchange rate risks. Specifically, if the short-term interest rate in dollar declines and the dollar depreciates against the pound sterling, the US bank may face a problem in covering its promised fixed-coupon and principal payments on the £-denominated note. Consequently, it may wish to transform its fixed-rate, £-denominated liabilities into variable-rate, US$-denominated liabilities.

The UK bank also faces interest and foreign exchange rate exposures. If the US interest rate rises and the dollar appreciates against the pound sterling, the UK bank would incur a loss in covering US$-based debt service with its fixed, £ sterling-based cash flows. Consequently, the UK bank may wish to transform its floating-rate short-term, dollar-denominated liabilities into fixed-rate pound sterling liabilities.

The risk management motivation may be restated in a risk–return framework. Firms may have differing ability in assuming risk. Consequently, their return requirement for assuming risk may differ. If that is the case, a party that has superior ability to assume risk may require smaller compensation for doing so than the going market price for such risk. This arbitrage process then helps both parties.[3] The UK bank's superior ability to withstand exposure in £ sterling and the US bank's superior ability to assume exposure in US$ underscore why swap transactions would take place. If the desired transactions were compatible in size and maturity, a currency swap would help both banks to avoid unwanted exposures in interest and foreign exchange markets.

6.2.4 Valuation of interest rate swap

Market makers, typically large commercial banks, who take the opposite side of any reasonable swap transactions, organize the market for the interest rate swaps. Interest payments are made on the basis of a notional principal amount, which is neither paid nor received.

Pricing swaps

There are two conventional ways to price an interest rate swap. One approach views a swap transaction in the bond valuation framework. The other approach considers it in the framework of an FRA, discussed in Chapter 4.

… approach. A bank with a *long position of a swap* transaction can be viewed … (B_F) nd investing in a variable coupon bond (B_V). Thus … ts and pays fixed-rate interest cost. By the same … *swap* issues a floating-rate bond (B_V) and utilizes … (B_F); hence, it pays at a variable rate and receives the … have a face value of P. The present value of the inter- … thus the present value of B_F minus the present value … terest rates r, that is,

hort position$] = B_F - B_V$

$$= \sum_{t=1}^{n} \frac{C}{(1+r_t)^t} + \frac{P}{(1+r_n)^n}$$

$$B_V = \frac{C_v}{(1+r_1)^1} + \frac{P}{(1+r_1)^1}$$

…ve, it can be seen that the C_V is the variable rate coupon and …nent date, B_V is always equal to the notional principal, P, …erest rate.

…p transaction, the value of the transaction should be zero. If it …s a positive value should pay the net value to the other party. …e value of the swap is not necessarily equal to zero. In fact, one …value while the other has a negative value. The party that has a …is likely to have a higher probability of default.

…d to pay six-month LIBOR and receive 10 percent per annum on …100 million. The swap has a remaining life of 1.5 years. The relevant …, and 18-month maturities are 11.0, 11.5 and 12.0 percent, per annum …urrent six-month LIBOR rate is 11.0 percent per annum, the six- …fixed-coupon bond of $5 million – that is, (10%/2) × 100 – will be discounted at 5.5 percent. The first six-month variable rate payment for the floating rate bond is $5.5 million – that is, (11%/2) × 100. Values of both bonds can be expressed as:

$$B_F = \frac{5}{(1+0.11/2)^1} + \frac{5}{(1+0.115/2)^2} + \frac{105}{(1+0.12/2)^3}$$

$$= \$97.37 \text{ million}$$

$$B_V = \frac{5.5}{(1 + 0.11/2)^1} + \frac{100}{(1 + 0.11/2)^1}$$

$$= \$100.00 \text{ million}$$

The value of the short swap position is $B_F - B_V$ which is equal to

$$\$97.37 - \$100.00 = -\$2.63 \text{ million}$$

If a bank has the long position (paying fixed and receiving floating), the value of the swap would be $+\$2.63$ million. In this case, the bank with a long position in the swap will pay $\$2.63$ million to the counterparty having the short position.

2 *Forward rate arrangements.* As described in Chapter 4, a forward rate arrangement (FRA) is a contract between two parties to fix an interest rate at a specified level at a future date for a specified future period. On the future date, if the market rate happens to be different from the contract interest rate, the losing party has to pay the winning party the interest differential between the market and contract rates. Specifically if the actual interest rate is higher than the contract rate, the interest rate moves in favor of the borrower-buyer of an FRA. In this case, the borrower will receive compensation from the seller-lender of an FRA. On the other hand, if the interest rate is lower than the contract rate, the buyer pays the seller of the FRA.

As an example, suppose that a six-month, $\$10$ million FRA has the contract (agreed-upon) rate of 10 percent in terms of 180-day LIBOR. Six months later, the benchmark (180-day LIBOR) rate is 12 percent. In this case, the interest rate is higher than the contract rate, and has moved in favor of the borrower. Given the loan amount of $\$10$ million, the lender will pay 2 percent (i.e., 12–10 percent) on the principal to the borrower for the amount of:

$$\$10 \text{ million} \times (180/360) \times 2\% = \$100,000$$

Because the compensation is paid at the *beginning* of the period instead of at the end, the cash payment is the *present value* of $\$100,000$, discounted at 12 percent for the six-month period.

An FRA is simply a forward contract between the two parties to exchange a floating-rate payment/receipt for a fixed-rate payment/receipt: the buyer pays the fixed rate, and the seller pays the floating rate. When the parties agree to a *series* of FRAs for a number of future successive periods, the contract becomes an interest rate swap. This is the reason why the interest rate swap is sometimes called the coupon swap. Thus

$$SWAP = FRA_{1,2} + FRA_{2,3} + \cdots + FRA_{n-1,n}$$

The FRA for any period can be computed using the term structure equation as follows:

$$(FRA_{n-1,n}) = \frac{(1 + r_{0,n})^n}{(1 + r_{0,n-1})^{n-1}} - 1$$

where $r_{0,j}$ is the spot interest rate for j periods.

The exchange of interest payment on the first payment date involves a floating payment of $C\star_1$ (which is known today and is equal to $r_1(P)$) and a fixed receipt C (fixed coupon rate which is also known today). The present value for the "seller" is thus:

$$\frac{C - C\star_1}{(1 + r_1)^1}$$

The value of the swap, taking place in period t, for the seller, that is, the party receiving the fixed coupon payment (C) while paying the floating payment ($C\star_t$), is the present value of the interest rate differential between the fixed and the floating rate payment shown as:

$$\frac{C - C\star_t}{(1 + r_t)^t}$$

For a six-month floating period,

$$C\star_t = 0.5 \times F_t \times P$$

where F_t, the implied floating forward rate, is based on the implied forward rate in the term structure of interest rates.

The value of a short forward contract is the present value of the amount by which the prevailing delivery price exceeds the forward price. Therefore, for the party receiving fixed and paying floating, the total (present) value of the swap transaction, V, can be expressed as:

$$V = \frac{C - C\star_1}{(1 + r_1)^1} + \Sigma \frac{C - C\star_t}{(1 + r_t)^t}$$

Example 6.2

Consider again the situation in Example 6.1 in which $C = \$5$ million, $C\star_1 = \$5.5$ million, and $P = \$100$ million. Given the term structure relationship, we have $r_{0,1} = 0.11$, $r_{0,2} = 0.115$, $r_{0,3} = 0.12$.

The forward rate, $F_{1,2}$ is computed as follows:

$$(1 + F_{1,2}/2) = \frac{(1 + r_{0,2}/2)^2}{(1 + r_{0,1}/2)^1}$$

$$= \frac{(1 + 0.115/2)^2}{(1 + 0.11/2)^1} = \frac{(1.0575)^2}{(1.055)} = 1.06$$

Thus, we have:

$$F_{1,2} = 0.1200$$

Similarly, the forward rate, $F_{2,3}$, is computed as:

$$(1 + F_{2,3}/2) = \frac{(1 + 0.12/2)^3}{(1 + 0.115/2)^2}$$

$$= \frac{(1.06)^3}{(1.0575)^2} = 1.065$$

$$F_{2,3} = 0.1300$$

or

Therefore, the value of the swap, V, is

$$V = \frac{5 - 5.5}{(1 + 0.11/2)^1} + \frac{5 - 0.5(0.1200)(100)}{(1 + 0.115/2)^2} + \frac{5 - 0.5(0.1300)(100)}{(1 + 0.12/2)^3}$$

$$= \$2.63 \text{ million}$$

The value of the swap is $-\$2.63$ million under the forward rate scenario and it is in agreement with the calculation based on the bond price valuation as demonstrated in the previous example.

6.2.5   Currency swaps market

Basic concept

A currency swap is a privately negotiated contract between two parties to exchange a series of cash flows denominated in two currencies. A usual form of currency swap is a **cross-currency interest rate swap**, which involves three distinct sets of cash flows:

1   the initial exchange of principals, which are chosen so that they are approximately equal to the exchange rate at the beginning of the swap's life;
2   the periodic interest payments to each other during the life of the swap agreement (the interest on either currency may be based on a fixed-rate set initially or on a floating-rate that will be reset periodically);
3   the final exchange (re-exchange) of principals at the same exchange rate used for the initial exchange of principals.

At times, the exchange of initial and/or ending principal payments is obviated.

In a cross-currency interest rate swap, the addition of the currency component adds a new basic dimension. For the Euro/US$ combination, we thus have the following types of swaps:

- fixed Euro versus fixed US$;
- fixed Euro versus floating US$;
- floating Euro versus floating US$; and
- floating Euro versus fixed US$.

To understand currency swaps, we begin with the simplest type of currency swaps – a **plain-vanilla** currency swap in the following example.

Example 6.3

A British firm wants to obtain US$75 million from an American firm for four years. In return, it will pay the American firm in £ sterling. The British firm agrees to pay annual interest payments as well as the final payment in US$ to the American firm, and in return expects to receive annual interest payments for four years and the final principal payment (at the end of four years) in £ sterling from the American firm.

Current exchange rate: US$1.50/£ sterling.
£ sterling interest rate = 8 percent
US$ interest rate = 10 percent

1   Initially, the British firm will receive from the American firm US$ 75 million and in return pays the American firm £50 million (= US$75 million/US$1.50/£ sterling).
2   Each year during the life of the swap, the British firm will receive 8 percent interest on the £50 million it initially paid, that is, £4 million (= 8 percent × £50 million) and it will annually pay the American firm US$7.5 million dollars (= 10 percent × US$75 million).
3   At the end of four years, the British firm will receive from the American firm £50 million and will pay the American firm $75 million.

This final payment terminates the currency swap.

As we mentioned earlier, a swap facilitator – a swap broker or a swap dealer[4] – often assists in the completion of a currency swap.

Valuation of currency swaps

1   *Relationship to bond prices.* In the absence of default risk, a currency swap can be decomposed into two bonds in a way similar to an interest rate swap. For instance, the value of a swap, V, to the party paying US$ interest rates and receiving foreign currency interest rates will be:

$$V = S(B_F) - B_D$$

where B_F is the bond value denominated and measured in the foreign currency; B_D is the value of the US$-denominated bond; and S is the spot exchange rate (expressed as the number of units of US$ per unit of foreign currency).

The value of a swap can therefore be determined from

- the term structure of interest rates in the domestic currency;
- the term structure of interest rates in the foreign currency; and
- the spot exchange rate.

Example 6.4

In a currency swap, a bank will receive 6 percent per annum in £ sterling and pay 9 percent per annum in US$ once a year. The principal amounts in the two currencies are $150 million and £100 million. The swap will last for another two years. Assume that the term structure of interest rates is flat in both currencies, with the £ sterling interest rate of 5 percent per annum and the US$ interest rate of 10 percent per annum. The current exchange rate is $1.45/£.

To determine the value of the currency swap, we first compute the value of the foreign bonds followed by the domestic bonds. Then, we compute the net value of these two bonds adjusted for exchange rate in order to obtain the value of the currency swap.

$$B_F = \frac{100(0.06)}{(1 + 0.05)^1} + \frac{100(0.06)}{(1 + 0.05)^2} + \frac{100}{(1 + 0.05)^2}$$

$$= \frac{6}{1.05} + \frac{106}{(1.05)^2}$$

$$= \pounds 101.86 \text{ million}$$

Similarly,

$$B_D = \frac{150(0.09)}{(1 + 0.10)^1} + \frac{150(0.09)}{(1 + 0.10)^2} + \frac{150}{(1 + 0.10)^2}$$

$$= \text{US\$147.40 million}$$

Hence,

$$V = S(B_F) - B_D$$

$$= (\text{US\$1.45}/\pounds)(\pounds 101.86) - \text{US\$147.40}$$

$$= \text{US\$0.30 million}$$

The value of the currency swap for the American bank, which receives pound sterling and pays dollar to the counterparty, would be US\$0.30 million.

2   *Currency swap as forward contracts.* An alternative valuation of the currency swap is to view the transaction as a series of forward contracts. Consider the bank in Example 6.4. Each year the bank has agreed to exchange an inflow of $\pounds 6$ million for an outflow of US\$13.5 million. In addition, at the final payment date, it has agreed to exchange a $\pounds 100$ million inflow for a US\$150 million outflow. Each of these exchanges may be construed as a forward contract.

Suppose r_t is the spot US\$ interest rate for time period of length t, and F_t is the forward exchange rate applicable to time t. The value of a long forward contract is the present value of the amount by which the forward price exceeds the delivery price. The value for the American bank of the forward contract corresponding to the exchange of interest payments, V_{1t}, at time t is, therefore,

$$V_{1t} = \frac{6F_t - 13.5}{(1 + r_t)^{(t)}}$$

Similarly, the value of the forward contract corresponding to the exchange of principal payments, V_P, at the terminal time, n, is

$$V_P = \frac{\pounds 100 \, F_n - 150}{(1 + r_n)^{(n)}}$$

This shows that the value of a currency swap can always be calculated from the term structure of forward exchange rates and the term structure of domestic interest rates.

The total value of the currency swap, V, is the sum of the interest payments, V_{It}, and the principal payment, V_P, that is,

$$V = \sum_{t=1} V_{It} + V_P$$

Example 6.5

Consider again the situation in Example 6.4. The current spot exchange rate is US$1.45 per pound sterling. It can be shown that forward exchange rates can be calculated by the following formula:

$$F_t = \frac{S_0(1 + r_t)^t}{(1 + r\star_t)^t}$$

where S_0 is the spot exchange rate; r_t is the domestic spot interest rate for time t; and $r\star_t$ is the corresponding foreign interest rate.

This formula gives the one-year and two-year forward exchange rates as follows:

$$F_1 = \frac{1.45\star(1 + 0.10)^1}{(1 + 0.05)^1}$$

$$= US\$1.5190/\pounds$$

and,

$$F_2 = \frac{1.45\star(1 + 0.10)^2}{(1 + 0.05)^2}$$

$$= US\$1.5914/\pounds$$

The exchange of interest involves receiving £6 million and paying US$13.5 million. Given the US$ interest rate of 10 percent per annum, the values of the forward contracts pertaining to the interest payments are:

$$V_{11} = \frac{6(1.5190) - 13.5}{(1 + 0.10)^1}$$

$$= US\$3.9873 \text{ million}$$

and,

$$V_{12} = \frac{6(1.5914) - 13.5}{(1 + 0.10)^2}$$

$$= US\$3.9873 \text{ million}$$

The final exchange of principal involves receiving £100 million and paying US$150 million. The value of the forward contract embedded in the final payment is

$$V_P = \frac{100(1.5914) - 150}{(1 + 0.10)^2}$$

$$= US\$7.5537 \text{ million}$$

The total value of the currency swap is

$$V = V_{I1} + V_{I2} + V_P$$
$$= -3.9873 - 3.2658 + 7.5537$$
$$= US\$0.30 \text{ million}$$

This is the same result as in the previous example.

6.2.6   Risks in swap arrangements

The bank as a swap dealer face two risks: market risk and credit risk. The market risk relates to the likelihood that exchange or interest rates may move against it in a way that turns the value of the swap negative. In this case, if the bank has to liquidate the position in the secondary market, it incurs additional cost to offset the negative value of the swap. The second risk, credit risk, results from the (bank's) counterparty default *when* the swap value for the bank is positive, that is, the swap value is negative for the counterparty. Now for a negative swap value, consider when interest rates decline; in this case, the fixed-rate payer will incur a loss because of the higher contractual fixed rate than the market rate. As a result, decreasing interest rates trigger the credit risk potential of the fixed-rate payer. Similarly, spiraling interest rates trigger the credit risk potential of the floating rate payer. This line of reasoning suggests that the probability of loss for the dealer (e.g., a commercial bank) depends on the compound events – falling interest rate *and* default by the fixed-rate paying counterparty, and increasing interest rate and default by the floating-rate payer.

Swap transactions have grown in volume from some insignificant amount in the early 1980s to an amount in excess of US\$6 trillion in recent times. At the same time, banks as intermediaries now rarely earn a spread in excess of 10 basis points. Thus a bank can find swaps profitable only if it has a sufficiently large volume. From the mid-1980s to today, the number of banks acting as intermediaries in swaps has dramatically fallen.

These observations have two alternative implications.

1   A pessimistic view. Explosion in the size of the swap market can come only from lowering of credit standards. Poor credit risk leads to an escalating number of failed swaps. Since only a few banks handle the explosive growth in swap transactions, a wholesale failure is likely to lead to dramatic failures of some large banks. This phenomenon may even lead to a systemic risk of a run on banks.

2   A sanguine view of the world. Credit risk has two components related to non-payment: inability and unwillingness. *Inability* to pay stems from lack of resources at the extreme. On the other hand, a debtor having inadequate resources to meet all obligations resorts to a hierarchy of claims against available resources, and meets obligations accordingly till he exhausts resources.

A creditor bank's strategy, then, is to

• upgrade the priority of its claims in the counterparty's hierarchy;
• have the debtor stretch his resources by only partial payments to creditors who are higher up in the hierarchy; or

- construct a swap that satisfies the need of the debtor indirectly by involving B as a counterparty where B has a higher priority accorded to the bank than the debtor would have.

These steps, either individually or jointly, enable the bank to reduce the effective credit risk of the debtor. Still, the third alternative may be more realistic than the first two.

A Pakistani firm needed a US dollar-denominated loan for augmenting plant capacity. The US bank it approached was unwilling to extend such a loan. But instead of outright rejection of the loan request, it created a chain of counterparties consisting of a French bank, a Moroccan bank, a Lebanese bank, and a Saudi Arabian bank to provide the funds. Thus the Pakistani firm swapped rupees for Saudi dinars (the Saudi bank needed Pakistani rupees to satisfy the demand of Pakistani immigrants who wanted to transmit funds home); the Lebanese bank was willing to act as an intermediary between the Moroccan bank and the Saudi bank; given the trade relations between Morocco and France, the French bank was willing to take a position in Moroccan dirhams; and finally the US bank swapped US dollars for French francs.

The alternative implication then suggests that

- nominal or notional amount of swap transactions may far exceed the genuine need for swaps; consequently, concern over the explosion in the notional amount may be overrated;
- the large number of transactions in the US bank–Pakistani firm example is not superfluous, as they serve a genuine purpose of reducing the credit risk of the last link in the chain;
- the fear of systemic risk involving bank failures may be exaggerated if not unfounded; and
- the low spread on a swap transaction may be viewed from two perspectives:
  - a bank, which serves as a link between two counterparties, is not assuming significant risk itself;
  - involvement of multiple links in the chain means that the initiating bank has to share its compensation with these links.

6.2.7   Swaptions

Swaptions are options related to swaps. A swaption call gives the buyer the right, not the obligation, to receive a fixed payment at the fixed interest rate (called the strike price) and to pay at the floating rate. A *swaption call* thus gives the buyer the right to go *short* on a swap. On the other hand, the writer of the swaption call has the obligation to go long on the swap if the call is exercised.

A swaption put is the right, not obligation, to pay at a fixed rate and receive at a floating rate. A *swaption put* is the right to go *long* on a swap. An American swaption can be exercised at any time prior to the expiration date while a European swaption can only be exercised at maturity.

6.3 Other Derivative Instruments

6.3.1 Interest rate cap

A common over-the-counter interest rate option offered by banks or other financial institutions is the interest rate cap. Interest rate caps are designed as an insurance policy to provide interest rate protection to the buyer (borrower) against floating interest rates above a fixed rate, which is called the cap rate. The cap buyer pays no more than the cap rate during the life of the contract.

Typically, the buyer pays the premium of the cap option up-front. When a cap on a loan and the loan itself are both provided by the same bank, the cost of the cap may be incorporated into the interest rate charged.

Example 6.6

On January 2, a corporation borrowed US$10 million for six months at 90-day LIBOR from Citicorp. The loan has a cap rate of 10 percent for a front-end premium of US$80,000. The payment schedule for the life of the loan is shown as follows:

Date	LIBOR Interest payment	Cap	Net cash flow	Due
January 2	9.0%	−US$80,000	+US$9,920,000	
April 2	10.2%	−US$225,000	−US$225,000	
July 2	11.0%	−US$255,000	+US$5,000	−US$10,250,000

Items in the last two columns are computed as follows.

- the cash flow received by the borrower on January 2 is US$9,920,000, a balance of US$10 million over the US$80,000 front-end cap premium.
- On April 2, the interest due is US$225,000 [= US$10 million × (90/360) × 9%]. The interest rate payment is computed using the interest rate set at the beginning of the period. Since it is below the cap rate, there is no cap payment.
- On July 2, the interest due is US$255,000 [= US$10 million × (90/360) × 10.2%]. Because the relevant interest rate is above the cap rate, the cap becomes effective. The bank has to pay the borrower an amount as follows:

$$\frac{\text{Loan} \times \text{Days in period} \times \text{Max}\,(0, \text{LIBOR} - 0.10)}{360}$$

$$= \text{US\$10 million} \times 1/4 \times (0.102 - 0.10)$$

$$= \text{US\$5,000}$$

As a result, the borrower will pay back the interest and principal net of the cap payment received, an amount of US$10,250,000 (US$10 million principal + US$255,000 interest − US$5,000 cap).

A relevant question pertaining to interest rate caps is how to determine the cap premium. Cap premium is typically expressed as a percentage of the notional principal amount. The primary factors, which determine the cap premium, are:

- The relationship of the cap level with the current and anticipated future levels of interest rate. Other things being equal, the lower the cap rate, the more expensive the cap premium.
- The duration of the loan. All else being equal, the longer the maturity, the more expensive the cap premium.
- Volatility of interest rates. All things being equal, the more volatile interest rates are, the more expensive the cap.

Valuation of caps

In general, caps may be viewed as a portfolio of call options.

- Cap interest rate is R_E;
- Principal is L; and
- Interest payments are made at the end of each of $t, 2t, \ldots, nt$ periods

At the beginning of period kt, the writer-lender of the cap (e.g., the commercial bank) expects to pay to the buyer-borrower an end-of-the-period amount equal to

$$t \times L \times \max(R_k - R_E, 0)$$

where R_k is the going market interest rate for time period kt.

Suppose the forward interest rate for period kt is F_k. The present value of the cap payment at the *beginning* of the kt period will be:

$$\frac{t \times L \times \max(R_k - R_E, 0)}{(1 + t \times F_k)}$$

where $t \times L/(1 + t \times F_k)$ can be viewed as the discounted value of the principal amount for each option.[5] [$\max(R_k - R_E, 0)$] is the call option value. In this way, we can regard each cap at kt as if it is a European option. Using Black's option on futures model (see Equation 5.12), we can derive the price of the cap at kt as:

$$\frac{t \times L \times e^{-r(kt)}[F_k \times N(d_1) - R_E \times N(d_2)]}{(1 + t \times F_k)}$$

where $d_1 = [\ln(F_k/R_E) + 0.5\sigma^2(kt)]/\sigma \times kt)^{1/2}$; $d_2 = d_1 - \sigma (kt)^{1/2}$; σ is the volatility of the forward interest rate; and r is the riskless interest rate.

Example 6.7

Given:

- the quoted IMM index is 92 for a Eurodollar futures contract that will mature in nine months;
- the implied standard deviation (ISD) for the future interest rate for a nine-month interest rate option is 0.15;
- the nine-month interest rate is 7 percent;
- the cap rate, the exercise price, is specified at 8 percent;

determine the price of a cap based on the three-month LIBOR rate in nine months' time for the US$10 million principal of a loan.

Given the IMM index for the Eurodollar futures is 92, its corresponding futures price per US$1 million contract value is computed as follows:

$$
\begin{aligned}
\text{Price} &= 1,000,000 \; [1 - (100 - \text{IMM})(90/360)/100] \\
&= 1,000,000 \; [1 - (100 - 92)(90/360)/100] \\
&= 1,000,000 \; [1 - 8(90/360)/100] \\
&= \text{US\$980,000}
\end{aligned}
$$

Hence, the future three-month interest (F) rate implied in the Eurodollar futures contract is:

$$
980,000 = 1,000,000 e^{-0.25F}
$$
$$
F = 8.08\%
$$

$$
\text{Value (Cap)} = (t{\star}L/(1 + t{\star}F)) \; e^{-rT}[F{\star}N(d_1) - E{\star}N(d_2)]
$$

where

$$
d_1 = \frac{In(F/\text{Cap rate}) + 0.5{\star}\sigma^2{\star}T}{\sigma{\star}(T)^{1/2}}
$$

$$
= \frac{In(0.0808/0.08) + 0.5(0.15^2)0.75}{0.15{\star}(0.75)^{1/2}}
$$

$$
= 0.4405
$$

Normal distribution tables give $N(0.4405) = 0.67$
Similarly,

$$
\begin{aligned}
d_2 &= d_1 - \sigma(T)^{1/2} \\
&= 0.4405 - 0.15{\star}(0.75)^{1/2} \\
&= 0.3106
\end{aligned}
$$

From the statistical table, we obtain

$$
N(d_2) = 0.6217
$$

After substituting all required variables into the cap equation, we obtain the value of the cap as:

$$\text{cap} = [0.25\star10\text{ m})/(1 + 0.25\star0.0808)]e^{-0.75(0.07)}[0.0808(0.67) - 0.08(0.6217)]$$
$$= (2,450,500)\,(0.94885)(0.0044)$$
$$= \text{US\$}10,230$$

6.3.2   Interest rate floors

Just as an interest rate cap is a series of call options that protects the borrower from an interest rate increase, an **interest rate floor** offers a lender an insurance against falling interest rates. Essentially the interest rate floor is a series of interest rate put options maturing at the payment dates. A borrower is basically writing a series of put options in the loan contract.

The payoff in an interest rate floor is quite similar to the interest rate cap. Suppose the floor is tied to the 10 percent LIBOR rate and the loan amount is US\$10 million. The floor payment will be:

$$\text{US\$}10\text{ million} \times (\text{Days in period}/360) \times \text{Max}(0, 0.10 - \text{LIBOR})$$

The applicable LIBOR rate for a period is, as usual, set at the beginning of the period. In addition, the pricing of the floor premium that the buyer-lender pays to the borrower can be determined in a way similar to the interest rate cap shown above.

6.3.3   Interest rate collars

Collars specify both the upper and lower limits for the rate that will be charged. A **collar** is a combination of a long position in a cap and a short position in a floor. It is usually constructed to equate the cost of buying the cap with the revenue from selling the floor. The net cost of the collar is thus zero, obviating the need for a front-end payment.

6.3.4   Cap floaters

A cap floater is a floating-rate note (FRN) with a periodic interest rate usually tied to the LIBOR, but the rate cannot exceed a certain "cap" rate. Thus the cap floater is an FRN with the interest rate cap. The cap floater usually provides 25–50 basis points higher coupon rates than the uncapped FRN.

6.3.5   Range forward contracts

Salomon Brothers introduced this derivative product in November 1985. A **range forward contract** is a currency contract that establishes an agreed upon range of forward rates between a buyer and a seller of the contract. If a multinational firm (the buyer of the range forward contract) wants to fix the *upper end* of the forward rates, FR_U, the bank (seller of the contract) will determine the *lower end* of the rates, FR_L.

Suppose FR_U is US$0.48/SF and FR_L is US$0.45/SF in a range forward contract. If, at maturity, the prevailing exchange rate is US$0.50/SF, the buyer purchases the German marks at US$0.48/SF, the upper range rate. In this case, the buyer gains the difference between US$0.50/SF and US$0.48/SF (i.e., US$0.02/SF).

If, on the other hand, the prevailing exchange rate is US$0.42/SF, which is below FR_L, the buyer will have to purchase the German marks at US$0.45/SF. In this case, the buyer suffers a loss of the difference between US$0.45/SF and US$1.42/SF (i.e., US$0.03/SF). Finally, if the prevailing exchange rate at the maturity of the forward range contract falls between US$0.45/SF and US$0.48/SF, the buyer will purchase at that prevailing rate.

Conceptually, the range forward contract (RF) is a combination of a call and put contract. Thus, it is similar to the interest rate collar except that interest rates are now replaced by forward currency rates. Specifically, buying a range forward contract is equivalent to buying a call (c) with an FR_U as the exercise price and selling a put (p) with an FR_L as the exercise price. Thus, we can express RF as:

$$RF = c - p$$

that is, a portfolio of a long call and short put.

This contract is a variation of the theorem of the put–call parity. Whereas the put–call parity requires the same exercise price for both options to create the conventional, unique-rate forward contract, the range forward contract permits two different exercise prices for the two options to create a forward contract with a range of forward rates.

Suppose a multinational corporation has a positive exposure in a foreign currency due to accounts receivable. Foreign currency appreciation will improve its cash flows in the domestic currency, while foreign currency depreciation will deteriorate these cash flows. If the corporation *sells* a call and *buys* a put, the combined – net – exposure of options and the account receivables will be contained on both the upside (a short call will wipe out the gain on the receivables) and the downside (the loss on the receivables would be absorbed by the gain on the put option). The range of the net exposure will depend on the exercise prices for the two options: the greater the difference between the exercise prices, the wider the range of the net exposure. Firms typically use this arrangement in order to offset the cost of buying the put option with the revenue from selling the call option. This combination is also known as a **cylinder option**. In effect, the cylinder option is just another range forward contract.

6.3.6   Indexed currency option notes

An **indexed currency option note** (ICON) is a financial derivative that was introduced on October 14, 1985 by Bankers Trust for the Long-Term Credit Bank of Japan. The ICON investors typically receive coupon payments at an interest rate *above* the market rate. However, the payment of the principal amount, say, US$1,000 is contingent upon the prevailing spot exchange rate at maturity, SR. Two exchange rates, SR_U (upper rate) and SR_L

(lower rate), are specified in the contract. These exchange rates are expressed in a direct quote, that is, US\$/Yen; and SR_L is $SR_U/2$ (i.e., the lower rate is half the upper rate). Three conditions are imposed on the note.

- If SR, the prevailing spot exchange rate at the maturity, is above SR_U, the bondholder receives nothing.
- If SR is less than the SR_L, the bondholder receives the face value e of the bond.
- If SR is within the range defined by SR_U and SR_L, the investor will receive a fraction $2 - SR/SR_L$[6] of the principal (i.e., US\$1,000).

Although the ICON looks somewhat complicated, it can be easily decomposed into simple options. In fact, for an investor, an ICON is a bundle of

- a straight bond, B, with a face value (e.g., US\$1,000);
- a long call option at exercise price SR_U (higher exercise price); and
- a short call option at the exercise price SR_L (lower exercise price).

Let us now consider various scenarios of the currency rate, and their impact on the investor.

If the prevailing exchange rate falls below SR_L, both call options (their exercise prices are at or above SR_L) expire. As a result, the investor will in effect have only the bond in the portfolio and the payoff is the bond's par value of

$$B = US\$1,000$$

If the prevailing exchange rate lies between SR_U (upper rate) and SR_L (lower rate), the long call option having the exercise price of SR_U expires while the investor's principal is reduced by the loss on the short call option, c, with an exercise price of SR_L. The loss on the call, $c(SR_L)$, which is sold by the investor, can be expressed as:

$$c(SR_L) = Max\ [0, 1000(1 - SR/SR_L)]$$

If the prevailing exchange rate exceeds SR_U (upper rate), both short and long call options are in the money. The investor will gain by the *long position* in the call with the exercise price of SR_U while the short position will entail a loss. The gain on the call, $c(SR_U,)$ which is bought by the investor, can be expressed as:

$$c(SR_U) = Max\ [0, 1000(SR/SR_U - 1)2]$$

(The expression in parentheses is multiplied by 2, as SR_U is twice the value of SR_L.) Thus,

$$ICONs = B - c(SR_L) + c(SR_U)$$

that is, a portfolio of a straight bond, short call with an exercise price, SR_L and a long call with an exercise price of SR_U.

The special feature of ICON is that its payoff at maturity is linked to the value of a currency. Some bonds whose payoffs are linked to other commodities (i.e., other than currency) can also be found in practice. For example, Standard Oil issued some zero-coupon bonds in 1986. The payoff of the bonds was linked to the oil price at the maturity of the bonds. If the price of the commodity (i.e., oil) went up, the company was in a good position to provide bondholders with additional payment.

Example 6.8

Suppose a US investor purchases a US$1,000 currency note for the Japanese yen. If SR_L (the lower contract rate) is US$0.005/yen, the principal to be received at maturity by the investor will be as follows.

Principal received (US$)	US$/yen rate at maturity
1,000	0.004
1,000	0.005
800	0.006
600	0.007
0	0.011

6.3.8   Knockout options

Knockout options resemble traditional options except that they are canceled when the underlying currency rate reaches a prespecified value even for a brief time period. These options became one of the most popular options by the mid-1990s. Suppose a one-month knockout *call* option has a strike price of US$1.65/£ and has a **knockout** (also known as outstrike) price of US$1.50/£. If, by the end of, say, the fifteenth day, the pound sterling reaches US$1.50 even for a minute, the option expires.

Similarly, the knockout *put* option may also have the strike price of US$1.65/£ and the outstrike price of US$1.50/£. In contrast to the call case, where the option is out-of money when the pound sterling reaches US$1.50, the outstrike price represents in-the-money situation for the put option. These options are also known as **down-and-out** calls and down-and-out puts, respectively, since the outstrike price is lower than – "down" – the strike price, and once the down price is reached, the parties are "out" of the contract.

Two characteristics of these options are noteworthy.

1   These options represent risk of earlier expiry than the corresponding standard option. Thus their effective maturity will be less than the stated or nominal maturity, depending on the volatility of the underlying instrument. As a result, they are cheaper than the corresponding standard options.

A US importer of goods from Germany has euro-based payment due in a month. She may buy a down-and-out *dollar* put (where US$ is quoted in terms of euro) to protect against a weakening dollar at a far more reasonable price than the standard put option. At the same time, if the dollar comes under unusual pressure during the month and keeps on losing the ground, the importer may find the option getting canceled, and facing further losses when the payment comes due. The premium paid for the option just adds to the loss.

A bank having an oversold position in euro may also choose to buy the knockout dollar put to contain the cost of hedging if its proprietary information leads it to assign very low probability for premature cancellation of the down-and-out put.

2   A bank *writing* the down-and-out put may find, as maturity comes nearer, that the put option is in the money but chances of the currency reaching the outstrike price (that would cancel the contract and release the bank from its obligation) is virtually nil. In this case, the bank may have to buy a standard put to protect itself against the losses, and it may find that the premium income from the down-and-out put is inadequate to meet the cost of buying the standard put later.

Suppose a bank writes a down-and-out SF put with the strike price of US$0.65/SF and the outstrike price of US$0.56/SF. The bank earns a premium of US$0.02. In this case, if the contract is not canceled before maturity, the bank would suffer loss for any price at maturity between US$0.56/SF and US$0.63/SF.

6.3.9   Basket option

A multinational company (MNC) has operations and activities in a number of countries with a variety of currencies. In order to minimize currency exposure, such a firm likes the convenience offered by the *basket option*, which allows it to hedge its global exposure in different currencies with just one option. Such an option can be a long-only (long in dollar) basket, short-only basket, or long/short or spread basket.

- A long-only basket option is used, for instance, by a firm in the US drug industry, which satisfies global demand with one manufacturing facility.
- A short-only basket option is useful for a manufacturer of standardized goods produced with standardized production processes, as it sources goods globally to satisfy the domestic demand. Apparels or color televisions, for instance, belong to this category of goods.
- As the MNC shifts from being a bundle of multi-domestic firms (each subsidiary essentially is a self-contained unit satisfying local demand with local production) to becoming a globally integrated network of sourcing and distribution, its exposure in various currencies is no longer just long or short. It requires a spread basket option.

These are truly customized options. Their maturity does not exceed one year. As the amount of exposure varies in each currency, even for a long-only or short-only option, its pricing depends on statistical correlation among the relevant currencies. A less than perfect correlation coefficient between a pair of currencies provides to an extent a natural hedge.

Essentially this is a problem akin to the risk determination of a portfolio: the difference is that currencies are used instead of securities, and position in a currency can be negative. Once, however, the "risk" of the portfolio is determined, the option pricing model can be employed to determine the price of a basket option.

Banks that write such options may find that their own currency exposure is complementary to these options. In that case, they are unwinding (at least a portion of) their exposure while earning premium income. When their own-account exposure moves in the same direction as the exposure assumed through writing the basket options, which are individually for large amounts but relatively few in number, the law of large number may not apply; instead, they may create greater volatility in earnings with a negative impact on share price on the one hand, and require a larger capital base (to be discussed in Chapter 10) that may negate the benefits of generating income from writing these options.

6.4 Credit Derivatives

A distinctive characteristic of credit risk embedded in an asset is that it cannot be readily traded in the secondary market, unlike the interest rate risk. The absence of a secondary market in credit risk trading stems from a lack of rating, opaqueness of default risk, and too small a size of individual transaction at the primary – rather than derivative – level. Credit derivatives circumvent these problems to a varying degree and provide credit insurance against fixed-income securities or loans. Thus, credit derivatives may be used to provide bond portfolio insurance against the default defined in terms of liquidation of the bond issuer, rating deterioration of various levels, or just illiquidity leading to non-servicing of debt. A credit derivative may be for one period or may encompass several years.

6.4.1 Basic types

Initially the credit derivative required the insurance buyer to pay a given amount of basis points, anywhere from 10 to 50 bps, to the seller. In return, the seller would compensate the buyer in case of default on the reference security (or portfolio). This form was not unlike the interest swap, since the buyer paid the fixed-rate compensation, and the seller assumed the contingent or floating-rate obligation. Thus the reference of contingency was not the LIBOR or T-bill rate but the default event.

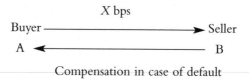

The subsequent form has been the Total Return (*TR*) credit derivative, where Party A which has a security *D* with default risk potential receives the return of LIBOR + agreed spread from Party B; and B receives the total return on the security *D* from A.

Return on security D is *total* in that it includes not only coupon but also capital appreciation or loss.

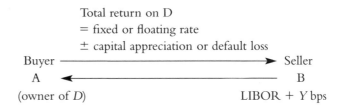

Total return on D
= fixed or floating rate
± capital appreciation or default loss
Buyer ⟶ Seller
A ⟵ B
(owner of *D*)   LIBOR + *Y* bps

A comparison between the two forms is instructive. In the first case, A, the buyer or the owner of security D, is keeping the coupon and any appreciation on security D. In the second case, A gives that up for [LIBOR + $(Y + X)$ bps], where X bps represents the cost incurred in the first case. A also gives up C, the compensation obtained in the case of default under the first case. Now the return of LIBOR + $(Y + X)$ bps is certain, whereas the return of coupon and appreciation on security D is available only when there is no default. Thus the second case is an improvement for the buyer A only if

$$p \times (\text{coupon} + \text{cap appreciation}) + (1 - p) \times C < \text{LIBOR} + (Y + X) \text{ bps}$$

where $(1 - p)$ is the probability of default on security D, and C is the compensation under default.

We can rewrite this as

$$p(\text{coupon} + \text{cap appreciation} - C) < [\text{LIBOR} + (Y + X)\text{bps} - C]$$
$$\text{i.e., } p < [\text{LIBOR} + (Y + X) \text{ bps} - C]/(\text{coupon} + \text{cap appreciation} - C)$$

Because default occurs during recession when interest rates are low, that is, p is low when LIBOR is low, there is no assurance that A would come out ahead under the *TR* alternative.

6.4.2   Credit derivative and synthetic repurchase agreement

It is possible to create a synthetic repurchase agreement or "repo" with the help of a credit derivative. Suppose A does not own security D, but B does; and A buys security D from B. A also enters into an agreement with B whereby A receives from B the compensation of LIBOR + agreed spread, and B receives from A the return on the security D. Thus the only change from the previous example is that now A does not initially own D.

Total return on D
= fixed or floating rate
± capital appreciation or default loss
Buyer ⟶ Seller
A ⟵ B
LIBOR + *Y* bps (owner of *D*)

In a repo, B, who initially owns D, also sells it to A, but agrees to buy it back at a predetermined price at the end of the period. The difference between the initial receipt and the later payment by B constitutes the interest payment LIBOR + agreed spread; and B receives any returns on D even when they are negative. Essentially, A does not own D but has the collateral of D. The combo (purchase of D + total return credit derivative) differs from the repo in two matters.

- A owns security D outright; and there is no agreement for sale of D at the end of the period.
- Typically the repo involves a treasury security, which does not have default risk.

As a result, a bank B owns D and likes the return but does not want to keep its ownership because of, say, capital requirements, can do so under the combo arrangement of the off-balance-sheet. If it were to do so under the repo, D would be deemed a collateral given to A; and B would be unable to escape the (higher) capital requirement.

The foregoing discussion suggests that when a repo exists for a risky security, proper pricing of a credit derivative will be when there is no arbitrage opportunity for profit, a situation akin to the IRPT where proper pricing of a forward contract would be linked to the interest rate differential in such a way as to remove any arbitrage opportunity.[7]

The discussion above was also based on the assumption that the seller has impeccable credit credentials. When that is not the case, there may be an intermediary, which has those credentials. In that case, the buyer A is likely to pay more for credit insurance because of compensation to the intermediary.

6.4.3   Alternative approaches to pricing credit derivatives

Pricing of the credit derivative follows from two distinct lines of reasoning: models that are based on the premise of usefulness of historical patterns; and models that are based on economic reasoning. Economic models have followed two approaches. The first one, due to Merton (1974), suggests that credit quality and stock prices go hand in hand: when credit deteriorates, stock price goes down. Hence, purchase of a put on the stock or shorting the stock of a firm allows one to hedge the bond investment in that firm. The other approach, due to Jarrow and Turnbull (1995), argues that credit risk should be measured in terms of the bond's spread over the riskless security.

Both these approaches have problems. The first one relying on a decline in stock value ignores the observation that if a firm facing bankruptcy risk is able to issue additional debt, the stock price goes up while the default or bankruptcy risk also increases. This may be due to an additional option value obtained by the stockholders: limited liability does not deteriorate their position while staving of bankruptcy enhances their chance of upside gain.

The second approach, on the other hand, assumes that the spread over the T-bill remains constant over a business cycle. Generally the spread related to credit risk moves in the opposite direction of the interest rate movement over the business cycle. Thus during recession when interest rates decline on government obligations, the default risk premium increases, leading to decreased volatility in the return on risky security over the interest rate cycle.

As a result, the proxy for risk should not be the spread over the T-bill rate, but the volatility in the yield on the security: the less the volatility, the greater the default risk for a fixed-income security.

Unlike interest swaps, there is lack of consensus on how credit derivatives should be priced. Further, the existing approaches are proprietary. Thus pricing of credit derivatives remains opaque. Hence it is not clear to what extent they include ad hoc adjustments, and whether they are justifiable. Of course, existence of a repo for a comparable security may provide a reasonable check on the pricing.

6.5 Conclusion

In this chapter, interest rate and currency swap transactions were first analyzed. Motivations of the swap transactions were also discussed. In addition, the two alternative approaches to pricing swap instruments were presented. Risks inherent in a swap transaction were clarified.

Subsequently, the discussion focused on additional derivative instruments such as swaptions, caps, floors, collars, range forward contracts, indexed currency note options, knockout options, and credit derivatives. Their analysis demonstrated that very often these complicated derivative instruments are simply a combination of basic call and put options. This insight makes it easier to understand pricing of these instruments. Instruments such as credit derivatives, however, are exceptions in that they do not have a widely accepted, direct linkage to the basic options. Hence their pricing remains controversial, if not shrouded in mystery.

DISCUSSION QUESTIONS

1 What is a parallel loan and how did it evolve into swap?
2 What are the advantages/disadvantages of swaps contract over the forward/ futures contracts?
3 Explain the pricing schedule for a swap
4 What market impediments give rise to swap transactions?
5 Two companies (A and B) are negotiating an interest rate swap arrangement of US$10 million 10-year contract as follows:

	Fixed	Floating
A company	8%	LIBOR + 0.5%
B company	9.8%	LIBOR + 1.5%

Company A would desire a floating rate loan while B wants a fixed rate loan. Design a swap that benefits both parties and at the same time the financial intermediary gets 0.2 percent.
6 Explain how swap transactions can be used for risk management.

7 The interest rates for the 6-month, 12-month, 18-month and 24-month rates are 10.25, 10.5, 10.75 and 11%, respectively. The current 6-month LIBOR is 10.25%. If a firm agrees to pay a fixed 10% and receives LIBOR for US$100 million notional value in the interest swap, how much should the firm pay or receive for the swap transaction?

8 A US company would like to borrow US$ at the floating rate while a UK firm wants to borrow pound sterling at the fixed rate. How should a bank make the swap arrangement that will benefit both firms, given the following parameters?

	US firm	UK firm
US dollars	LIBOR + 0.6%	LIBOR + 1.1%
Pound sterling	5.1%	6.6%

9 Under what condition(s) do proliferation of interest rate swaps not increase the credit risk of banks?

10 What are swaption call and put?

11 Assume you have a US$1 million floating rate (LIBOR) loan with a cap of 8% on March 1. The premium of the cap is US$2,000. What is the cash flow for the loan if the LIBOR is 8, 8.5, 9 and 7% on March 1, June 1, September 1 and December 1 respectively?

12 What are range forward contracts, indexed currency option notes, knock-out options, and basket options?

13 What is credit derivative? What valuation approaches are used in credit derivatives? Discuss the limitations of these valuation approaches.

14 On June 15, 2000, Bank of Tokyo entered in a currency swap transaction with the Bank of Philadelphia to hedge the **exchange risk** exposure of its operations in the USA. Bank of Kyoto swapped its three-year floating rate Japanese yen bonds with a fixed-rate US$ bonds. The details of the currency swap are as follows:

Initiation date	June 15, 2000
Maturity	Three years
Principal amounts	500 million Japanese yen and US$5 million
Fixed rate payer	Bank of Philadelphia
Fixed interest rate	5%
Fixed date count	30/360
Fixed rate receiver	Bank of Tokyo
Floating rate index	LIBOR
Floating day count	Actual/360
Payment frequency	Every six months
Settlement day	June 15 and December 15

LIBOR rates (%) are projected as follows:

June 15, 2000	5.0
December 15, 2000	5.1
June 15, 2001	5.2

> | December 15, 2001 | 5.3 |
> | June 15, 2002 | 5.5 |
> | December 15, 2002 | 5.8 |
>
> a What are the expected cash inflows for the Bank of Tokyo?
> b What are the cash inflows for the Bank of Philadelphia based on the interest rate projections?

NOTES

1 The World Bank reportedly decreased its borrowing cost by 10 percent.

2 These interest rates need not be "domestic" rates. As a matter of fact, they are likely to be Eurocurrency market rates.

3 This argument resembles the comparative cost advantage. However, the comparative cost advantage stresses the market imperfection manifest in differing ability in accessing a given market, whereas the risk assumption argument does not require market imperfection.

4 A currency swap broker acts strictly as an agent, without taking any financial position in the swap transaction. A currency swap dealer may actually take one side of the transaction to help complete the swap.

5 Here t is the fraction of the year for which the interest rate is set. Thus, $t = \frac{1}{4}$ for a 90-day floating reference interest rate, and $t = \frac{1}{2}$ for a semi-annual floating reference interest rate.

6 The expression in parentheses is equal to $(SR_U - SR)/SR_L$.

7 Both situations are also analogous in that they regard interest rate differentials in the one case, and pricing of the repo agreement in the other as exogenously.

CHAPTER 7

International Credit Function for Private Business

LEARNING OBJECTIVES

- To examine the cross-border transaction and its financing
- To discuss the letter of credit and its role in the trade financing
- To consider the role of different agencies (private as well as governmental) in financing international trade
- To analyze countertrade and the bank's function in countertrade
- To explore project financing and the role played by the commercial bank in project financing

7.1 Introduction

In recent years, a relentless surge in international trade and investment has led to a concomitant increase in the demand for credit and credit-related services. Formerly, the main focus of foreign trade financing centered on risk management: goods-in-transit risk; political risk such as the freezing of foreign exchange; commercial risk reflected in default risk on the part of the buyer or importer; or volatility in the currency rates.

In more recent times, a major shift has occurred in which trade financing is not so much a tool for risk management as it is a weapon in executing global marketing strategies. In the face of crumbling trade barriers, electronic commerce and banking, and an uptick in volatility of goods, financial and foreign exchange markets, the importance of this new role for foreign trade financing cannot be ignored.

Banks, both large and small, recognizing a growing source of fees and revenues from these activities, have begun to market their cross-border credit-related services far more aggressively than ever before. Banks provide such services to private businesses in a global environment in several ways. First, banks facilitate cross-border trade and arrange its financing.

Second, they provide credit services along with other services for cross-border investments. In addition, banks provide (or facilitate) loans to private entities and corporations establishing business in foreign countries. (Loans to sovereign governments and their related risk characteristics will be discussed in the following chapter). A theoretical framework for analyzing private credit is presented in Appendix I.

We also discuss **countertrade** and how banks play an important role in the process. Countertrade has been gaining importance in recent years despite the fact that many trade barriers among countries have been lowered or removed. Finally, the process of project financing is analyzed and the role of the bank is highlighted in this process because of its growing importance everywhere in the world.

7.2   Cross-border Trade Transaction and its Financing

We discuss below the unique or special features of the cross-border trade, its mechanics (with special emphasis on the letter of credit), the shipment-related documents, and traditional payment modes.

7.2.1   Unique or special characteristics of cross-border trade

A cross-border trade transaction involves two basic aspects: delivery of goods and funds transfer. This transaction differs from its purely domestic counterpart in several respects:

- cross-border trade typically involves a foreign currency (at least for one party);
- customs for conducting business (especially for negotiating agreements) differ; and
- legal structures differ in enforcing the agreement or seeking retribution in case of its violation. For instance, the importer does not know whether the exporter has capability (or, worse still, willingness) to deliver goods (or services) of agreed-upon specifications (in terms of both quality and quantity) in time. For the exporter, the problem is whether the importer has the capability and willingness to meet agreed-upon payment in time. A bank primarily plays the role of minimizing the risks of non-performance by a party in the agreement and assuaging the concerns of the party it represents.

The major roadblocks such as tariffs, regulations, quotas, and laws necessitate special documents. At times these documents facilitate the trade; at other times they hinder the trade process.

7.2.2   Mechanics of the cross-border trade transaction

A typical cross-border trade transaction involves the following steps:

- First, a tentative agreement – regarding the quantity, quality, and price of the goods; their shipment mode and timing; and timing of payment and guarantors of the payment – is reached between the exporter and the importer. Frequently, this agreement is represented by a **proforma invoice**.

- Second, the exporter requires that the importing firm start negotiating with its bank to provide the exporter with a **letter of credit** (L/C) whereby the importer's bank guarantees to pay the exporting firm if the exporting firm fulfills its obligations spelled out in the L/C – typically by providing the issuing bank (or its designated agent) with specified documents as evidence of proper shipment of goods. From a bank's perspective, L/C is a payment mechanism, which is based solely on documentary evidence.
- Third, after the shipment of goods is made, the exporter forwards the shipping documents and the payment order or *draft* through the exporter's domestic bank to the importer's bank (or its designated agent), which issued the L/C.[1]
- Fourth, after reviewing and checking that all the documents conform with the conditions specified in the L/C, the importer's bank either makes payment on the sight draft or accepts the time draft from the exporter for future payment.[2] A time draft, when accepted – endorsed – by a bank becomes the **bankers' acceptance** (B/A). The B/A is a way to finance the trade transaction because the exporter's acceptance of future payment implies that the importer does not have to come up with payment till a later date. At the same time, the B/A is a negotiable obligation of the bank that endorsed the draft, that is, the owner of the document has the right to collect from the endorsing bank; hence, the exporter is able to sell it on a discounted basis (assuming the credit standing of the bank in the financial markets). Thus, financing of the trade transaction is taken over from the exporter to third parties.
- Finally, the bank collects payment from the importer and liquidates the B/A upon its maturity.

Most payment settlements are accomplished through interbank account transactions.[3] In recent years, electronic instructions have primarily replaced telexed instructions as a means of effective transfer. Two major networks owned by the banks for international payments are the **Society of Worldwide International Funds Transfer** (SWIFT) and the **Clearing House Interbank Payments Systems** (CHIPS).[4]

To the extent that payments involve a foreign currency, the bank also helps the importer in procuring it. (Issues regarding whether it should be obtained in the spot market when the payment is due or earlier in the forward market – or its variation in the spot-money market – so as to lock in the future spot rate have been discussed at length in Chapter 3; hence, they will not be discussed here.)

Special aspects of letters of credit

The most formalized payment mechanism in international trade is the L/C, which allows the importer to obtain more favorable terms as it assures the exporter of the payment guarantee by the L/C issuing bank. The nature of the guarantee depends on the type of the L/C.

An L/C may be issued in revocable or irrevocable form. An **irrevocable L/C**, which is more common in international trade transactions than the revocable L/C, cannot be modified or canceled without the consent of all parties involved. Another type of L/C is called the **transferable L/C**, which can be transferred from the original beneficiary to another beneficiary. Several conditions are required for this type of L/C. First, the instrument must be irrevocable. Second, the actual word "transferable" must appear on the document. Third, the transfer can take place only once. Partial transfers are allowed only if the L/C explicitly allows partial shipments. Finally, the applicant has to be informed about the identity of the secondary beneficiary at an appropriate time.

The bank, usually the exporter's bank, will try to verify that the L/C meets the guidelines under the Uniform Customs and Practice 500, the legal standards of the export/import industry in the USA. The L/C is then called an **advised L/C**. The advising bank does not have the obligation to fulfill the payment if the (L/C) issuing bank defaults. The advising bank charges a fee for this service.

When a foreign bank issues an L/C, the exporter faces payment risk of refusal of the foreign bank to honor the agreement at a later date and inability of the exporter to enforce the agreement in the court of law of the country where the foreign bank is domiciled. The exporter may request, as a result, its domestic bank to assume responsibility jointly with the bank that has issued the L/C. When another (typically domestic) bank adds its confirmation to the L/C, it is now called the **confirmed L/C**. The confirming bank is then required to act in the same way as the issuing bank as long as the guidelines of the L/C are met. This type of confirmed L/C means that the confirming bank has exposed itself to country and political risks associated with the transaction. The confirming bank charges a much higher fee (normally 0.125 percent of the invoice value) than the advising service bank because of this additional risk assumption.

Two aspects regarding the L/C are noteworthy. *First*, while the issuing bank relies on documents referred to in the L/C to ascertain fulfillment of the necessary conditions, the tasks of defining

- what are the requisite conditions,
- who are the proper agents to verify various conditions, and
- what documents the agents need to provide

rest solely on the shoulders of the importer. (Some typical documents associated with the L/C are briefly described below.)

If documents contain discrepancies that are at odds with the terms stated in the L/C, the bank should immediately notify the importer, who in turn decides whether these discrepancies are significant enough to violate the agreement. If there are discrepancies (the documents are not in order), and the bank fails to notify the importer, the importing firm may choose not to honor its commitment; in this case, the bank remains liable to the exporter. We will not pursue here issues of notification to the exporter and resolution of agreement violation, given their legal ramifications. Suffice it to note here that different legal jurisdictions may imply different rights and obligations for the bank than in, say, the USA.

Second, an L/C represents a contingent liability for the bank – liability arising if the importer defaults on the payment obligation defined by the L/C. Payoffs for the bank are the "premium" income or fees for originating the L/C, offset by the expense of reimbursing the exporter when the importer defaults. Essentially, the bank sells a put option.

Why would a bank accept such an asymmetric payoff? It is because the expected benefits are larger than the expected cost of paying off the exporter in case of the importer default. Three different scenarios are likely.

- First, the bank insists on having a solid collateral (e.g., T-bills or CD) from the importer. This collateral minimizes the bank's loss in case of default by the importer. For the importer, a bank's insistence on a liquid asset (T-bills or CD) as a collateral is a signal that the bank considers the importer's business too risky to be important currently or in the future. Of course, the importer would go through this trouble rather than paying off the exporter immediately because of recourse difficulties when the exporter does not fulfill its obligation. In this case, the bank is performing an agency function.
- Second, very likely, the collateral is illiquid; in this case, the bank is performing liquidity transformation in addition to being the agent for the importer by interposing its credit-worthiness.
- Third, when a bank does not have any explicit collateral, it is looking at the implicit collaterals such as current or future profitable business with the importer, and the consideration that the transaction is too small in comparison with the net worth of the importer.

7.2.3 Shipment-related documents

To avoid confusion in international trade transaction, there are **in**ternational **co**mmercial **terms** (**Incoterms**). Incoterms serve as benchmarks for interpretation of trade terms and are utilized by governments, legal authorities and practitioners worldwide for avoiding or resolving ambiguity in cross-border trade agreements.[5]

These are some of the typical documents used in a trade transaction.

1 *Commercial invoice*. It describes the product, unit amount, and price for the particular item being shipped. It also contains the names and addresses of the exporter and importer, the number of packages, the payment terms, the name of the vessel, and the ports of departure and destination.
2 *Packing list*. It outlines what invoices are being filled for the current shipment.
3 *Certificate of insurance*. All cargoes going abroad are insured. Most of the insurance contracts used today are under an open (or floating) policy. This policy automatically covers all shipments made by the exporter, thereby eliminating the need for arranging individual insurance for each shipment. Certain transactions require insurance on the product due to the expense of replacing the goods if lost, stolen, or damaged.
4 *Bill of lading*. It is a title document that shows ownership. The **bill of lading** (B/L) serves three main functions.
    - It is a contract between the carrier and the exporter (shipper) whereby the carrier agrees to carry the goods from port of shipment to port of destination.
    - It is the shipper's receipt of goods.
    - It is a document that assigns control over the goods (a holder of the bill of lading is able to obtain possession of goods).

A B/L is usually prefaced with the means of transportation, such as **Ocean bill of lading** (for the purpose of sea transportation) or **Airway bill of lading** (for air transportation purpose). Once the bill of lading has been received, the transaction cannot be reversed. It is the final document before shipment begins.

Specific situations may call for additional documents. For instance, a **Certificate of Origin** is required when goods from a country are not allowed, are subject to quota restrictions, or are given preferential tariff treatment in the importing country. Similarly, when quality is critical, both parties may agree to appoint a third party as the arbiter of quality, and its certificate has to be included by the exporter with other required documents.

7.2.4   Bilateral payment or financing modes

We have already seen the role played by a draft and an L/C in settling a trade transaction. There are three traditional alternatives where financing is provided by one of the two parties in the transaction: cash advance, open account, and consignment. These alternatives involve a bank only peripherally. Still, all five alternatives imply different degrees of risk assumed by a bank's client, and the choice reflects the client's risk preference. Hence, these three alternatives are described here.

Cash in advance

The exporter receives funds in advance or when the product is shipped. The advantage to the exporter is the immediate cash inflow and use of the money. The importing firm, on the other hand, loses an important leverage against the exporter in case of tardy delivery, non-delivery, or delivery of unacceptable products. Advance payment is typically requested when

- the importer's order requires custom-made parts that cannot be used elsewhere by the exporter or a tailor-made product that has no market elsewhere;
- the importer's credit is marginal;
- the importer's country faces unusual uncertainties; or
- a combination of the factors listed above.

If the justification for such payment is significant out-of-pocket-cost for the exporter, the importer's bank may suggest that the exporter post a **performance bond** that insures the importer against non-performance by the exporter. Alternatively, the exporter may be offered an installment payment schedule against the portion of the job completed. Marginal credit becomes an issue only when the importer's bank is unwilling to issue an L/C or its L/C is unacceptable to the exporter. A constructive solution would be to obtain confirmation of the L/C from an acceptable bank. Similarly, risks arising from uncertainties in the importer's country may be mitigated by the importer depositing funds in an escrow account in a neutral country. These alternatives to cash-in-advance will not compensate the importer for lost time, but they would certainly assuage the exporter's concerns and at the same time minimize the importer's loss of prepayment in case of non-performance by the exporter.

Open account

In an open account arrangement, the exporter establishes payment conditions and ships the goods before payment is received. The exporter thus relies on the importers' ability and willingness to pay after shipment. The open account method is used when there is an ongoing relationship between the two parties, and there is stability in the political environment in which the importer conducts business. The bank's primary role is centered on conversion of currency.

Consignment

In a consignment transaction, the exporter ships the merchandise and sends the shipping documents to the importer. The exporter retains title of the merchandise. When the importer sells the goods, the proceeds less the markup are sent to the exporter. The bank is usually not involved in this transaction (except for fund transfers or payment) because the importer serves as an agent for the exporter for a fee.

7.3 Trade-related Financing and Risk Insurance

Trade financing methods mentioned above are either strictly documentary credits or do not involve outside parties. There are additional avenues for arranging trade financing. Three major parties help promote trade and facilitate trade finance:

- financial institutions (primarily commercial banks and insurance companies);
- government agencies; and
- private organizations.

These entities frequently work together to finance or facilitate trade.

7.3.1 Financial institutions

We will consider financing made available to exporters as well as importers.

Financing for importers

When an importing firm orders goods from the exporter, it may not have adequate liquidity to finance the transaction. Instead, it borrows from its local bank. Normally, the lending bank requires the importer to provide a **trust receipt**, which transfers the title of the goods to the bank. The importer is able to withdraw goods by arranging requisite funds or showing the bank a confirmed order for the goods. In the latter case, the bank may be assigned the accounts receivable that arise from the trade. Sometimes the bank and the importer can make an arrangement whereby the bank can withdraw money from the importer's account on designated dates.

As discussed in more detail in the later section, banks in the exporting countries can arrange with their export-import banks to provide financing to importers. Foreign governments and government agencies promote exports by guaranteeing loans made to the buyers (importers).

Financing for exporters

The major source of financing for exporters, in addition to discounted banker's acceptance and trade acceptance, is either *discounting* the foreign receivables or assigning them to a *factor*. The major difference between the two methods is that **factoring** is typically *without recourse*, that is, the exporter is not liable for non-payment by the importer. The factoring of exports is more highly developed in Europe than elsewhere but it is gaining recognition among exporters outside Europe.

Forfeiting is typically used in a transaction encompassing multi-period payments. The importer provides a set of promissory notes (each one representing individual payments) to the exporter; and notes are fully guaranteed[6] by the importer's bank. The exporter is able to discount *without recourse* these notes with the forfeiter, who in turn assumes the risk of collecting payments on the notes upon maturity from the importer or the guaranteeing bank.

Forfeiting, common in several European countries, is not unlike factoring in the USA. The major differences are:

- Factoring involves the seller's accounts receivables; thus the transaction does not require direct acknowledgment of obligation by the buyer-importer. Forfeiting is based on the importer's promissory notes and requires guarantee by the importer's bank.
- The short-term nature of factoring contrasts with the multi-period character of forfeiting.
- Factoring does not provide full hedging of risks since it typically requires coinsurance by the seller-exporter. For instance, the exporter may obtain, say, 90 percent in the gross proceeds from the factor; the balance is paid upon satisfactory settlement of the transaction by the importer.

Both forfeiting and factoring are expensive ways of financing trade, partly because the acquiring parties do not trade the instruments, but hold them till maturity; in the process, they assume the liquidity risk. Further, no efforts have been made to standardize the documents; hence, transaction costs for originating the arrangements are not insubstantial. Banks undertake these activities either directly or through a stand-alone unit of the **bank holding company**.

Attempts have been made in the USA to adapt forfeiting by developing **export trade notes** (ETNs) that would preserve the feature of non-recourse to the exporter. Adaptation is designed to overcome problems of factoring or forfeiting, specifically, to improve legal enforceability of ETNs by standardizing the agreements and laws in different jurisdictions. Such an adaptation, in turn, would improve marketability of the notes in the secondary market. To our knowledge, ETNs have not become a workable alternative for export financing.

Leasing

Financial institutions frequently provide lease financing to importers of durable goods. Two considerations are typical in the lease transactions. First, although the importing firm is able to enjoy the benefits of the use of the asset, it does not have title to the ownership. This precludes it, for instance, from using the asset as a collateral for financing. Second, the term of the lease is multi-period, often approximating the economic life of the goods. Thus it is clearly a financing (rather than an operating) lease.

A bank plays two different roles in lease financing. It may (a) provide on its own such financing, or (b) arrange to bring additional parties for the predominant portion of financing. In either case, its familiarity with imperfections in financial or goods markets enables it to partake a portion of the profit from arbitraging such imperfections. In the second case, it also requires an extensive network of connections with other financial institutions and an understanding of their needs.

7.3.2 Government agencies

Export–import bank

Governments all over the world try to increase exports by providing loans, guarantees, subsidized credit, and insurance for commercial and political risks. They justify the support on a variety of grounds: domestic growth in economic activities, employment, foreign exchange earnings, enhancing competitiveness of key domestic industries, to name a few. It is easy to see that an aggressive program by a country can provide its exporter a significant – or unfair – advantage over competitors from other countries. In 1978, the OECD nations agreed to abide by guidelines on matters such as the nature of subsidies in the interest rate charge and length of credit period, in order to prevent escalating distortions that may ultimately harm the growth in the global trade. Still, the opaque nature of programs allow countries to create favorable distortions for their own industries at the expense of competition elsewhere.

The US **Export-Import Bank**, also known as the **Eximbank**, is an autonomous agency that obtains funds from the US Congress and provides exporters the necessary financial assistance to compete with other countries through a variety of export financing and guarantee programs.[7] All are designed to support US exports, irrespective of whether the eventual recipient of the loans or guarantees is foreign or domestic.

Major programs include the following.

(a)   *Direct loans*. To help finance big-ticket items (costing $10 million or more) on extended terms, the Eximbank makes direct loans, typically not exceeding 65 percent of the contract amount, to foreign importers. Loans are in US$ and payments are made directly to the US exporters. The foreign buyer has to come up with a 15 percent down payment. The balance of 20 percent (or more), which generally comes from a commercial bank (or a consortium like PEFCO described below), may be covered for commercial and political risks through guarantee from the Eximbank. The bank may also obtain fixed-rate funding from the Eximbank for funneling credit to foreign buyers. The Eximbank requires amortization of the direct loan over a period of 5–10 years.

(b) *Guarantees*. The Eximbank provides unconditional guarantee to a US commercial bank for repayment on the loan extended by the bank to the foreign buyer. Both commercial (default by the buyer) and political (e.g., payment freeze by the foreign government) risks are covered under this guarantee.

Sometimes, an exporter extends credit to the foreign customer over a number of years and then sells the installment receivables to a commercial bank or another financial institution. The Eximbank extends its guarantee to the commercial bank to induce it to buy the receivables without recourse. In this case, the guarantee typically covers all political risk but only 10 percent of the commercial credit risk.

Under the **Working Capital Guarantee Program** that encourages lenders to make working capital loans to US exporters, the Eximbank provides repayment guarantees to lenders on secured, short-term working capital to qualified exporters. Such a loan is important for the exporter fulfilling a custom order that has a gestation lag of several months. If the exporter defaults on the loan, the Eximbank covers 90 percent of the principal of the loan and interest.

(c) *Short-term discount loan program*. This program was initiated in early 1972 to make an additional financing source available to exporters. Under this program, short-term export paper is discounted to supplement, and not supplant, private sources of funds. Hence, each applicant must certify to the Eximbank that a discount is necessary to complete the transaction and that it cannot be financed in, say, the B/A market. The B/A market is limited to 180 days while the discount loan program allows loans with maturity up to 364 days. Thus, this program complements the private financing source.

Commodity Credit Corporation

The Commodity Credit Corporation (CCC), an agency within the Department of Agriculture, provides assistance in the production and marketing of US agricultural commodities or other related functions.

Since agricultural commodities are consumed in a relatively short period of time, a prudent bank does not normally extend export credits more than 180 days. The CCC has initiated a program that makes financing available for up to three years.

The CCC also has other programs to promote agricultural products. For example, the CCC can enter into an agreement with a commercial firm in the importing country that buys the agricultural commodities from the CCC on the long-term credit and resells them locally. The commercial firm, using the proceeds, agrees to either promote US agricultural commodities or help economic development in other friendly nations.

Overseas Private Investment Corporation

The **Overseas Private Investment Corporation** (OPIC) established in 1971 is wholly owned by the US Treasury. Its objective is to stimulate and facilitate US private equity and loan investments in, as well as trade with, friendly developing countries.

To assist US companies investing in developing countries, OPIC provides investment insurance for political risks but does not offer insurance for normal business or exchange rate risk. Loans made to private enterprises in developing countries are guaranteed 100 percent by

OPIC; the proceeds of such loans may be used to buy raw materials, equipment or services either from the USA or less developed countries.

7.3.3 Private institutions

Private Export Funding Corporation

The **Private Export Funding Corporation** (PEFCO), organized primarily by a group of US commercial banks in 1970, has the objective of facilitating medium- and long-term credit to foreign buyers of US goods. It obtains funds through issue of its own securities in the USA or abroad. The Eximbank guarantees interest payments on PEFCO's own debt obligations, thus making these securities more attractive.

PEFCO helps finance US exporters to sell big-ticket items such as power plants or wide-bodied jet aircraft on a long-term basis. Its financing is complementary to other major sources in two ways. First, as stated above, financing by the Eximbank (e.g., 65 percent) and commercial banks (up to 20 percent) is supplemented by PEFCO for the remaining 20–25 percent of the total amount. Second, big-ticket financing normally requires a credit term of 10 years. The commercial bank may typically finance loans up to the first five years; PEFCO finances the middle parts (usually 5–10 years) and the Eximbank will finance the final part of the loans.

Foreign Credit Insurance Association

The **Foreign Credit Insurance Association** (FCIA) was formed under the aegis of the Eximbank by a group of insurance companies in 1962. The FCIA works closely with the Eximbank and is a private sector entity that provides coverage for commercial and political contingencies.

The FCIA covers various types of commercial risks including non-payment risk by importers and preshipment risk. The latter risk occurs if the order obtained by the US exporter for manufacturing special goods is canceled before shipment and receipt of payment. Its coverage of political risk includes a government freeze on debt service or cancellation of a previously approved import license by the government.

Insurance from the FCIA is normally sold through insurance brokers and agents to the exporter. Many large insurance brokerage houses have an FCIA specialist on their staff that can underwrite insurance and offer general assistance to exporters. In addition to insurance brokers and agents, the FCIA obtains a good deal of insurance business from the commercial banks that recommend their clients to buy the insurance protection.

The exporter then both assigns the policy (that provides 90 percent of the coverage) and sells the foreign buyer's promissory notes to a commercial bank. Although the sale of the promissory notes is without recourse to the exporter, the exporter is required to bear 10 percent of the risk through coinsurance.

Opportunities and challenges for banks

For a business interested in foreign trade, funding and insurance programs are not only bewildering but also a source of uncertainty and anxiety. Even if it identifies the right program for funding and insurance, there is no assurance that it is qualified to obtain the program. As mentioned above, the opaqueness of programs to an extent is deliberate: to camouflage the extent of aid or assistance that may even violate the OECD covenants – if not in letter, then in spirit.

A bank can invest resources in making sense out of bewildering and changing requirements imposed by a variety of programs. The resultant familiarity would enable it to help clients determine their eligibility for desirable programs, select the right program with minimum cost and risk, fill the necessary forms, complete laborious paperwork, and obtain non-overlapping complementary sources of funding and insurance in a reasonable amount of time.

If a bank is able to generate sufficient trade-related financing business, it can securitize these financing credits by issuing securities against them. These securities raise funds immediately, and they are serviced by the cash flow generated by the credits. This way, the bank is able to liquidate its investment in the financing credits. Securitization of export credits backed by government agencies has managed to lower the cost of trade financing. A major problem, however, is the Eximbank's insistence on coinsurance for interest cost. When an importer defaults, the Eximbank provides interest rate compensation of only the prevailing T-bill rate + 1 percent; hence the bank bears the loss of interest income it originally anticipated over and above the compensation guaranteed by the Eximbank. Further, the Eximbank charges guarantee fees of 0.5 percent per annum. Since a sale of **securitized assets** is normally without recourse to the seller bank, the seller bank obtains fewer funds, increasing thereby the effective cost of securitization.

7.4   Countertrade

Countertrade refers to a wide range of business arrangements in the sale of a good where payment involves forms other than (or at times, in addition to) cash.

Countertrade can be conducted in a variety of alternative forms as discussed below.[8]

(a)   **Barter**. Barter entails a simultaneous exchange of goods between two parties. However, it is possible that one party may fulfill its obligation earlier than the other party. We will designate the party fulfilling its obligations earlier as "exporter," and the other party as the "importer," although both parties are exporters in the final analysis. The following aspects of a barter trade should be noted:

- Although each party may have an idea of the value of its purchase, a value is never assigned. When pricing is opaque due to, say, significant amount of fixed cost, the seller is able to employ price discrimination without any adverse reactions from other customers.
- Although currency risk does not exist, other risks may be present. Specifically the default risk still exists for the "exporter" (party fulfilling its obligation earlier). As in the case of ordinary transactions, a bank can provide a standby L/C to alleviate this risk.
- The exporter may not have familiarity with the marketing of goods it imports. As a result, it incurs additional cost of marketing these goods.

- Proceeds from the sale of such goods may involve time delay; hence, the cash cycle for the exporter may lengthen, necessitating additional external financing.
- A barter transaction may be viewed as a combination of export and a forward import contract by the exporter, and vice versa by the importer.

A barter transaction can be extended to include a variety of products. For example, in a triangular barter transaction, company A buys fruits from company B, which in turn buys wheat from company C. Company C will buy rice from company A to complete the barter arrangement.

(b) **Counterpurchase**. Counterpurchase or a *parallel barter* has two separate and independent contracts each specifying the commodity to be purchased by a party in a designated time period. The value of each commodity to be traded is typically specified. For example, in the first contract, company A (in one country) will buy wheat from company B (in another country) with cash. The second contract, which is conditional on the first contract, specifies that company B buys an equivalent amount (in value) of another product (say, wine) from company A within a given time span, also for cash. The performance of the second contract is guaranteed via a performance bond or provision of penalties.

The transfer of credit by the exporter to third parties is typically not permitted in developing countries. These countries encourage or require counterpurchases because they do not have access to financing imports and demand for their exports is sluggish or shrinking; a transfer to, say, an existing buyer of the export defeats the goal of expansion of the market for exports.

If the exporting firm cannot use the counterpurchase itself, costs of searching and identifying user-customers as well as other marketing costs may deter it from entering into a counterpurchase agreement in the first place.

(c) **Buy-back**. Buy-back typically involves the building of a manufacturing or processing facility by a company in another country, in return for partial or full repayment in the form of products generated by the facility. The company is likely to have operating control for a specified period, at the end of which the control is transferred to the local government. This arrangement is known as **build–operate–transfer** (BOT). This arrangement may last anywhere from one year to multi-years (5–10 years).

The buy-back agreement shares one trait of the counterpurchase arrangement: there are two separate contracts covering each leg of the transaction. Hence the agreement contains flexibility for financial settlement, guarantees, and deliveries for each leg.

Typically, the exporting company agreeing to the BOT arrangement under a buy-back agreement is not just building a facility; it agrees to transfer technology in the form of equipment or processes. Given its technical edge, its bargaining position is stronger than that of the exporter under the plain counterpurchase agreement.

(d) **Switch**. A switch is a counterpurchase agreement where the original exporter is allowed to transfer credit to a third party. Thus it overcomes the exporter's problem of first buying and then distributing designated counterpurchase goods in the pure counterpurchase arrangement.

(e) **Offset**. An offset agreement typically involves purchase of a big-ticket item by an importing country. This purchase entails a broad range of commercial and industrial compensation schemes. Purchase of aircrafts or a satellite communications system by a country, for instance, may require the supplier to construct a production facility that produces components utilized in the product or system.

Typically, an offset is a counterpurchase arrangement without any restrictions on the exporter for finding a third party that would buy the excess credit. Thus it has an edge over the switch arrangement where the exporter has to find a third party that can use the credit for specific products or services.

A countertrade survey (Bussard 1987) found that, among all the barter trade arrangements, counterpurchase (55 percent) is the most important in terms of usage, followed by offset (24 percent), buy-back (9 percent), switch trading (8 percent) and barter (4 percent).

7.4.1 Bank's role in countertrade

A countertrade transaction minimizes use of a currency in settling the transaction. Two interrelated issues arise:

- Are currency market impediments the sole source of stimulus for countertrade?
- Does the bank have profit potential that would justify its involvement in countertrade activities?

Although currency shortage was a major force during the Bretton Woods period, today there are other equally, if not more, significant factors for countertrade. A major source of funding for LDCs dried out when commercial banks redirected their lending activities to entities in developed countries in the aftermath of sovereign debt crisis in the 1980s. At the same time, increased competition in the volatile goods markets forced producers in the industrialized nations to come up with creative financing solutions for maintaining or enhancing their sales. Furthermore, a need for keeping competition at bay has meant that these solutions should be proprietary or opaque. Because countertrade is a bundle of marketing and financing activities, it allows the supplier considerable flexibility in providing price concessions, for instance, without generating adverse reactions from either competition or existing customers.

Finally, consider the perspective of a business firm in a developing country that does not have problems in obtaining foreign exchange. To date, the firm has marketed its products exclusively in the domestic market; however, it would like to exploit the potential of an unfamiliar, industrialized market. A countertrade transaction with a supplier from the industrialized market allows it to forge a "partnership" with the supplier. This relationship serves as a foundation for overcoming impediments in the goods market, whether they are a maze of regulations or structural impediments such as tastes and prejudices, that affect the acceptance of its product.

In brief, impediments in the goods market as well as in financial markets foster countertrade.

What role can a bank play in countertrade? For countertrade transactions, the bank can utilize its organizational resources and global network of partners and clientele to identify opportunities for countertrade, especially potential markets requiring specific products, and link exporters (who have a countertrade requirement) with the interested buyers in the identified pool of countries.

Investment in developing the organizational expertise is essential; however, it can be parlayed into profitability by paying attention to another critical dimension. Bundling of different functions in a countertrade transaction also means that the transaction represents a bundle of different types of risks, such as performance risk, marketing risk, and the agency risk.

These risks are not only dissimilar for the two parties, but are also different from a conventionally financed trade transaction.

The bank's advisory role in countertrade business thus involves

- assessing the risk of the transaction by identifying and evaluating individual sources of the overall risk,
- unbundling and apportioning those risks to a party which has unique capacity to bear them,
- shifting risks to third parties in a cost effective way, and
- determining that such reduction in cost and risk justifies for each party not to employ the conventional trade transaction.

A bank helps a US computer manufacturer in entering into a counterpurchase agreement with a Malaysian company, whereby the US company sells subassemblies to the Malaysian firm on a 90-day payment basis, and it buys computers from the Malaysian firm on a credit period of 120 days. In order to avoid financial hardship on the Malaysian firm, the bank agrees to provide a standby L/C on behalf of the US company to the Malaysian firm, enabling it to obtain local financing on the strength of the L/C.

This transaction allows the US company to contain both performance risk and credit risk in a rather simple way: it would hold up payments on its obligation if the Malaysian firm produces computers of unacceptable quality or is tardy in its delivery or payment to the US company. Note that currency or financing risk is not the central issue here, and the bank's financing role is peripheral.

In recent years, a new instrument facilitating countertrade agreement has been devised, as illustrated in the following example.

Suppose Mosaic, a US exporter, is about to enter into a countertrade transaction in Romania. Mosaic has been given a menu of goods for which it has to locate prospective buyers in the USA. With the help of its bank, Mosaic has located prospective US buyers who would buy a given quantity of goods that meet precise specifications at prices not exceeding appropriate ceilings. Rather than locating and negotiating with Romanian exporters who would supply these goods, Mosaic may issue a transferable instrument for imports, called the *international trade certificate* (ITC), and its Romanian holder is entitled to export to the USA specified goods of requisite quality within a designated time period for US$. Mosaic's bank can play several of the following roles, directly or through its correspondent bank network:

- get the certificate endorsed by the Romanian Central Bank;
- place (sell) the certificate with (to) Romanian exporters;
- confirm the certificate (i.e., guarantee payment on the ITC) for the Romanian exporters.

7.5   Banking Services and Multinational Corporations

An MNC contemplating business activities in a local economy may be unfamiliar with the local environment and thus would need more than money to carry out business activities. A bank can play a constructive role in facilitating access to pertinent information on issues such as

- timing for undertaking investment in light of the local regulatory, political, and economic climate;
- location of the plant in terms of considerations such as
  - local government structure as well as its ability and receptiveness to facilitate the MNC's investment;
  - state of the local economy, including availability and prices of real estate, taxes, labor pool and wage structure, banks' health and capability and eagerness to provide conventional and unique services needed by the MNC; and
  - infrastructure of transportation, telecommunications, health services, as well as educational and training facilities.

At this initial exploratory stage, the MNC may decide to enter the country on a joint venture basis. The bank can provide valuable information on the prospective partner's

- financial health;
- connections in the local business community and government bureaucracy;
- reputation for integrity and professionalism; and
- familiarity with unique or special aspects related to marketing and production of contemplated products.

Furthermore, it may help its client analyze the (a) congruency and consistency of goals of the two parties, and (b) complementarities of resources each brings to the table.

Financing of the initial investment may be local – in the home country – or in the international or offshore markets. Maturity, terms, and denomination of currencies have ramifications in terms of not just the cost but also risk, flexibility, and control. To what extent and at what price undesirable aspects can be mitigated is an area where the bank can play an important advisory role.

One example for creativity in financing is through identifying disparity in regulations, laws, and taxation locally, in the offshore markets, and in the USA.

Suppose a plant in a foreign country can be financed through debt financing or leasing. In the case of debt, it can be structured in a way that represents equity for investors (giving them a tax shield on a portion of "dividend" income) and rating agencies (no adverse impact of financing on the MNC's rating that would have increased its cost of raising funds) but is debt for the local MNC affiliate, allowing it to deduct interest for tax purposes.

A lease, on the other hand, is defined differently in different countries. One critical issue is to distinguish a lease from an installment purchase. If it is a lease, ownership and thereby tax deductibility of depreciation expense on the asset rests with the funds providers.[9] If it is installment finance, the borrower owns the asset and is able to deduct the depreciation expense for tax purposes. Countries follow disparate practice in defining this distinction. Some countries follow the *letter* of agreement underlying the financial arrangement. Other countries consider the *spirit* of agreement. In this case, it is possible to structure an agreement in such a way that tax deductibility of depreciation expense is allowed for funds providers (a lease) in one country and the asset user (an installment purchase) in the other country, a practice of "double dipping." The asset may be destined for a third country, where its classification as a lease may be preferred because the asset user may not have initially any income to offset depreciation income, and lease payments may not require "interest withholding" tax, a tax levied on income earned by foreign, non-resident sources of financing. A lease that is structured to encompass three different locations enables the firm to pay tax and regulations arbitrage by lowering the cost without raising the risk of financing.

Once operations are set up locally, the bank can arrange for a full range of banking services to the MNC's local affiliate that include cash management services (including foreign exchange procurement and currency exposure), employee services (payroll, pension, and profit sharing), private banking services to upper level management, short-term loans, and capital expenditure financing. A bank with a well-established retail (or branch) banking or strong correspondent bank network has a decisive advantage over others in providing special services.

Lockbox Service is an example of such a service. When an MNC affiliate has a high volume of checks from customers all over the country, check receipts, their deposits and clearance each require time to clear, that is, each step has a float. Under a lockbox system, the bank enables the affiliate to avoid or minimize the "transit" float required in postal transmission of the check to the affiliate's offices, the "process" float for recording and depositing payments at the affiliate's office, and "clearance" float for clearing checks locally where the customer maintains the account.

The bank also helps design payment products to control their outgoing payments and hence increase their efficiency because it takes time for the paid checks to clear. The bank will try to fully utilize these floats to earn extra interest for its clients.

7.6 Special Financing Needs of Customers

Bank customers, especially large MNCs, are often able to bypass banks and directly access, for instance, offshore or domestic financial markets for routine financing needs. Commercial papers and floating rate notes by these firms have allowed them to reduce the need for short- and medium-term financing from commercial banks.

There are, however, two areas where a bank can play a vital role: project finance and financing of cross-border merger and acquisition.

7.6.1 Project finance

Historically, large-scale projects, particularly those related to infrastructure in the economy, were the exclusive domain of the government or quasi-government autonomous agencies. Over the last two decades, construction, financing and management of projects such as pipelines for oil and gas, tunnels, bridges, electricity generating facilities and hospitals are routinely undertaken by private businesses all over the world. In LDCs, a major challenge faced by these businesses is that the domestic financial market is not well organized and hence project organizers cannot raise needed money.

Projects may be classified into two categories.

- *Stock-type project.* The project exploits the existing stock of the goods. Examples include mines, oil and gas field project, which terminates when the stock is exhausted.
- *Flow-type project.* The project generates a flow of business or traffic. Examples are pipelines, power generating facility, toll bridges, toll highways, tunnels, and hospitals.

Unique or special features of project finance

Project finance has several features that distinguish it from the traditional financing method.

1 The sponsor(s) sets up a separate legal entity for the project; this entity assumes all risks of the project.

- The project's feasibility, construction, financing, and operations involve a considerable amount of time and uncertainty, in addition to an enormous amount of financial resources. The distinct identity allows the sponsor to obtain funding without recourse to itself, in effect creating a firewall between the project and its ongoing business.
- Independent entity also means that funds providers do not face the problem of contamination of the project flows with those of the sponsor's ongoing business. To the extent that information on the sponsor's business is not transparent, the potential contamination will only manage to raise the cost of funding for the project (Shah and Thakor 1987).
- While "without recourse" qualification gives the sponsor a legal escape hatch, any unfair treatment accorded to the lenders would have a serious deleterious impact on its future ability to access financial markets. Consequently the legal protection is resorted to by the sponsor for failure of the project on "reasonable" grounds, typically causes that are beyond its control and could not have been anticipated under normal circumstances.

2 The project (vehicle) company has *well-defined objectives* achievable in foreseeable future; and the legal entity has a *finite life*, which ends upon achieving the objectives.

- Statements on objectives may include, for instance, "operation of the plant 5 years after it comes on stream and is utilized at least 50 percent of the capacity".
- End of the project company's entity may be in terms of handing over the project and its management to the government, or floating equity that would transfer the ownership of the project to stockholders at large.

3 The project company enters into comprehensive contracts with different parties: contractors, suppliers, project manager, lenders, and even government. These contracts are to mitigate **agency problems** and risks associated with the project.

- Each party has greater familiarity with a facet of the project it is responsible for than the sponsor. As a result, there is information asymmetry and potential problems of adverse selection and moral hazard.[10] Avoidance of these problems may require detailed specification of covenants, warranties, and incentives, among other things.
- These contracts are very likely customized; as a result, they are not only time consuming but also entail substantial legal expertise and expense to ascertain covenants' legal enforceability that increases the front-end cost of the project.

4 The project company employs a *high degree of financial leverage*.

- The parent company or sponsor retains a portion of the equity of the company. Expenses of the initial feasibility study and efforts for involving other parties before the project company is formed are only partially reimbursed to the parent and other parties whose expertise is used for determining the feasibility of the project. All these parties are compensated through equity participation.
- Equity participation, a form of incentives, is provided to different parties so as to mitigate the agency problem of moral hazard.
- Initial public offering of equity in the project company allows the sponsor to transform the narrow clientele (a few owners) structure into a broad clientele base with many stockholders. The conversion of a "private" firm into a public company, subjects the project to closer scrutiny and reporting requirements by different regulatory bodies. Financial flexibility is thereby achieved at the cost of increased inflexibility in other areas.
- Timing is very crucial for an initial public offering. At an early stage, the complex and delicate negotiating process contains proprietary information that cannot be made public;[11] public ownership, however, requires transparency that is antithetical to such negotiating process. Further, incentive schemes employed to resolve agency problems are likely to be misunderstood or misinterpreted when they are made public. It is only when these problems have been resolved or have receded in significance that an initial public offering of equity can be seriously contemplated.
- Lenders, assuming hefty risk, rely heavily on the sponsor's credibility based on successful completion of similar project(s) in the past.
- Banks provide substantial capital investments either through a loan syndicate or on their own. Reliance on bank financing (which is relatively short-term with maturity of 5–7 years) instead of alternative long-term sources like a bond issue reflects the agency cost of debt financing. It is expedient to share the proprietary information on the project with private lenders than a large number of bondholders. Banks are thus likely to monitor the project more effectively than the scattered body of bond holders.
- To ensure loan service, banks may require debt service linked to the project's output (rather than its operating cash flow).
- The project sponsor enters into a "working capital maintenance" arrangement with banks to insure sufficient liquidity for the project during the construction phase.
- Besides the bank loan, there are other financing components in project financing such as sponsor loans (loans advanced by the sponsors), supplier credits, customer credits, and leasing.
- Often multilateral agencies, such as the World Bank (in particular, its agency, the International Finance Corporation) and Regional Development Banks, as well as government agencies like OPIC may be involved in the project finance. Although financial

contributions by these agencies are relatively small, their participation lends credibility to the project thus facilitating financing and in general enhancing viability of the project.

- Third-party assurance may also be given to the lenders.
- A bond issue for project financing is only likely for a low-risk project. By the same token, when the front-end uncertainties of the project are resolved, bond financing may replace existing bank loans.
- In contrast, conventional financing of a capital project typically
  - does not call for a separate legal entity;
  - may have risk that is, while significant, not overwhelming;
  - does not allow predominance of debt finance when operating risk is significant;
  - allows predominance of debt financing in the face of high operating risk only at a very high cost, under stringent constraints on managers, under significant provision of collateral by the parent, or a combination of all of the above provisions.

Illustration of stand-alone project financing

Below we show how the payoffs to the project company and creditors differ under the project finance vis-à-vis the conventional finance.

Assumptions:

- Existing debt obligation of the parent or sponsors without the project = $100.
- Debt obligation for the project = $100.

Given the above assumption, the company that undertakes a project without using the project financing arrangement (i.e., setting up a separate company) will have to pay $200 debt service in the next period. Assume there are four states in the next period that illustrates the importance of project financing that can separate the cash flows from the parent. The cash flows from the existing assets and projects taken together are as shown in Table 7.1.

- If state 1 occurs, both with and without project, the cash flows are insufficient to service debt of both the parent and the project. Thus the firm fails.
- If state 2 occurs, the parent will fail but the project by itself survives.
- If state 3 occurs, the project fails because the cash flows are insufficient to service its debt, but the parent survives because its cash flows exceed its debt service. (This case illustrates the importance of project finance and without recourse debt.)
- State 4 illustrates the coinsurance aspect. The cash flows of the parent by itself are sufficient to service the total debts (parent and project) while the project has insufficient funds to service its own debt.

All these states show the importance of how financing affects the likelihood of bankruptcy for the firm.

Risk of project finance

For the project finance, various parties (the bank, the project manager, sponsors, and others) assume different types of risks. Table 7.2 shows the different types of risk involved in many typical project financing arrangements.

Table 7.1 Payoff scenarios for project finance

State of nature	1	2	3	4
Cash flows – parent	60	60	120	250
Cash flows – project	60	120	60	60
Panel A: Payoffs in traditional finance (i.e., without project finance)				
Debt	120*	180*	180*	200
Equity	0	0	0	110
Panel B: Payoffs to parent and project (given project financing)				
Parent debt	60*	60*	100	100
Parent equity	0	0	20	150
Project debt	60*	100	60*	60*
Project equity (sponsors)	0	20	0	0

* Denotes short of paying the debt services (i.e. cases of default).

Table 7.2 Typical risk of project finance

Risk type	Nature of risk	Who bears the risk?
Input	Basic raw materials may be unavailable	Suppliers
Market	Market conditions change due to changes in demand	Banks/project managers
Operating	Operating costs such as labor and materials may change	Bankers/project managers
Political	Expropriation, civil unrest, terrorism	Government and indirectly all parties
Technical	Cost overrun	Project managers
Timing	Possible delays affecting cash flows	Project managers/ Equity holders

Structuring project finance and allocation of risk: An illustration

The success of project finance rests on the ability of the sponsors to obtain requisite financing at the least cost without constraining management flexibility or increasing bankruptcy risk. Enormity of operating or business risk implies that predominant or exclusive funding by lenders would mean lenders' demand for very high returns. Thus the most critical task in a project finance is to unbundle risks and apportion risks to parties which are best suited to assume the allotted risk without additional compensation that a party unfamiliar with the risk would demand; and partition cash flows among these parties.

As an illustration, consider a mining project that would take three years for completion. Demand for the mineral is very strong but volatile. Prices have increased over the last decade at a rate higher than inflation. The government's attitude can be best described as "benign neglect." The sponsor has completed the feasibility study, and found that viability of the project depends on it obtaining funds for no more than the going rate for an investment grade company. The sponsor funds the project in the following way.

1   It obtains a subordinated loan from a customer for 25 percent of the construction finance at an interest rate 60 bps below the current rate for an investment grade bond. In return, the customer agrees to buy 50 percent of the projected output annually at a current price adjusted for cumulative inflation rate. If the customer chooses not to buy in a given year, the proportional debt service scheduled for that year will be postponed without additional compensation. If the customer needs additional output up to 10 percent, the price would be the average of the adjusted price and the prevailing market price.

In effect, the customer has been able to lock in a favorable price schedule for a sizable quantity; further, it has purchased an option on an additional 10 percent of the output; in return, it pays the premium of accepting lower compensation on the debt financing it provides. The customer also obtains flexibility in purchasing lower output by forsaking proportionate debt service for that period.

At the same time, the debt subordination serves as an equity for senior debt.

2   It signs a contract with an insurance company for the balance of financing need at the interest rate of 20 bps above the investment grade bond issue today. The insurance company would provide the funds only upon construction of the plant in three years.

There is no margin for error in the construction phase; furthermore, funds are needed for financing the construction phase.

Favorable terms of the insurance loan reflects containment of (a) market risk due to customer contract, and (b) avoidance of construction risk.

3   Its bank agrees to provide a bridge loan for three years at an average rate of 20 bps below the investment grade bond issue. It would disburse funds only when the designated portion is completed and certified; further, it would hold 10 percent of the amount billed in escrow; and release the escrow when an outside agency certifies satisfactory completion of the job.

The bank was able to charge the lower rate because it does not provide the entire loan. Further, if the job is satisfactorily completed, it has little risk in obtaining funds from the insurance company. Finally, it is also monitoring the contractor's performance on construction, and in return is able to access the funds held in escrow.

4   The contractor posts a performance bond that would reimburse the project for the unfinished portion of the construction, if the contractor withdraws from the project. The sponsor agrees to provide a bonus in terms of equity participation of 2 percent if the project construction is completed on time and within budget.

The contractor assumes a major portion of construction risk, and indirectly helps obtain construction financing at lower cost through the escrow arrangement.

Penalties for infractions are offset by rewards for proper completion. Furthermore, rewards do not require cash.

5   For equipment finance, the bank helps make the following arrangements. An offshore subsidiary of the Project Company is established in a tax haven. A consortium of insurance companies makes a commitment to fund equipment purchase (at a designated time in future) through purchase of cumulative preferred stock issued by the subsidiary. The subsidiary obtains commercial and political insurance commitment from the Eximbank.

6   The tax haven-based subsidiary agrees (a) to purchase the equipment with funds to be provided by the consortium (for delivery at proper time), and (b) sell it on an installment basis to another subsidiary of the Project Company in a country that has liberal depreciation allowances for tax purposes.

The second subsidiary in turn will lease the equipment to the Project Company for lease payments just sufficient to cover financing service required by the consortium.

- Preferred dividends are tax sheltered for the consortium, lowering the cost of financing. Given the tax-sheltered status, the subsidiary is not affected by the lack of tax deductibility of preferred dividends.
- The Eximbank guarantee manages to lower the cost of preferred stock.
- Lease payments avoid the interest withholding taxes in the country where the project is located.
- The second subsidiary's lease agreement enables it to retain the title to equipment, and deduct its depreciation for tax purposes. It passes this benefit in the form of a lower lease payment to the Project Company.

In brief, the Project Company is able to lower the cost of acquiring equipment by arbitraging tariff (negative in the form of export incentives by the Eximbank) and taxes (uneven impact in the USA, the tax haven, the Second Country, and the Project Country).

Bank's role in project finance

A commercial bank can play a vital, if not the critical, role in every phase of the project's life.

1 At the inception, a bank can be instrumental in assembling a project finance advisory service group for feasibility assessment, trade credit, international finance experience, overall project development, and management skills (i.e., negotiation and documentation).
2 Formation of the project company allows a complex contractual negotiation process as well as putting in place financial arrangements. The bank is part of the group that anticipates behavioral and financial ramifications of agreements and creates a bulwark of incentives and covenants that safeguards the long-term viability of the project. The bank also plays a crucial role in devising a proper financial structure so that requisite financing is obtained at minimum cost without adversely affecting liquidity. As pointed out above, this process requires identifying parties that are best able to assume a given risk, and exploiting market imperfections. Moreover, the bank helps locate lenders who provide permanent financing. The bank, either by itself or as a syndicate member, may arrange for **bridge financing**.
3 During the construction phase, the bank is in charge of providing remittance to contractors; a more significant task shouldered by the bank, however, is construction risk management, that is, monitoring that construction is on time, within budget, and able to meet the specified standards.
4 Once the project is completed, the bank can help in risk management. Specific risks may include foreign exchange rate risk, interest rate risk, and commodity risk. The bank may also offer services for tax and transaction cost related arbitrage that enhance the profitability of the project without increasing its risk.
5 Finally, the bank plays an active role when the project company is about to go public with the initial public offering of the equity. Determination of the size of the offering,

acceptable price range, selection of the lead underwriters, and evaluation of their bid are some critical issues where the bank can be helpful.

The recent trend followed by commercial banks in project finance is to bundle the project finance services such as those listed above (Forrester 1995), often apportioning these services among members of a coalition. In these cases, no clear trend is discernible as to whether banks tend to price their services on the project individually or as a group.

7.6.2 Merger and acquisition financing

Use of debt financing has been increasingly noticeable in financial restructuring, a trend started by corporate America in the early 1980s and followed elsewhere in the world in recent years. Financial restructuring is often associated with divestiture of divisions by multi-divisional firms, takeovers, and mergers. These reorganizations commonly end up with 80 to 90 percent of debt in the new or modified financial structures. Because of the high degree of financial leverage, these corporate restructures are called **leveraged buy-outs** (LBOs).

LBO financing is a natural market for both domestic and international banks. Bank loans to support LBO transactions are essentially similar to traditional commercial loans. This is because banks are senior creditors; and other debt, subordinated to bank claims, serves as an equity cushion. However, the earning pie of the leveraged firm is predominantly gobbled up by interest charges. The corporate liquidity turns anemic, making it extremely vulnerable even to mild downturns in business cycles. The ensuing bankruptcy proceedings and difficulties of achieving consensus often render the "equity cushion" of subordinate debt meaningless. Thus a bank should exercise extreme caution in treating a senior position in an LBO in the same vein as an ordinary loan.

Some banks have been lulled by the stand taken by regulators on LBO financing. New capital adequacy guidelines established by the Basel Committee consider loans to highly leveraged companies in the same risk category as traditional commercial and industrial loans. The risk characteristics of the LBO loan may be substantially different from other loans. Thus, the bank needs to adopt adequate controls and procedures for evaluating, pricing, and managing risks of this type of lending activity, and negotiate a contract with covenants that would protect its interests in adversity, more likely in the highly leveraged firm than in the traditional commercial and industrial loans.

7.7 Conclusion

In this chapter, we have discussed different aspects of cross-border financing of private, as opposed to official or government, activities where a commercial bank plays an important role. These activities run a gamut from episodic foreign trade transactions (including countertrade) to financing and investment activities of MNCs as well as projects whose financing cannot be accomplished through conventional methods.

One common theme runs through the role of a bank in these activities: assessing various dimensions of risk; identifying which entities have the most capacity to bear or assume the risk; and whether risk can be bundled or unbundled for the purpose of efficiently pricing it or for other strategic reasons. In the process we find that availability of foreign exchange or currency risk is not the sole critical element in international activities. Instead, obstacles in the goods and financial markets in the form of disparate laws, regulations, taxes, and transaction costs create distortions and give rise to not only risk but also return.

DISCUSSION QUESTIONS

1 What are cross-border services provided by banks to private businesses? Are banks indispensable for providing these services? Why?

2 Which services are gaining in importance in recent years? Why?

3 What is the unique role of banks in cross-border trade?

4 Describe briefly the process of cross-border trade transaction.

5 Briefly describe the following terms and their role in cross-border transactions: documentary L/C; irrevocable L/C; confirmed L/C; advised L/C, bill of lading; banker's acceptance; International Trade Certificate.

6 What are the principal means of financing international trade?

7 Discuss why an L/C is a put option written by the issuing bank. Do you think that the bank receives adequate compensation for assuming the underlying risks?

8 What risk is assumed by a bank when it confirms a L/C?

9 What does the US Eximbank do? Do you think that it is worth the resources provided by taxpayers?

10 Explain how (a) the Private Export Funding Corporation and (b) the Foreign Credit Insurance Association help promote US exports. Why do we need two such organizations?

11 Which bank services are needed most by foreign firms in a local economy? As financial markets become increasingly integrated, will there be any change in their needs? Why?

12 "Countertrade essentially avoids settlement of a transaction through currency transmission. When there were exchange controls, the practice of counter trade made a great deal of sense. Since governments now increasingly let their currencies trade on a floating rate basis, countertrade will soon be a historic relic." Discuss.

13 What role does a bank play in countertrade? What, if any, changes has it undergone over the last two decades?

14 What is project financing? Discuss its relationship with loan syndication.

15 Discuss unique features of project finance.

16 What is the role of banks in project financing? Why has the bank's role changed from credit lending to other services?

17 Discuss the role played by banks in merger and acquisition financing.

18 Commerce Bank, based in Columbus, Ohio, issues a letter of credit (L/C) at the request of St Louis Clothing Company in favor of Cheung Kong Exporting Inc., a Hong Kong-based company. St Louis Clothing Company is importing $10 million worth of apparel to be supplied by Cheung Kong Exporting Inc. Under the terms of the L/C, the face value of the import order is payable in six months after the Commerce Bank accepts the draft drawn by the Hong Kong exporter. The current discount rate on six-month acceptances is 9 percent per year and the acceptance fee is 1.5 percent per year. Furthermore, there is a flat commission, equal to 0.5 percent of the face amount of the accepted draft if and when it is sold. How much does Commerce Bank have to pay if the exporter holds the acceptance until maturity? How much will the bank pay for purchasing the acceptance accompanied with the draft?

19 Smart Bank has a client firm in Wichita, Kansas, which has exported machine tools to Japan. The client needs financing on the 90-day account receivables of $10 million. The bank proposes to discount the receivables at a 2.5 percent discount rate per month; however, the bank will have to be reimbursed by the client for face value in case the bank cannot collect from the Japanese importing company or the bank issuing the L/C. For a non-recourse financing option, the bank proposes to charge an additional 1.75 percent fee. How much will the bank pay the exporter for the recourse and non-recourse options?

APPENDIX I: PRIVATE CREDIT (LOAN) ANALYSIS

Estimating the default risk on a loan is not a straightforward exercise. The analysis involves various aspects for the credit conditions of the borrower. Conventionally, the analysis starts with the financial statements of the borrowers (or firms) and examines ratios related to liquidity, asset utilization efficiency, financial leverage and profitability. Below we provide the basic framework for credit analysis and its modification in the international environment.

Basic Analytical Structure

A credit decision for a business enterprise (firm) involves weighing the benefit of granting credit against the cost emanating from such a decision. From a slightly different perspective, benefit of granting credit is the cost for selecting the alternative of "rejecting the credit request." Hence, the credit extension decision requires consideration of

- Cost of rejection alternative; and
- Cost of acceptance alternative.

It follows, then, that the alternative that has the lower cost, should be selected.

Rejection Cost (RC)

If a credit request is rejected, the firm loses profitability of the transaction or relationship. From the simple transaction perspective, the excess of revenue over the avoidable cost gives profitability. This excess is known as the contribution margin. Since fixed costs are unavoidable, they are not reflected in the cost estimate. Hence,

$$
\begin{aligned}
\text{Contribution margin } (CM) &= \text{Revenue} - \text{Avoidable cost} \\
&= \text{Revenue} - (\text{Total cost} - \text{Fixed cost}) \\
&= (\text{Revenue} - \text{Total cost}) + \text{Fixed cost} \\
&= \text{Profit} + \text{Fixed cost}
\end{aligned}
$$

Since revenue is collected in future, it is not certain whether the firm will be able to collect it. As a result, the CM is weighed with the likelihood or probability that the credit receiver will pay the obligation. This probability is concisely stated as probability of payment, p (pmt).

In brief, the rejection cost, RC, is given by

$$ P\ (pmt) \times CM $$

Acceptance Cost (AC)

Acceptance cost results from credit extension that does not entail payment by a credit receiver on a timely basis.

An extreme case is when the credit receiver fails to pay. This is the "bad debt" or "default" cost. A less severe case is when the credit receiver is tardy in making payments, and the creditor firm has to take extra efforts for reimbursement. The cost of extra efforts is the "collection" cost.

Finally, irrespective of when the credit receiver pays, the firm incurs the opportunity cost of resources tied up in credit extension. This is the "investment" cost.

The sum of these cost components is the acceptance cost, AC. In turn, these cost components are defined as follows.

- Bad debt cost = (probability of non-payment) (Avoidable cost)
  Since p (pmt) $+ p$ (non-payment) $= 1$,
  Bad debt cost $= [1 - p\ (pmt)] \times$ (Avoidable cost)
- If the credit receiver is expected to take, on average, T periods to pay; and the cost of capital for investment in credit extension is r percent per period, then

$$ \text{Investment cost} = (r) \times T \times \text{Avoidable cost} $$

  where the term in the bracket is the compounding factor for T periods at the discount rate r.

- Collection Cost is the cost affiliated with special efforts made to collect from tardy customers. In brief,

$$ AC = [1 - p(pmt)] \times (\text{Avoidable cost}) + [(1 + r) \times T] \times \text{Avoidable cost} + \text{Collection cost} $$

versus

$$ RC = p(pmt) \times CM $$

Select the alternative that entails lower cost.

Applicability to Foreign Borrowers

The above framework is applicable to both financial and non-financial firms. We highlight below some salient aspects of its applicability to a bank considering a loan to a foreign entity. We have

$$\text{Avoidable cost} + \text{Contribution margin} = \text{Total cost}$$

- *CM*. With an increase in *CM* as a proportion of total cost (*CM* proportion, henceforth), the proportion of acceptance cost will decrease because of an implied reduction in both the bad debt and investment cost components. Thus the alternative of granting credit to a marginal credit request will be perceived more favorably than that of credit rejection.

  In a bank's case, the *CM*, primarily reflecting the bid-ask spread, is heavily constrained. Still, when a bank has direct access to the Eurocurrencies market but its competitors or the borrowers do not (a situation more likely encountered in a less industrialized economy), loans to foreign borrowing entities become an attractive proposition.[12]

- *p(pmt)*. Payment probability reflects both the ability and willingness of the borrower to pay. Ability is related to the **generation of operating cash flows** as well as the **equity cushion** of the borrowing entity.
- The basic framework assumes full payment on only one date. When payments are distributed over several periods, one uses a time-discounting framework.
- *(r)*. The discount rate *(r)* contains a risk premium for both the country risk and the borrowing entity. Chapter 8 discusses country risk in detail. Some of the roadblocks, either unusual or unique in foreign environments, are as follows.
  - Regulatory practices such as accounting conventions may render financial statements opaque and estimating (a) future cash flows and (b) equity in the enterprise very difficult.
  - *Legal enforcement* of the contract may not be swift. Nor may it be possible for a lender foreign bank to repossess the real property for the borrower's default. Thus a conventional **collateral** may not have the same comfort level abroad as in the home country.
  - Enforcement of a contract (or at the extreme a bankruptcy) may entail substantial *transaction costs* necessitated by complex bureaucratic procedures.
  - *Tax* write off of a bad loan may not be permissible.
  - A different *structural environment* may prevent the lending bank from enforcing the contractual obligations in a straightforward fashion, even when it is legally permissible. The standing of the borrower in the community may inflict the cost of ill will on the bank "coldly and impersonally" enforcing contractual provisions.
  - An issue related to risk is whether one should consider "systematic" risk defined in the CAPM framework, or total risk in a given credit situation. A useful and reasonable guideline is to use the systematic risk notion when the portfolio of similar loans follows the actuarial risk concept or the law of large numbers, and the default eventuality for the loan portfolio does not threaten the survival of the bank. Thus unless the loans, individually or jointly, are significantly large for the size of the bank, and their default prospects are closely intertwined, a "beta-based" adjustment (through the CAPM framework) in the discount rate *r* would be reasonable.

Some Additional Remarks on Implementing a Credit Evaluation Framework

Today, banks utilize sophisticated quantitative analysis to guide them in making credit decisions. Quantitative analysis involves the use of discriminant analysis or **credit scoring** models to assess the credit worthiness of a borrower. Credit scoring models are basically regression-type models. These models are based on a number of useful variables as inputs relating to the creditworthiness of the borrower. The model then gives a credit score or probability distribution of default of the borrower on the basis of the input factors. On the basis on the derived credit scores, the bank classifies credit requests in the acceptance and rejection categories. This classification is modified to reflect "regulatory realities," as described below.

The LDC debt crisis in the 1980s caused many medium and smaller-sized banks to exit from international lending activities. This change was driven partly by regulatory changes in major industrialized countries.

- Central banks and regulatory authorities from 12 industrialized countries form the Bank for International Settlements (BIS) Committee that has developed international guidelines for banks to conduct business. These guidelines have specified risk weights for various bank assets and off-balance-sheet transactions in order to assess capital adequacy.
- In addition, a minimum standard of capital adequacy is set up for all the banks.

Implementation of the new risk-adjusted capital guidelines has a significant impact on a bank's portfolio decisions that include country risk analysis. If a bank finds that those business lines do not meet the risk-adjusted guidelines, it has to avoid loans to those businesses.

Furthermore, the BIS guidelines (see Chapter 10 for more details) require banks to use an integrative approach to assess country risks and relate these risks to the bank's capital. Clearly, there is no uniform decision-making structure across banks regarding the loan risk analysis. For example, Bankers Trust (now a unit of Deutsche Bank) uses an integrating approach that incorporates three components: *amount, duration of risk*, and *risk factors*. This system is called risk-adjusted return on capital (RAROC).

- The amount of the loan in RAROC is measured in terms of the exposure amount. Percentages, similar to the BIS guidelines, are applied to measure the exposure.
- The duration of risk is measured along the time dimension in terms of maturity of the exposure. Exposures longer than one year are considered riskier and thus require a cushion of additional capital.
- The risk factor index, similar to the traditional credit rating index, has a scale range from 1 to 8, reflecting respectively the best quality risk and the most doubtful credits.

NOTES

1   Information technology has enabled banks to issue electronic L/Cs. The importer is able to avoid paperwork and minimize time involved in opening the L/C through the electronic communications network. Further, the negotiations process between the importer and the exporter is considerably abbreviated by the use of electronic mail. Nevertheless electronic presentation of documents by the exporter to the issuing bank has not made great strides because of ambiguity regarding their legal status in different jurisdictions.

2   Although a trade transaction typically involves both the L/C and the draft, a bank may be a party in only one or the other document in a given transaction.

3   The international payment instruments (L/C, draft and bankers' acceptance), which were originally developed and used for international transactions, are still widely used in industrialized nations (e.g., France and the USA) as well as emerging economies (e.g., Latin American countries).

4   Because of increasing flows of payments and automation, banks are vulnerable to many techno-logical errors. For example, on November 21, 1985, Bank of New York could not receive payment on their securities purchased due to an in-house software failure. As a result, the Federal Bank of New York had to extend $23.6 million overdraft to cover the bank's shortfall at the end of the day. This cost the bank overnight interest of several million dollars (Smith and Walter 1990).

5   For details on the Incoterms, see http://www.foreign-trade.com/schedules.htm; http://www.spindrift.co.za/incoterms.htm; and http://lawlibrary.ucdavis.edu/LAWLIB/Dec01/0116.html

6   In the absence of forfeiting, the exporter still faces the risk of non-payment by the guaranteeing bank, if any legal defect makes the guarantee inoperative.

7   The Eximbank also provides help to US importers on occasions. Budd Company was provided with subsidized import financing so that it might compete against a foreign firm.

8   There is no standardized vocabulary for describing various forms of countertrade. Hence definitions used here may be inconsistent with those used elsewhere. Terms here closely follow definitions used by the American Countertrade Association.

9   Cost of funding also depends on the standing of a creditor in case of default by or bankruptcy of the borrower. A lease has an advantage in a bankruptcy because the ownership resides with the funds provider.

10   In the absence of an independent entity for the project, the increased cost of funding reflects the cost of "adverse selection" by funds providers. Moral hazard occurs when, for instance, the contractor bids a low amount on the job fully realizing that the sponsor has overlooked some vital construction portions; and that the subsequent "add-on" would allow an amount over and above the loss built in the initial low bid. Often adverse selection is designated as "hidden information," and moral hazard, "hidden action."

11   Suppose a project sponsor has a secret "collateral" against the government to be used in case of project expropriation or equivalent adverse measures. This collateral is revealed to the lenders and its maintenance is a pivotal covenant in the debt contract so as to lower the cost of debt financing. It is obvious that such information cannot be made public.

12   Naturally, as markets become more integrated and provide greater access to participants especially from a less industrialized nation, this advantage diminishes.

CHAPTER 8

Sovereign Risk Analysis

LEARNING OBJECTIVES

- To understand the traditional approach to country risk analysis
- To learn about assessing country risk for a bank's loan portfolio
- To learn about (a) country debt crises in the 1980s and policy responses to contain them, and (b) subsequent changes in market practice
- To understand various factors leading to the banking and financial crises since the early 1990s

8.1 Introduction

Country risk is the risk of doing business in another country. It consists of unique cross-border risks borne by a bank due to its claims against economic agents in a foreign country. When that economic agent (borrowing entity, for instance) is the government, country risk is defined as *sovereign risk*. In this chapter, our focus will be on the government as a borrower; hence we will use these terms interchangeably.[1]

The history of encountering country risk can be traced back to the cross-border lending activities in the eastern Mediterranean region during the fourth century BC (Dil 1987). From the fourteenth to sixteenth centuries, many nations such as England and France defaulted at least once to external creditors. In the nineteenth century, several colonies in the Americas also failed to meet their debt service on obligations held by foreigners. In the twentieth century, the decades of the 1930s and 1980s witnessed defaults by many countries notably in Latin America.

For country risk analysis, the bank assesses both the political and economic environments of a country in order to determine the likelihood of timely service on obligations held against economic entities in that country. This analysis helps the bank decide on both the acceptability of the risk of the loan and appropriate terms for the loan, especially the interest premium. A follow-up periodic analysis is also undertaken to monitor changes in conditions affecting delinquency or default potential.

Like any credit risk analysis,[2] the fundamental issue of country risk comprises of assessing a borrower's ability and willingness to service obligations on a timely basis. The *ability to pay* is constrained by the adequacy of a country's foreign exchange reserves or its ability to raise funds externally. A government may have access to resources to meet the debt service obligation; however, it may not undertake such a service due to domestic economic or political ramifications. The *willingness to pay* then becomes more critical than the ability to pay.

- Non-payment or default may have beneficial political implications domestically (e.g., a "macho" image of the government).
- The direct cost of a punitive action by the lender may be marginal, as sovereign immunity of the government places significant constraints on the lender's ability to pursue a suitable course of legal actions in case of default.
- External financial markets may deny access to the defaulting country even for trade financing. Such actions may disrupt the smooth running of the economy.

A government's willingness to pay thus depends on its calculations of relative costs and benefits of non-payment.

Early twentieth-century bankers and their predecessors primarily used a heuristic approach to country risk analysis on a case-by-case basis. In recent years, developments in the portfolio theory, aided by robust statistical methodology and sophisticated computer technology, have permitted a more refined or comprehensive approach to country risk analysis. However, overriding importance of unquantifiable and ever-shifting political realities clearly shows why commercial banks continue to emphasize the heuristic, qualitative approach.

We discuss below the traditional and portfolio approaches to country risk measurement. The LDC (less developed countries) debt crises in the 1980s as well as their resolution (partial or otherwise) have a clear implication for a bank's assessment and assumption of country risk; hence, a brief description of these crises and attempts for their resolutions follows. The last section looks at the banking crises – involving not only the LDCs but also some industrialized nations – since the 1990s. Various explanations and rationale for individual crises have important policy ramifications for decision makers who manage the exchange rate system and for banks that evaluate country risk.

8.2 Traditional Country Risk Analysis

Traditional country risk analysis has two dimensions: economic and political. Whereas the economic analysis primarily focuses on the financial characteristics of the country, the political analysis examines the politico-legal aspects of country risk.

In 1977, the US Eximbank conducted a survey of country risk analysis processes employed by 37 US banks. The sample banks included the 12 largest US banks, which accounted for 30 percent of the total US banking industry assets and over 50 percent of the total US bank international assets at that time. The survey highlighted four frameworks for country risk analysis.

1 Many banks did not use any specific format across the board; instead, they employed an in-depth, subjective analysis on a case-by-case basis. By its very nature, it is difficult to ascertain effectiveness of this approach.

2 Some banks used a structured method with a standardized format. Such an approach has the potential for facilitating comparison between different countries on a timely basis; however, its heavy reliance on subjectivity makes it difficult to evaluate the efficacy of this approach.

3 A variation of the previous approach was the checklist of observable variables such as inflation rate or government deficit. Still, selection of the variables and the weight assigned to each variable remained arbitrary. In a setting of rapidly changing environments requiring a shift in the list of relevant variables and their weights, effectiveness of this approach remains suspect.

4 Only a small percentage (2 percent) of banks used some forms of quantitative method for country risk analysis. Typically, such methods paid special, if not exclusive, attention to the current account of the balance of payments (e.g., surplus of exports over imports). Since such a surplus has a favorable impact on a country's reserves required for debt service, current accounts surplus was considered good, and deficit bad. One predictable result of this emphasis on the current account was that the potential borrowers tended to consider seriously either currency devaluation or import substitution for improving the current account and thereby obtaining debt on more favorable terms. Unfortunately, devaluation is generally only a short-term solution, as it leads to inflation especially when demand for imports is inelastic. Before long, the resultant inflation also makes exports more expensive and less competitive in the foreign markets. Import substitution policies are no more effective than devaluation, since they violate the fundamental comparative advantage principle ensuring efficient allocation of resources.

A major flaw of the focus on the current account, however, is the ignorance of the capital account or the assumption of passive capital flows. The economic analysis must consider the whole balance of payments, not just one part.[3] Autonomous capital flows (those not directly linked with trade or current account flows) need special attention, because they may mask an imminent debt crisis even when reserves show healthy levels. Countries facing the problem of reserve depletion often skirt the fundamental maladies and beef up the reserves by borrowing foreign currencies on a short-term basis, thus postponing the crisis and making it even worse. Similarly, long term direct investment flows in low-priority industries may heat up inflationary forces that adversely affect competitiveness of the traditional exports.

A discussion of some desirable attributes of a sound quantitative method is now in order. A general model of country risk relates the measure of country risk to various economic and other indicators as follows:

$$P_i = \exp\{-(a + \Sigma_{j=1, m} b_j X_{ij})\}/[1 + \exp\{-(a + \Sigma_{j=1, m} b_j X_{ij})\}] \qquad (8.1)$$

where P_i is the conditional probability of (non)payment for a country i, a surrogate for country risk given X_{ij}, a country characteristic; a and b_j are parameters. To estimate Equation 8.1, we can make a logarithmic transformation to obtain a linear form as:

$$Y_i = \log(P_i/(1 - P_i)) = a + \Sigma_{j=1, m} b_j X_{ij} \qquad (8.2)$$

Equation 8.2 can be estimated by the ordinary least squares regression (OLS) method. We now discuss measurement of various variables for regression analysis.

8.2.1 Default probability P_i

Various measures of probability P_i have been used.

- Some studies have used the *premium* charged by banks for a loan to a particular country over the LIBOR. In syndicated loans, the front-end fees to the syndicate often lower this premium, and this compensation is not routine public information. At the same time, a loan with an unusually long grace period or great flexibility for the borrower with respect to the principal of the loan will carry a large premium. Whether these biases will cancel each other out cannot be ascertained a priori.
- A variant is the yield on the sovereign state's bonds that are traded on the market. Relatively thin markets and infrequent trading diminish the utility of this index in terms of timeliness and reliability.
- Another popular index of the probability P_i is the rating score from publications like the *Institutional Investor* or *Euromoney*. These scores range from 0 to 100, where 100 is the most desirable score of country risk. The *Institutional Investor* scores are survey responses of individual bankers and thus represent their personal assessment of countries' creditworthiness. On the other hand, the *Euromoney* scores reflect actual financial market conditions based on different variables.
- Credit rating by agencies such as Moody's and Standard & Poor (S&P) is still another index to represent P_i. Cantor and Packer (1995, 1996) have shown that (a) these ratings significantly influence yields, i.e., rating agencies have credibility in the marketplace; and (b) they adequately capture impact of pertinent macroeconomic variables.
  - Out of eight macroeconomic variables (per capita income; GDP growth; inflation; fiscal balance; external balance; external debt; economic development; and default history), five (per capita income, inflation, external debt, economic development, and default history) were highly significantly correlated, and ratings correctly anticipated the impact of these variables. Indeed, ratings appear to provide additional information beyond that conveyed in the standard macroeconomic country statistics incorporated in market yields (Cantor and Packer 1996: 83).
  - The market relies on the rating agencies especially for the speculative issues, presumably because of the high level of information noise in these issues.
  - Although the market seems to *anticipate* a change in ratings and incorporate it in revising the yield, the actual announcement still affects the market in a correct way, especially

for the speculative issues. Presumably, the market consistently underestimates the impact of revision in rating, and adjusts for correction upon actual announcement.

In light of the fact that yields themselves suffer from problems of timeliness and reliability, validation of the Cantor and Packer studies for country risk assessment via ratings cannot be ascertained without further empirical investigation. Episodic evidence also suggests the rating agencies were as much taken by surprise as others in the Asian crisis of 1997, discussed later. Suffice to state at this juncture that Moody's and S&P's ratings of long-term sovereign debt of Indonesia, Malaysia, the Philippines, South Korea, and Thailand remained unchanged up to July 1997, when the crisis hit these countries. As a matter of fact, there was an *upgrade* for the Philippines just prior to the beginning of the crisis (Radelet and Sachs 1998).

In general, a problem with the use of an index in Equation 8.2 is that the regression only links the index with a set of hypothesized factors. Whether the index can accurately predict the likelihood of default by a country still remains an issue.

8.2.2 Economic factors X_{ij}

Traditionally, country risk analysis is based on the financial performance of many economic indicators including *liquidity, profitability*, and *debt structure*. These economic indicators affect the country risk in either a positive or negative way.

Liquidity

Banks use various ratios to measure a country's liquidity for debt service. One such measure is the ratio of export receipts to the debt service obligation. The second is the ratio of the country's foreign exchange reserves to imports. A higher ratio in both cases is a stronger indicator of liquidity adequacy; hence, it is inversely related to country risk.

A related measure is the coverage ratio of the net capital flows to the debt service obligations. The net capital flows, in turn, are measured by the current account surplus plus unused credit lines available to the country.

Essentially, these measures correspond to short-term indicators of a country's ability and access to generate funds for debt service.

Debt structure

The debt structure of a country is similar to the debt structure for a firm: it reflects the financial risk of the entity. One measure of debt structure is the total external outstanding debt to exports ratio. A ratio relating debt to gross national product (GNP) is another common measure of a country's debt structure. A larger number implies greater country risk.

Profitability

The profitability measure reflects the potential for generating profits in the country. Higher profitability not only generates larger liquidity in itself but also enhances prospects for future capital inflows. Thus higher profitability connotes higher growth and lower country risk.

Various measures including growth in GDP, growth in exports, and growth in per capita income are used to measure profitability.

Willingness to pay

Measuring the willingness of the country to pay is not easy. If a country is committed to economic growth, and imports are required for sustaining or improving economic growth, then a ratio of imports to GDP may reflect the country's willingness to repay its external debt. Thus, the higher this ratio, the more likely the country will be willing to repay its debts.

8.2.3   Political factors X_{ij}

Events such as the civil war in Lebanon, revolution in Iran and the invasion of Afghanistan by Russia in the late 1970s highlighted the change in the creditworthiness of countries involved. The invasion of Kuwait by Iraq in 1990 and the subsequent Gulf War had wide repercussions on the wellbeing of a large number of countries around the globe. These political events demonstrate their critical role in country risk analysis.

The opening up of the communist world for foreign investments necessitated careful assessment of non-economic risks, stemming from deep-seated ethical, religious, and nationalistic chasms. The political upheavals in Central and Eastern Europe instigated the still-ongoing, arduous process of building democratic institutions; and success of this process is not a foregone conclusion. The political future of the former Soviet Union and China remains very much an enigma in spite of an impressive array of political and economic reforms in these two countries. The financial crisis in South-East Asia did not have a uniform impact: Indonesia suffered the most, because of the political unrest that paralyzed the process of economic reform, while Taiwan remained unscathed. Finally, the third world is undergoing continual changes especially with respect to the role of private business in their economies.[4] As a result, political realities are likely to be more volatile in the future than in the recent past, suggesting the vital importance of political factors in country risk analysis.

Methodology

Basic methodology in political risk analysis involves a subjective-objective approach (Simon 1992). First, the subjective, individual assessment on political risk is obtained. For example, an analyst or expert who has contacts within the host country provides special assessment. Objective data may be supplemented.

Second, political risk is assessed by a group of analysts that use the inputs from the first stage. Again, objective as well as subjective criteria may be used to predict the likelihood of civil war or other manifestations of political instability.

The drawback of this approach is the potential for bias and a lack of consistency and comparison across countries. Further, it may be extremely expensive; worse still, it may not yield relevant input for decision-making on a timely basis.

Identifying political risk variables

Political risk assessment requires, among other things, appraisal of a given variable in terms of its impact on a given foreign interest. Some variables, for instance, have a broad-base impact on foreign entities' interest in the country; others affect only particular entities or industries originating from a specific geographical region or country.

General factors include *mismanagement* of the economy and widespread *corruption* that may make the government unable to meet its obligations. The Russian government's inability to collect taxes has had an adverse impact on all foreign investors. On the other hand, a US manufacturer of oil extracting machinery had less to worry about the Russian government debility because of the insulation of the Russian oil industry that primarily would export its products and keep the lion's share of foreign exchange earned from such export.

A variety of political risk variables have been used and tested in the literature. Brewer and Rivoli (1990) examined the impact of three political risk variables: (1) governmental regime shift (i.e., the frequency of change or smoothness of transition in political leadership), (2) political legitimacy (i.e., the extent to which political process is democratic or authoritarian) and (3) armed conflict (i.e., the length of time the country is involved in armed conflicts). They found that governmental regime shift had a greater impact on creditworthiness than the other two factors.

Empirical investigations by Thapa and Mehta (1991) supported the idea of Agmon and Dietrich (1983) that *perceived* country risk is lower if there is a high probability of political bailout from the bank's government. Such a bailout results from the strategic – geographic, economic, or military – importance of the host or borrowing country to the bank's government. One intriguing implication of this line of reasoning is that greater instability makes the borrowing country more creditworthy, contrary to the widely held assumption of the favorable impact of political stability on the borrowing country's creditworthiness.

8.3 Portfolio Approach

Modern portfolio theory provides a useful framework for analyzing the risk-return trade-offs in a bank's loan portfolio. For illustrative purposes, consider a country loan for Chile with an expected return of 10 percent with a standard deviation of 8 percent, while the loan for Venezuela has an expected return of 12 percent with a standard deviation of 10 percent. Because both loans offer a similar risk-return tradeoff, that is, higher return with higher risk (standard deviation), there is no apparent reason to choose one investment over the other. Nevertheless, when considered in the context of the bank's loan portfolio, one of the two alternatives may emerge superior to the other. Suppose the correlation of Chile's loan with the bank loan portfolio is high because the loan portfolio is dominated by primary goods industries or agricultural economies that have a business cycle pattern similar to Chile's. On the other hand, Venezuela, an oil-based economy, has much less in common with the bank loan portfolio. In that case, lending to Venezuela, other things being equal, appears superior from the portfolio perspective.

To formally describe the portfolio approach, let R_i be the expected return on the loan to the ith country, and R_m be the average (weighted) return on the bank's global loan portfolio. Then, we can link R_i and R_m as follows:

$$R_i = a + b_i \star R_m + e_i$$

where b_i represents the risk sensitivity of the ith country risk to the overall risk of the bank loan portfolio, and e_i is the residual risk factors that are affecting R_i.

Expressing the above equation in variance (Var) terms, we have:

$$\begin{array}{ccc} \mathrm{Var}(R_i) & = & b_i \star \mathrm{Var}(R_m) + \mathrm{Var}(e_i) \\ \text{Total Risk} & & \text{Systematic Risk} \qquad \text{Unsystematic Risk} \end{array}$$

In the modern portfolio theory, risk is thus decomposed into two categories: systematic and unsystematic. **Systematic risk** refers to the asset's relationship with respect to the market, and it is a product of the asset's beta and the variance of the average return on the global portfolio. Systematic risk is influenced by economy wide conditions such as the business cycle and fluctuations in the financial markets. When these factors are transmitted across countries and regions, returns would exhibit similar volatility everywhere, and returns volatility of an asset in one place cannot be offset – diversified – by returns elsewhere. This undiversified portion of the volatility then is the systematic risk component of that financial asset.

Unsystematic risk is also called the *residual* risk, which is supposed to be diversifiable. If the portfolio is large enough, the unsystematic risk will reduce to zero. Thus country-specific risk reflecting unique characteristics of the country and corresponding to the unsystematic risk will disappear when loans are made to a large number of countries.

Using this portfolio approach, the goal of international asset allocation is to maximize return for a given level of risk. This process requires estimation of the expected return and risk associated with each loan (or asset). When the portfolio approach is considered for bank loans to the sovereign governments, many theoretical and practical issues arise.

- Expected return and its volatility are not easy to measure. Their estimates depend on the likelihood of timely repayment of principal and interest, which are not directly included in the loan documentation itself and may not be easily quantifiable.
- Portfolio theory requires estimation of return and risk in terms of the market value of the financial asset. Since many of these loans are not traded in the marketplace, accuracy of the estimates remains questionable. Also, the measurement and relevance of the bank's own portfolio in place of the market portfolio remain questionable, since the systematic component in the bank portfolio would contain a portion of the diversifiable component in the context of the global market portfolio.
- Issues of asymmetric information (the borrowing government has more information on its creditworthiness than the bank) and adverse selection (the less creditworthy borrower is willing to pay higher interest charges) raise the fundamental question on applicability of the portfolio theory based on efficient markets (or symmetric information).
- Finally, the portfolio theory assumes solvency of investments and their ready disposal or liquidity. These assumptions have little applicability to sovereign debt. As mentioned

earlier, creditors or banks do not have a deterrent in the form of direct recourse to the assets of a government in default. Political means of pressure remain perhaps the one generally effective tool; however, our understanding of this tool has a long way to go.

Although loan liquidity has significantly improved in the wake of bank securitization of its assets (from mortgage loans to credit card receivables), securitization of loans to sovereign governments has remained elusive because these loans, relatively large in amount but too few in number, have indivisibility or lumpiness that makes their securitization difficult.[5]

Because of these difficulties, many analysts have tended to de-emphasize application of the portfolio-theory approach to managing country risk. Instead, their analyses have endorsed focus on individual country factors in place of their relative importance in the global context.

Still, the portfolio theory approach offers great promise and opportunities for country risk analysis. Regulatory authorities in the USA have emitted a strong, favorable signal in this direction. The Security Exchange Commission (SEC) requires banks to disclose in their financial reports exposure to any individual country exceeding one percent of total outstanding loans. In the same vein, the Federal Reserve Board requires banks to provide similar country exposure information in their quarterly reports.

8.4 Debt Crisis Management in the 1980s

After Mexico announced debt payment difficulties in August 1982, other Latin American countries and countries from other regions soon followed Mexico's example. By the end of 1985, the so-called Baker 15 countries (Argentina, Bolivia, Brazil, Chile, Columbia, Ecuador, the Ivory coast, Mexico, Morocco, Nigeria, Peru, the Philippines, Uruguay, Venezuela, and Yugoslavia) with two others (Jamaica and Panama) had $9.6 billion interest arrears on their long-term obligations (Kim 1993).

There were several major external reasons for the debt crisis. First, the Federal Reserve's tight money policy led to double digit T-bill interest rates before markets believed that the Federal Reserve was serious about curbing high inflation. Consequently the debt-service cost for the debtor countries, typically based on LIBOR, substantially increased. Further, industrial nations including the USA were in recession at that time (1980–82) and thus had substantially reduced imports from the LDCs. As a result, the value of the LDC commodity exports fell sharply. Finally, the dollar denomination of these debts made things worse for the borrowers because the dollar value rose against all major currencies. Internal factors such as diverting foreign exchange reserves from genuine development needs to domestic political ends as well as capital flight only precipitated or worsened the crises.

8.4.1 Loan default and negotiations

Loans to sovereign governments are seldom by a single bank; instead, a syndicate is formed whose members hold varying proportions of the loan. A large number is prima facie attractive because of the notion of risk sharing or insurance discussed in Chapter 1: default risk when shared becomes manageable for an individual bank. When a government defaults or declares its inability to service debt obligations, the syndicate form has some interesting ramifications.

One would presuppose that banks having a common interest would present a solid front for default-related negotiations. In general, this is a reasonable assumption; however, the game theory predicts behavior that contradicts this general presumption. For instance, consensus is difficult to achieve due to the *free rider* problem. Suppose the debtor government proposes a grace period for debt service as well as interest rate concessions that are sensible under the circumstances but imply a lower loan value. A syndicate member bank with a sufficiently small share of the loan can reasonably surmise that (a) its actions will have no impact on the aggregate outcome, that is, other members will not be affected or concerned about its action, and (b) if it chooses to hold out, the lead bank in charge of negotiations will regard the cost of protracted negotiations higher than buying out its (the holdout member's) share at a price higher than the price embedded in the offer by the borrower. Then it will hold out and obtain the free ride from the lead bank. In this case, every member will see the advantage of holding out or free-ride, and the offer will not be accepted. Note that the critical variable responsible for ineffectiveness of the lead bank here is the small size of the stake held by individual members; and a small number of participants does not necessarily mean an individually large stake.

What can the lead bank do to expedite agreement among member banks? Finance theory examining the takeovers in the context of the game theory suggests notions of *exclusionary provisions* and the *supermajority rule* that have applicability here. An example of exclusionary provision is when the lead bank is able to inflict penalties on the holdout bank through excluding it from some other lucrative deal. Supermajority rules say that an agreement by a designated majority (in terms of the aggregate number or size and typically different from a simple majority) is binding on all members.

Two implications for the lead bank are clear.

- It should be very careful in initially identifying the potential membership group. Thus banks with which it has ongoing, mutually beneficial relationships should be invited to join the syndicate in the first place (the club membership has justifications, after all!).
- It should devise membership covenants that avoid problems like free-ride. It is also important for the lead bank to obtain side payment from the defaulting nation, such as treasury management or trade financing contracts, and use it for rewarding acquiescing membership.[6]

The discussion so far focused on the obligation of the sovereign government; however, default by a private borrower may result from foreign exchange sanctions imposed by the government. The government some time offers debt-for-cash buy back to lender banks whereby banks agree to sell their loans directly to the government; the government in turn agrees to make smaller payment(s) in future (or for similar concessions) but in the original currency of denomination. The FICORCA (Fideicomiso de Cobertura de Riesgo Cambiario) agreement offered by the Mexican government in the early 1980s is one example of this kind. Naturally, the terms represent a loss for the banks. On the other hand, banks are assured by the government of debt service in the original currency of the loan agreement; further, the loans do not have to be written off; and, in the final analysis, the alternative of not accepting any proposal entails even greater *expected* losses. Still, in order to avoid a divide-and-conquer strategy of the government, most syndicated loan agreements have a sharing clause prohibiting individual banks from renegotiating with the debtor, unless waivers are granted by other participating banks.

In some instances, a debt crisis led to a special form of *debt securitization*. Debt securitization involved an exchange of LDC loans held by banks for new securitized instruments issued by the debtor nation at a reduced interest rate or face value. Banks thus exchanged non-tradable loans into tradable securities that could be sold in secondary markets. (Frequently, the purchasers were citizens of the debtor country who had managed to get the money out of the country earlier.) In effect, conversion allowed banks to facilitate creation of secondary markets for syndicated loans. Further, many banks preferred loan conversion in bonds to avoid the rescheduling process. As a result, these debt-securitized transactions were primarily debt-for-bond swaps. These swaps turned out to be safer than the loans because the debtor countries by and large faithfully serviced their foreign bonds throughout the debt crisis even when they suspended the rescheduled payments on their foreign loans.

Successful debt-securitization transactions were conducted between banks and the borrowing nations such as Mexico and Brazil. The main advantage for these countries was the debt reduction worth billions of dollars.

Negotiations have encompassed some unconventional solutions in recent years. We discuss highlights of some of them below.

Debt-equity swaps

The **Debt-equity swap** was the most dramatic form of debt conversion. This swap transaction involved reimbursement of debt claims in local currency. These funds were then used for direct private investment or acquisition of equity securities in the debtor country. The initial swap as well as the eventual repatriation of income or principal was often subject to the specific host-country rule. For instance, the Mexican government did not allow all lender banks to participate in the debt-equity swap program. The US money center banks such as Citicorp, Bankers Trust, Chase Manhattan and Morgan Guarantee were some of the major players in these transactions in the past. The amount of swaps by these commercial banks was still small in magnitude due to the complexity and time-consuming nature of the process. For instance, willing and able US banks faced problems of

- the accounting treatment of markdown associated with the potential exchange and its contaminating effect on other loans elsewhere or in the negotiating nation;
- requiring permission from the Federal Reserve or other regulatory authorities;
- identifying suitable, sound investment opportunities; and
- dealing with uncertainties of
  - time-consuming approval in principle of undertaking the swap in the first place;
  - approval of the investment target(s); and
  - repatriation of proceeds in future.[7]

Government proclivities for approving swaps on a case-by-case basis made matters worse in terms of time delay!

Typically investment of the local currency denominated proceeds involved an MNC. In effect,

- A bank with access to a swappable LDC loan would contact the MNC considering direct investment in the LDC.
- Given the MNC need for funds in local currency, the bank would sell the requisite amount of debt (denominated in a hard currency) to the central bank for local currency.
- The bank would exchange these funds for hard currency with the MNC.

In the process, the MNC would obtain the local funds at a much better exchange rate than the official rate; the debtor nation would be able to pay back hard-currency debt in local currency; and the bank would obtain debt service in hard currency provided by the MNC, and clear some spread on the transaction, thereby shrinking the net loss on the loan.

Governments (or the debtor nations) would have been the net gainers when the debt-equity swap brought in new investments. This was not, however, the case, according to some knowledgeable observers at that time. In the absence of new investments, the opportunity loss for the government was the loss of foreign exchange the MNC would have brought to the country in the first place. In fact, MNCs were the largest users of the debt-equity swaps; and they managed to obtain local currencies at a big discount, creating political embarrassment for the governments in some instances. Further, the swap transactions had an unacceptable side effect on the economy: repurchase of the entire loan in local currency meant expansion of the money supply; and unless it was sterilized inflationary forces gathered further momentum.

Debt-equity swaps were initiated in early 1982 in Brazil and 1984 in Nigeria. In 1985, Mexico formally allowed debt-equity conversions, only to be suspended in 1987. From 1984 to 1989, at least 17 different LDCs had active debt-equity conversions. The deals were concentrated in only four countries (Argentina, Brazil, Chile, and Mexico) that accounted for 92 percent of the total value of debt-equity transaction during this period (Dropsy and Solberg 1992).

Debt-for-nature swap

The structure of this swap transaction is similar to that of the debt-equity swap except that the investor spends the acquired local currency to manage programs in forest conservation, scientific study, and environment education.

Debt-for-commodity swap

This is another debt conversion in which the bank-held external debt claim is exchanged for a claim on physical commodities. These commodities can be sold to the world market for cash. The lender banks return some portion of the proceeds to the debtor nation and keep the remainder as debt repayment. This swap transaction is also called the debt-for-export swap.

8.4.2   Alternative solutions

Three general approaches for handling a debt crisis are possible, when negotiations between the creditor banks and the debtor government fail to reach a satisfactory compromise. They include:

- use of secondary market mechanisms by banks to reduce the debt burden;
- a coordinated effort by three parties (creditor commercial banks, their government(s), and the debtor government) to resolve the debt issues;
- involvement of multilateral agencies.

Secondary market approach

A lender bank may sell a loan to (or swap it with) another financial institution. Typically the bank resorts to the secondary market when it sees protracted or fruitless negotiations with the debtor nation. This passive approach signals the "throwing in the towel" by the bank. Consequently, it is not difficult to see that the buyer has no incentive to offer a fair price of the loan. At times, developing countries themselves participated in the secondary market in an attempt to reduce the debt burden cheaply. (The problem of moral hazard arises because the defaulting nation would in the first place have no incentive to propose reasonable terms to the lenders.)

There may be reasons other than anticipated intransigence of the debtor nation. For instance, disclosure requirements by US regulators for bank exposure to any individual country in excess of one percent of total loans, coupled with their insistence on adequate loan loss reserves for loans in default, could also have encouraged banks to diversify through secondary markets, and balance their portfolio geographically.

Finally, there was also the "herd effect" in reverse: just as banks (particularly US regional ones) earlier could not subscribe to loan syndicates fast enough, later they could not get out of these loans fast enough.

Unlike the debt-for-equity swap between a bank and an MNC, a bank can use the secondary markets (if they exist) for not only loan sales but also debt-for-debt swaps.

1   *Loan sale.* A bank loan sale occurs when a bank, which originated the loan, sells it (with or without recourse) to another party. If the loan is sold without recourse, the loan is removed from the bank's balance sheet and the bank has no obligation for the loan.

Trading in LDC loans often took place in the high yield (or junk bond) departments of the participating banks, which as market-makers would provide quotes for LDC loans. Some of the buyers in the market were wealthy investors and, as mentioned above, the debtor nations themselves. The largest buyers of the loans were, however, multinational corporations that utilized these loans in debt-equity swap transactions described above.

The secondary market for LDC debt has grown rapidly since 1983 and has achieved by now both depth and breadth: the number and average size of annual transactions have increased along with the number and types of market participants. Before 1987, the amount of loans sold by US banks was small. In 1987, banks had sharply accelerated their sales for reasons stated above and presumably because many banks had built sufficient loan loss reserves that would permit them to sell off their LDC loans without substantially reducing current profit reports.

2 *Debt-for-debt swap.* Debt-for-debt swap refers to a situation in which one bank exchanges debt claim on one country for that on another country with another bank. Initially the secondary market was mainly driven by these inter-bank swaps; later, exchange of debt for cash started taking place.

The debt-for-debt swaps were estimated to be around 75 percent of the secondary market transactions. Bankers Trust was one of the first US banks to conduct sizable transactions in this debt swap market. For instance, in the early 1980s, Bankers Trust bought $190 million of Mexican loans with Brazilian debt valued at $100 million, plus cash worth US$90 million (Hector 1983).

Tripartite negotiations

The critical element added here is the active role played by the government(s) of the lender banks. These governments do not relish the role. Such a role is likely to generate the glare of publicity that may paint the debtor government in the corner and harden its position. Success or effectiveness of such involvement works well when there is a carrot-and-stick approach whereby direct aid coupled with concessions by lender banks is offered in return for promises of better-disciplined economic policies by the debtor government. Unfortunately, local political considerations may prevent the debtor government from agreeing to keep (or keeping) promises; and the aid of multilateral agencies is sought. The following two plans illustrate the role played by governments of the lender banks.

1 *Baker plan.* After three years of the LDC debt crisis, James Baker, the US Secretary of Treasury, proposed a plan, known as the **Baker plan**, in 1985 to provide solutions for improving the debt crisis. The plan called for (a) commercial banks to lend an additional $20 billion and extend loan maturity dates, (b) governments of industrialized nations to use the conduit of multilateral agencies like the IMF, the World Bank and the Inter-American Development Bank to provide fresh loans to the heavily indebted countries, and (c) debtor countries to adopt market-oriented approaches such as trade liberalization policies for promoting economic growth.

The Baker plan attempted to augment the debt capacity of debtor nations through promoting growth facilitated by new lending as well as structural changes in the debtor countries. However, bankers were reluctant to provide additional credits and kept insisting on the World Bank guarantee for at least a portion of new loans. Critics complained that appraisal and monitoring of reforms by the LDCs were inadequate or non-existent in the plan.

2 *Brady plan.* In 1987, Nicholas F. Brady, the US Secretary of Treasury, proposed a new approach to the debt crisis, known as the Brady plan. The basic element of the Brady plan was to exchange defaulted sovereign loans for tradable 30-year bonds or **Brady bonds** issued by the defaulting government. In turn, zero-coupon US Treasury bonds purchased by the defaulting nation collateralized the principal of these bonds. In turn, the Brady issue was comprised of par, level-coupon bonds or zero-coupon bonds. Both alternatives offered flexibility to banks in terms of debt relief or debt forgiveness plans. Typically, debt relief called

for interest rate cuts annually up to three percentage points for a par issue; debt forgiveness involved a reduction of 30–50 percent on principal payable at the LIBOR-based interest rate for a zero-coupon issue.

The Brady plan also assigned an important role to the IMF and the World Bank in establishing economic structural adjustments in debtor countries (which might even necessitate loans by these bodies to the indebted countries). Finally, the plan urged waivers of the sharing clause in the loan syndication agreements, which prohibited individual members from directly negotiating with the debtor government.

Initially the major opponents of the Brady plan were the bankers themselves. They were not excited about getting locked into a commitment to reduce either the principal of their loans or interest rates on the loans. But debt forgiveness in one form or the other was the reality they had to face, and the Brady plan only underscored that reality. Unfortunately, the waiver of sharing clause, allowing side payments to some members of a syndicate, only vitiated or protracted the negotiation process by debilitating the bargaining position of the majority in the syndicate. Furthermore, the plan was also criticized by sympathizers of LDCs that the plan catered to banking interests.

Basically the Brady plan amounted to securitization of non-tradable loans into tradable securities, initially for Mexico and later for other countries. This securitization process helped create a secondary market for bank debt. By 1994, the annual trading volume in the Brady bonds had reached $1.684 trillion, registering an increase of 64 percent from the previous year, according to the Emerging Market Traders Association (EMTA). In the 1997 EMTA Survey, Brady bonds represented 41.4 percent of total reported trading volume.

Role of multilateral agencies

The change in bankers' attitude toward multilateral organizations like the IMF since 1973 reflects the changing role of these agencies. Since the IMF was the lynchpin of the Bretton Woods Agreement, the demise of the Agreement in 1973, some thought, would signal graceful fading away of the IMF. US bankers perceived the IMF as an anachronistic organization, and contributions by the US government to the IMF as useless and wasteful. The image of IMF as a champion of the Third World countries did not help the matter. However, during the debt crisis in the 1980s, these multilateral agencies were not only found useful to administer the bitter medicine of tightening the belt (in terms of both the monetary policies and government expenditures or subsidies to inefficient public and private enterprises), increasing taxes, and undertaking structural reforms such as privatization and deregulation, but also to be partners in additional loans (additional funds injected by the IMF went at least partially for debt service).

Banks' calculations were simple: default on a loan where a multilateral agency is a partner would also be a default against the rest (or at least, the majority) of the world; this implication would make the defaulting country at least pause before resorting to such an action. Further, the borrowing government would have a tough time pushing for loan term revisions to achieve its political goals at the expense of lenders when a multilateral agency is also a lender.

8.5   The Debt Crisis of the 1980s

Several stylized observations on the debt crisis of 1980s are possible.

- Unlike the 1970s, when banks handled in their stride the structural changes in the world economy in the aftermath of the oil shock, the debt crisis of the 1980s caught banks by and large unprepared. As a result, they handled the crisis in a tactical fashion that ignored the long-run objective of facilitating the long-term economic growth of LDCs that would improve their creditworthiness. Indeed, banks made an about-turn on extending loans to LDCs.
- Banks implemented policies that failed to discriminate among countries with varying degrees of creditworthiness, and imposed uniform penalties across the board.
- Banks shifted to extending loans to sovereigns in the *industrialized* nations often at a razor-thin margin or lower.
- Banks abandoned the area of syndicated loans as high quality clientele moved to securities-related areas such as NIFs and Euro-CP as well as swaps. The move of banks as facilitators of NIFs and Euro-CP called for skills and perspectives of investment bankers who, in contrast to commercial bankers, were more sensitive to market-based risks than to strictly credit risk.
- Banks became very active in LBOs; they not only provided senior financing but also arranged for cross-border financing.
- Finally, the universal vogue of market-based economies since the mid-1980s has spawned two developments: virtual end of central planning and privatization. In turn, these developments, along with increasing integration of financial markets across nations, have rendered conventional analysis of country risk out of focus, if not irrelevant, and changed the scope of bank activities.

8.5.1   Shift to market-based economies

The privatization movement in yesteryear's LDCs has been accompanied by foreign investment, reduced restrictions or removal of foreign exchange controls, and deregulation in general. Foreign investments come in two forms: portfolio investments and direct, private investments.

- Privatization creates attractive opportunities for investment in securities of privatized enterprises, since these enterprises have better prospects for productivity improvement than ever before due to deregulation and potential competition.[8] (Privatization, at least theoretically, helps the government reduce the drain on the treasury, not only initially – through sale of the public enterprise – but later through avoiding or reducing subsidies to these privatized enterprises; and still later these enterprises may even start contributing to the treasury upon reaching a profitable stage.)
- Similarly, deregulation and improved growth prospects attract MNCs that undertake real investment at an accelerated pace.

Both forms of foreign investments bring in foreign exchange that replete the official reserves, allowing the government to relax foreign exchange controls (without necessarily abandoning the fixed exchange regime). Real investment by both the MNCs and the local business create the need for expanding the capacity of infrastructure such as transportation, energy, and communications. (This capacity expansion typically requires huge capital outlays, made possible through project financing, discussed in detail in Chapter 7.)

Several characteristics of this shift toward market economy are noteworthy.

- Local securities markets are thin and thus lack depth, accentuating volatility of returns on portfolio investments.
- Financial infrastructure for trade or transaction settlement is either non-existent or woefully inadequate. The distinction between returns on paper and those upon settlement becomes critical because of transaction costs and time delay.
- Capital inflows generate further momentum for inflationary forces through money supply expansion; an antidote of sterilization (effective reduction of money base) is either not possible or desirable.
- Deregulated markets are susceptible to unsettling global forces, in particular to transmission of interest and foreign exchange rate volatilities; exaggerated volatility in the securities market make markets more susceptible to speculative capital flows.
- Infrastructure bottlenecks become critical, as the plans for expansion, their actual implementation as well as the related project financing become complex and time consuming; at the extreme, these bottlenecks adversely affect productivity and thus the country's competitive edge in the global markets.
- Private enterprises assume unprecedented importance in the global financial markets, shifting the focus away from the sovereign governments. Their need for funds requires issuance of both debt and equity instruments; however, equity issues require placement skills and tend to be more lucrative for banks than debt issues.
- Productivity improvement especially in privatized enterprises calls for pruning employee roll; lack of marketable skill and unavailability or inadequacy of training facilities result in structural unemployment that has both welfare and political ramifications.
- Social dislocation caused by, among other things, inflation and structural unemployment as well as the adoption or nurturing of political processes of democracy allow political and/or religious extremists to inject instability in the socio-political fiber of the country. Although this instability is unlikely to unravel the process of market orientation (except in the wake of a cataclysmic global event), it has a real potential for slowing down the process. Implications of these characteristics for the scope of bank activities need careful consideration.

8.5.2　Changing scope of bank activities

The LDC debt crisis in the 1980s caused many medium and smaller-sized banks to exit from international bank lending, or restrict their international banking activities to trade finance. Multinational banks, on the other hand, have retained a global focus, but the scope of their activities has undergone transformation. The discussion above enables us to explain some of the developments and chart a possible course for the future with respect to their country risk exposure.

First, the LDC governments do not figure prominently on the banks' balance sheets, nor for that matter, loans in general. The activities of banks in future will significantly overlap with those of investment banks: in arranging for funds locally and in offshore markets for their clients; in facilitating foreign portfolio investments in the LDC; in risk management (banks having an advantage over investment banks with respect to credit derivatives); and in arranging project financing and possibly providing bridge financing before construction of the project is completed or the project comes on stream.

Second, increasing attention is being devoted to cross-border services related to cash management in particular and treasury management (for private businesses as well as government) in general. Banks have a differential advantage over investment banking houses in this arena.

Third, in spite of its competitive nature, banks will maintain their presence in the Euromarket. Euroequities for firms will draw more attention in this market than their debt issues.

Fourth, increasing integration of the market will transmit shocks originating from one segment of the market to another very quickly; however, as the depth of the market increases, the amplitude witnessed during the transition period will subside. This will have a significant impact on risk management demanded by the bank clientele and required on its own account, both during transition and later on.[9]

Finally, the increasingly competitive field of project financing will require differential services such as

- identifying suitable local partners;
- arranging for foreign developers cheap-cost financing that goes beyond the use of export-import banks and relies on, for instance, tapping tax- and transactions cost-related arbitrage; and
- helping them hedge against not only economic exposure related to volatility in foreign exchange, interest rates, and commodities but also socio-political exposure of the projects.

8.5.3   Modifications in the notion of country risk

The conventional notion of country risk revolves around credit risk. A transition of LDCs to emerging market-based economies and a transformation of banking activities have some of the following implications.

- Since banks will be arrangers of funds (and not the major providers), credit risk would be less pertinent than *market* risk in the country risk analysis. On the other hand, banks selling credit derivatives on foreign entities, private or public, would face greater risk that does not even appear on the balance sheet.

- Conventional analysis of country risk, a facet of credit risk, regards foreign exchange availability as a critical constraint on a country's ability or willingness to service debt obligations. Foreign exchange reserves or foreign trade would have much less relevance now, especially if countries move away from a fixed exchange rate system to a floating (or at least, managed floating) system.
- Infrastructure capabilities for transactions settlement would be an important component of country risk analysis, although it would be less significant than adequacy of social overhead-related infrastructure.

In brief, modifications in country risk analysis will require in general a shift of focus at the macro level from credit risk to interest or market risk. In specific, this analysis will downplay foreign exchange reserves related factors, and give more prominence to (a) factors signaling socio-political instability with potential for setback to the market-orientation process, and (b) indicators for settlement risk, hitherto ignored in the analysis.

8.6   Recent Financial Crises since 1990

8.6.1   Crises in the 1990s

One major issue in conducting country risk analysis is whether (and to what extent) a country is vulnerable to a financial crisis. Such a crisis is characterized by financial markets beset with unusual volatility that may impede carrying out financial transactions in a normal fashion. In the 1990s, several financial crises have occurred, both in industrialized nations and in newly industrialized nations. We briefly describe these crises and analyze at length the South-East Asian and Argentine crises and a near-crisis in the USA, and relate them to other crises for drawing some generalizations.

Sweden

In the early 1990s, Sweden, a member of the EU, faced a banking crisis.[10] Economic growth in Sweden had been sluggish since the early 1970s: heavy tax burden, extensive social welfare benefits and rigid regulations crippled capital investment and adversely affected the country's competitive position. Credit market deregulation in 1985 led to monetary expansion and the fixed exchange rate system only further exacerbated potentially destabilizing conditions. Reserve depletion due to current account deficits and capital outflows was accommodated with increased interest rates that brought in short-term capital inflows. Ultimately, the high interest rates led to collapse in security prices. In 1991, GDP dropped by 6 percent, the unemployment rate shot up from 3 percent to 12 percent, and bank provision for loan losses climbed to 12 percent of GDP. During September 1992, monetary authorities nudged overnight rates to 500 percent to stem the hemorrhage of capital outflow.

Withdrawal from the ERM[11] in November 1992 (in effect abandoning the fixed exchange rate system) immediately led to significant depreciation of its currency. This depreciation, coupled with an explicit inflation target policy, stabilized the Swedish economy and brought down the domestic interest rates.

UK

In September 1992, the UK interest rate was at an unusually high level of 13.75 percent. This was partially because of the government policy to support the pound sterling – necessitated by the pound parity in the German mark established at too high a level when the UK joined the ERM. Still, the market was not convinced whether the monetary policy was adequate to defend the parity, and sustainable over the long run. Speculative capital outflow ensued, and its escalation led the UK to intervene in the foreign exchange market with its reserves to prop up the pound sterling vis-à-vis the German mark. It was estimated that the Bank of England reportedly spent between $15 billion and $20 billion in just a single day to support the pound. The Bundesbank helped by spending another $50 billion worth of German marks. The Bank of England even borrowed German marks to defend the pound. However, these efforts failed. The UK was forced to let its currency float and thus dropped out of the ERM.

France

In July 1993, Bundesbank, the leading member of ERM, left its high interest rate unchanged in order to contain inflationary forces which might be fanned in the wake of integration of Germany: the restructuring of East Germany, in updating both manufacturing facilities and the woefully inadequate infrastructure framework, would mean government support and expenditure; and the anticipated increase in unemployment and retraining of the work force would add a further burden on the federal budget. Speculators questioned the willingness and ability of France, a member of the ERM, to defend the parity rate by either keeping the interest rates at a level consistent with the German rate or intervening in the foreign exchange markets. As a result, they anticipated parity rate adjustment, that is, French franc devaluation, and dumped the French franc in the foreign exchange market. Bundesbank alone spent about $35 billion to support the French franc but the efforts did not seem to work. By the end of July, the French government along with other ERM members decided to widen the parity rate range to 30 percent.

In essence, the French government abandoned the fixed exchange rate system. As a result, the attack on the French currency subsided.

Latin America

In 1994, Mexico faced another currency crisis. Earlier in 1982 when Mexico suspended its debt service, it came as a surprise to Mexico's lenders and created tremors in global financial markets. This time the crisis was also a surprise, but the market was not totally unprepared. Abolition of controls in the goods and financial markets over the previous decade had led to a rapid increase in imports. High interest rates to contain inflation, combined with the fixed exchange rate, induced significant capital inflow from abroad. This inflow was accompanied by growing imports that were financed through bank loans. Thus the bank-financed imports managed to contain inflationary forces without creating a serious drain on the country's foreign exchange reserves and allowed the government to postpone the day of reckoning for devaluation.

Mexican banks' short-term borrowing from foreign sources increased either because of their own volition or due to foreign lenders' preference.[12] In either case, Mexican banks aggressively expanded their loan portfolios by financing household consumption as well as domestic businesses. This aggressiveness meant an increase in marginal loans. In turn, such marginal loans led to acceleration in non-performing loans. Macroeconomic indices, however, remained positive in terms of low inflation rate and fiscal budget surplus.

When the bubble burst, the IMF called for restructuring of the Mexican banking sector and fiscal reforms in return for a loan package. The IMF and the Clinton administration took exceptional steps to assemble a $50 billion rescue package that would allow the Mexican government to maintain debt service until it could retire the outstanding stock of its dollar denominated debt. At the same time, Mexico responded to the currency crisis by removing the impediment of the fixed exchange rate, that is, it allowed the exchange rate to float. The destabilizing impact of the currency crisis was contained within a relatively short time period.[13]

In 1995, domestic and foreign investors became skittish about Argentina's commitment to a quasi-currency board system (known as "convertibility system") under which the peso was pegged to the dollar. They began to withdraw funds from Argentine banks in the aftermath of the Mexican currency collapse.

Argentina, like Mexico, returned to normalcy quickly after receiving a financial bailout from the USA, multilateral agencies (the IMF, the World Bank, and the Inter-American Development Bank), and some private creditors.[14] Both countries had suffered a sudden drop in GDP but did manage a swift recovery in 1996 and 1997.

Venezuela had maintained a stable managed exchange rate with the US dollar for several years, and it traditionally relied on oil for about 50 percent of its fiscal revenues. Lower oil prices resulting from global competition in 1997–8 substantially reduced Venezuela's revenues and by April 1998 the budget deficit was anticipated to climb to 4.5 percent of GDP. Capital flight ensued, creating a panic in its foreign exchange market. On August 24, 1998, the Venezuelan bolivar closed at 576.5 to the dollar, down 14.7 percent for the year.

Russia

After the demise of the communist regime, the successor Russian government stabilized the Russian ruble through heavy intervention in the foreign exchange market with the help mainly from the IMF. In August 1998, the Russian government forced restructuring of the country's $40 billion treasury bill (GKO) market. Domestic debt restructuring along with the fear of higher inflation and rising unemployment led to a rapid deterioration in the value of the ruble. Seeking to avert a free fall as well as protect its dwindling foreign reserves, Russia's Central Bank on August 27, 1998 acted to cancel indefinitely any trade on the Moscow Interbank Currency Exchange, in effect, withdrawing its support for the ruble.

Although foreign investors favored economic liberalization policies of the Russian government, fiscal deficits resulting from an impotent tax collection system and weak banking system saddled with uncollectible loans seemed to hamper the effectiveness of these policies, thereby stretching the process of transforming Russia into a vibrant market-based economy.

In early September 1998, the Russian Trading System of leading shares dropped 17.1 percent to 63.2 points. Earlier default on debt service and suspension of currency support coupled with the stock market fall sent shockwaves to the world securities markets, especially for bank shares. Many US and European banks had significant exposure to Russia, as Table 8.1 portrays.

Table 8.1   The bank claims on Russia by different countries

Country	Claims (US$ billions)
Germany	30.4
USA	7.0
France	6.9
Italy	4.2
Austria	3.5
Netherlands	2.2
Japan	0.9
UK	0.9

Source: *Wall Street Journal*, August 27, 1998.

The 19-bank syndicate that originally loaned money to Russia formed an international committee to negotiate settlement on loan payment default in August 1998. By March 1999, a 5-bank subcommittee had already recommended to file a suit against Russia to recover the money, but it was unable to convince other members for such action. As a matter of fact, it came to light in early March of 1999 that Deutsche Bank, the leader of the 19-member committee, had unilaterally accepted the restructuring terms offered by Russia, under which international investors would receive

- 70 percent of face value in interest-bearing securities known as OFZs, with maturities from four to five years;
- 20 percent on **zero coupon bonds** with a three-year maturity; and
- 10 percent in cash installments.

In addition, Deutsche Bank was reportedly negotiating with the Russian government for settlement of debt from the Soviet era. To compound the confusion, Chase Manhattan Bank, another member of the international committee, also broke ranks with other members and apparently joined Deutsche Bank in accepting terms proposed by Russians on not only the more recent debt but also the older, Soviet-era debt.

This development clearly illustrates that

- **bank syndicates** are not a monolithic group;
- keeping tight reins on the group in the face of a default is extremely difficult since different members have different agenda; and
- banks do not learn (or tend to forget) lessons from their own experiences (and much less from others').

Brazil

Following the Russian crisis in August 1998, investor attention turned to Brazil. Apparently, some investors who had invested in Russia on margin had to liquidate their investments elsewhere to meet the margin calls. Brazil was supposed to be the target of their reaction. Brazil's economy was suffering from twin problems of the fiscal deficit in excess of 6 percent of GDP, and its overvalued currency peg. An aid package arranged by IMF for $42 billion in

Table 8.2 Currency value changes for different Asian countries

Currency	FX: US$1 June 30, 1998	FX: US$1 June 30, 1997	% change
Chinese yuan	8.281	8.289	+0.09
HK dollar	7.745	7.747	+0.03
Indonesia rupiah	14568.890	1760.000	−87.92
Japanese yen	138.310	114.610	−17.58
Malaysian ringgit	4.100	1.827	−55.44
Korean won	1370.000	641.400	−53.18
Philippine peso	41.500	19.080	−54.02
Thai baht	42.160	17.900	−57.54

Source: *Wall Street Journal*, various dates.

exchange for Brazil's promise to reduce the fiscal deficit helped abate the crisis. Brazil also increased the interest rate to prevent runs on the real, the Brazilian currency.

The crisis, however, flared up again in January 1999, when one of the Brazilian states defaulted on its dollar-denominated obligations. Also, in the interim, the Brazilian government was unable to make any progress on containing the fiscal deficit. Brazil's initial response was 8 percent devaluation. This was hardly adequate. Within days, Brazil decided to let float its currency (reportedly without the IMF's blessing), and on the first day it depreciated by 30 percent. The stock market's reaction, however, was very positive. Although initially it was feared that devaluation would unleash destabilizing inflationary forces, such fears proved groundless. Some observers felt that capital controls in Brazil ruled out capital flight, and devaluation just gave a shot in the arm to Brazilian exports.

South-East Asia

Starting in 1997, many Asian countries encountered financial upheaval whose tremors were felt all throughout the world. This crisis differed in several respects from other crises that preceded as well as those that followed: it was not a balance-of-payment crisis like Mexico; it was a crisis where economic fundamentals were sound, if not strong; and as noted earlier, it took the rating agencies completely by surprise. Its extensive analysis elsewhere has failed to reach an agreement on the causes responsible for the crisis as well as their implications. We discuss below the chronology, analysis of causes, and implications of the crisis.

In the early half of 1997, Thailand's non-bank finance companies suffered from defaults on real estate loans that were financed by foreign debt. Initial ambiguity and later resistance of the Thai government to rescue these companies started the exodus of foreign capital. Thailand chose to let the baht float on July 2, 1997. Capital flight followed in Malaysia and the Philippines. During the first half of 1997 in Korea, two chaebols (conglomerates), Hanbo Steel and Sammi Steel, declared bankruptcy, only to be followed by default by Kia Motor Company; so the stage was set for crisis, but it did not hit Korea before October 1997. The crisis hit Indonesia in August, and threatened both its economic fabric and political stability.

Table 8.2 displays the currency value changes for the Asian countries one year after the crisis.

The stock markets in the countries hit by the currency crisis followed suit in the last quarter of 1997; its impact was felt in both Hong Kong and Russia, and to a lesser extent

Table 8.3 External financing for the Asian region

	1994	1995	1996	1997★
Private flows, net	40.5	77.4	93.0	−12.1
Equity investment	12.2	15.5	19.1	−4.5
Private creditors	28.2	61.8	74.0	−7.6

★ Denotes estimates only. The Asian region in the table includes Indonesia, Malaysia, the Philippines, South Korea and Thailand.
Source: Institute of International Finance, Inc., *Capital Flows to Emerging Economies*, January 1998.

in Latin American countries. The magnitude of capital flight in the crisis-ridden region is provided in Table 8.3.

Given the export-orientation of these Asian countries, a disappointing performance of their exports coupled with a decline in their currency value led to a dramatic increase in the *misery index*, a sum of the unemployment rate and inflation rate. Responses were a combination of (a) the financial commitment and bailout by various multilateral agencies (Indonesia, US$18 billion; Korea, $35 billion; Thailand, $6.7 billion) with attached conditions for financial reforms; and (b) countries' unilateral actions often antithetical to the financial reforms asked by the multilateral agencies. A noteworthy example of the latter was Malaysia.

On September 1, Malaysia imposed stringent currency controls to pull its currency, the ringgit, out of international markets.[15] The ban on ringgit included:

- trading or investing in instruments of offshore banks;
- payment to non-residents on a foreign investment transaction in excess of aspecified amount without prior government approval;
- imports by non-residents unless purchases are paid in foreign currency;
- preventing
  - Malaysian residents from taking out of the country an amount in excess of M$10,000 worth of foreign currency;
  - Malaysian institutions from offering domestic credit facilities to non-resident banks and stockbrokerage companies;
  - foreigners from repatriating proceeds from the sale of local securities;
  - foreigners from repatriating earnings for a year.

8.6.2 Analysis of the Asian financial crisis

Several causes have been ascribed to the Asian financial crisis, but before we investigate them, it is worthwhile showing why conventionally favored economic fundamentals *fail* to yield a satisfactory explanation. We consider a few of them below.

Decline in the export earnings

One reason for the currency crisis is ascribed to capital withdrawal due to the declining earnings potential of the country. Since the Southeast Asian countries are export-oriented,

Table 8.4 Regional annual growth rate of exports (%)

Countries	1990	1991	1992	1993	1994	1995	1996
China	18.2	15.8	18.1	7.1	33.1	22.9	1.6
Indonesia	15.9	13.5	16.6	8.4	8.8	13.4	9.7
Korea	4.2	10.5	6.6	7.3	16.8	30.3	3.7
Malaysia	17.4	16.8	18.5	15.7	24.7	24.7	26.0
Philippines	4.0	8.7	11.2	13.7	20.0	31.6	16.7
Thailand	14.9	23.2	14.2	13.3	22.7	25.1	−1.3
Mexico	17.7	0.7	1.4	9.2	14.2	40.3	22.6

Source: Radelet and Sachs (1998).

performance of their exports is pertinent. Table 8.4 displays the export performance of different countries in the region.

The slowdown of export growth in several countries in the region during 1996 has been primarily attributed to the fall in the demand for semi-conductors (Corsetti et al. 1998) creating sector-specific shocks in these countries. The decline in countries such as Indonesia and the Philippines was, however, far less than the decline in the value of their currencies shown in Table 8.2. Further, the positive growth rate throughout the period suggests that the export performance was not a triggering force.

Current account deficit

The Asian financial crisis has been attributed to weakness in the current account of the Asian countries. The current account as expressed in terms of GDP for various countries is shown in Table 8.5.

Entries in Table 8.5 show that the 1996 current account behavior in South-East Asian countries is not unusual in the context of either their own historical experience or similar countries elsewhere.

Overvalued currency

Several Asian countries (Thailand, Korea, Indonesia, and the Philippines) have pegged their exchange rates to a benchmark currency like the US dollar. As the purchasing power of a pegged currency declines vis-à-vis the benchmark currency, the pegged rate will be in excess of the intrinsic value, that is, the real (inflation-adjusted) exchange rate will be overvalued. The more overvalued a currency, the greater the likelihood of its devaluation. Thus overvaluation will trigger loss of confidence by foreign investors in the pegged currency. Table 8.6 reports the real exchange rates of the Asian currencies for the period 1990–6.

The results indicate that while the real exchange rates for the Asian countries may be overvalued, its magnitude was not severe for the pegged currencies.[16] Also, the Korean won, an undervalued pegged currency, did not escape onslaught of the currency crisis.

Table 8.5 Current account surplus (deficit) in terms of GDP (%)

Countries	1990–95	1996
(Average)		
Asian countries		
China	0.9	0.9
Hong Kong	3.3	−1.2
Korea	−1.2	−4.8
Singapore	12.7	15.5
Taiwan	4.0	4.0
Indonesia	−2.5	−3.7
Malaysia	−5.9	−4.9
Philippines	−3.8	−4.7
Thailand	−6.7	−7.9
Latin America		
Argentina	−1.6	−1.4
Brazil	−0.6	−3.3
Chile	−2.6	−5.4
Colombia	−1.7	−5.5
Mexico	−5.1	−0.6
Other countries		
Israel	−3.9	−7.4
Africa (average)	−11.1	−7.8
Hungary	−4.0	−3.7

Source: Bank for International Settlements, 68th Annual Report, June 1998.

Table 8.6 Real exchange rate (end of year data)

Country	1990	1991	1992	1993	1994	1995	1996
Hong Kong	99.7	103.9	108.5	115.9	114.5	116.6	125.5
Indonesia	97.4	99.6	100.8	103.8	101.0	100.5	105.1
Korea	97.1	91.5	87.8	85.2	84.7	87.8	86.8
Malaysia	97.0	96.9	109.7	111.0	107.1	107.0	111.9
Philippines	92.3	103.1	107.1	97.4	111.6	109.5	116.0
Singapore	101.2	105.7	106.0	108.6	111.9	112.7	117.9
Thailand	102.2	99.0	99.7	101.9	98.3	101.7	107.6

Note: The base figure (100) is the average for the year 1990.
Source: J.P. Morgan.

Excessive short-term foreign debt

A country with a pegged currency often raises short-term interest rates to stem the capital out-flow, and may even manage to attract short-term capital flows from abroad. In a crisis situation, the latter may not be renewed, and the former may resume the flight abroad – adversely affecting the reserves in both cases. Thus a small ratio of short-term foreign debt to reserves suggests relatively little vulnerability of a country to a potential non-renewal of short-term foreign debt.

Table 8.7 Ratio of short-term foreign debt to reserves

Countries	June 1996	June 1997
Asian countries		
Indonesia	1.724	1.704
Korea	1.623	2.073
Malaysia	0.252	0.612
Philippines	0.405	0.848
Taiwan	0.189	0.244
Thailand	0.992	1.453
Other countries		
Argentina	1.325	1.210
Brazil	0.702	0.792
Mexico	1.721	1.187
Pakistan	0.740	2.440
South Africa	4.050	3.124
Zimbabwe	1.319	1.635

Source: Bank for International Settlements and IMF (1998).

Table 8.8 Size of banking sector

	1995 % of GDP	
	Bond market	Bank lending
USA	110	54
Japan	74	152
Malaysia	56	100
Philippine	39	54
Thailand	10	100
Indonesia	6	57

Source: *Wall Street Journal*, October 16, 1997.

Table 8.7 displays this ratio of the short-term foreign debt to reserves. Several observations are pertinent. First, an increase in this ratio for all Asian countries suggests a faster increase in short-term indebtedness than in reserves. Second, several Asian countries have ratios exceeding one, indicating their vulnerability to potential withdrawal of credit facilities. Still, the ratios for the Asian countries are in line with other countries including Pakistan and South Africa that did not experience any financial crisis.

Excessive reliance on bank credit

The debt (bond) markets in South-East Asian countries have been underdeveloped. Companies that need long-term financing would then resort to short-term financing from banks and other financial institutions. As a result, the banking sector of these countries would play an important role in allocating funds to the companies in need of external financing. Table 8.8 illustrates the relative share of the banking sector.

Table 8.9 Expansion of bank credit to private sector

Country	Annual rate of expansion 1990–97	% of GDP 1997
China	13	97
Hong Kong	8	157
Indonesia	18	57
Japan	1.5	111
Korea	12	64
Malaysia	16	95
Philippines	18	52
Singapore	12	97
Thailand	18	105
USA	0.5	65

Source: Bank for International Settlement, Annual Report, 1998.

Table 8.9 provides another perspective on the historical growth of bank loans. Both indicators show that domestic bank loans expanded quickly throughout the region in the years preceding the crisis.

As the Asian economies continued to grow, the banking sector accommodated the need for funding the expansion. Normally, sustained economic growth over time leads to (and presumably requires) development of the securities market that complements banks in financing such growth. Hence, the relative importance of the banking sector declines over time. Laws and regulations, however, may hamper the growth of the non-bank financial sector. It is also possible that borrowers eschew security issuance and keep relying on banks for funding needs to circumvent public scrutiny of their operations, especially when banks are prone (or jawboned) to allocate funds on the basis of non-economic considerations. For example, state-owned banks in Indonesia and Korea were reportedly allowed to circumvent many regulations without penalty and extend loans where "strategic" considerations outweighed the absence of economic justifications. Finally, several major corporations in Indonesia had their own banks and thus the arm's length evaluation of credit request by the parent would not have been plausible. We now examine this line of reasoning.

Expansion of loan activities by itself does not mean indiscriminate lending. Non-performing loans provide a good signal in this instance. Table 8.10 reports that the quality of loans, in inverse proportion to the non-performing loans, has not been out of line historically or in the context of other emerging economies.

In brief, historical records show that while reliance on bank credit did not decrease over time, banks did not provide credit indiscriminately, if non-performing loans are any indication.

Excessive investment in risky projects

As the foreign capital inflows (especially Japanese capital with low cost and equally low economic return domestically) increase, banks may extend credit for marginal investment, that is, investment in risky projects with low or inadequate expected profitability.

Table 8.10 Non-performing loans (% of total loans)

Countries	1990	1994	1995	1996
Indonesia	4.5	12.0	10.4	8.8
Korea	2.1	1.0	0.9	0.8
Malaysia	20.4	8.1	5.5	3.9
Thailand	9.7	7.5	7.7	N/A
Mexico	2.3	10.5	14.4	12.5
Argentina	16.0	8.6	12.3	9.4

Source: Bank for International Settlements.

Table 8.11 Incremental capital-output ratio (ICOR)

Country	1987–92	1993–96
China	3.1	2.9
Hong Kong	3.7	6.1
Indonesia	3.8	4.9
Korea	4.0	4.9
Malaysia	3.7	4.8
Philippines	6.0	5.5
Singapore	3.6	4.0
Taiwan	2.4	3.9
Thailand	3.4	5.1

Source: Corsetti et al. (1998).

The attribute of excessive investment is often tested by a standard measure of investment efficiency – the *incremental capital output ratio* (ICOR). ICOR is defined as the ratio of the *incremental* investment (as a percentage of GDP) to the rate of economic growth. The higher the ICOR, the lower the investment efficiency. The low productivity of investments in the Asian countries as measured by the ICOR is demonstrated in Table 8.11.

Although ICOR indicates some increases, the increases for some countries are only moderate. Further, this ratio presumes that investment proportion in infrastructure projects (that have considerable lead time before coming on stream) is stable over time. Increased undertakings of infrastructure projects in South-East Asia cast doubts on negative inference of the increased ICOR.

Property market bubbles

Another facet of marginal or risky investment is related to real estate. One common reason cited in the press for the Asian crisis was the burst of the real estate market bubble that increased the banks' and other financial institutions' portfolios of non-performing loans on marginal real estate projects. However, as shown in Table 8.12, the real estate property prices hardly increased over the 1991–6 period in Bangkok Grade A office space or in Jakarta.

Another indicator of the real estate price movement is the vacancy rate. A high vacancy rate may indicate excessive (or presumably speculative) construction of real estate, sluggish demand for rental space, or a combination of the two. Table 8.13 displays the vacancy rate for

Table 8.12 Land values of Grade A office space for Thailand and Indonesia

Period	Sales price: Bangkok (baht/m. sq.)	Capital value Jakarta ($/m. sq.)
Q4, 1990	66.0	3019
Q4, 1991	67.0	2788
Q4, 1992	60.0	2482
Q4, 1993	59.5	2327
Q4, 1994	60.5	2358
Q4, 1995	60.5	2179
Q4, 1996	60.4	2250
Q2, 1997	43.0	2267

Source: Data Stream.

Table 8.13 Central business district office vacancy rates

City	1997 (%)
Bangkok	15.0
Hong Kong	6.0
Jakarta	10.0
Kuala Lumpur	3.0
Manila	1.0
Singapore	8.0
Shanghai	30.0

Source: J.P. Morgan, *Asian Financial Markets*, January 1998.

various cities in South-East Asia. The vacancy rate for every Asian city (except Shanghai) is below 15 percent, which is low compared to many US cities such as Dallas and Houston, and far less below the 30 percent vacancy rate in several major American cities during the 1980s. The results further suggest that in terms of both cash flow (vacancy rate) and market value, real estate investments in Asian cities do not appear to suffer from pressure perceived in the press.

In sum, data cited above do not permit denoting the Asian crisis as the balance of payments crisis, where policy responses to balance of payments maladies (such as inadequate reserves and current or trade account deficits) unleashed destabilizing forces and distorted the resource allocation process.[17] Nor does it justify unequivocally placing blame on banks for their "unsound" loans or on risky, low-return real estate investments for the crisis.

8.6.3 Economic fundamentals of the Asian crisis

One interesting aspect of the Asian financial crisis is that fundamental economic factors were sound. Over the period of 1992–6, the GDP growth of the Asian countries was sustained and in the respectable range of 6–8 percent; the inflation rate range was 3–9.5 percent

(Corsetti et al. 1998); the savings rate range was 18–36 percent (Statistical Appendix, IMF 1997); and there were improvements in the life expectancy rate, literacy rate, and the lowest income bracket group (Radelet and Sachs 1998).

Although paucity and lack of reliability of data prevent one from making a definitive case, the current thinking seems to support the notion that a *combination* of factors, such as excessive short-term borrowing from foreign sources and distortion in allocation of financial sources, was responsible for the crisis. Furthermore, where such combinations were not in the danger zone, the impact of contagion cannot be ruled out.[18]

Implications of this result, however, have been controversial. One school, the capital myth school, blames *speculative* capital flows harming these countries, which were by and large in sound economic shape;[19] and it recommends regulation of capital mobility. The other school, a jawbones school, blames governments for jawboning and thereby distorting the resource allocation process that forced or scared the foreign capital into exiting,[20] and its prescription is a removal of government interference in the market place.

We present now a case, which focuses on a country that has a government

- which has not jawboned the investment decisions under normal circumstances and still faced speculative capital flows; and
- in the face of speculative capital movement, introduced measures that were perhaps as harsh and sweeping as those employed by Malaysia, and was less effective than expected.

To set the stage, consider a country, which has a fixed or quasi fixed exchange rate system while its capital and/or current accounts have been freely convertible.

As we stated in Chapter 3, under the fixed exchange rate system (an impediment for the competitive foreign exchange market), a government defines conversion of its currency into a benchmark (reserve) currency such as the US dollar at a fixed rate, and stands ready to buy or sell the benchmark currency with its own currency at that rate, that is, the parity rate. Over time, it is not unusual to find that the parity rate is no longer realistic, because the pegged economy's relative strength diverges, especially due to divergent inflation rates. If the inflation rate in the pegged currency is expected to increase significantly above that in the benchmark currency, the government of the pegged currency needs to devalue its currency or remain ready for an assault on its foreign exchange reserves.

Unfortunately, the government is generally too reluctant to undertake appropriate devaluation on a timely basis; and eventually when it does devalue, the magnitude of devaluation (reflecting cumulative deterioration) is very likely to be large. During this lead time (time between when devaluation should occur and when it actually occurs), speculators play essentially a no-loss game. When they perceive the current parity rate is unsustainable, they borrow the pegged currency, convert and invest the proceeds in the reserve currency for a given period of time. If the pegged currency devalues within this time period, speculators will require conversion of only a fraction of the reserve currency proceeds to cover the debt obligation in the pegged currency. The only downside risk for speculators is when the devaluation[21] does not materialize within the expected time period. In that case, the cost to the speculators is the interest differential in the two currencies, the (high) borrowing rate in the pegged currency and the (low) investment rate in the reserve currency.

Thus, under the fixed exchange rate system, as the distortion in parity rate increases over time, the government's reluctance to bring it in line with reality allows currency speculators to profit through creating a synthetic call option. Essentially, this creation calls for (a) borrowing the currency under stress at a presumably high interest rate, and (b) converting and investing the proceeds in the reserve currency at a low interest rate (hence, the premium on the synthetic option is defined by the interest differential). This call option yields lopsided payoffs of downside risk of just losing the premium but significant upside gain potential. Speculators are able to undertake such an activity because the current or capital account convertibility is permitted.[22]

The speculative bet on the fixed exchange rate system is best illustrated in the situation of Hong Kong during the 1997 currency crisis. Since 1983, the Hong Kong dollar has been pegged to the US dollar under the currency board system that ties its money supply to its US dollar reserves to ensure parity credibility in the market. While the real value of the Hong Kong dollar (HK$) was high (Table 8.6), and very likely as a result it did have a current account deficit (Table 8.5), these numbers were within the acceptable range. Hong Kong did not have either state-owned banks or regulation and laws that would be deliberately violated by banks to lend to marginal, high-risk firms.

In October 1997, speculators borrowed money from local banks or other local sources and started to sell the HK$ spot (or instead of borrowing in the money market, they just shorted the HK$ in the forward market), exerting substantial pressure on the HK$.

Anticipating that the Hong Kong Monetary Authority (HKMA – the central bank of Hong Kong), would raise the interbank interest rate, these speculators also shorted the Hang Seng Index Futures. When the interest rate climbed, as per speculators' expectation, the stock market decline allowed speculators to pocket a profit of about HK$3.6 billion from the futures contracts. Although the HKMA was able to defend the pegged exchange rate system by (a) prohibiting local banks from loans to speculators,[23] and (b) tapping huge reserves to intervene in the foreign exchange market, the speculators were able to reap the benefit of the "call option" of the pegged exchange rate system.

The Hong Kong government also undertook an extraordinary action of jawboning in the stock market in order to scare away speculators anticipating to profit from a decline in the stock market. It bought a substantial amount of blue chips stocks for two weeks starting mid-August of 1998. The argument for intervention was to restore confidence in the Hong Kong financial market. The intervention in the stock market by a government (which, under normal circumstances, observed a hands-off policy in the financial markets) might have taken observers and market participants totally by surprise. While it is difficult to ascertain which was most effective – the strong action, the surprise it contained, or the no-nonsense directive to banks to refrain from loans to speculators – in ultimately calming down the speculative fever, the crisis underscored the notion that a country cannot have unregulated financial markets when its government finds it necessary to defend the fixed exchange rate system.

Some observations are pertinent in light of the Hong Kong case.

- Before mid-1997, its government did not follow regulatory or economic policies that would have made the country vulnerable, as denoted by Tables 8.14–15, and contrary to the prediction of the Jawbones school.

Table 8.14 12-month percentage change of total loan for use in Hong Kong for 1992–7

1992	1993	1994	1995	1996	1997		
					Mar	June	Sept
11.4	18.2	17.1	11.1	17.1	23.2	26.1	30.7

Source: Mihaljek et al. (1998).

Table 8.15 Non-performing loans

	1992	1993	1994	1995	1996	1997 (June)
Non-performing loans (% of credit exposure)	–	–	–	2.38	2.31	1.81
Default (write-off) rate (%)	0.08	0.23	0.20	0.13	0.10	0.10

Table 8.16 Capital flows of Hong Kong (in HK$ millions), 1993–5

	1993	1994	1995
Capital inflows	316,696	371,305	387,278
Capital outflows	306,350	363,965	372,767
Net flows	10,345	7,340	14,511

Source: Mihaljek et al. (1998).

Credits were readily available in the Hong Kong financial market, but still non-performing loans as well as the default rates were low if not unremarkable.

- Speculators' participation in currency markets was not spontaneous; nor was capital account convertibility a factor initiating the crisis, contrary to the assertions of the Capital Myth theory. Speculators were just the messengers of the bad news and not bad news themselves.

Table 8.16 shows the capital flows for Hong Kong. The results do not support emergence of a trend for capital withdrawal from the Hong Kong market.

- The bad news was: the country's fixed exchange rate was overvalued; and the union with China in June 1997 generated uncertainty[24] or risk that required additional compensation, making investments relatively unattractive.
- Speculators' moves in both the security and the currency markets thus can be explained in terms of selling or shorting stocks that had turned unattractive investments *and* the expectation of ensuing capital flight that would put additional pressure on the overvalued currency.

We now turn to a case which is unusual in that it avoided a potentially systemic crisis, but has implications not only for economic theories that can explain or predict a crisis but also for bank management.

8.6.4 Experience in the USA

In September 1998, reports surfaced that Long Term Capital Management (LTCM), a hedge fund, was in serious trouble. Toward the end of the month, not only were these reports confirmed, but its critical nature was also underscored by a hastily arranged package of $3.625 billion to rescue the fund, at the behest of the Federal Reserve Bank of New York. The following observations are based on press reports at the time.

- LTCM has been in the business of global risk management. Its owners and clients included banks from the USA, Germany, Switzerland, and China.
- It analyzed the unfolding situations, and took positions for its clients and on its own account.
- It started out in 1994 with $1billion of capital. It managed to attract this capital from major financial institutions all over the world by assembling a group of some of the sharpest analysts as well as experienced traders who could efficiently implement implications of sound analysis. It managed to provide its investors returns in excess of 40 percent for each of the years 1995 and 1996.
- In September 1997, LTCM announced to return in January 1998 $3billion, or about one-half of its capital, to investors. The move was consistent with downsizing by similar funds, such as Soros and Paul, Tudor and Jones.
- Among the strategies that backfired for LTCM in 1998 were:
  - *Credit spread* based transactions that involved shorting treasury securities and investing in higher-risk corporate or **mortgage-backed securities** on the expectation that an *upward movement* in interest rate affects more adversely lower-risk securities than higher-risk ones. A *decline* in yield on treasury securities in July 1998 (stemming from investors' anxiety, especially due to the Russian crisis, that led them to park their funds in US treasury securities) had an adverse impact on LTCM's profitability.
  - *Convergence trade* related transactions, where LTCM (expecting a rise in the German interest rates because of the need for convergence in the interest rates in anticipation of the single currency for the European Monetary Union on January 1, 1999) shorted German bunds and invested in Danish securities. A decline in the German interest rate apparently racked up additional losses.
  - Investment in Russian securities was financed through credit lines. This leverage move backfired when in August Russia rescheduled its obligations.
  - LTCM's capital base, which was $3 billion at the beginning of 1998 had shrunk to around $500 million by mid-September; but that did not reflect the impact of impending margin calls: liquidating securities to meet margin calls at the wrong time[25] would only have decimated the battered equity base (LTCM's equity multiplier was anywhere in the range of 25× to 50×).

- Strategic partners of LTCM had capital contributions of $100 million apiece at the beginning of the year. Bank of China (a quasi government organization), UBS (a Swiss bank), and Dresdner bank (Germany) were among this group of partners. UBS reported after-tax losses of $685 million on a 15 percent equity stake in LTCM. Dresdner Bank reported roughly $143 million in write-down of its investment in the third quarter of 1998.
- By the end of September, another hedge fund, reporting losses worth 30 percent of its capital base for the year, blamed the losses on LTCM.
- On September 16, Alan Greenspan, the Fed chairman, testified in the US Congress that hedge funds are not that large in the total context of the system; hence are not a threat for the stability of the financial system.
- On September 23, a week later, Greenspan stated that policy-makers around the world have to be especially sensitive to the deepening signs of global distress, which can impact their own economies. On the same day, the Federal Reserve Bank of New York, which had hastily assembled major financial institutions, announced infusion of $3.5 billion equity in LTCM by a group of 16 commercial and investment banks.
- The UK Financial Services Authority and the Swiss Bank Commission opened investigations specifically related to LTCM and other funds to determine their banks' exposure.

It is obvious from the above description that a single institution had generated significant losses for its sophisticated investors,[26] including major banks around the world. These losses could have been responsible for the Brazil crisis, either because of the need for rebalancing investor portfolios or due to liquidity shortfall for investors in Brazilian securities. These losses, furthermore, came as a surprise to these investors as well as regulatory authorities in the industrialized world (information asymmetry due to opaqueness or lack of timely reporting). Their potential for generating *systemic* risk has been underscored by (a) the direct involvement of the Federal Reserve Bank of New York in the work-out package; (b) pronouncements by the Fed chairman in a week that showed a dramatic reversal; and (c) banking authorities elsewhere specifically investigating the impact of a single entity's transactions. Perhaps because of swift regulatory involvement or just sheer good luck, the dire consequences were averted. But it does raise the following questions:

- What measures can ensure adequate transparency in transactions in terms of both timeliness and clarity in terms of implications? Should they be made a part of regulation? Would such requirements adversely affect efficacy of organizations subject to such transparency regulations?
- Do we have the capability for accurately assessing implications even if we have timely access to information? For instance, as an owner of a 15 percent equity stake in LTCM, UBS presumably had access to whatever information it wanted. The size of the loss suggests that the bank management was unaware of what was going on. If, on the other hand, it was fully aware of the risk, was assumption of such risk consistent with the bank's mission to its stockholders and other stakeholders?
- Can the financial market be relied on to charge an appropriate premium to a firm assuming excessive risk? Can the market contain the contagion stemming from failure

of a big firm? Or would the market participants reduce their individual risk and in the process destabilize the system?

Naturally, there are no easy answers, if they exist at all. However, banks treading uncharted but interconnected waters may have to be prepared for them as much as Japan and California are prepared for earthquakes.

8.6.5   Crisis in the 2000s – Latin America

In the aftermath of the early 1980s crisis, recovery of emerging nations was not uniform. Argentina was still vulnerable to bouts with hyperinflation. After his election in 1989, President Menem proceeded to streamline the taxation system, cut tariffs, privatize state enterprises, and encourage foreign investment through deregulation. Above all, in 1991, his administration adopted a quasi-currency board system (known as the "convertibility system") under which the peso was pegged to the US dollar. The critical difference from the currency board system was that the mechanical rule of tying money supply exclusively to the stock of the reserve currency (a hallmark of the orthodox currency board system) was replaced by a discretionary power granted to the central bank to regulate money supply.

During 1991–4, these measures generated respectable growth, tamed hyperinflation, reduced fiscal deficits, and attracted foreign capital. However, the 1995 crisis in Mexico also infected Argentina, which suffered from both capital outflows and a decline in its GDP by 2.8 percent. Although the economic growth resumed during 1996–8 (5.5 percent in 1996, 8.1 percent in 1997), it came at a price of worsening current account deficit and increasing debt burden.

The 1997 Asian financial crisis had repercussions throughout Latin America. At first, Argentina seemed less affected by this crisis than its neighbors. But while Brazil bounced back in 1999 following the real devaluation, Argentina's situation worsened. Insistence on maintaining parity in the face of the strengthening US$ resulted in an overvalued peso that in turn rendered Argentine exports uncompetitive and its imports attractive. The net result was growing trade deficits; deepening recession; high unemployment and business bankruptcies; industrial decline; heightened sensitivity to external shocks; and capital flight (stemming from the fear of imminent peso devaluation).

In 2000, the new administration of De La Rua obtained from the IMF a three-year $7.2 billion stand-by arrangement by accepting the condition of a strict fiscal adjustment. The IMF had assumed 3.5 percent GDP growth in 2000 (actual growth turned out to be 0.5 percent).

In January 2001, multilateral agencies including the IMF agreed to an aid package of $40 billion in response to deteriorating economic conditions. In June, the government announced conversion of short-term debt of $29.5 billion, primarily owned by banks, into long-term debt at higher interest rates. In September, based on Argentina's commitment to implement the "Zero Deficit Law," the IMF increased its lending commitment by another $7.2 billion. Another debt restructuring, this time of longer maturity, worth $60 billion followed in November. This action signaled imperiled liquidity and led to a bank run in

December. The administration responded by restricting deposit withdrawals. To add insult to injury, the IMF withheld a $1.24 billion loan installment, citing Argentina's chronic inability to meet fiscal targets. The government announced default on its debt obligations, in the wake of resignation by De La Rua on December 20.

In January 2002, President Duhalde announced

- devaluing the peso by 29 percent (to 1.4 to the dollar) for major foreign commercial transactions, and a floating rate for all other transactions;
- converting all debts up to $100,000 in pesos (passing on devaluation cost to creditors, notably foreign banks);
- imposing capital and bank account controls;
- levying a new tax on oil to compensate creditors for future losses;
- renegotiating public debt; and
- promising a balanced budget.

By the end of January 2002, the peso had lost 30 percent of its value in US$.

The financial crisis has still not abated (by April 2003). Nor has the economy responded to a variety of ad hoc measures. If anything, these measures have muddled the already-confusing picture. But the worst part, from our perspective, is that the Argentine banking system has been left in shambles.[27]

To start with, foreign banks that owned about 73 percent of the banking assets were the major holders of claims issued by the federal and provincial governments during the late1990s. JP Morgan estimated total exposure of the banking sector to the federal and provincial governments at 30.7 billion pesos, 180 percent of the total banking sector equity. Many of these claims were dollar-denominated. At the same time, the impending crisis, widely anticipated, led depositors to convert or maintain their deposits in dollars: the share of deposits in US dollars relative to local currency in Argentina went up dramatically from about 52 percent in mid 1998 to 72 percent by the end of 2001 (Perry and Serven 2002). The de-dollarization (conversion from dollar denomination to the peso by decree) in 2002 had a disastrous impact on banks' balance sheets: dollar-denominated assets were converted into pesos at 1 : 1 peso-dollar parity, while dollar deposits were converted into pesos at 1.4 pesos per dollar. In addition, both de-dollarized assets and liabilities were to be indexed to the emerging hyper-inflation. Thus banks suffered from not only illiquidity, aggravated by net deposit outflows, but also insolvency stemming from debt restructuring and conversion losses.

As if this was not enough, in May 2002, the Argentine crisis spread to Uruguay, which still had not recovered from the fallout of the South-East Asian crisis of 1997–8 as evidenced by a fall in its GDP by 2 percent in 2000. In order to contain damage, Uruguay effectively matched the devaluation of the Argentine peso by widening the band of parity to 12 percent. This has managed to push the dollar-denominated debt to more than 50 percent of its GDP. In order to obtain help from the IMF, the government also prepared a plan for cutting the budget deficit from 5 to 2.5 percent of GDP by cutting expenditures and increasing taxes. It did receive roughly $750 million of a three-year standby loan, far below what the government hoped to receive. In the interim, its dollar reserves plummeted by Argentine nationals' liquidation of dollar-denominated deposits in Uruguay. In July 2002, the crisis spread to Brazil, whose currency, the real, lost 20 percent of its value. By August 2002, the crisis – deepened by capital flight from Brazil and its potential default on $250 billion of external debt – managed to further weaken the situation in Uruguay, and to a lesser extent in Mercosur (the Latin American trade block) partners Chile and Colombia. The US hastened to provide Brazil with a bridge loan of $1.5 billion for defence of the real. The IMF agreed to provide Brazil an aid package of $30 billion with $25 billion to be made available in 2003 only if Brazil agrees to maintain its budgetary surplus through 2005.[28]

There is still no agreement regarding the relative importance of critical factors that contributed to the Argentine (and Latin American, in a broader sense) crisis: policy measures such as free-market policies (deregulation, privatization, trade and financial liberalization) and the convertibility system (often confused with the currency board system), as well as external factors like the stance of the multilateral agencies and the US government have been both extolled (or exonerated) and blamed! Fiscal measures or government corruption have been deemed either critical or irrelevant for the crisis. Similarly, recommendations to resolve the ongoing crisis have embraced conflicting measures. As an example, a range of alternatives – from (a) "dollarization" (replacing the peso with the dollar); (b) a two-track system that would retain the peso for transactional purposes while using the dollar for storage of value function; (c) a linkage of the peso to a basket of currency, which may or may not contain dollars; (d) devaluation; to (e) flexible exchange rate for the peso – has been recommended or condemned either for transitional stability or for the long run.

For bank management, Argentina has provided a painful experience. In the early 1990s, Argentina held out a very appealing promise for banks to get on the ride before it was too late. Even as late as 1998, the World Bank ranked Argentina second after Singapore among developing countries because of the good quality of its regulatory environment. And yet, two years later, foreign banks in Argentina did not know which way to turn and extricate themselves from an untenable situation.

Both the Asian and the Latin American crises suggest that there is no single panacea. For instance, devaluation enabled Brazil to pull itself out, while it has failed to work in Indonesia and (so far) in Argentina. The IMF help, as well as insistence on open markets along with fiscal responsibility, worked in Mexico, while it has failed so far in Argentina.

The following generalizations, however, may provide helpful guideposts for cross-border banking activities.

- Countries are comparable to firms with respect to volatility or risk. A combined measure of operating risk (volatility of the external trade-related flows of an economy) and financial risk (debt burden owed to foreigners or in foreign currency) determines the degree of vulnerability of the economy.
- Emerging economies are likely to have a fixed exchange rate system of one kind or another, especially since their capital markets lack breadth or depth. In turn, the fixed exchange rate is accompanied with capital account inconvertibility that safeguards the economy against swift and volatile short-term capital flows.
- Stability provided by fixed currency rates creates distortions over time as the economic performance veers away from the standard provided by, say, purchasing power parity or relative inflation rate. Unless timely and appropriate adjustments in the currency rates are made, currency value distortions spill over in financial and goods markets.

- In order to prevent a crisis that exacerbates these forces in capital/goods markets, proper controls need to be in place before or on the eve of the crisis. This brings us back to the hierarchy of goods-financial-currency markets. Pegged currencies, in conjunction with proper capital (or goods) market controls have prevented economies from getting swept into a self-feeding downward spiral; for example, Malaysia and Hong Kong. On the other hand, countries such as Indonesia and Argentina have prolonged crises because they missed the window of opportunity that would have been provided by timely controls in the capital/goods markets. Banks need to tread gingerly in such territories.

8.7 Conclusion

This chapter discussed various issues concerning country risk analysis. The traditional, heuristic approach was contrasted with the portfolio approach: whereas the latter's systematic treatment of country risk analysis is appealing, practical estimation of required parameters severely limits its applicability.

The traditional analysis using a quantitative model that links country risk to qualitative variables was then discussed. Perception of country risk, reflected in terms of either risk premium embedded in bond yields or judgmental scores of country rating, is linked under this approach to explanatory variables including both economic and political indicators that include liquidity, debt structure, coverage ratio, profitability, and political risk factors.

International debt crisis during the 1980s was discussed and alternative unilateral (loan sales in the secondary markets), bilateral (debt-for-equity swaps), and multilateral (Brady plan) solutions were analyzed. Additionally, modifications needed in the conventional country risk analysis were highlighted in the context of emerging trends of a shift toward market-based economies and banking industry's response to changing environments.

Finally, the financial crises from 1990 onward were examined. Although a financial crisis is caused by a combination of factors that may vary in different situations, a key common factor is the incompatibility of different policies pursued by a government. Specifically, a country that pegs its exchange rate while it liberalizes its current or capital account (or capital market) will be vulnerable to such crisis. Still, the example of LTCM demonstrates that crises do not have to emanate from or be confined to emerging nations; they can also germinate in advanced, market-based economies. Indeed, the potential for emergence of a destabilizing event is much greater than ever before in an interconnected market.

DISCUSSION QUESTIONS

1 Since the 1980s, banks have shunned the LDCs. Why are we then concerned with country risk?

2 What have been the traditional approaches used by US banks for country risk analysis? What developments in recent years have cast doubts on their effectiveness?

3 a Describe briefly how the portfolio approach can be used in country risk analysis.
   b In Chapter 1, it was stated that the modern portfolio theory is based on the premise of efficient financial markets. What implications does this statement have, if any, on extending it to country risk analysis?
   c Are there any other problems or issues that have a bearing on such extension?

4 How and why were the financial crises in the 1980s different from or similar to those in the 1990s? What expectations do you have for potential financial crises in the first decade of the twenty-first century?

5 Why do debt negotiations collapse in the wake of default in loan syndication? Discuss measures that would prevent such collapse(s), and implementability of these measures.

6 This chapter introduces swaps that can be used to mitigate country debt problems. What is their relationship with swaps introduced in Chapters 3 and 6?

7 The discussion on the South-East Asian crisis suggested that security markets diminish the importance of the banking sector by directly providing funds to the needy businesses. Earlier it was suggested that banks having a country debt problem could reduce their losses through the use of secondary (security) markets. How would you reconcile these two statements?

8 How were the Baker plan and Brady plan different from each other, especially in terms of their effectiveness? What factors were responsible for their differing effectiveness?

9 What developments led to the South-East Asian financial crisis? Could they have been prevented from occurring in the first place?

10 Since early 1990, Smart Bank has extensively loaned money to foreign businesses. During the Asian financial crisis, a South Korean customer defaulted on its US$-denominated loan of US$5 million from Smart Bank with an interest rate of 12 percent. During negotiations for loan restructuring, Smart Bank suggested that it would roll over the loan for another year, if the customer would grant Smart Bank the choice of payment between US$5 million and 6,500 million won for principal, when the loan matures. (The won payment was arrived at by multiplying the principal amount of US$5 million with the prevailing exchange rate of won 1,300/US$).

   a Suppose the currency rate has an equal probability to depreciate to won 1,700/US$ or appreciate to won 1,300/US$. What is the value of the option to Smart Bank, assuming the interest cost for the bank of 10 percent?
   b What will be the value of an option for 12 percent interest cost for the bank?
   c If probability is 80 percent for the currency rate won 1,300/US$ and 20 percent for won 1,700/US$, what will be the new value of the option for 10 percent interest cost for the bank?

> d Discuss the issues involved in using the prevailing exchange rate (won 1,500/US$) for the option feature in the loan covenant.
>
> 11 Chaste Bank of New York extended a US$10 million loan (with annual interest payments to a Thai bank in 1996. Due to the rapid decline of the baht currency in 1998, the Thai bank was unable to repay the interest payments. After extensive negotiations, Chaste Bank agreed to reduce the interest rates from 8 percent to 5 percent and lengthen the maturity of the loan from three years to five years. The only concession that the Thai bank made was to pay an upfront fee of $250,000. Analyze the ramifications of the concession for Chaste Bank if its cost of capital is 6 percent.

APPENDIX J: CHRONOLOGY OF THE ASIAN FINANCIAL CRISIS

1997	Events
Early 1997	Heavy interventions by the Thai government in spot and forward baht markets
May 15	Thailand introduces controls for the onshore and offshore Thai baht markets
July 2	Floating of the Thai baht
July 11	(1) The Philippine Central Bank widens unspecified band for the Philippine peso
	(2) The Support band for the Indonesian rupiah is widened from 8 to 12 percent
July 28	(1) Thailand asks the IMF for financial help
	(2) Malaysian ringgit falls by about 4.8 percent
August 14	Floating of the Indonesia rupiah
August 20	IMF approves $3.9 billion loan for Thailand
October 20–23	(1) Hong Kong Hang Sang Index falls by 23 percent in three days
	(2) Korean won comes under pressure in the currency markets
October 27	(1) US stock prices decline by 7 percent
	(2) Sharp declines in Latin American stock markets
October 28	Russian stock prices drop by 23 percent
October 31	Central Bank of Brazil doubles its intervention rate by 43 percent
November 5	IMF approves $10.1 billion for Indonesia
November 10	Russian interest rate increases by 7 percent and the intervention band for the ruble is widened from 5 percent (both sides) to 15 percent
November 20	Support band for Korean won is widened from 2.25 to 10 percent.
November 21	Korea applies for IMF credit
December 4	IMF approves credit of $21 billion for Korea
December 16	Floating of Korean won
1998	
January 29	Korean government and external creditors agree to exchange $24 billion of short-term loans for government-guaranteed loans at floating rates of 2.25–2.75 percentage points over six-month LIBOR.
February 9–10	IMF and external creditors oppose Indonesian currency board proposal
March 4	IMF relaxes certain macroeconomic policy restrictions for Thailand

August 27	Russian Central Bank stops intervention in currency markets to support ruble
September 1	Mahathir Mohamad, the Malaysian Prime Minister imposes stringent currency controls to pull the ringgit out of international financial markets
	(A decree prohibits foreign portfolio investors from repatriating profits to Korea for 12 months).

NOTES

1 For private entities, country risk will be the added dimension to the credit risk considered in Chapter 7.
2 See Appendix I in Chapter 7.
3 A caveat should be noted. Some observers today find the balance of payment document less reliable due to cross-country derivative transactions that obscure, for instance, a country's true free reserves.
4 Some observers contend that a sudden rush to privatization without ensuring an adequate infrastructure only worsens the situation: this process, among other things, permits plundering by a few of the populace at large. Their pessimistic assessment of Russia, for instance, is based on this contention. The same premise leads them to be cautiously positive about China because of the Chinese gradual approach in liberalizing the Chinese economy.
5 Securitization basically calls issuing securities on a bundle of a large number of assets that share similar risk characteristics; the investor in these securities is able to hold a small portion of each of the asset and thereby achieve actuarial risk experience.
6 For an interesting twist on the leadership issue, see the discussion in Section 8.6.1 on the Russian crisis in 1998 and Deutsche Bank.
7 The last hurdle would be irrelevant when a multinational firm seeking local direct investment was identified early on for a swap transaction.
8 Even when an erstwhile state enterprise is able to retain its monopolistic power in the *goods* market, it still has to compete with other enterprises in *financial* markets.
9 By their very nature, lucrative over-the-counter derivatives offered by banks are opaque. Adverse publicity generated by Enron's extensive use of complex derivatives will put banks active in this field on a defensive vis-à-vis other investors, regulators, and the public at large.
10 Finland encountered a similar banking problem.
11 As mentioned in Appendix B in Chapter 2, the ERM is essentially a grid of the fixed exchange rate system. Its one distinctive feature is that its members have a joint, bilateral responsibility to defend the parity rate range. Thus if the Swedish krona were to come under pressure as compared to the German mark, both Sweden and Germany would come to defend the parity rate.
12 Foreigners' expectation that IMF would bail out banks in case of troubles – a moral hazard – made banks an attractive conduit for their investment.
13 The oil price decline in 1998 did not result in a rerun of 1982 because the Mexican economy diversified its exports by 1998. Oil exports represented only 5.9 percent of the total exports in 1998 as compared to 70 percent in 1982 and 29 percent in 1986. Further, even if there were adverse impact, very likely it would not have been magnified because of the floating exchange rate system adopted by Mexico in 1995. At the same time, the IMF bailout was administered across the board, and banks which had provided speculative loans managed to obtain protection as much as banks with conservative management policies – a moral hazard.
14 During the turmoil, Argentina (a) maintained neutrality of monetary policy governed strictly by currency reserves, and (b) refused to bail out weak banks with public sources. It is conceivable

that this stance bolstered the credibility of Argentina in financial markets and prevented further capital flight that would have seriously damaged the Argentine economy.

15 These measures were directed to stem capital outflows. But under normal circumstances, such measures would likely discourage long-term capital flows (including private, direct investment).

16 The Hong Kong dollar has a currency board system. As noted in Appendix A in Chapter 2, the US$ reserves determine the basic money supply of the Hong Kong dollar.

17 This statement warrants a qualification. Nusbaum (1997) reported that the IMF had been concerned about cross-border derivatives worth roughly $26 *trillion* in 1995 that did not appear in the balance of payments statistics, and that would inject as much as a 25 percent bias in the reported data as a result. Consider a Thai bank facing a ceiling on domestic equity exposure that entered in a *total return credit derivative* (see Chapter 6) whereby it would purchase US Treasury securities and swap its return for total returns on Thai equity purchased by a foreign financial institution. With the collapse of the Thai baht and the domestic equity market, the Thai bank would face a double-barreled liquidity drain – a higher (dollar-based) debt service charges in baht precisely when its indirect equity investments were presumably generating negative total returns. Indeed, any problem faced by the Thai bank would be easily transmitted to another country in the region, especially when the "foreign" institution was based in the neighborhood country.

18 Marshall (1998) defines contagion as coordination failure that stems from asymmetric information where investors take their cue from each other in the absence of adequate international regulatory oversight.

19 See, for instance, Bhagwati (1998).

20 Barth et al. (1998).

21 Although up valuation is theoretically possible, it is not a realistic scenario under the given circumstances.

22 A current account convertibility allows unregulated access to foreign currencies for current transactions such as export or import of goods and services. Capital account *in*convertibility, on the other hand, requires obtaining permission from authorities for a foreign-exchange denominated financial transaction. Such inconvertibility is designed to thwart speculative activities. But the current account convertibility can readily undermine the intent of capital account inconvertibility: nothing can prevent, say, an exporter or an importer from undertaking speculative activities under the guise of a current account related activity.

23 Such a ban could have been easily circumvented by a short forward-forward swap, as explained in Chapter 3.

24 The Chinese government's reassurances notwithstanding, this uncertainty might have at least added to the economy's vulnerability. Traders and financial analysts in Hong Kong were very vocal in expressing their concerns about the likelihood of the Chinese government's interference in the free-market economy after reversion of Hong Kong to China.

25 One market estimate put the forced liquidation to be anywhere between $80 billion and $100 billion.

26 Several banks reportedly were connected to LTCM in various capacities such as partners, lenders, and clients.

27 Some observers compare the Argentine situation to that in Indonesia, both mired in a multi-year economic morass.

28 Luiz Inácio Lula da Silva was elected as Brazil's president in 2002. As a leader from a left-wing party, likely to favor increased welfare expenditures, he has added to the uncertainty about economic stability. So far (April 2003), he has struck a moderate note, and has continued his predecessor Cardoso's economic reforms that include (a) reducing government expenditures, (b) increasing taxes for infrastructure, and (c) increasing the investment rate, including direct foreign investment. Still, any increase in the prevailing high unemployment rate only further complicates a meaningful prognosis.

CHAPTER 9

Asset and Liability Management

LEARNING OBJECTIVES

- To learn about gap and duration gap tools that a bank uses to deal with interest rate risk
- To understand the impact of foreign exchange risk on the overall risk of the bank
- To learn about the impact of non-parallel shift in the term structure of interest rate on the bank's hedging strategy
- To learn the different balance-sheet and off balance-sheet strategies that deal with interest rate risk

9.1 Introduction

For a non-financial firm, the MM theory provides at least a starting point for the resource allocation process: the firm should find the net present value of the prospective real asset first as if it is being financed exclusively by stockholders; and if it is positive, then the appropriate asset financing should take advantage of existing financial market imperfections. For a financial firm or bank, such a dichotomy of investment and financing decisions creates one major problem. The bank's assets are as much financial as its liabilities. But more fundamentally, as we saw in Chapter 1, the basic premise for the existence of banks is rooted in financial market inefficiencies, and this premise is at odds with the MM theory. Indeed, such inefficiencies signify a joint consideration of investment and financing decisions, and the computation of the cost of capital (as suggested by, for instance, MM) as a cutoff rate becomes less meaningful for a bank than for the non-financial firm.[1] Furthermore, any investment project cannot be considered in isolation or by itself. Instead, its impact on the owners must be analyzed in the context of other investments of the firm.

Bank management practice that focuses on joint consideration of (a) investment-financing decisions, and (b) an investment proposal with existing investments (rather than the proposal in itself) is consistent with the above conceptual implications. Hence, this chapter concentrates on bank management practice that emphasizes asset-liability management, rather than consideration of a single project. In turn, the asset-liability management practice has highlighted the risk (rather than return) dimension.[2] Its objective has been to optimize three components of risk: liquidity risk, credit risk, and interest rate risk. Liquidity risk is typically monitored by liability and liquidity managers; Chapters 4–6 extensively discussed management of this risk. Similarly, most banks delegate the management of credit risk to the bank's loan and investment centers; credit risk, specifically pertaining to the international dimension, was analyzed in Chapters 7 and 8. Hence we concentrate here on the interest rate risk dimension as it relates to asset-liability management.[3] One risk typically ignored in the domestic, single-currency dimension is the foreign exchange risk. As we saw in Chapters 3–6, currency risk is intimately interrelated to the interest rate risk. Therefore, for expository ease, we will first focus on a single-currency scenario, and later modify the analysis to include the multi-currency consideration.

This chapter discusses and explains various traditional methods that banks use to manage interest rate risk. It also considers non-traditional methods that employ derivative instruments to achieve similar objectives. In both cases, the presumed objective is to optimize the impact of interest rate change (or related risk variables) on the bank's market (or equity) value.

9.2   Interest Risk Measurement

Given the mix of a bank's assets and liabilities, interest rate changes may raise or lower the spread or net interest income as well as the market value of assets and liabilities, and thereby affect the equity value. Suppose a bank makes 30-year fixed-rate loans and finances these loans with short-term deposits (say, three-month to one year). If there is an unforeseen increase (decrease) in interest rates, a concomitant increase (decrease) in interest expense will narrow (widen) the spread. Alternatively, an unexpected increase (decrease) in interest rates will lower (raise) the value of 30-year loans.[4] Changes in the regulatory outlook, increased bank participation in offshore markets, and greater volatility in interest rates accompanied with narrower spreads in face of stiffer competition have made interest risk management more critical than ever before.

Interest rate risk is primarily measured in terms of the volatility of (a) net interest income, or (b) the bank's value due to changes in the interest rates. Although these two measures are closely related, they do not always convey similar information. The share price volatility reflects only the systematic component of the interest rate risk; thus interest income volatility may not translate in share price volatility on a one-to-one basis. By the same token, a bank with a portfolio of marginal loans may show greater stability in net interest income but higher volatility in its share value over a business cycle; on the other hand, an extremely volatile net interest income from risk-free securities may not translate into high volatility in its share value (Fung et al. 1996). In the final analysis, the share price volatility is the most comprehensive measure of the three in that it reflects information on the (proximate) ratio of expected net interest income to the risk-adjusted rate of return required by shareholders, where the risk-adjustment considers systematic contribution of risk on all dimensions.

Two commonly employed conventional methods for measuring and managing interest rate risk are the gap and duration models. The gap model focuses on net interest income as the target measure of bank performance, while the duration models target primarily the market value of bank equity. We examine below these two methods.

9.2.1 Gap analysis

The objective of this approach is to stabilize or increase the expected net interest income. At a given point, net interest income is managed by dividing the planning period into several intervals, and for each interval a gap is determined, where the gap is the difference between the dollar amount of *rate-sensitive assets* (RSAs) and the dollar amount of *rate-sensitive liabilities* (RSLs). The basic steps of gap analysis are as follows:

- Select a planning period (say, 12 months) for determining the rate-sensitivity of both assets and liabilities.
- Group together assets and liabilities in arbitrarily defined compartments either in terms of their maturity or when the market will revalue them; the principal portion of the asset or liability that is revalued is categorized as rate-sensitive.
- Determine the gap in terms of the dollar difference between RSAs and RSLs for each time compartment.
- Let management evaluate gap information directly and/or through sensitivity analysis.

In short, we have:

$$\text{Gap} = \text{RSAs} - \text{RSLs} \tag{9.1}$$

Example 9.1

The following assets and liabilities ($ million) of a hypothetical bank illustrates the measurement of the gap analysis:

Compartment	Assets	Liabilities	Gap
0–7 days	9,100	10,200	−1,100
7 days–3 month	80,500	90,500	−10,000
3–6 month	95,000	75,000	20,000
1–2 year	4,000	3,000	1,000
above 2 years	20,100	10,000	10,100
	118,700	98,700	20,000

In the above example, the assets and liabilities are divided into five re-pricing intervals, such as 0–7 days and 3–6 months. Each interval contains assets and liabilities that mature in that time interval and thus provides an indication of direction and magnitude of the impact of interest rate change.

As a result, bank management uses the above gap information against expectations of interest rate changes either to hedge net interest income or to speculatively change the size of the gap for each time interval. Hedging removes the volatility of net interest income by either changing the dollar amount of assets and liabilities sensitive to interest rate changes or using less traditional instruments such as forwards, futures, option contracts, and interest rate swaps. Speculation, on the other hand, focuses on improving profitability in the wake of the anticipated interest rate change. If the anticipated change does not materialize, profitability is likely to worsen.

The impact of interest rate changes on the bank's value depends on the bank's rate-sensitivity with respect to earnings, portfolio mix, and gap value. Thus, changes in interest rates can increase, decrease, or have no effect on the overall bank's net interest income. A *negative* gap indicates that the bank has more RSLs than RSAs; thus more liabilities than assets are to mature during the entire period encompassing the gap. When interest rates decrease with a negative gap, the bank will pay lower interest charges on all re-priceable liabilities and earn lower yields on all re-priceable assets. Since such liabilities exceed the counterpart assets, the saving in interest expense will be higher than the loss in interest income. Therefore, net interest income increases with a negative gap, when interest rates decline. The reverse occurs when interest rates increase: such increases lead to losses with a negative gap.[5] In short, a negative gap helps during declining interest rates, and hurts during rising interest rates.

A positive gap indicates that a bank has more RSAs than the RSLs. When interest rates rise in that interval, interest income increases more than interest expense because more assets are re-priced, thus net income increases. Decreases in rates have the opposite effect: interest income falls more than interest expense causing net interest income to fall.

If the bank has zero gap, the RSAs equal the RSLs and interest rate changes have no impact on net interest income. The relationship between gap and changes in interest rates is outlined in Box 9.1.

A bank may choose to speculate on future interest rates by actively managing the gap. For example, if management expects an interest rate increase in a given time interval, it may move its gap in the positive direction, that is, decrease the maturity of its assets and/or increase the maturity of its liabilities belonging to longer time intervals. Of course, such an action is predicated on not only an accurate interest rate forecast but also the ability to manipulate maturities at reasonable cost.

The preceding discussion also suggests that when a bank has non-zero gap, it is speculating. Thus a bank with a positive gap is explicitly or implicitly betting that the interest rate is going to increase.

The primary strength of gap analysis is that its calculations are easy and its results are readily understandable. Many asset/liability software programs are available to produce a gap report and analyze a bank's general interest rate sensitivity. Nonetheless, this method suffers from some weaknesses also.

- It yields ex post measurement errors; for example, rate-sensitive loans linked to a bank's prime rate may not move in step with the CD rate at which the bank raises funds.

Box 9.1 Gap analysis summary

If gap is *positive* (+), interest rates and net interest income move together:
- When interest rate increases, bank's net interest income increases because the increase in interest income is larger than the increase in interest expense;
- When interest rate decreases, bank's net interest income decreases because the decrease in interest income outweighs the decrease in interest expense.

If gap is *negative* (−), interest rates and net interest income move in opposite directions:
- When interest rate increases, bank's net interest income decreases because the increase in interest expense exceeds the increase in interest income;
- When interest rate decreases, net interest income in bank increases because the decrease in interest income is less than the decrease in interest expense.

If gap is *zero* (0)
- Interest rate changes (increases or decreases) have no impact on net interest income because interest income equals interest expense.

- It ignores the time value of money within each interval; thus assets and liabilities may mature at the "front" or the "back" of an interval and are still lumped together without differentiation within that interval.[6]
- This method ignores the cumulative impact of interest rate changes on a bank's position. Gap measures should be calculated over the entire range of re-pricing, yet they often focus on only near-term changes in net interest income. Interest rate changes also affect the value of fixed-rate assets and liabilities and the total risk beyond one year. These cumulative changes on the bank's overall position (i.e., its impact on equity position) are ignored by the gap analysis.
- Gap analysis assumes a parallel shift in the term structure of interest rates. Thus it ignores changes in the *slope* of the term structure that causes variable impact on values of different instruments.

Even when a bank's gap is perfectly matched, a shift in the slope triggered by, say, a Federal Reserve's action may have a dramatic impact on the bank's profit. This volatility in interest rates is commonly known as the *basis risk*. Gap does not account for basis risk. This is a particularly serious problem for a bank with assets or liabilities denominated in different currencies, since interest rates in different currencies do not move in consonance; and the net impact of returns from these foreign currency-denominated instruments on the bank's overall profitability remains even more muddled as those returns require translation in the domestic currency.

9.2.2 Duration gap model

The concept of duration is closely related to the maturity. As a matter of fact, it is a "weighted" maturity.

$$D_A = \sum_t^T [(t) \star CFA_t/(1 + r)^t]/[CFA_t/(1 + r)^t]$$

where D_A is the duration of an asset with periodic cash flows for T periods; T is the maturity of the asset; CFA_t is the cash flows from the asset in period t; and r is the discount or interest rate.

The numerator of the above definition is the "weighted average" of discounted values of payments throughout the life of the asset. Thus the present value of the second period payment will be multiplied by 2, the third period payment by 3, etc. The numerator gives more weight to a more remote payment than a less remote one. The denominator is simply the present value of all periodic payments. This definition then leads to the following generalizations.

- Suppose two assets with the same (present) value have the same maturity, but asset A obtains earlier payments, while asset B receives payments later. In that case, the duration of asset A is smaller than the duration of asset B.
- If an asset has only one payment at maturity, that is, a zero-coupon bond, the maturity and duration will be identical. Any payments received on an asset in the interim reduce its duration. Hence, duration can never exceed maturity of an asset.

Duration is in effect "elasticity" of asset value with respect to interest rate change. Bank management thus uses duration measures to evaluate interest rate risk. Analysis in Appendix K suggests that (ignoring the foreign exchange market and foreign sector) ΔE, a *change* in the bank's equity, would be equal to:

$$\Delta E = -[A \star D_A - L \star D_L] \, \Delta r/(1 + r) \tag{9.2}$$

where A is the value of the bank's assets; L is the value of its liabilities; r is the interest rate and D_A (D_L) is the duration of the assets (liabilities).

If we factor out the assets, A, from Equation 9.2, we obtain:

$$\Delta E = -[(D_A - k \star D_L)][A][\Delta r/(1 + r)] \tag{9.3}$$

where k is the ratio of liability to total assets, or the debt ratio, which measures the bank's financial leverage.

From Equation 9.3, it can be seen that the bank's equity value is affected by three major factors:

1 The *adjusted* (or leverage-adjusted) *duration gap*, $-(D_A - k \star D_L)$,
2 The size of the bank, A, and
3 The size of the interest rate shock, $\Delta r/(1 + r)$.

Equation 9.3 is called the **duration gap model** (d-gap), which features managing the market value of stockholders' equity in light of interest rate movement. It focuses on the adjusted duration gap for stabilizing or enhancing bank equity's market value. Management can either hedge the interest risk by minimizing the adjusted duration gap or speculate by widening the gap.

Example 9.2

The following is the ABC Bank's simplified balance sheet:

Assets ($ m)	Liabilities ($ m)
A = 100	L = 80
	E = 20

Suppose:

Asset duration	$D_A = 6$;
Liability duration	$D_L = 4$;
Interest rate change	$\Delta r = 1\%$;
Current interest rate	$r = 10\%$.
We have:	
Debt ratio	$k^\star = 80/100$

- The adjusted duration gap will be:

$$-(D_A - k^\star D_L) = -6.00 + (0.8)\,4 = -2.8$$

- The change in the bank's equity value will be as follows:

$$\Delta E = [-(D_A - k^\star D_L)](A)\Delta r/(1 + r)$$
$$\Delta E = [-2.8](\$100 \text{ million})(0.01/1.1)$$
$$= -\$2.55 \text{ million}$$

That is, a 1 percent interest rate increase will reduce the equity value by $2.55 million.

To gain a better understanding of the impact of interest rate on the equity value, Box 9.2 summarizes the impact of interest rate change on the equity value for a given value of d-gap. A comparison between the duration and gap analyses is instructive:

- A *positive* gap or d-gap responds favorably, for instance, to a positive interest rate change.
- **Duration analysis** concentrates on the stockholders' equity value; the gap approach only looks at net earnings for stockholders.
- Duration measures are additive. Hence the bank can match assets with liabilities, instead of matching individual accounts.
- The d-gap method takes a longer-term viewpoint.

Most sophisticated asset/liability management software systems can compute duration of a bank's total asset and total liability structures.

Box 9.2   D-gap analysis summary

If adjusted d-gap is positive (+), interest rates and equity value move together
Duration of assets is less than duration of liabilities.

- As interest rate rises, a decrease in the asset market value is less than the decrease in the value of liabilities. Thus, equity market value increases.
- As interest rate falls, an increase in the asset value increases less than the liability. Thus, equity value decreases.

If adjusted d-gap is negative (−), interest rates and equity value move in the opposite directions
Duration of liabilities is exceeded by duration of assets.

- As interest rate rises, a decrease in the asset value is larger than the decrease in the liability. Thus, equity value decreases.
- If interest rate falls, an increase in the asset value is larger than that of liability. Thus, the equity value increases.

If d-gap is zero (0), the equity value will be unaffected by interest rate movement

- If interest rate rises (falls), decrease (increase) in the asset value is the same as that of the liability. Thus, the equity value remains unchanged.

As the d-gap differs from zero in either direction,

- A given change in interest rate has a magnified impact on the equity value.

Some weaknesses of the d-gap approach are as follows:

- Reliability of the duration measure hinges on reasonably accurate forecasting of (a) the *timing* of base rate change, and (b) the *magnitude* of base rate change.[7]
- A bank must monitor and adjust the duration of its portfolio on a continuous basis; the related effort and transaction costs may turn out to be excessive.
- The d-gap analysis, like the gap measure, does not consider basis risk or changes in the shape–slope of the yield curve.

An illustration contrasting the two approaches is provided below.

Example 9.3

XYZ Bank has the following financial statement:

Balance sheet *before* interest rate increase ($ million)

Assets		Liabilities	
Rate-sensitive loan	$50.00	Rate-sensitive deposits	$40.00
Fixed rate		*Fixed rate*	
Reserves	12.00	5-year zero-coupon bonds	82.20
20-year zero-coupon	64.60	($110 at 6%)	
($250 at 7%)		Net capital	4.40
	$126.60		$126.60

From the balance sheet, we can compute the gap for the bank as

$$\$10 \text{ million (i.e., RSA} - \text{RSL} = \$50 - \$40)$$

When the reference interest rate increases by 2 percent for both loans and deposits, the positive gap will generate additional interest income of $200,000 (i.e., 2% × $10).

However, the balance sheet of the bank after the interest rate increase will appear as follows:

Assets		Liabilities	
Rate-sensitive loan	$50.00	Rate-sensitive deposits	$40.00
Fixed rate		*Fixed rate:*	
Reserves	12.00	5-year zero-coupon bonds	74.86
20-year zero-coupon bonds	44.61	($110 at 8%)	
($250 at 9%)		Net capital	(8.25)
	$106.61		$106.61

A 2 percent increase in interest rate will lower the bank asset value by $19.99 million ($126.60 million − $106.61 million), leading to a *decline* in the equity value by $12.65 million ($4.4 million + $8.25 million) that ushers the bank into bankruptcy.

Now we consider the impact of foreign-exchange denominated activities on interest rate management.

9.3 Foreign Exchange and Gap Management

The d-gap rule needs to be modified when a bank is involved in lending and borrowing in a foreign currency. The modified rule for immunizing the bank's equity (E) from interest rate risk is (see Appendix K) as follows:

$$\partial E/\partial r = (LD_L - AD_A)/(1 + r) + (A^\star - L^\star)S_0/(1 + r^\star) \tag{9.4}$$

where A and $A^\star$ are the present values of the domestic loans (assets) and foreign loans, respectively; L and $L^\star$ are the domestic and foreign liabilities, respectively; r and $r^\star$ are domestic and foreign interest rates, respectively; S_0 is the current (observed) spot exchange rate; and D_A and D_L are the duration of the domestic assets and liabilities, respectively.

This formulation is based on the assumptions of (a) the Fisher Open[8] effect which links exchange rate change to the differential in interest rates in two currencies, and (b) only the domestic interest rate changes. For a complete immunization, Equation 9.4 should be set to zero.

Example 9.4

Loan receipts and debt payments for PQR Bank that has domestic and foreign loans and debts are as follows:

Year	Domestic ($)		Foreign (SF)	
	Loan	Debt	Loan	Debt
	10%	6%	10%	5%
1	100	200	1,500	2500
2	100	200	1,500	
3	100	–	1,500	
4	100		–	
5	100		–	
6	100		–	
Present value	435.53	366.68	3,730.4	2,381

If the domestic loan interest rate is 10 percent, the present value (PV) of the loans will be:

$$100/(1 + 10\%)^1 + \cdots + 100/(1 + 10\%)^6$$
$$= \$435.53$$

If the domestic interest rate on debt is 8 percent, the present value of debt (PV) will be:

$$200/(1 + 6\%)^1 + 200/(1 + 6\%)^2$$
$$= \$366.68$$

Similarly, we can compute the present value of the foreign loan (assuming 10 percent interest rate) SF 3,730.4, and the foreign debts (assuming 5 percent interest rate) SF 2,381.

The duration (D_A) of the domestic loans (assets) can be computed as before:

$$D_A = \frac{100(1)/(1 + 10\%)^1 + 100(2)/(1 + 10\%)^2 + \cdots + 100(6)/(1 + 10\%)^6}{435.53}$$

$$= 3.224 \text{ years}$$

And the duration of the bank's debts (liabilities) will be

$$D_{\mathrm{L}} = \frac{200(1)/(1 + 6\%)^1 + 200(2)/(1 + 6\%)^2}{366.68}$$

$$= 1.485 \text{ years}$$

Suppose we are given the following information:

- The current spot rate $0.50/SF,
- The EuroSF interest rate is 10 percent.

The overall equity exposure due to interest risk measure from Equation 9.4 will be:

$366.68 \times 1.485/(1 + 6\%) - \$435.53 \times 3.224/(1 + 10\%) + (3730.4 - 2381)\$0.50/(1.1)$
$= \$513.70 - \$1276.50 + \$613.36$
$= -\$762.80 + \$613.36$
$= -\$149.44$

In the example above, the bank has

- Domestic exposure of $-\$762.80$.
- Foreign division exposure of $613.36.
- Consolidated exposure of $-\$149.44$.

This example illustrates several important aspects of asset-liability management.

- If a multinational bank manager strictly concentrates on the domestic immunization rule for the domestic assets and liabilities and ignores foreign-exchange based operations, the overall position of the bank will likely be different from the targeted one envisaged by the management.
- Separate immunization of domestic and foreign positions will only manage to increase the immunizing costs due to undertaking redundant actions, and may even land the bank in an undesirable position.
- The consolidated net exposure immunization rule will be a sound practice as it would hedge the firm wide operations. This is because the bank's interest exposure due to mismatched maturity/duration of asset-liabilities is also likely to be partially offset (or magnified) by the exchange risk exposure due to the Fisher Open effect on the initial exposure: as the interest rate risk increases, the exchange rate will move in a similar fashion so as to reduce (or increase) the exposure of the bank's equity value.

9.4 Convexity

In the duration and gap analysis, we focused on interest rate risk that would arise from the *parallel shift* of the term structure of interest rate.[9] The decision rule for interest rate immunization strategy is that the product of the duration of the assets times the asset value should equal the duration of the liability times the liability value.

In many instances, the term structure does not have a parallel shift. In fact, the slope of the term structure changes at different rates because the change in interest rates for different maturities is not constant. For example, when the Federal Reserve increases the short-term rate, the long-term bond interest rates may show smaller (larger) increases. In this scenario, the slope of the term structure will be flatter (steeper). In turn, a smaller change in an interest rate for a given maturity will show a smaller change in the value of the associated bond. Thus a general change in the term structure induces smaller or larger price changes.

Convexity reflects the rate of change in the bond price increase (decrease) as a result of the rate of change in the interest rate decrease (increase). A larger value of convexity suggests greater sensitivity of the bond price to a given change in its interest rate. A smaller convexity value means less bond price sensitivity to its interest rate change.

If there is a non-parallel shift in the slope of term structure, immunization of the bank's portfolio requires that the general condition depicting equity value (see Appendix L for the derivation of the general condition) should be zero. Two alternative simplifying assumptions are possible:

1 Only interest rate risk matters; that is, we are concerned with only the first two duration measures.
2 When there is only slope shift.[10]

In the first case involving two duration measures, the general condition will be reduced to

$$\Delta E = -(AD_A - LD_L)\Delta r + (AD_A^2 - LD_L^2)\Delta r^2/2 = 0 \tag{9.5}$$

where D_A^2 is the second duration of the asset while D_L^2 is the second duration of the liabilities. The second duration is to capture the convexity of the interest rate. D_A and D_L are the conventional measure of (first) duration for the asset and liability of the bank described earlier in Section 9.2.2.

Inspection of Equation 9.5 reveals that the condition will be fulfilled, if

$$AD_A = LD_L \tag{9.6a}$$
$$AD_A^2 = LD_L^2 \tag{9.6b}$$

The first approach embodied in Equations 9.6a–9.6b requires that the first duration of asset has to be equal to the first duration of liability and the second duration of asset should equal the second duration of liability. Although it is not easy to achieve this by arranging the asset and liability alone, it can be accomplished by using interest rate futures contracts, as we shall see later.

Example 9.5: Computation of Two Duration Measures

We are provided with the following information.

Interest rate, $r = 10\%$

Maturity (t)	Cash flows (CF)	Present value $PV = CF/e^{rt}$	First duration $PV \star t$	Second duration $PV \star t^2$
1	$100	$90.483	$90.483	$90.483
2	100	81.873	163.746	427.492
3	100	74.082	222.245	666.736
Total		$246.438	$476.474	$1,184.711

$$\text{First duration} = \$476.474/\$246.437$$
$$= 1.933$$
$$\text{Second duration} = \$1,184.711/\$246.438$$
$$= 4.807$$

In the alternative approach involving the first three duration measures, the general condition will reduce to:

$$\Delta E = -(AD_A - LD_L)\Delta r + (AD_A^2 - LD_L^2)\Delta r^2/2 - (AD_A^3 - LD_L^3)(\Delta r^3/6) = 0 \quad (9.7)$$

Equation 9.7 will be more complicated as it requires additional restrictions on the set of duration measures.

9.5 Managing Interest Rate Risk

It is essential that an asset/liability manager in a multinational bank understand how the interest rate risk is linked to the asset and liability transactions. This section will discuss the strategies available for managing this interest rate risk. For expository convenience, we will focus extensively on immunization or hedging strategies, and will refer to aggressive or speculative management only in passing.

9.5.1 Basic immunization procedure in gap versus d-gap models

Gap model

We have already seen that gap reports are useful for isolating areas of the balance sheet that are most sensitive to interest rate movements. When a bank chooses to have a zero gap, its net interest income should not change irrespective of any change in the interest rate. The bank can take the following steps in achieving the gap to zero:

- Calculate periodic gaps over short time intervals.
- If the gap is positive, rate-sensitive assets should be decreased, or rate-sensitive liabilities should be increased, through a combination of actions such as the following:

  (i) Match funding of re-priceable assets with similar re-priceable liabilities so that periodic gaps approach zero.

    (ii)   Match funding of long-term assets with short term, interest-sensitive liabilities in the positive-gap slots.

    (iii)   Use off-balance sheet transactions, such as financial futures and interest rate swaps, to construct "synthetic" securities for hedging purposes.

Duration model

In the duration model, calculation of the adjusted d-gap is required. If it is positive, the duration of assets is greater than the leverage-weighted duration of liabilities. Hence, a combination of strategies is possible:

- Decrease the duration of assets.
- Increase the duration of liabilities.
- Increase debt ratio.

Illustrative actions for immunization will be along the same lines as for positive gap above.

Strategies of interest rate risk management can be implemented by two categories of actions: balance sheet related; and those belonging to the off-balance sheet category. Balance sheet-related actions attempt to change the bank's interest rate sensitivity by altering various components of the assets and liabilities on the balance sheet. These actions are basic tools for interest rate risk management and have been extensively used by banks.

Off-balance sheet strategies involve more recent financial instruments, such as financial futures and interest rate swaps. We now discuss specific balance-sheet related actions first and then consider off-balance sheet activities.

9.5.2 Balance sheet management strategies

Altering the investment portfolio mix

One basic balance sheet strategy to alter a bank's interest rate exposure is to restructure the bank's asset composition of the balance sheet. If a bank's asset portfolio income is, for instance, excessively sensitive to interest rate changes (i.e., more assets re-pricing in a given period than liabilities), the first course of action is to lengthen the maturities of such assets.

For a multinational bank, the menu for asset liquidation and resource redeployment is extensive. What is undiversifiable risk for a smaller portfolio can be partially reduced in a larger portfolio, especially when financial markets are not fully integrated. As a result, the bank can assume what may be considered excessive risk but is in fact reasonable in light of the bank's involvement in several markets.

Before implementing new portfolio mix strategies, the bank should consider the following factors.

- Risk implied by the strategy. Suppose a bank's one-year gap position is found too "asset sensitive" (more assets re-pricing in the next twelve months than liabilities). Selling a

Treasury bill with a 60-day maturity and reinvesting the proceeds in a Treasury bill maturing in 13 months will solve the problem only temporarily.

- Basis risk. To become less liability sensitive, a bank could purchase floating-rate, long-term securities instead of assuming a short-term obligation that needs to be rolled over.
- A selection of floating-rate securities with an index rate that does not move in tandem with the bank's cost of funding will not significantly reduce the basis risk.

> Many floating-rate securities, for instance, use Treasury rates as their basis for resetting the interest rate on the security. If the bank's cost of funding does not change by the same amount as the change in the Treasury rates, variation in the net interest margin will occur. It is possible that LIBOR and prime rate may more closely reflect a bank's cost of funds. Floating-rate investments with these bases then will be more effective for protecting the net interest margin.

- Profitability. Profitability considerations may involve a tradeoff between capital gains today and reduced future earnings. Or profitability may be improved by lowering the credit standards. The following illustrations amplify these considerations.

> A five-year Treasury note purchased three years ago at 10 percent yield to maturity will continue to earn 10 percent for the next two years. If the bank's two-year gap position is too asset-sensitive and it sells the 10 percent Treasury note at the current two-year Treasury note yield of 8.5 percent and reinvests in a new five-year Treasury note yielding 9 percent, a 100 basis points reduction in the yield will occur for the next two years. Selling the 10 percent note at a time when the two-year Treasury note yield is 8.5 percent will produce a (capital) gain in the current year. Thus the bank has to consider whether a 100 basis point reduction of the net interest margin on the securities for the next two years is worth the security gain in the current year.

> One way to offset the 100 basis points reduction in the net interest margin is to reinvest in five-year agencies or some high-quality corporate notes with higher yields than that of Treasury notes. However, the bank's asset/liability committee must resist the temptation to push the investment manager to purchase lower-quality and/or longer-term securities for bolstering the net interest margin.

Pricing and developing new products

In the early 1980s, many US thrift institutions experienced massive losses when interest rates rose to record levels. For years, they had aggressively priced and marketed one- to five-year certificates of deposits to fund 30-year fixed rate mortgages. Creative bankers, however, developed adjustable-rate mortgages with interest rates that would be reset every one, three, or five years, and funded the mortgages with time deposits of matching maturities. Banks were thus able to produce a satisfactory net interest margin while assuming low-level interest rate risk.

One inherent limitation of the above strategy was the low level of acceptance by the borrowers seeking residence mortgages – a structural impediment, so to speak. As a result, its impact on the balance sheet was only gradual. Many US thrift institutions in the early 1980s had already had too much risk exposure and too little capital to survive long enough to benefit from this change in the pricing strategy.

A structural challenge may also present an opportunity, especially for a multinational bank. The cost of developing a product that has lackluster performance in one market can be recovered through introducing that product in another market.

Automobile financing at consumer level, only a marginally profitable activity due to cut-throat competition in a well-developed market, may be extremely lucrative in an emerging market.

Securitization and loan sales

Securitization occurs when a bank unloads a given bundle of assets and issues securities to the new owners who can trade these securities in the secondary markets. More formally, it is a process of efficiently financing assets that generate actuarial experience (thereby improving accuracy of their expected financial behavior) when these underlying assets are properly combined together and segregated from other assets of the originating bank. The following characteristics are typical in effective securitization of assets.

- Individual assets in themselves are too small or their cash flows are too unpredictable to raise funds against them in an economic way.
- Assets in themselves cannot be readily traded in the market place.
- Assets' behavior is more erratic singly or individually than when they are combined in a bundle.
- Assets in the bundle share some basic traits, that is, they are homogeneous in some ways.

> Credit card charges by individual customers may show erratic payment behavior and may be too small to enable a bank to issue securities against them.

When these customers are properly classified in various categories (e.g., customers making full payments on charges that avoid interest charges; customers who pay the requisite minimum amount without fail; customers who pay a differing amount over the life of a charge; and so on), these categories yield aggregated payment behavior that is stable and predictable.

- Improved predictability of financial behavior should not be vitiated by other unrelated assets of the firm. Often a *special-purpose vehicle* (SPV) or entity is needed; and the originating firm "sells" this asset bundle (transfers the title irrevocably) to the SPV.[11]
- The SPV is a pass-through that obtains funds and passes them to the originating bank.

- Greater accuracy of estimates allows prospective lenders to avoid the additional charge related to uncertainty.
- Credit rating of the securities may be enhanced by a stand-by letter of credit or a guarantee from a government agency (or a financial institution with higher credit rating). Naturally the cost of obtaining the guarantee may not be negligible. Still, they should be considered against lowered borrowing cost that may result from improved secondary markets for these securities.
- The bank is able to obtain cheaper financing than otherwise.[12]

Loan securitization enables the bank to turn illiquid assets into liquid obligations that can be readily traded in the secondary market. It also enables the bank to make loans to customers on terms that might have been unacceptable to the bank because of the interest rate risk connotation.[13]

> A bank does not want to extend additional 30-year fixed rate mortgages, in spite of their popularity among homebuyers. By providing 30-year fixed-rate mortgages, converting them into agency-guaranteed securities, and immediately selling them in the security market, the bank can meet its customers' demands for 30-year fixed-rate mortgages without incurring additional interest rate risk.

Loan securitization greatly increases liquidity of the bank's balance sheet and accelerates its asset turnover. Therefore, the bank management should carefully consider its use for asset/ liability management.

For a multinational bank, even when loan securitization is only marginally profitable in the domestic market, it may still be worth undertaking. This is because the internalized organizational expertise built from the domestic experience enables the bank to reap handsome returns abroad. Caution should be exercised to ensure that the proper external environment exists in the foreign market. For instance, the existing legal framework may not be conducive for securitization.[14] Further, local financial market conditions may not be favorable for security placement. Resorting to foreign or Euromarkets may not be a viable alternative since they may create foreign exchange exposure that increases the net cost of financing.

Loan securitization activity ranges from mortgages to credit card receivables. Sovereign loans, as we saw in Chapter 8, have also been securitized, allowing banks to unload unprofitable assets. Finally, conventional bonds and loans have become a popular vehicle for banks to securitize through *collateralized bond obligations* (CBOs) and *collateralized loan obligations* (CLOs) that permit investors to obtain higher returns by assuming higher risk (Goodman 1998).

Use of brokered deposits

Depositors are typically slow in responding to deposit pricing or marketing of traditional deposit gathering activities. If a bank requires a large amount of fund for immediate use or wants to alter its interest rate risk posture, it has to offer an interest rate substantially above the market rate. Such a practice may entail significant cost to the bank in addition to the explicit interest cost: cannibalization of the existing deposit base may, for instance, force the bank to pay higher interest on the *existing* deposits without bringing in new funds. Further, competitive reprisal may not allow a bank to attract customers from other banks.

In light of these problems, brokerage firms have developed retail offices to develop a nationwide market in placing regional bank CDs for a moderate fee ranging from 25 basis points to 60 basis points on the principal amount of large deposits. One big advantage of the **brokered deposits** is that it avoids competitive reprisals because of opaqueness of these transactions. Still, the costs on these deposits can be excessive.

A multinational bank often encounters opportunistic situations that may allow it to obtain brokered deposits at an attractive cost from other markets.[15] Political crises lead investors from a country to seek refuge in safe currencies of the industrialized nations. A multinational bank with a reputation need not have a physical presence in that country. It may want to obtain brokered deposits from that country which carries a lower cost (including brokers' commission) because of its ability to offer flexibility of location and timing.

Use of borrowed funds

Bank borrowing falls into short-term and long-term categories. Each category of borrowing serves a very different function in the asset/liability management process. In an asset/liability management strategy, short-term borrowing serves as a source of funding through interest rate-sensitive liabilities that can be created quickly and in large quantity.

The two common sources of short-term borrowing are the federal funds purchase and the use of reverse repurchase agreements. Purchased federal funds are usually an overnight inter-bank unsecured loan that must be paid back the next business day and thus should not be relied on as a permanent source of funding. Furthermore, its availability for rollover becomes doubtful as the bank's financial condition deteriorates. Still, a strong correspondent bank network may enable a bank to meet expediently its unforeseen short-term needs.

A *reverse* repurchase agreement (reverse repo) is the immediate *sale* of securities (e.g., Treasury bill) with a simultaneous agreement to repurchase them back at a fixed price on a specific date. The interest rate paid in this transaction is usually slightly below the federal funds rate because the borrowing is secured by the underlying securities (typically government obligations), and the lender avoids transaction costs of initially buying and later selling the securities.

Essentially, a reverse repo is a temporary liquidation of high-quality securities. When a bank faces liquidity problems or finds market conditions inopportune for raising funds through preferred means, it can either undertake a reverse repo transaction or outright liquidate high-quality securities. The reverse repo conveys a strong signal to the market that financial problems are only temporary.

It is possible for a multinational bank to lower the borrowing cost on deposits through tax arbitrage. A bank, for instance, establishes a subsidiary in a tax haven. It arranges with a US multinational firm to have its subsidiary park its funds in the bank's tax haven subsidiary as limited term preferred stock. "Dividends" paid to the MNC subsidiary are then passed on to its parent. This increases the size of dividend payout ratio in that tax-related "basket" for the parent, and the parent is able to obtain larger global tax credit against its US tax liabilities than would have been possible. The MNC may not mind receiving a slightly lower return on deposits, as long as it can generate adequate tax savings. On the other side, the tax haven subsidiary provides funds from the "preferred stock" issue to the parent bank in the form of deposits that carry tax-deductible interest rate charges.[16]

Long-term borrowing on a fixed-rate basis allows a bank to lock in the fixed interest rate cost for a long time period and thus reduce the bank's liquidity risk as well as interest rate sensitivity of its liabilities. By the same token, a bank can reduce its asset-sensitivity by issuing floating-rate, long-term debt.

Long-term debt can be in the form of unsecured debt called debentures. Debentures are listed as debt in the liability section of the balance sheet, but are considered as (second-tier) capital by the regulators because the owners of the debentures have an unsecured position. Interest expense on debentures is tax deductible.

The bank can also issue preferred stock to raise money. Preferred stock is a hybrid form of long-term debt and the interest on preferred stock is referred to as a dividend. Although the dividend is paid from the after-tax earnings of the bank, this disadvantage is partially offset by the fact that corporate investors are willing to accept a relatively low compensation on preferred stock because 70 percent of the dividend income received by a corporation is exempt from US income taxes.

Again, a twist is possible by establishing a subsidiary in a tax haven. This subsidiary issues preferred stock to US corporate investors, such as insurance companies, and funnels the funds to the parent in the form of a loan that carries tax-deductible interest charges for the parent. Corporate investors are able to lower their tax liability on dividend income, and the parent bank is able to deduct interest charges on the funds. It is even possible to have the issue rated as preferred stock by the rating agencies (thus not increasing the debt ratio) and regulators regarding the issue as capital rather than debt for capital adequacy purposes!

Box 9.3 summarizes the balance sheet strategies described above.

9.5.3 Off-balance sheet activities

Interest rate swaps

As we saw in Chapter 6, an interest rate swap is an agreement between two parties to exchange a stream of interest payments over a designated period. Because it is an exchange of interest payments and involves no principal payment, it is a very direct way to alter the interest receipt or payment pattern on a financial instrument. An interest rate swap transaction can extend to several years; thus it is a hedging instrument to manage long-term interest rate risk.

A bank with access to the Eurocurrency market can also fund a loan request by taking advantage of a favorable borrowing condition in one currency and entering in a currency-cum-interest rate swap to contain the exposure without incurring significant cost. The major risk in such a swap, however, lies in the possibility that the borrower may default or pay off the loan prior to the maturity date. In the prepayment case, if the interest (or currency) rates had moved against the bank's position, the bank would incur substantial cost to unwind the swap. This is why it is important to recognize prepayment possibility and its cost for a loan that is funded through swaps.

Box 9.3 Strategies for reducing (increasing) asset and liability sensitivities

Reduce (increase) asset sensitivity:
1 Extend (decrease) investment portfolio maturities.
2 Increase (decrease) floating-rate deposits.
3 Increase (decrease) short-term deposits.
4 Increase (decrease) fixed-rate lending.
5 Sell (extend) adjustable-rate loans.
6 Increase (decrease) short-term borrowing.
7 Increase (decrease) floating-rate long-term debt.

Reduce (increase) liability sensitivity:
1 Reduce (increase) investment portfolio maturities.
2 Increase (decrease) long-term deposits.
3 Increase (decrease) adjustable-rate lending.
4 Sell fixed-rate loans.
5 Increase (decrease) fixed-rate long-term debt.

Financial futures contracts

International banks use financial futures trading on organized exchanges to manage the interest rate risk associated with their assets and liabilities. A futures contract represents a commitment between a buyer (seller) and the exchange's clearing house with regard to a standardized financial asset at a specified time in the future and a specified price. In contrast to relatively illiquid and long-term swaps, futures contracts are very liquid, short-term instruments. In addition, because of the guarantee by the clearing house for the performance of all contracts, the credit risk of these instruments is negligible.

Consider the following example to see how an asset-sensitive bank can use futures to reduce its interest exposure.

A bank expects interest rates to decline 100 basis points during the next six months. The fall in interest rate can cause a decline of $250,000 in its net interest income because of *positive* gap. The asset/liability manager can, thus, use the interest rate futures to hedge this risk by *buying* six-month T-bill futures contracts. A 100 basis points decline in interest rates will produce a $250,000 increase in the value of T-bill futures contracts. If the interest rate increases 100 basis points, a result contrary to expectations, a $250,000 loss would result on the futures contracts to be offset by the gain in the net interest income.

> As a result, if the appropriate hedge is put in place, the current net interest margin will be assured regardless of the direction in which interest rates move in the next six months. A loss/gain generated by the futures position will offset the counter movements in the bank's net interest margin.

The above example helps us to see the basic similarity between gap and duration analyses in managing the bank's asset and liability. (As we saw earlier, the gap analysis is carried out to manage the interest income (expense), while the d-gap analysis is for managing the change in the bank's equity position.)

Suppose a bank has a positive d-gap (refer to Box 9.2 above). A decline in the interest rate will lead to a decline in the bank's equity value. To offset the loss in equity value, the bank should long the interest rate futures that would generate a gain when interest rates decline. Thus, the use of a long position in the interest rate futures contracts for hedging a positive d-gap is consistent with the long futures position for hedging a positive gap.

Future (forward) rate agreement

An FRA allows a buyer bank to lock in the interest rate cost on an agreed amount at a designated time in the future for a defined period.

> A bank may purchase a three-month FRA for a nine-month contract at the benchmark interest rate of 6 percent on $25 million. If three months from now the spot benchmark rate is 7 percent, the bank receives immediate compensation of [$25million $\times$ (0.07 − 0.06) $\times$ 3/4] / [1 + 3(0.07)/4]. If the rate were lower than 6 percent, the bank will have to compensate the seller.

The need for hedging through purchase of an FRA is obviated when the bank, for instance, funds a $25million one-year loan today by accessing a one-year deposit market. However, when the bank finds an unusual opportunity to obtain a $25 million deposit for three months at below-market bid rate, it may take advantage of the opportunity *and* buy the FRA to avoid potential losses due to an interest rate increase in three months. Similarly, for a multinational bank, it is possible that the bank may have a window of opportunity in the three-month market in another currency. By hedging that risk and purchasing the FRA, the bank is able to lock in the profitability without incurring commensurate risk.

The FRA is a viable alternative to other derivative contracts, including the repos mentioned earlier. The alternatives represent different types of risks (e.g., credit and settlement), timing of cash flows, and transaction costs. A careful analysis may reveal an opportunity for arbitrage along one or more of these dimensions.

Option contracts

Multinational banks can also use options as alternative instruments to manage their interest risk. Options, used as hedging devices, have advantages and limitations. However, if properly used, they can provide an effective hedge against volatile interest rate movements.

There are two types of options on interest rates – one on cash market and the other on the futures market (see Chapter 5). Options on the interest rate futures are more widely used by financial institutions because of their liquidity.

- Suppose a bank anticipates excess liquidity at the end of two months. The bank buys a call option that gives it the right to purchase the Eurodollar time deposit (or futures contract) at the contractual rate, say, 10 percent.
  - If the market rate at the end of the two months turns out to be higher (say, 12 percent) than the contract rate (10 percent), the bank will let the option expire.
  - However, if the market rate turns out to be below the contract rate, the bank will exercise the call option.

  A put option is the right to sell the Eurodollar time deposit (or Eurodollar futures contract) at a contractual rate.
- A multinational bank buys a put option on the Eurodollar futures to hedge interest rate increases. The put option is bought for premium of 0.14 at the strike price of 92.00.
  - The contract rate (which is called the discount yield) is at 8 percent (i.e., 100–92).
  - An option premium of 0.14 will correspond to $350 because one basis point (bp) in the Eurodollar futures contract is equal to $25 (i.e., 14 bp × $25/bp = $350).
  - With a strike price of 92.00 and premium of 0.14 for the put option, the break-even price is 91.86 (i.e., 92–0.14). The break-even point is the price at which that the option buyer will incur neither gain nor loss. The option will thus be in the money if the reference Eurodollar futures rate rises above 8.14 percent.

As a matter of fact, the bank will be better off if all interest rate declines sharply. In this case the option will be out of the money, but the cash Eurodollar rates will enable the bank to incur low cost of issuing the CDS in the cash market that would offset the premium paid in buying the insurance (put option).

The following example illustrates a concrete scenario.

Example 9.6 Buying put options on Eurodollar futures to hedge borrowing costs

Cash market:

1 On August 2, 2000, a bank plans to issue a series of $1 million, three-month Eurodollar CD apiece in the following months: November, March, and May. The current (August) three-month CD rate is 8 percent.
2 The bank intends to hedge interest rate increases.

Option market: The bank buys one contract for each of the put options:

1 December 2000 put option with a strike price of 92 (i.e., yield of 8 percent) and a premium of 0.14, i.e., the premium is $350 (14 × $25);

Box 9.4 Use of derivative instruments for asset/liability management

Positive duration gap
- Short interest rate futures, e.g., use of Eurodollar futures to hedge future interest rate movement to longer–maturity asset;
- Long interest rate puts, i.e., use of put option to hedge interest rate rise;
- Long forward rate arrangement (FRA) to lock in longer-term interest rate in liability;
- Long swap (pay fixed; receive floating rates).

Negative duration gap
- Long interest rate futures;
- Long interest rate calls (hedge interest rate drop);
- Short FRA;
- Short interest rate swaps (receive fixed; pay floating rates).

---

2 March 2001 put option with a strike price 92 (i.e., 8 percent yield) and a premium of 0.21, i.e., the premium is $525 (i.e., 21 × $25);
3 June 2001 put option with a strike price of 92 (i.e., 8 percent yield) and a premium of 0.2, i.e., the premium is $500 (i.e., 20 × $25).

November 1, 2000
Cash market: The bank issues $1 million three-month CD at 8.25 percent. The bank thus incurs additional interest cost of $625 as compared to 8 percent on August 2, 2000 (i.e., (0.25 × (0.0825 − 0.0800) × $1million)).
Option market: December 2000 put option has a premium of 0.2 as its underlying futures contract gives a yield of 8.31 percent (i.e., its IMM index is 91.69, which is 100 less 8.31). The bank sells this December put option and receives $500 (i.e., 20 × $25).
March 30, 2001
Cash market: Bank issues $1 million three-month CD at 7.90 percent; thus its gain as compared to 8 percent is 10 bps, which translates into $250 gain.
Option market: March put option is out-of-the-money because the futures rate is 7.85 percent.
May 1, 2001
Cash market: The bank issues $1 million three-month CD at 8.5 percent; its loss as compared to 8 percent is 50 bps, or $1,250 (50 × $25).
Option market: The futures rate for June is 9.6 percent. Thus, June 01 put is in-the-money and can be sold for 0.5. The bank realizes $1,250 (i.e., 50 × $25).

Summary of the cash and option transactions

Date	Cost of issuing CD plus option
November 1, 2000	8.05 percent (i.e., 8.25 percent cost of CD less 0.2 percent gain from option)

March 30, 2001	7.9 percent (CD cost and no return on option)
May 1, 2001	8 percent (i.e., 8.5 percent cost of CD less 0.5 percent gain from put option)
Average	7.98 percent

The average cost is 7.98 percent (i.e., (8.05 percent + 7.9 percent + 8 percent)/3), which is quite close to 8 percent the prevailing on August 2, 2000.

Box 9.4 summarizes the use of different derivative instruments for hedging interest rate risk.

9.6 Conclusion

When a bank is exposed to the interest rate risk, it can measure the exposure by calculating its gap report, duration analysis, or the change in the net present value of equity. These measures also serve as tools for managing the bank's interest risk exposure.

The balance sheet strategies are essential tools for managing both interest rate and liquidity risks.

As to the off-balance-sheet strategies, financial derivative contracts including futures, options, and swaps each possess distinct characteristics. Futures and options reflect the change in the value of a fixed-income instrument as interest rates change. Therefore, they are better suited to hedging the value of a specific asset or the net asset value of a financial institution than for hedging changes in net interest income. Interest rate swaps are more appropriate for hedging variations in net interest income caused by a change in interest rates.

While all of the tools provide a hedge against interest rate movements, they all have one thing in common: none of them is foolproof and thus each entails some opportunity costs. As a result, costs of various alternatives should be carefully examined in light of the bank's expectations regarding interest rate volatility. Indeed, such analysis may suggest that bank asset/liability management should not rely on one single strategy; instead, it should consider a *combination* of alternate strategies for managing the interest rate exposure.

DISCUSSION QUESTIONS

1   What is interest rate risk from a bank's perspective?
2   The MM theory recommends that investment and financing decisions should be separately considered and a firm need not consider existing investments (especially their future cash flows) in evaluating discounted cash flows of an investment project.
    a   Do you think that a gap analysis for asset-liability management is consistent with both these prescriptions?
    b   If there are inconsistencies, where and why do they exist?
    c   Is the d-gap measure consistent with the MM theory?

3   The CAPM considers only the systematic risk relevant. Bank management not only considers the total risk (including the unsystematic risk component) but it also investigates various components of the overall risk (e.g., liquidity, credit, and interest rate risk) that are often interrelated. How would you reconcile these conflicting approaches?

4   A bank has $10 million assets whose duration is five years while the duration of its liabilities is three years. Liabilities are about 85 percent of the bank's total assets. What will be the change in the bank's equity if the interest rate is expected to increase by 1 percent above its current 8 percent level?

5   a   What is the significance of a bank's position in foreign exchange in asset-liability management of interest rate risk?

    b   Suppose ABC bank has cash flows from domestic and foreign loans and debts as follows:

	Domestic		Foreign (€-denominated)	
Year	Loans	Debt	Loans	Debt
1	100	250	200	400
2	100		300	
3	100			

Assume that the domestic loan rate is 9 percent and deposit rate is 5 percent; and the foreign loan rate is 10 percent and deposit rate is 4 percent (both for €-denominated transactions). The current spot exchange rate is $0.95/€. Assuming that the Fisher Open relationship holds, what is the equity exposure of the bank arising from domestic interest rate risk?

    c   Suppose the research department of the ABC bank estimates that the impact of the domestic interest rate change on the spot exchange rate is −0.1 ($/€), implying that the Fisher Open relationship does not hold. In this case, what will be the ABC's equity exposure of the interest rate risk given the information in the above table? Explain under what conditions that domestic interest rate and spot exchange rate has a negative relationship? Elaborate and discuss how the interest rate–spot exchange rate relationship affects the bank's equity exposure arising from interest rate risk.

6   Discuss why convexity is important in the interest risk management by the bank.

7   Discuss various balance sheet strategies to manage interest rate exposure.

8   What are off-balance strategies that deal with interest rate exposure?

9   ABC bank has extended a 10-year $50 million loan at 10 percent interest rate. In addition, the bank has on its books two-year, floating rate loans for $110 million; the interest rate is linked to the LIBOR, which is 7 percent currently. ABC is also a net investor in the fed funds market for $20 million. The average time to re-price the floating loans is three months, while the time for re-pricing the federal fund rate is two months. The core liabilities of the bank are for two years with an interest rate

of 8 percent, adjusted every six months. All fixed and floating rate payments are due annually.

The balance sheet of the ABC bank (in millions of dollars) as of December 31, 2000 is shown as follows:

Assets		Liabilities	
Cash	30	Core deposits	60
Federal fund	20		
Fixed loans	50	Euro CDs	110
Floating loans	100	Equity	30
	200		200

    a Compute the duration of the fixed rate loans portfolio and its total assets

    b What is the duration of the core deposits and its total liabilities?

    c If duration gap is used to measure the interest rate risk, what is the bank's interest rate exposure?

10 Bank of Missouri reassesses its interest rate exposure by using a planning horizon of six months. Its balance sheet (in millions) is as follows:

Assets		Liabilities and Equities	
Short-term loans (10%)	40	Demand deposit (0%)	35
L/T loans (12%)	30	Savings deposit (6%)	20
Buildings	5	Equity	20
	75		75

    a Calculate the bank's re-pricing gap using six months as a horizon.

    b What is the expected net interest income for the Bank of Missouri?

    c Assuming an interest rate decline by 50 basis points over the six-month period, what will be the impact on the net interest income? For an increase in the interest rate by 100 basis points, instead, what will be the impact on its net interest income?

    d Discuss the interest rate exposure for the bank and possible hedging strategies to be used to hedge its interest rate risk.

11 On August 1, Trust Bank makes a $25 million, three-month, fixed rate loan at an interest rate of 13 percent to a company. The bank finances the loan by issuing a one-month Certificate of Deposit (CD) that pays an interest rate at LIBOR. When the one-month CD matures, the bank will roll it over at a new rate. The current LIBOR is 10.2 percent. As per the IMM index at the Chicago Mercantile Exchange, September Eurodollar futures are now trading at 89.34 and December Eurodollar futures are at 88.89. The bank CD will be rolled over on the following dates: September 1 and October 1.

> a   What transactions should the bank undertake in the futures markets to hedge the interest rate risk?
>
> b   On September 1 (the first roll-over date), September futures trade at 90.54 while December futures are at 89.95. The LIBOR is 9.12 percent. Describe the bank's position (gain or loss) for the futures market transactions.
>
> c   On October 1, the December futures are at 90.56. The LIBOR is 8.64 percent. Describe the bank's transactions.
>
> d   On November 1, the borrower closes the loan and the bank pays back the maturing CD. Compute the total net gain or loss to the bank for the transactions taken including the futures transactions.

APPENDIX K: HEDGING RULE FOR A BANK FACING A PARALLEL SHIFT IN TERM STRUCTURE

Let A and L be the bank's domestic market values of assets and liability, respectively. Similarly, $A^\star$ and $L^\star$ are its foreign assets and liability, respectively. Then, the equity of the bank, E, is

$$E = (A - L) + s(A^\star - L^\star) \tag{K.1}$$

where S_0 is the spot exchange rate, expressed as the dollar per foreign currency (\$/FC). The market values of the domestic assets and liabilities of the bank are simply the present value of its future cash flows (CF), which are discounted at the domestic interest rate, r, for its asset and liability maturity, ma, and ml, respectively. Thus, we have:

$$A = \sum_{t}^{ma} CFA_t/(1 + r)^t, \tag{K.2}$$

$$L = \sum_{t}^{ml} CFL_t/(1 + r)^t \tag{K.3}$$

Similarly, the foreign cash-flows are discounted at the foreign interest rate, $r^\star$:

$$A^\star = \sum_{t}^{ma^\star} CFA_t^\star/(1 + r^\star)^t, \tag{K.4}$$

$$L^\star = \sum_{t}^{ml^\star} CFL_t^\star/(1 + r^\star)^t \tag{K.5}$$

Differentiating Equation K.1 with respect to the domestic interest rate (while assuming foreign interest rate remains unchanged), after some manipulations, yields:

$$\partial E/\partial r = -(AD_A - LD_L)/(1 + r) + (A^\star - L^\star)(\partial s/\partial r) \tag{K.6}$$

where D_A, and D_L are the duration of the domestic assets and liability, respectively.

Apparently, spot exchange rate is dependent on interest rate. The precise impact on the spot rate from the change of interest rate, $\partial s/\partial r$, depends on the types of economic models to be used for their relations. For simplicity here, let us assume that the spot exchange is endogenous in the interest rate as described by the Fisher Open relation. That is, $s = S_0(1 + r)/(1 + r\star)$, S_0 is the observed spot rate. Other relationships between the spot exchange rate and interest rate are possible. Given the Fisher Open relation, the impact of change in the domestic interest rate on the exchange rate will be:

$$\partial s/\partial r = S_0/(1 + r\star)$$

Then, we can simplify Equation K.6 to:

$$\partial E/\partial r = -(AD_A - LD_L)/(1 + r) + (A\star - L\star)S_0/(1 + r\star) \tag{K.7}$$

The terms in the first parentheses on the right-hand side of the equation represents the traditional measure of interest rate exposure. If there is exchange rate risk, setting the domestic interest rate exposure to zero cannot optimally immunize interest rate risk. Instead, the exchange rate risk resulting from the interest rate effect should be considered.

APPENDIX L: DERIVATION OF THE DURATION IMMUNIZATION RULE FOR A BANK FACING A NON-PARALLEL SHIFT IN TERM STRUCTURE

In the following proof, we use continuous compounding to simplify the procedure.

$$E = A - L$$

where E is shareholder equity; A is the present value of asset cash flows, i.e., $\Sigma A_t e^{-r + t}$; and L is the present value of the cash flows from liabilities, $\Sigma L_t e^{-rt}$.
Thus,

$$
\begin{aligned}
\Delta E &= \text{New equity value} - \text{Old equity value} \\
&= \left(\Sigma A_t e^{-(r+\Delta r)t} - \Sigma L_t e^{-(r+\Delta r)t}\right) - \left(\Sigma A_t e^{-r+t} - \Sigma L_t e^{-rt}\right) \\
&= \left(\Sigma A_t e^{-rt} - \Sigma L_t e^{-rt}\right)\left(e^{-\Delta rt} - 1\right)
\end{aligned}
\tag{L.1}
$$

$$e^{-\Delta rt} = 1 - \Delta rt + (\Delta rt)^2/2 - (\Delta rt)^3/3! + \cdots$$

Substituting $e^{-\Delta rt}$ in Equation L.1 and simplifying, we obtain:

$$
\begin{aligned}
\Delta E &= \left(\Sigma A_t e^{-rt} - \Sigma L_t e^{-rt}\right)\left(-t\Delta r + t^2\Delta r^2/2 - t^3\Delta r^3/6 \cdots\right) \\
&= \left(\Sigma A_t e^{-rt}t - \Sigma L_t e^{-rt}\ t\right) - \Delta r + \left(\Sigma A_t e^{-rt}t^2 - \Sigma L_t e^{-rt}t^2\right)\Delta r^2/2 \\
&\quad - \left(\Sigma A_t e^{-rt}t^3 - \Sigma L_t e^{-rt}t^3\right) - \Delta r^3/6 + \cdots \\
&= -\left(AD_A - LD_L\right)\Delta r + \left(AD_A^2 - LD_L^2\right)\Delta r^2/2 \\
&\quad - \left(AD_A^3 - LD_L^3\right)\left(-\Delta r^3/6\right) + \cdots
\end{aligned}
\tag{L.2}
$$

where $D_A = \Sigma A_t e^{-rt}t$, the continuous compounding measure of duration of assets; $D_L = \Sigma L_t e^{-rt}\ t$, the continuous compounding measure of duration of liabilities; $D_A^2 = \Sigma A_t e^{-rt}t^2$, the second duration measure of assets; $D_L^2 = \Sigma L_t e^{-rt}t^2$, the second duration measure of liabilities; $D_A^3 = \Sigma A_t e^{-rt}t^3$, the third duration measure of assets; $D_L^3 = \Sigma L_t e^{-rt}t^3$, the third duration measure of liabilities.

If the goal is to immunize interest rate risk completely, ΔE is required to set to zero. That is, all duration measures have to set to zero to achieve this purpose.

Similarly, if only interest rate risk matters in terms of changes and convexity, i.e., only Δr and Δr^2, the first and second duration measures, will matter since higher duration measures will vanish.

NOTES

1 This does not mean that the cost of capital is irrelevant. It still has uses for acquisition of real estate, for instance. Similarly, it has an important role to play in assessing performance of a division or subsidiary, as we shall see later.

2 Traditionally, regulations have played an important role in constraining the returns – a kind of quid pro quo for restricting competition for banks. This may explain stress on risk rather than returns. Since regulations are promoting *financial* market inefficiency, this viewpoint is not inconsistent with our stance here.

3 Naturally, the three components of risk are interrelated. Consequently, focus on one component at the exclusion of others is only for expository convenience.

4 We assume here that loans will not be refunded when interest rates drop.

5 A forward-forward swap with near-term short and long-term long positions (or a "repo" sale), discussed in Chapter 3, leads to results similar to a negative gap with a change in the interest rate.

6 Given that the gap analysis rarely exceeds two years, and a compartment is at the most of one year, the intra-compartmental differences are hardly likely to be material.

7 This problem is also encountered in the gap analysis.

8 See Chapter 3 for discussion on the Fisher Open effect. As shown in Appendix K, $\partial s/\partial r = s_0/(1 + r^\star)$ implies that a change in the spot exchange rate due to the domestic interest rate change will be inversely proportional to the foreign interest rate. Although the above result is based on constancy of the foreign interest rate, it is in the spirit of the relative interest rate relationship of the Fisher Open effect.

9 The authors benefited greatly from fruitful discussions with Sanjay Nawalkha on the interest rate immunization decision rules in this section.

10 If we allow for, say, a curvature shift or changes in other shape parameters of the term structure in addition to the slope shift, the decision rule will be even more complicated, and incremental benefits would have to justify the cost of this additional refinement.

11 As these assets are typically sold without recourse to the bank, the bank may be able to lower the regulatory (equity) capital requirement to be discussed in the next chapter. In this way, the bank is "arbitraging the regulation", i.e., lowering the regulatory cost by avoiding the regulatory requirement. It is similar to the bank raising funds in the Eurocurrency market and escaping thereby the cost of deposit insurance imposed on funds raised in the domestic market.

12 When liquid assets are segregated and sold to the SPV, the remainder of the bank assets becomes less liquid and their quality deteriorates. Hence, the bank's shareholders or other existing claimholders will demand higher compensation that may offset the cost savings achieved through securitization.

13 Securitization, however, does not allow the bank to eliminate credit risk inherent in the loan portfolio, since the-without-recourse loan sales requires the bank to either bear the actuarial risk or obtain lower discounted value. Credit enhancement either carries higher fees or has to follow strictly the guidelines set by the guaranteeing entity.

14 Knowledgeable observers contend that the common law tradition (e.g., in the USA and UK) is more conducive resolving issues pertaining to securitization than the civil law (e.g., France and

Italy). Issues revolve around matters such as when an asset sale is a true sale and how an SPV should be treated for tax, reporting and regulatory purposes.

15 During the late 1970s, a low inflation rate and perceived advantage of secrecy of accounts spurred foreigners to deposit funds in Switzerland to such a great extent that the Swiss government imposed a tax of 10 percent per *quarter* on non-resident deposits – effectively letting these deposits earn a negative return of 40 percent a year! A Swiss bank could offer a customer an account denominated in a foreign currency (e.g., US dollar) in a tax haven with compatible secrecy assurances at nominal return far below the going market rate.

16 Complex legal and accounting issues arise on matters such as when dividends are interest payments and vice versa; also whether the IRS would accept the transaction with the shell company as a legitimate one.

PART IV

Trends and Future Directions

Capital Adequacy

10.1 Introduction

In Chapter 9, we already saw that the MM propositions have limited applicability when financial markets are inefficient. When taxes, transaction costs and bankruptcy-related costs are not insignificant, varying proportions of debt and equity in the capital structure of a business enterprise will have an uneven impact on its value. For instance, when taxes or transaction costs are introduced, debt becomes a preferred funding source because of its ability to enhance the value of the enterprise. But debt also enhances the potential for bankruptcy and adversely affects the values of both the enterprise and its stock. Thus bankruptcy prospects serve as a deterrent for extensive use of debt. Balancing these opposing forces[1] so that they may lead to the desirable capital structure (how much debt there should be in the capital structure) becomes an important policy or strategy issue for its management.

Historically, banks have almost exclusively relied on deposits – short-term debt – for funding loans and other investments. Hence bank *preference* for debt is well accepted, and not a controversial matter for capital structure consideration. But what about the deterrent of bankruptcy? Given the critical role of banks in the money creation process, a government is motivated to maintain safety and soundness of the banking system. It is widely perceived that the government will prop up banks facing bankruptcy out of its concern that failure of individual banks, particularly large financial institutions, might erode public confidence and thus create chaos in the financial system. In turn, the government inclination to bail out banks in trouble suggests that the threat of bankruptcy would not be critical for a bank. Given this safety net, a bank would not have any qualms for utilizing debt to the fullest extent. Nor would it hesitate to undertake excessively risky investments with lopsided payoffs for its stockholders. This potential moral hazard has led the government to regulate a bank for both the scope of its activities (that primarily affects its asset choice) and capital adequacy (that prohibits it from funding through an excessive amount of debt). Regulations related to the capital adequacy serve as a critical deterrent on the bank's ability to employ debt to the extent desired by the bank in its capital structure.[2] To put it differently, capital structure design is not just a management issue; instead, it is shaped by the regulatory constraints imposed on bank management.

It is generally believed that recent developments – such as globalization of financial markets with the unregulated Eurocurrency market at its epicenter and banks' preferences for risk assumption through off-the-balance-sheet contingent financing – have added urgency to regulators' anxiety regarding stability of the global financial system. The US regulatory bodies have responded to these significant changes by (a) increased supervisory co-ordination at not only national but also international level, (b) increased disclosure to investors, (c) increased insistence on proper assessment of asset quality, and, above all, (d) radically redefining minimum capital requirements for individual banks.

The issue of capital adequacy for banks has been a concern of regulators since 1930. In 1986, the US bank regulators proposed to require US banks to maintain capital that reflects riskiness of bank assets. By 1988 the proposal had been transformed in the **Basel Accord**, an international banking agreement for risk-based capital standards by the central bank representatives of 12 industrialized nations.[3] Although the stated motive for the Accord was "the level playing ground" for banks domiciled in different countries so as to foster competition across borders, it is believed that its ulterior motive was "to eliminate the funding-cost advantage of Japanese banks that allowed them to capture more than one-third of international lending during the 1980s."[4]

Although what constitutes capital and how the requirement should be enforced is left to the discretion of individual regulatory authorities, the Basel Accord reflected consensus on several important elements.

First, a bank's minimum capital requirement is specified by a formula that attempts to determine primarily the default (credit) risk of the assets. The general idea is that greater credit risk requires a larger capital base.

Second, the definition of assets includes off-balance sheet instruments containing contingent risk elements. For this purpose, a common formula was devised for conversion of these items into equivalent assets.

Third, stockholders' equity is viewed as the most critical component of the bank capital. Each bank is expected to operate with a minimum amount of equity vis-à-vis credit risk of its assets.

Fourth, the bank is required to maintain core, or "Tier I," and secondary, or "Tier II," capital at a level so that the combination of the two tiers may not be less than 8 percent of the risk-adjusted assets. The capital requirements were approximately standardized among countries in order to have a level playing field for competing banks domiciled in different countries.

The risk-based capital standards (the Basel standards) have been evolving ever since 1988. Modifications reflect both desire for fine-tuning and need to keep up with changes in the global environment. These modifications have a significant influence on bank management decisions pertaining not just to financing but also to investments.

This chapter first provides a general discussion on the role of capital in bank management. It then covers the development of capital-based regulation and illustrates the mechanics for capital requirements under the Basel standard. Further, it discusses the impact of the capital-based regulation on bank management decisions. Finally, it traces modifications in the regulatory stance since 1988 and its impact on bank management.

10.2   The Key Role of Capital

As we saw in Chapter 1, regulators concerned with the systemic risk of bank runs do not like to rely exclusively on reserve requirements, deposit insurance or being a lender of last resort because of the potential for moral hazard. As a result, regulators aiming at minimizing the moral hazard problem impose equity capital requirements as a fraction of the bank's assets.

Conventionally the strong bank capital base reduces risk in two basic ways:

- it provides a cushion for absorbing losses from investments that have defaulted or gone sour (credit risk);
- it allows the bank to meet liquidity needs arising from unanticipated deposit outflows either through sale of assets without duress or by maintaining uninterrupted access to financial markets (liquidity or interest risk).

Recently, capital has assumed significance for still another reason. With the intensified competition and abridged product life cycle, banks have been under heavy pressure to develop new products. Risks related to the development process, successful introduction in the market place and competition are often unanticipated or underestimated. The cushion of equity capital is vital for bearing the cost of these risks.

Strong capitalization is intended to benefit the banking industry in the following ways (Caesar 1992).

- It reduces incentives for banks to take excessive risks and to minimize misallocation of credit, thereby avoiding an oversupply of funds to high-risk ventures and an artificially low supply of capital to low-risk loans earmarked with low returns.
- For strong, healthy banks, it mitigates the burden of partially subsidizing inefficient or weak banks through deposit insurance premiums that are uniform across the board.

- It reduces the likelihood of a credit crunch. In an economic downturn, a well-capitalized bank will probably not have to contract its asset base in the face of non-performing loans. Rather, such a well-capitalized bank will probably be able to absorb substantial losses and to maintain its previous lending levels.
- Given the uniform applicability of regulations (even across borders, albeit, to a less extent), price-cutting competition is likely to lose momentum, thereby improving profitability as well as its predictability.

Several qualifications should be noted with respect to desirability of a large capital base, especially given its definition in terms of book value. It is difficult to establish a plausible link between book value based bank capital and its ability to withstand the risk of failure. Also, "one size fits all" is questionable since well-managed banks that are run efficiently may require a low capital-to-asset-ratio cushion.

Further, a large capital base does not automatically translate into liquidity. Although it may help the bank in raising additional external funding, ultimately it would depend on the quality of other assets. In the final analysis, as long as the market value is sufficiently positive, banks can resort to external markets for sale of assets or additional securities to offset liquidity problems. Failures, then, are tied directly to market value, and not the accounting value.

10.3   Development of Capital-based Regulation: Background

Several important events relating to international banking took place in the 1980s. First, defaults by many sovereign governments eroded the quality of bank loan portfolios and banks (especially the US based) were forced to report this deterioration. Second, many investment-grade corporations accelerated the pace of directly resorting to the financial market for financing needs, bypassing the banks. As a result, the quality of bank loans declined. Third, volatility of interest and foreign exchange rates continued to remain significantly high. Finally, commercial banks faced increased competition due to deregulation from banks as well as other financial institutions.

The bank responses on international dimensions broadly adhered to the following patterns.

- They shifted the loan portfolios in favor of sovereign debt of industrialized nations, especially via the Euro-currency and Euro-bond markets, even when margins were razor thin. Some government agencies of industrialized nations were able to reduce their borrowing cost on FRNs from LIBOR + 0.25 percent in the early 1980s to LIBID − 0.5 percent in the mid-1980s!
- They lowered the acceptable credit standards, shifted to other forms of investments (such as bridge loans for project development or for mergers, acquisitions, and LBOs), or both. They also facilitated non-financial firms' direct access to financial markets through devices such as NIFs, MOFs, and Euro-CP.
- They developed OTC derivative instruments such as swaps, FRNs, options, and futures that enabled firms to shift the increased unpredictability of interest and currency rates to

banks. These instruments by and large contained contingent liabilities and risk that did not appear on the bank balance sheets, but managed to fortify their income statements with fees income. What was worse, upper level management in banks often did not understand risks inherent in these instruments or other new products. On the positive side, products like FRNs and loan sales or securitization enabled banks to reduce the maturity (and thereby lower the interest exposure) of their asset portfolio. Similarly, banks showed greater sensitivity to geographical diversification by swapping or selling sovereign loans, a development at least partially due to requirement for disclosure to investors of problem (or disproportionately large) sovereign loans.

- They created complex organizational structures, often under the umbrella of the bank holding company, where different units started pursuing business that did not fall within the scope of typical banking activities. Further, these other units were not subject to regulation.

Banks' actions to offset decreased returns and/or increased risk were woefully inadequate, and systemic risk in the framework of integrated but largely unregulated financial markets still remained a matter of concern for the bank regulators.

This concern did not translate into swift regulatory measures. Partially, this was because domestic supervision of banks had not kept pace with the banks' expanded activities in the international arena. National supervisory authorities were ambivalent about supervision of foreign banks operating in their territory. Sharp differences in domestic regulatory philosophies over matters such as disclosure requirements and information sharing did not help the matter. Finally, individual national authorities were reluctant to change their regulatory policies out of fear that the changes might put their own banking industry at a competitive disadvantage.

In the 1974 meeting in Basel, Switzerland, the central bank governors of the **Group of 10** (G-10) countries formally established a framework to ensure the long-term health of the international banking system under the auspices of the Basel Committee of the Bank for International Settlements.

In 1975, the Basel Committee issued the Basel Concordat that established guidelines for banks operating in more than one country. The Concordat recognized the primary responsibility of host country authorities for bank supervision but acknowledged the implied duty of parent country authorities to ensure the solvency and liquidity of the foreign branches of their nationals. A major goal of the Concordat was to eliminate supervisory gaps and to emphasize that banking authorities should exercise supervisory responsibility rather than simply assuming the role of a lender of last resort. That this was a wishful proclamation, especially with respect to the goal of seamless supervision, was clearly brought out in the failure of BCCI in 1991, a Third World bank, established in Luxemburg but primarily operating in the UK, that managed to escape supervisory scrutiny in both these countries.

10.4   Development of Capital Requirement in the USA

Regulatory interest in capital adequacy surfaced in the USA in the aftermath of the banking crisis of the 1930s. The large losses of depositors resulting from the bank failures of the Great Depression ultimately led to the introduction of federal deposit insurance. Deposit insurance marked a fundamental change in the function of capital. Capital had previously served to protect the depositors, but there was no protection for the small depositor. The Federal Deposit Insurance Corporation (FDIC), a government agency selling an insurance policy to banks, was created to protect its small depositors in case of bank failure. Over the years, the initial limited deposit insurance has been increased to $100,000 per account (thereby increasing the protection several times for an individual); and in the last 25 years, most bank failures have been resolved by mergers (where the acquiring bank has assumed the total deposit liability) rather than by liquidations. Thus, deposit insurance has evolved from small depositor protection to a safety net for all bank depositors. As a result, the potential threat of bank runs no longer motivates banks to maintain high capital ratios or hold a large precautionary cushion of liquid assets. (As a matter of fact, it creates a perfect opportunity for moral hazard, as discussed in Chapter 1, in terms of bank management undertaking risky investments that increase the likelihood of bank failure.) Thus, the burden of maintaining bank capital at an adequate level fell largely on the regulators.

Capital ratios declined sharply during the 1950s and 1960s. By the 1970s, the continuing postwar decline in capital ratios was thought to pose a danger to the banking system. As deregulation in the banking industry progressed, it was widely perceived that capital ratios had fallen too low to absorb losses. By 1982, the ratio of total capital to total assets for all insured banks had fallen to 6 percent, less than half its 1929 level.

With rising bank and thrift failures and declining capital ratios, the Federal Reserve System, FDIC, and Office of Comptroller of the Currency (OCC) in 1981 began to reestablish uniform minimum capital standards. The Federal Reserve System and OCC considered two measures of capital adequacy: the ratio of primary capital to total assets, and the ratio of total capital to total assets. Primary capital was defined as equity capital plus loan loss reserves. Total capital was defined as primary capital plus limited-life preferred stock and qualifying subordinated notes and debentures. The FDIC chose to consider only one ratio: the ratio of equity capital to total assets.

The 1981 capital standards quickly became outdated. First, banks increased their off-balance sheet activities, which increased risk while enjoying, by default, exemption from the capital standards. Second, the 1981 standards permitted loan-loss reserves to count without limit toward primary capital; and by 1985, any *realistic* charge for loan losses would have completely wiped out equity capital of some large US banks.

Initially, the Federal Reserve chose to exhort banks to reinforce the capital base and improve monitoring of risks. By the end of 1986, it announced an accord with the Bank of England that established a higher capital ratio and required banks to account for off-the-balance-sheet instruments for such capital requirements. Eventually, this accord became the basis for the 1988 Basel Accord. The Basel Accord established total capital to risk-weighted assets as an international bank capital measure, and set 8 percent of the risk-adjusted assets as the minimum acceptable level of capital, as previously described.

In 1989, Congress passed the Financial Institutions Reform, Recovery and Enforcement Act (FIRREA), which took a keen interest in depository institutions' insolvency risk and in the policy measures to control this risk. The Act calls for a core capital requirement of 3 percent of total assets.

In late 1991, Congress passed the Federal Deposit Insurance Corporation Improvement Act (FDICIA) calling for rigid regulatory capital requirements for banks beginning in

Table 10.1   Capital categories for the prompt corrective actions

	Total risk-based ratio	Tier 1 risk-based ratio	Leverage ratio
1. Well-capitalized	10% or above	6% or above	5% or above
2. Adequately capitalized	8% or above	4% or above	4% or above
3. Undercapitalized	Below 8%	Below 4%	Below 4%
4. Significantly undercapitalized	Below 6%	Below 3%	Below 3%
5. Critically undercapitalized	Below 2%		

December 18, 1992. According to the FDICIA, a bank's capital is assessed by the **leverage ratio** (more accurately, the equity ratio) that measures the bank's core capital in terms of its assets. Core capital is a bank's common equity plus qualifying perpetual preferred stock plus minority interest in equity accounts of consolidated subsidiaries.

This Act tries to strengthen the importance of bank capital by establishing five capitalization categories (see Table 10.1 for these five categories) with additional regulatory actions (called Prompt Corrective Actions) triggered by classification of a financial institution into lower categories.

- If a bank is classified as well capitalized, there is no mandatory action required.
- If the bank falls into the adequately capitalized category, it is not allowed to take brokered deposits, except with FDIC approval.
- In the undercapitalized category, the bank is required to (1) suspend dividends and management fees, (2) require capital restoration plans, (3) restrict asset growth, (4) require approval for acquisitions, branching and new activities and (5) reject brokered deposits.
- In the significantly undercapitalized category, in addition to satisfying the mandatory provisions in the undercapitalized category, the bank has to (1) resort to recapitalization, and (2) restrict inter-affiliate transactions, deposit interest rates and officers' pay.
- In the critically undercapitalized category, the bank has to satisfy all conditions in the above category. In addition, the bank has to suspend payments on subordinated debt along with other restrictions. Regulators are directed to place the bank into receivership or conservatorship.

Consistent with the Basel Accord, the US bank regulators also adopted a risk-weighted framework for assessing capital adequacy. This framework was fully phased in by January 1, 1993. The original guidelines stressed the importance of equity capital and established a minimum requirement for so-called "Tier 1" or *core (primary) capital*, composed of common equity, non-cumulative perpetual preferred, plus certain reserves net of intangible assets like goodwill, plus minority interest in consolidated subsidiaries. The book value of Tier 1 capital must equal at least 4 percent of risk-weighted assets. *Secondary capital* (Tier II) consists of other kinds of reserves and other classes of stock, plus certain liabilities, including subordinated term debt. In assessing the adequacy of its capital, a bank cannot include any secondary capital in excess of primary capital or any subordinated debt in excess of half of primary capital.

Under these guidelines, a weighted average measure is employed for total assets corresponding to four different categories of assets group represented by an appropriate percentage

(0, 20, 50, or 100 percent) plus the off-balance sheet items weighted by the appropriate percentage (0, 20, 50, or 100 percent).

Subsequently, these guidelines were modified to permit netting of off-balance sheet derivatives (1995). The Basel Committee also issued a proposal to change supervisory standards from periodic monitoring of the bank's transactions to evaluation of the bank's internal control systems (1998), as discussed later.

10.4.1 Details of the risk-based capital requirements

Bank managers must follow a four-step procedure to determine the minimum capital requirements:

1 Classify bank assets into one of four risk categories, which are represented by 0, 20, 50, and 100 percent.
2 Classify off-balance-sheet activities into the appropriate risk categories represented by 0, 20, 50, and 100 percent.
3 Multiply the dollar amount of assets in each category by the appropriate risk weight (i.e., the percentage) to obtain the risk-adjusted assets.
4 Check whether the bank capital satisfies the requirement by comparing the desired percentage, either 4 percent or 8 percent (as shown in Table 10.1) to the risk-adjusted assets.

On-balance sheet items

All bank assets are required to be classified as one of the four categories for computing the ratios. Box 10.1 illustrates these classifications.

Box 10.1 Four categories of bank asset classification for the risk-based capital requirements.

1 *0 percent category.* Cash (domestic and foreign) Trading Accounts, Federal Reserve Bank Balances and claims, Securities of the US Treasure, OECD governments and some US agencies
2 *20 percent category.* Cash items in the process of collection, US and OECD inter-bank deposits and guaranteed claims, some non-OECD bank and government deposits and securities, general obligations municipal bonds, and some mortgage-backed securities.
3 *50 percent category.* Loans fully secured by first liens on 1–4 family residential properties, revenue municipal bonds and credit equivalent amounts of interest rate and exchange rate related contracts.
4 *100 percent category.* Loans to private entities and individuals, some claims on non-OECD governments and banks, real assets, claims on foreign banks with an original maturity greater than a year, instruments issued by other banking organizations that qualify as capital and investments in subsidiaries.

Example 10.1

The following are the assets (in thousands) appearing on the Capital Bank's balance sheet.

	(1) Assets	(2) Risk weights	(3) = (1)×(2)
Cash and Reserve	100	0%	$0
T-bills and T-bonds	100	0	0
General obligated bonds	50	20	10
CMO backed agencies	100	20	20
Domestic depository institution	60	20	12
CMO backed by mortgage loans	200	50	100
State and municipal revenue bonds	100	50	50
Commercial loans	500	100	500
Other investments	40	100	40
Risk-adjusted assets			$732

Their risk-weights are provided in column 2. The last column provides the risk-based assets.

Off-balance items

Estimation of risk-adjusted assets for off-balance sheet items involves segregation of these activities into two categories: contingent guarantee contracts and derivative instruments.

1 *Contingent guarantee contracts.* The key point in the estimation process is to convert values of these contingent guarantee contracts into credit equivalent amounts similar to the balance sheet assets. Box 10.2 illustrates the conversion.

Box 10.2   Credit conversion factors for contingent guaranteed contracts

1 *0 percent conversion factor.* Loan commitments less than one year maturity and unconditionally cancelable at any time.

2 *20 percent conversion factor.* Short-term, self-liquidating trade-related contingencies such as commercial letters of credit and bankers' acceptances.

3 *50 percent conversion factor.*
   • Performance-related standby letters of credit
   • Unused portions of loan commitments with original maturity of more than one year
   • Revolving underwriting facilities, note issuance facilities and other similar arrangements.

4 *100 percent conversion factor.*
   • Direct credit substitute standby letters of credit
   • Agreements to purchase assets
   • Sale and repurchase agreements and asset sales with recourse.

Once the credit equivalent amounts of the contingent guaranteed contracts are established (i.e., the dollar value of the contract times the appropriate conversion factor), the risk class of these converted assets must be determined. In fact, the counterparty behind the guaranteed contract dictates the risk class of these converted assets. For example, if the counterparty is a private agent, then the appropriate risk weight for these assets will be 100 percent. On the other hand, risk weight will be less than 100 percent, if the counterparty is a state agency.

Example 10.2

Suppose the following commitments are made by the St Louis Bank.

1   $200,000 standby letter of credit to back a commercial paper issue;
2   $150,000 commercial letter of credit;
3   $100,000 loan commitments to a corporation; its maturity is more than one year.
4   $400,000 standby letter of credit to back an issue of general obligation (GO) bonds by the state government.

	(1) Face value	(2) Conv. factor	(3) = (1) × (2) Credit equiv. amount	(4) Risk weight	(5) = (3) × (4) Risk-adjusted asset value
Commercial paper	$200	1.0	$200	1.0	$200
L/C	150	1.0	150	1.0	150
Loans	100	0.5	50	1.0	50
GO bonds	400	1.0	400	0.5	200
Risk-adjusted assets					$600

2   *Derivative instruments.* According to the risk-based capital rules, exchange-traded derivative contracts have zero risk; only OTC derivatives carry risk. Specifically, for the OTC contracts such as swaps, interest and currency related futures and options, their nominal or face values are converted into credit equivalent amounts (defined below), which are then multiplied by 0.5 (risk weight) to yield the risk-adjusted assets.

The credit equivalent amount is the sum of the replacement cost and potential exposure of the derivative instruments. The replacement cost or mark-to-market cost is the *present value* of the cost of replacing a contract if a counterparty defaults today. The replacement cost is computed by using the current rate for the value of the derivative instruments. For example, suppose last year a bank entered into a two-year forward contract to buy £300,000 at $1.50/£. Today, one year later, the one-year forward rate is $1.60/£. Then the replacement cost of the forward contract will be $30,000, that is, ($1.60 − 1.50)/£ × £300,000). However, if the one-year forward rate is $1.40/£, the replacement cost will be zero because it will be smaller at the market rate than at the contract rate.

Table 10.2 Conversion factors for interest rate and currency contracts for potential exposure

Maturity	Interest rate contracts (%)	Currency contracts (%)
One year or less	0	1.0
One to five years	0.50	5.00
Over five years	1.00	7.50

The potential exposure of the derivative contracts relates to the *credit risk* of these instruments. The conversion factors for the interest rate and currency related instruments are shown in Table 10.2.

Example 10.3

A bank has (a) a five-year fixed-floating interest rate swap with a principal amount of $5,000,000 with $40,000 replacement cost, and (b) a two-year forward contract of $1,500,000. The potential exposure and risk-adjusted asset value (in '000s) are computed in the following two steps as:

Contracts	Face value (1)	Conversion ratio (2)	Potential exposure (3) = (1)×(2)
Swap	$5,000	0.005	$25
Forward	1,500	0.050	75

	Potential exposure (1)	Replacement cost (2)	Credit equiv. amount (3) = (1) + (2)	Risk weight (4)	Risk adjusted value (5) = (3) × (4)
Swap	$25	$40	$65	0.5	$32.5
Forward	75	0	75	0.5	37.5
Risk-adjusted assets					$70.0

Netting

Under the modification adopted by the Federal Reserve Board, netting is permitted when a bank enters into an agreement with a counterparty for *a set of transactions* (e.g., a swap), which explicitly requires their settlement on a net basis. Calculations above with respect to potential exposure and current exposure now would be carried out on a net basis in the following way.

- Net current exposure. Compute the sum of replacement cost, calculated just as earlier, for each transaction; designate it as $G[c]$. Net current exposure, $N[c]$, will be given by the sum; but it will be 0 if the sum is negative.

- *Net potential exposure.* Compute the gross potential exposure, $G[p]$, as a *sum* of potential exposure, calculated as earlier, for each transaction.
- Compute the ratio of net to gross current exposure, designated as $R = G[c]/N[c]$.
- Net exposure, $N[p] = [0.4 + 0.6 \times R] \times G[p]$.

The credit equivalent amount is the sum of the two net exposures. Essentially, the modified procedure reduces the capital requirements on transactions like swaps.

Example 10.4   Risk-adjusted assets and capital

Given the data in Examples 10.1–10.3, we now determine total risk-adjusted assets and capital.

- The total of the risk-adjusted assets is the sum of the risk-adjusted assets on and off the balance sheet.

$$\$1,402,000 \text{ (i.e., } \$732,000 + \$600,000 + \$70,000)$$

- Next, we compute the Tier I, Tier II and total capital position of a bank. According to the capital rule shown in Table 10.1, Tier I capital must equal or exceed 4 percent of weighted risk assets.

$$0.04 \times \$1,402,000 = \$56,080$$

Core capital (Tier I) consists of common stockholders' equity and minority interest in common stock accounts of consolidated subsidiaries less goodwill amounts.

- Supplementary capital (Tier II) is limited to

$$1.00 \times \text{Tier I capital} = \$56,080$$

Tier II capital consists of items such as allowances for loan and lease losses (limited to 1.25 percent of weighted risk assets), perpetual and long-term preferred stock (no limit), hybrid capital instruments including perpetual debt and mandatory convertible securities (no limit) , and subordinated debt and intermediate-term preferred stock whose original weighted average maturity of seven years or more (limited to 50 percent of Tier I)

- Total capital is the sum of Tier I and Tier II capital less deductions and must equal or exceed 8 percent of weighted risk assets.

Deductions consist of investments in unconsolidated banking and finance subsidiaries, reciprocal holdings of bank-issued capital securities and other deductions as determined by supervisory authorities.

10.4.2   Implementation of the capital standards in the USA

While the Basel Accord established common, *minimum* standards across countries for measuring and controlling risks, the FDICIA has supplemented the Basel standards, as shown in Table 10.1, by launching prompt corrective action instigated by any *one* of the three criteria. Early detection of problem banks results in mandatory implementation of a system of discipline in which *penalties escalate with the extent of violation of capital standard requirements*. This escalation of penalties is meant to sharply curtail the extent to which private stakeholders in an undercapitalized institution can transfer the insolvency cost to taxpayer-supported safety nets.

Regulatory discipline embodied in the FDICIA is also envisaged to supplement as well as increase the role of market discipline. Regulators will choose the least cost regulation alternative when failures occur.

Most banks in the USA as well as Europe have had little difficulty meeting the standards. In 1990, a majority of the US banks were already in compliance with the new risk-based capital requirements. When the FDICIA was first applied in December 1992, among 15,000 US commercial banks, fewer than 100 banks were in the lowest capital category – critically undercapitalized. Still, this initial situation does not ensure that a bank that has met the requirements will always be able to comply with the standards. Thus two interrelated issues surface.

- What can a bank do to avoid being subject to prompt corrective action?
- What are the alternative courses of actions for a bank when it faces the constraint of regulatory standards?

We now examine these two issues.

10.4.3   Ramifications of capital requirements

Clearly, capital adequacy has become a major benchmark for assessing the performance of banks. The risk-based capital regulation has had a far-reaching impact on bank management.

Constraint on asset growth and its financing

Minimum capital requirements are likely to constrain a bank's ability to grow. Given the growth opportunities in the international field, these requirements are more likely to be a binding force for a bank with international orientation than a bank strictly focused on domestic business. Additions to assets by a bank also require it to augment its capital base so as to meet the capital-to-asset ratio requirement. Each bank must limit its asset growth to some percentage of retained earnings plus new external capital.[5]

A bank can augment its capital base in four ways.

1   It generates increased earnings. Increased earnings allow the bank to increase retention without lowering the dividend payout ratio. But competition may prevent the bank from raising the spread on loans or generating a large fee income from services.

2   It finances growth internally by decreasing dividends. However, this option may induce the shareholder to sell stock, especially if they are skeptical about growth prospects, and thus may lower share prices. Depressed share prices increases the bank's vulnerability to takeover attempts.

3   It finances part of the assets growth with new capital, such as new common stock or perpetual preferred stock. However, such equity is considerably more expensive than debt, and is available only if the bank actually has access to the stock market.[6]

4   Finally, a bank may merge with another financial institution (bank or non-bank) that has deep pockets and/or subject to minimal regulatory oversight. Popularity of the bank holding company format has been partially due to this motivation.

In practice, although a bank would likely pursue some combinations of these strategies, it may simply choose not to grow, or cease to be a bank.

Change in the capital mix

By the early 1990s many large banks had responded to the impending capital requirements by issuing new capital securities including convertible debt and adjustable-rate, perpetual preferred stock.[7] Several banks also entered into sale and leaseback arrangements with bank real estate properties to generate one-time infusion of capital. The net effect was an increase in the proportion of total capital represented by common and preferred stock and their hybrids.

Change in asset mix

Banks may respond to the capital requirements by changing their asset composition. Risk-averse managers may resort to *inter-category* switches, that is, shift assets from high-risk categories such as commercial loans with a 100 percent risk weight to lower-risk categories such as US government securities with zero weight. Alternatively, a bank may resort to intra-category shuffling, that is, shift from low-risk commercial loans to high-risk ones in order to generate higher returns without requiring additional capital contribution.

Modifications in pricing policies

The risk-based capital requirements clearly imply that riskier investments need greater equity support. As a result, banks are forced to re-price their services to reflect these equity requirements. For example, if a bank has to have capital in support of a loan commitment, it may raise the fee to cover the cost of this capital.[8] In addition, all off-balance sheet items require capital, and thus may also be priced properly.

The Basel standards have been adopted by a larger number of countries than the G-10 countries. Banks in some countries have a stronger capital base than banks from other countries. Aggressive, strongly capitalized institutions can exploit cross-border opportunities that remain unfunded by poorly capitalized institutions in a given country.

Emerging trends

The new capital standards have spawned several trends in the wake of their evolution and implementation. First, the risk-based capital requirement has spurred all types of asset securitization activities. Financial institutions have become the largest issuers of asset-backed securities. Consumer receivables (e.g., automobile, mobile home, and credit card loans) are high-quality, liquid assets, which make them natural candidates for securitization. Securitization and sale of these high risk-weighted loans allow banks to reinvest the proceeds in assets with lower risk weights (or, again, alternatively, in higher-risk assets in the same category).

Second, domestic residential lending has received increased attention in comparison with other traditional forms of lending. In essence, banks are taking advantage of the void in housing finance left by thrift institutions.

Third, banks have started to securitize loans through collateralized loan obligations (CLOs). During 1996–7, these loans included not only high yielding commercial loans (reflecting high credit risk) but also emerging market assets. Securitization of bank loans implies that a 100 percent risk-based capital charge applies only to the balance held by the bank, and not the full loan amount.

This is not the only type of "regulatory arbitrage" a bank can undertake. Consider, for instance, an insurance company interested in purchasing a portfolio of loans from a bank. It has two alternative choices: (a) to acquire *securities* backed by the bank loans, and (b) to purchase the loan portfolio directly. The insurance company would be required to have less capital under alternative (a) than under alternative (b)![9]Thus a "double-dip" regulatory arbitrage – where both the bank and the insurance company have been able to reduce capital requirements – occurs as a result of securitization.

10.4.4   Limitations of the risk-based capital standards

Inconsistency of the standards with stated purposes

The Basel Committee explicitly stated that the purpose of the capital adequacy standard is (1) to strengthen the international banking industry and (2) to provide a level playing field for banks competing in more than one country. Because the Basel standards for capital, especially Tier II capital, are left up to the discretion of banking authorities in a given country, the defined standards would not be likely to be out of reach for the banks domiciled in the country. In this respect, the "soundness and stability" goal of the Basel standard seems farfetched. Further, as this discretion extends to approval of various capital instruments, the competitive equality objective is also undermined. For example, in both Germany and Japan, banks are permitted to count substantial hidden reserves – in the form of unrealized gains on share portfolios, industrial participation and property – as part of capital.[10]

Bank portfolio considerations

The risk-adjusted asset ratio provides an objective basis for risk assessment. However, the current system for risk weights is crude and inadequate.

- It uses a coarse classification system. For example, weak commercial loan credits have the same risk weight as high-quality ones. Banks may prefer weak loan credits to high-quality ones because of higher returns prospects for identical capital requirement – a classic example of what Stiglitz and Weiss (1981) call the *incentive effect*. The danger thus is that banks' decisions along these lines might actually increase overall portfolio risk.
- It fails to reflect risk differences across countries, especially for C&I loan category. For instance, Japanese banks' loans to a member of the family concerns (keiretsu) are significantly different from, and presumably less risky than, US and UK banks' loans to unrelated independent entities. The US bank's loan terms, for instance, can be reasonably characterized as the result of arm's length bargaining. No such characterization is possible for the Japanese bank's loan terms.
- It fails to distinguish two aspects of credit risk: delinquency risk (timing of cash flows) and default risk, the extreme of delinquency risk; instead, it focuses strictly on default risk. Delinquency may have liquidity implications.
- It reflects only one dimension of risk – credit risk. Market or interest risk is ignored for on-balance sheet items. Thus an investment in a 30-year government bond from an OECD country has zero risk weight whereas a one-year loan to an investment-grade firm carries 100 percent risk weight. Similarly, a 30-year fixed-rate home mortgage, which is vulnerable to interest-rate risk, requires only half the capital of a three-month commercial loan with virtually no interest-rate risk.

  The capital standards also ignore liquidity risk. Short-term loans and securities are inherently less risky than long-term assets, yet the new capital standards do not discriminate between portfolios with shorter-term maturities and those with longer-term ones.
- It measures individual asset's risk. Modern portfolio theory has demonstrated, and investors have closely followed the lesson, that the riskiness of a portfolio cannot be measured by examining each asset individually. The overall riskiness of the portfolio heavily depends on the interrelationships among individual assets. Diversification through different types assets, different industries, and different geographic regions can significantly reduce the risk of a bank's portfolio.
- A more critical but subtle problem is the joint consideration of risks that may change the asset rankings. Suppose an investment in a five-year, AAA-rated FRN has the same credit risk characteristics as the investment in a five-year BBB-grade, fixed rate obligation *combined with* credit enhancement. Still the BBB-grade may be a preferred investment choice because its return estimates show greater stability over a business cycle than the AAA-rated FRN, and its deficiency with respect to credit risk is removed with credit enhancement.
- Focusing solely on the riskiness of each individual asset also overlooks the risk associated with possible asset–liability mismatches. Funding long-term assets with short-term liabilities adds to liquidity risk, since withdrawal of the short-term funding may call for premature liquidation of the long-term assets. Further, rising interest rates can increase the cost of the short-term funding. A portfolio of relatively safe long-term assets can, therefore, become excessively risky if funded by short-term liabilities.
- The Basel standards for balance-sheet assets are based on book values. The book value does not necessarily correspond to the economic or market value. Book value, for instance,

ignores changes in the market value of assets, the value of unrealized gains/losses on bank investments, the value of a bank charter, and the value of federal deposit insurance. All these ignored factors are likely to have a significant impact on the bank's ability to access the market for additional funding during emergency. At the same time, the regulatory stance embedded in the Basel standards allows a bank to exploit the arbitrage opportunity. The practice of securitization discussed earlier illustrates an application of regulatory arbitrage.

- The standards' treatment of off-balance sheet items considers the counterparty (default) risk, but fails to reflect trading or position risk.

These criticisms should be put in perspective: the standards were not envisaged by regulatory bodies as a panacea. They had regarded them as a necessary first step in the evolutionary process, as the modifications below suggest.

10.5   Modifications in the Basel Standards

In 1998, the Basel Committee adopted a proposal to modify bank supervision. Currently a US bank's records are periodically reviewed in detail by regulators. Electronic transactions, off-balance-sheet transactions pertaining to derivatives, and increased gyrations in fundamental economic forces (e.g., interest rates, inflation rate, and currency values) make it difficult and time consuming for the examiner to identify and assess the bank's risk profile and determine the bank's ability to withstand the normal risk.

The modification advocates a choice for a bank: continue with the standard, transaction-based review or opt for examination of the bank's own internal control mechanism for measuring, controlling and adequately providing for exposure to not only credit risk but also interest rate, liquidity, position (related to, e.g., options), and foreign exchange risks. The thinking behind giving a bank such a choice is that *ex post* examination of past transactions, and that also periodically, is of little value in the volatile world of today especially when banks have a preponderance of derivatives-based transactions. For the sake of stockholders and for survival, management has to have an internal control mechanism. So long as that mechanism is not functioning against the interests of depositors (pose the systemic risk), adoption of the proposed approach would allow a less regulatory cost burden on banks.

The mechanism will be assessed along the following five dimensions:

1   *Management oversight and the control culture.* Setting up the organizational structure, a responsibility of the board of directors and top management.
2   *Risk assessment.* Identifying and assessing internal and external factors that affect or are affected by various facets of risk, such as country risk and credit risk of bank activities in light of changes in the industry or economy.
3   *Control activities.* Essentially sound internal auditing activities that would avoid problems of verifications, reconciliation and reasonably objective review.
4   *Monitoring.* Continual monitoring and periodic review of the internal control system.
5   *Supervisory responsibility.* Insistence on a strong control culture with a focus on risk assessment and monitoring at the top management level.

In June 1999, the Basel Committee proposed one additional modification that would replace the earlier arbitrary risk weights assigned to different categories with weights based on external credit ratings. For instance, a loan to a borrower (business or government) rated AAA by Moody's would carry the weight of 20 percent, while a loan to an entity rated B- would carry the weight of 150 percent. If a borrower is not rated at all, the weight would be 100 percent, as is the case now.

10.5.1   VAR model

The Basel Committee on Banking Supervision also considered effectiveness of **value-at-risk** (VAR) models utilized by some multinational banks, and found them, as a class, a viable alternative.

Basically VAR constructs a probability distribution of returns. This distribution is converted into a **cumulative probability** function (i.e., corresponding to each alternative outcome, it shows the sum of probabilities for outcomes equal to or worse than the outcome under consideration). If management selects one such probability number as a benchmark, the corresponding loss (or return) number is the V.

Example 10.5

We have the following outcomes (column 2) corresponding to economic conditions (column 1), and the associated probabilities (column 2). Column 3 provides cumulative probabilities, the sum of all probabilities from the rows above including the current one.

Value at risk illustration

State	Outcome (%)	Probability	Cum. Probabilities
(1)	(2)	(3)	(4)
Depression	-12	0.01	0.01
Severe recession	-8	0.02	0.03
Recession	-5	0.025	0.055
Mild recession	2	0.10	0.155
Status quo	7.5	0.25	0.405
Growth	9.0	0.575	0.98
Boom	20	0.02	1.00

In this case, if management deems the 3 percent – 0.03 – experience as a benchmark, the outcome of -8 percent under the Severe recession category is relevant for VAR on a portfolio of, say, $30 million. Thus the VAR will be

$$-8\% \times \$30\text{million} = -\$2.4 \text{ million}$$

The Basel Committee's recommendations have a direct bearing on the choice of parameters in a VAR model:

1   The model has to consider return data of at least 12 months to generate probabilities.
2   The holding period for which the return is calculated should be 10 days.

3   The benchmark should be 1 percent.

4   The capital requirement should be the larger of (1) the current VAR estimate, and (2) the average of VAR estimates over previous 60 days multiplied by 3.

The recommendation did not cover which model or approach is preferable.

Alternative VAR models

Several models exist for VAR analysis: J.P. Morgan's *Credit Metrics* and Credit Suisse Financial Products' *Credit Risk* are the two leading models. These and other models either employ the assumption of a given distribution or avoid making such assumptions and generate distributions from simulating the past experience (the example above falls in the second category). In both cases, the assumption is that past experience is relevant.[11]

Models that employ known, standard distributions generally use joint normal distributions that are stable over time, and facilitate generating combined estimates of correlated returns. Still, they often differ in terms of a narrow focus on default versus one that highlights delinquency. The delinquency approach generates a loss (return) when the internally generated credit rating of a loan undergoes a change. In contrast, the strict default approach generates a loss only when a loan registers default, say, due to bankruptcy.

Which model should a bank choose? Even the cursory discussion above underscores the complexity of the issue.[12] Still, a management may want to keep in mind the following considerations.

- Stability of parameters and relevance of past experience are red herrings in the volatile world. However, the issue is not *whether* to implement a VAR model. The regulatory bodies are going to opt for the VAR approach; hence, predilection regarding worth of a (any) VAR model will be a moot question.
- Regulatory bodies may allow management an alternative approach, provided such an approach considers jointly different dimensions of risk and shows accuracy of its generated estimates. This may be an expensive proposition.
- The alternative still may be worth investigating, if management needs an internal model that realistically portrays risk. The scope of activities may have a critical bearing on this matter.
- Even when a bank finds a particular VAR model incompatible with its goals, it may still want to assess whether the gain in flexibility outweighs the cost of incompatibility in implementing the model. If, for instance, a model strictly using default risk is unacceptable to the bank but acceptable to regulators, its adoption may permit the bank to select assets with greater potential for delinquency without entailing additional capital contribution.
- Potential for sabotage by subordinates should not be underestimated. The model may permit subordinates to chain the bank to a more risky path than management wants. As a result, a VAR model should not supplant other internal control mechanisms.

These recommendations are a major departure from current regulatory practices: currently regulators apply, as we have mentioned above, purely mechanical rules to evaluate the instruments in order to determine their risk and thereby the need for capital; the recommendations urge regulators to evaluate instead the bank's internal system – the VAR – in terms of its assumptions, models, and their robustness, and its monitoring devices. The basic premise is that the bank should know their products' risk better than regulators; this knowledge better be reflected in a coherent risk management system; and capital adequacy will be determined on the basis of this system, if the system is deemed sound by regulators.

These recommendations also suggest that the bank need not have one internal risk management and monitoring system and, at the same time, another one for determining its capital adequacy requirement. Indeed, smart management would overhaul the bank information system(s), and create one integrated system that is capable of satisfying various needs, such as planning; internal risk management and resource allocation for divisions, geographic regions, activities, and products; commensurate performance monitoring; regulatory and prudent capital requirements; investor reports; and reports for regulators.

10.5.2   External credit rating

The Basel Committee's proposal for replacing the coarse risk-screening categories with categories based on credit rating by external credit rating agencies recognizes the problem we raised earlier regarding incentives for a bank to bias intra-category investments toward the riskier end. Naturally, external agencies are not always accurate, nor their downward revisions timely, as our discussion of the South-East Asian crisis in Chapter 8 indicated. Still, this is a great deterrent against biases in investment decisions. Table 10.3 shows the proposed weights for banks.

The new proposal has several potential implications.

1   In a majority of cases, the proposal is either neutral or favorable to banks in terms of capital adequacy. Unrated entities would not call for additional bank capital. On the other hand, top-rated entities would require less capital contribution for the bank. As a result, top-rated entities would enjoy "preferred habitat" related lower cost than currently:
   • They require less contribution of higher-cost bank equity.
   • Their fewer number combined with banks competing to land their business would give them negotiating leverage with banks.
2   Speculative businesses – those with ratings of B– and below – will have a harder time or higher cost consequences because of higher capital contribution (150 percent versus the current 100 percent) requirement.
3   Still, the speculative businesses may not be passed the entire cost of additional equity contribution. It is possible that top-rated non-regulated businesses may arbitrage by "enhancing" low-rated businesses' credit-rating through, say, standby letters of credit.[13] It is even possible that banks may entice top-rated firms to lower their borrowing cost further through such intermediation.[14] We present below a hypothetical example.

If this happens, the excessive risk currently assumed by banks would shift to other market participants, and the threat of systemic risk would recede – as the regulators would prefer!

Table 10.3 Proposed weights for calculating capital requirements

	Assessment (%)					
Claim	AAA to AA−	A+ to A−	BBB+ to BBB−	BB+ to B−	Below B-	Unrated
Goverments	0	20	50	100	150	100
Banks Option 1[a]	20	50	100	100	150	100
Option 2[b]	20	50[c]	50[c]	100[c]	150	50[c]
Corporates	20	100	100	100	150	100

[a] Risk weighting based on risk weighting of sovereign in which the bank is incorporated.
[b] Risk weighting based on the assessment of the individual bank.
[c] Claims on banks of a short original maturity, for example less than six months, would receive a weighting that is one category more favorable than the usual risk weight on the bank's claims.
Source: Stevens (2000).

Metro Bank lends to Universal Electric, with an AAA rating, at LIBOR − 5 bp. Corner Computer is another customer of Metro Bank with a rating of CCC. Metro can lend to Corner Computer at LIBOR + 250 bp.

Universal provides a standby letter of credit to Corner and charges 75 bp for this enhancement. Due to enhancement, Metro charges LIBOR + 25 bp to Corner. Hence,

- Corner's cost is reduced to LIBOR + 100 bp (from LIBOR + 250 bp);
- Universal's cost is reduced to LIBOR − 80 bp (from LIBOR − 5 bp); and
- Metro enjoys not only the business of Corner at reduced risk for itself but is able to beat out competition in obtaining Universal's business.

10.6 Conclusion

This chapter discussed the function of bank capital and development of capital requirement regulations. Details of the current risk-adjusted capital requirements were also discussed and illustrated. Finally, some likely modifications in the current regulatory practices were noted along with their possible ramifications.

The risk-based capital requirements are not irrelevant in the face of systemic risk posed by (a) current volatile environments in which banks function, and (b) banks navigating in uncharted waters. Whether (1) systemic risk is really a matter of concern, (2) capital requirements takes care of the risk in case it is a matter of concern, and (3) there are better or more effective ways of handling the systemic risk than capital requirements are unresolved issues to date. However, regulators cannot be expected to refrain from taking actions in the absence of unambiguous answers on these issues. Initial adoption of the Basel Accord and the recent proposals for modification of the regulations underscore both regulators' sensitivity to market forces without going overboard and their flexible attitude. Needless to say, regulations in their current form have a significant potential for affecting banks' growth, capital mix, asset composition, and pricing policies, as well as controlling risk-taking activities taken by banks. Adoption of proposed modifications would offer banks both the additional flexibility and a new challenge to streamline their information systems as well as organizational setup.

DISCUSSION QUESTIONS

1   In the Eurocurrency markets, government regulation especially regarding the reserve requirements is conspicuously absent. Still, the money-multiplier, which could be theoretically infinite, is in reality close to one. This suggests that banks follow prudent policies, and those who do not are not welcome to participate in the markets. If banks behave in such a responsible way, why do we need bank capital adequacy regulation?

2   What general consensus was reached by the Basel proposal of 1988? What were the objectives behind the agreement?

3   What roles does bank capital play in the banking business?

4   Discuss briefly the history of capital adequacy requirement for banks in the USA.

5   What are the different risk categories of bank assets for determining the risk-based capital requirements? What problems does such a classification scheme entail? Do you think that replacing these categories with the proposed reliance on external ratings by agencies such as Standard & Poor and Moody's will be an improvement? Why?

6   Explain Tier I and Tier II capital for a bank.

7   Global National Bank has $30 million in commercial standby letters of credit and $100 million interest rate swap contracts with more than an eight-year maturity. The bank's balance sheet (in $ million) on December 31, 20xx is shown below.

Assets		Liabilities and Equity	
Cash	15	Deposits	150
Mortgage loans	100	Long-term debts	10
Commercial loans	60	Equity	15
	175		175

a   Compute the risk-adjusted assets and their corresponding capital requirement.

b   Explain if the bank has sufficient capital to meet the capital requirement.

8 What are the revisions envisaged by the Basel Committee regarding capital adequacy? What impact would they likely have on bank management, vis-à-vis the previous standards?

9 Currently the banking industry is undergoing consolidation worldwide. At the same time distinction among different financial intermediaries is getting blurred through mergers and acquisition. What impact would these trends have on regulatory supervision regarding bank capital adequacy maintenance?

10 Explain the concept of the value-at-risk model for bank regulation.

11 Bank of St Louis has substantially expanded its international operations in recent years. It has estimated holdings of ¥150 million and £40 million, which are subject to exchange rate fluctuations. Currently, the spot rates are $0.0098/¥ and $1.50/£. The daily standard deviation of ¥ and £ is 0.0012 and 0.005, respectively. Assume the exchange rates are normally distributed. Use a 95 percent of confidence interval to address the following issues.

a What is the VAR for the ¥ holding for a day (i.e., VAR is assumed to be measured in terms of standard deviation) at the 95 percent confidence level? For the £ holding? What is the combined VAR?

b What is the VAR for the portfolio of the ¥ and £ for the four scenarios of the correlation between their exchange rates as −0.5; 0; 1; and 0.5? (hint: use the concept of portfolio theory)

c If the bank holds the portfolio for 10 days, what is the value-at-risk for the bank, assuming that the correlation of exchange rates is −0.5, 0, 1, and 0.5, respectively? (hint: use the fact: $\sigma T = \sigma 1 \sqrt{T}$ where T is the time interval)

d As a bank regulator, what other factors should be considered for assessing the capital charge for the bank?

12 During the credit crunch of the 1970s, banks could not lend to even top-rated businesses because of disintermediation in the wake of the interest ceiling on deposits (Regulation Q). Banks "arbitraged" the Regulation Q by encouraging these businesses to tap the money market by issuing commercial papers. Initially they earned fee income by placing commercial papers and when needed, by enhancing the issue by the standby letters of credit. A consequence was that these businesses over time learnt to access the market directly bypassing the banks! Do you think that in the wake of adoption of the external credit rating proposal, the top-rated businesses would similarly threaten banks by taking over loaning funds to speculative businesses? Explain your reasoning.

NOTES

1 Corporate finance literature has also highlighted, among other things, agency and corporate governance or control considerations for defining desirable or optimal capital structure.

2   Would banks employ more debt in their capital structure, if the capital adequacy standards were abolished? A priori, it is not possible to state that banks would. A parallel with the reserve requirements and the Eurocurrency markets is instructive: banks do not face the reserve requirements in these markets; still they have self-imposed reserve standards; and when some of them do not, the industry polices them (e.g., BCCI in the 1980s had the image of imprudent behavior in the banking industry; as a result, even prior to its demise (1991) it was not welcome during the 1980s to access the Eurocurrency market, according to knowledgeable practitioners). It is also possible that a threat of re-regulation may prevent banks from excessive reliance on debt, even in the absence of regulations.

3   For a detailed discussion on the chronology of the Basel Accord, see Wagster (1996).

4   Wagster (1996: 1321–2). Japanese banks benefited from high savings rate in Japan that presumably lowered the interest cost. The cost of equity capital depends on the risk premium demanded by the stock market participants. The buoyant Japanese stock market, coupled with the lack of its integration with the global equity market in the 1980s lends plausibility to this assertion of cost advantage for Japanese banks.

5   In the parlance of finance discipline, this is defined as the sustainable growth rate.

6   Because US bank stocks typically trade for less than their book value, capital standards based on book value will require excessive issuance of stock. Existing stockholders may not take kindly to additional external equity financing.

7   It is also conceivable that a bank issues preferred stock that is debt for the purpose of taxes but is preferred stock from the perspectives of both regulators and rating agencies. Existence of offshore subsidiaries can facilitate such a transaction.

8   Requiring each activity to be self sustaining (in terms of required capital contribution) also implies that banks would be moving away from relationship-based business to transaction-based business.

9   Goodman (1998: 22).

10 It is instructive to note that Deutschebank voluntarily disclosed these "hidden reserves" in 1996, thus putting pressures on other German banks to follow suit. One may conjecture that the bank's action might have been aimed at listing its stock on the New York Stock Exchange.

11 A study by Jackson et al. (1998) indicates that the two basic approaches do not yield significantly different volatility estimates for well-diversified fixed-income portfolios; however, they significantly differ in accurately generating the benchmark probability. The simulation-based approaches had an edge over the models employing known distributions.

12 Non-financial corporations have been exposed to the VAR approach for determining debt capacity in Donaldson's work (1961).

13 If this happens, it would be an interesting twist where the task of intermediation in financial markets would pass from banks to presumably non-financial businesses.

14 Naturally the issue for a top-rated business will be whether it obtains compensation in excess of the premium it demands for assuming additional risk.

CHAPTER 11

Toward Investment Banking Activities

LEARNING OBJECTIVES

the historical development separating the investment bank
l banks

the distinction between the transaction and relationship
(investment and commercial) banks

the basics of major investment banking activities

dissimilar nature of activities for a commercial and an
k

the merger and acquisition activities of commercial and
nks

ted with the recent capital adequacy standards for US
nks

er 1, the conventional approach envisages the role of a commercial bank as a money lender, which funds the loan with deposits. In the process, the bank transforms highly liquid deposits (presumably short term) into illiquid loans with long-term maturity. Thus the commercial bank performs a liquidity creation or asset transformation function. An investment bank, on the other hand, is a financial intermediary that performs primarily the brokerage function of bringing together buyers and sellers with complimentary needs. It thus reduces the search cost for market participants.

This chapter first traces the historical development of barriers in the USA, and its impact on the twin branches of banking. In Section 11.3, it describes in detail major activities of an investment bank. In Section 11.4 relative strengths of the two banking institutions are assessed in areas of overlapping activities. Section 11.5 looks at the recent trend of acquisition of an investment bank by a commercial bank. Section 11.6 investigates capital adequacy for an investment bank with a backdrop of capital for a commercial bank. Section 11.7 briefly considers challenges and opportunities in the path of a commercial bank embarking on principally investment banking activities. The final section summarizes the highlights of the chapter.

At the outset, it should be noted that the distinction between these banking activities, created and reinforced historically by legal and regulatory barriers in some countries, has undergone a radical change in response to evolution of these barriers. In the USA, for instance, the distinction between an investment bank and a commercial bank has been blurred with the repeal of the Glass–Steagall Act. Why are we then stressing the distinction? The following reasons may clarify the picture.

First, the discernible trend toward deregulation of commercial banks as a result of the demise of the Glass–Steagall Act has suffered a setback due to scandals and bankruptcies involving firms such as Enron and WorldCom. A striking case illustrating potential or de facto re-regulation is highlighted by a recent series of judgments against leading banks (such as Citigroup, Credit Suisse First Boston, Goldman Sachs, Morgan Stanley, Lehman Brothers, Deutsche Bank, and UBS) that have agreed to the "Chinese wall" separation between underwriting activities and research activities (typically affiliated with the brokerage function) in an investment bank.

Second, the phenomenon of mergers and acquisitions (M&A) between investment banks and commercial banks has led to the daunting task of integrating these banking activities – a task that has partially emanated from differing, if not incompatible, cultural orientation of these two branches of banking activities.

Finally, integration of these banking activities has been confined to a small, albeit significant, segment of the banking industry. The remainder of the firms in the industry, both commercial and investment banks, face the urgent task of defining their niche for survival and prosperity.

11.2   Historical Background

11.2.1   Laws and regulations

Prior to the great depression of the 1930s, many large (especially money-center) banks in the USA sold (or underwrote) securities and simultaneously conducted conventional commercial banking activities of accepting deposits and granting loans. In the wake of the failure of several commercial banks (roughly about 40 percent of all banks), the Banking Act of 1933, also known as the Glass–Steagall Act, was passed to prohibit commercial banks from handling either investment banking activities or insurance underwriting. Specifically, this Act made it illegal for a commercial bank to

- underwrite public offering of securities;
- buy and sell securities to public; or
- underwrite insurance.

The argument for separating the commercial bank from the other two financial intermediaries was that potential losses of underwriting securities or insurance could undermine interests of a bank's depositors; or, bad loans (paid off from security sales proceeds) of the commercial bank could be foisted on purchasers of securities.

This Act has now been repealed. The ongoing movement of deregulation in the last several decades had already significantly weakened the impact of sanctions imposed by the Glass–Steagall Act:

- Domestically, the first crack in the Glass–Steagall Act occurred when commercial banks were permitted to underwrite municipal and state revenue bonds in the 1960s.
- In the late 1960s and 1970s, the rise of the Euromarket created a great opportunity for US commercial banks to underwrite securities and trade in corporate securities in offshore markets where the Glass–Steagall Act was inoperative. Bank regulators in foreign countries would not impose the same separation of investment and commercial banking activities so far as their domestic markets were concerned; and they closed their eyes to the activities in the offshore (eurocurrency and securities) markets.
- Prior to 1991, the Federal Reserve Board granted special exemption to a few large bank holding companies to engage in a limited number of investment banking activities.
- The FDICIA 1991 allowed bank holding companies to engage in underwriting activities through separate subsidiaries, given adequate capital and limited underwriting loss.
- In March 1997, the Federal Reserve Board (Fed) began allowing Section 20 subsidiaries[1] of bank holding companies to raise the ceiling on the "prohibited source" (i.e., underwriting) of revenue from 10 to 25 percent.
- The Fed also started to allow that some employees could deal with both commercial loans and high-yield bond offering.

After several abortive attempts especially during the decade of the 1990s, US Congress in 1999 finally granted powers to the regulators to repeal the Glass–Steagall Act that separated the investment and commercial banking activities. Its ramifications are:

- securities firms and insurers can buy banks;
- banking regulators cannot discriminate against insurers;
- banks can underwrite insurance and securities;
- states retain regulatory authority over insurers;
- mutual insurance companies are allowed to relocate to another state;
- the OCC gets the authority to regulate bank subsidiaries that underwrite securities issues;
- the Federal Reserve has umbrella authority over bank affiliates undertaking risky activities;
- the SEC retains authority over securities products offered by all financial firms.

Separately, the SEC initiated partial deregulation of underwriting activities by adopting

- in 1982, Rule 415 that allows corporations to issue security in a piecemeal fashion any time within two years of its registration without any waiting period; and

- in 1990 (modified in 1992), **Rule 144a** which allows "private" placement of a firm's securities with qualified institutional buyers (QIBs).

While participation in international markets broadened the scope of activities by the commercial bank, competition especially from non-bank sources adversely affected its traditional monopoly on twin activities of deposit acceptance and straight loans. Thus, the commercial bank has, voluntarily or involuntarily, tended to

- give up extending short-term loans to large customers, who have managed to access directly financial markets often with the help of investment (and, at times, commercial) banks; and when it makes loans to such customers, these loans (a) are barely profitable in their "plain vanilla" form, and hence (b) have whistles and bells, that is, are packaged with derivatives of various types, so as to fatten the thin margins;
- finance its loan portfolio with comparable, fixed-term CDs or purchased money (often coming from other banks!);
- sell off a portion of its loans via **securitization**, and in general
- employ strategies to manage the interest rate risks by using derivatives and/or matching duration of their assets and liabilities.

For the US investment bank, the picture has also changed. It faces the competitive pressure as deregulation gathers momentum. Euro-security markets, especially the Eurobond issues, have required its physical presence in foreign markets. **Shelf registration** under Rule 415 has permitted an issuer to seek competitive bids from underwriters, and sometimes even bypass underwriters.[2] Commercial banks, at times foreign-domiciled, have started competing with it in the government (including municipal and state) bond underwriting. Its scope of activities has undergone a significant transformation, as the next section describes.

It should be noted here that the international dimension has a critical bearing on these two types of banks. Across national borders, laws and regulations pertaining to the separation of the two banking activities are neither uniform nor enforced with equal force. For instance, the universal banking system of Germany allows a bank the legal opportunity to offer financial products in the broadest sense: to lend money to a business firm, to underwrite its securities offering, to sell insurance, and even invest in its equity. On the other hand, Japan has followed the USA in keeping separate these two branches of banking; still, Japanese banks are permitted to hold equity in non-financial firms. The resultant "uneven playing ground" has managed to create both opportunities and challenges for competing (and otherwise comparable) commercial banks domiciled in two different countries. Ongoing changes in these laws and regulations – exemplified perhaps most dramatically in the USA by the repeal of the Glass–Steagall Act – underscore the urgency of investigating these twin banking activities.

11.2.2 Relationship versus transaction orientation

Ever since the separation of commercial and investment banking in 1933 and through the 1960s, both sets of banking activities had been governed by relationship orientation. That is, clients conducted their transactions with the bank with which they had established a comfortable relationship. These transactions covered a range of products and services offered by the bank, although the range was typically limited. From the perspective of the bank, the relationship orientation exhibited the following characteristics.

- Costing of a product or service was rarely undertaken in a systematic fashion.
- Pricing of an individual product was not an important consideration; instead, the focus was on the overall profitability of the relationship.
- Pricing concession in a particular case was made with an eye toward thwarting potential competition.
- Still, stealing a customer from a competitor through aggressive pricing tactics was not deemed "professional."
- Relationship orientation was carried over internally: an employee had a de facto lifetime tenure with the firm.

This situation changed in the 1970s due to a variety of reasons, such as

- Customers of commercial banks felt "betrayed" during the early 1970s when they could not procure funding from banks during tight money market conditions.
- Creditworthy customers of commercial banks found financing through commercial paper flexible and cheap.
- Creditworthy customers of both banks found financing in Euro-markets less expensive and swift (by obviating regulatory requirements).
- Multinational companies, hampered by regulatory constraints, also found it expedient to finance their foreign subsidiaries in the Euro-markets.
- Deregulation and market volatilities (in terms of inflation, interest and foreign exchange rates) induced greater competition, lower margins, and customer desire for risk management products.

All these forces have tended to tilt toward the transaction orientation, where the customer selects the supplier who promises the right product at the right price and in time for a given transaction; and where the supplier, realizing that winning the right to sell a product currently may not assure future sales, pays close attention to the transaction's profitability, that is, accurately costing the product. Often, products are just sufficiently differentiated to make it difficult for the customer to compare prices. Finally, the analytical ability of employees has started receiving preference over their "social" ability; employee productivity, rather than their ability to be Dr Feelgood with the clients, has become more paramount in deciding whether he or she should be promoted and retained for the foreseeable future.

While the pressure to shift the orientation from relationship to transactions was exerted on both sets of banks, the commercial bank delayed the shift as it had greater flexibility in terms of clientele, and it chose to focus on the domestic clientele of the smaller size. Also, the oil crisis in the 1970s gave the commercial bank an extraordinary opportunity to intermediate in the international markets where the clientele were the sovereign governments. The picture changed dramatically in the 1980s when the country debt crisis forced commercial banks to turn inward to private businesses, and they felt the pressure of deregulation of not only financial markets but also financial intermediaries. In turn, these developments heightened the awareness and the need for the requisite shift in orientation, albeit gradually. On the other hand, the investment bank feeling the pressure in the 1970s on its major activity of underwriting securities, an activity that has always been episodic and infrequent, began broadening its menu of services and exercising ingenuity in pricing the products. This tendency naturally accelerated transition to transaction orientation.

Ironically, over time, the critical importance of new products with their characteristic short life span has meant that the commercial bank moves more in the direction of transaction orientation, especially by paying attention to the costing of individual products, while the investment bank has come to realize that razor-thin profit margins can be overcome by bundling services contemporaneously (e.g., arranging or underwriting debt financing at a sufficiently high price to compensate for a currency swap provided at a throw-away, low margin).[3] The net result is: while initially the chasm in terms of orientation grew between the two institutions' orientation, over time, these differences have narrowed – with both institutions moving away from the extreme positions.

11.3 Major Investment Banking Activities

In order to sharpen the focus on distinction between the two types of banking activities, we first discuss in some detail major investment banking activities. As noted in Section 11.1, the primary function of an investment bank centers on brokerage. The important attribute of a broker is to (a) identify who are potential investors or fund-seekers; (b) know their particular needs and preferences; and (c) bring together the two parties (buyers and sellers) with congruent needs and preferences so that they may successfully conclude the business transaction. An important subset of brokerage activities is underwriting, which entails guaranteed proceeds to the seller – who happens to be the issuer – of the security.

Although underwriting remains pivotal for the investment bank, it has aggressively pursued many additional activities in recent years. Portfolio management (including initiating and managing mutual funds), development of new products for managing risk, corporate finance advisory services (e.g., for acquisitions and divestitures as well as LBOs), and arrangement of infrastructure project financing are some noteworthy additions. Finally, the investment bank has broadened its scope to include activities like loan syndication and money management that closely resemble traditional services of the commercial bank.

11.3.1 Underwriting new issues

The core of investment banking business is underwriting. The underwriting activity includes both basic securities like equity and bond issues and hybrids such as preferred stock and convertible bonds. An issue may be placed with the investors either on a best-effort basis or as a "sold" (or underwritten) basis. An underwritten issue requires the investment bank to purchase the entire issue at a predetermined price and then resell it to investors in the market; thus it guarantees the proceeds to the issuer (in effect, the underwriter sells a put option to the security issuer).

Typically the investment bank provides many services related to the underwriting activities.

Advising

When a firm decides to issue a security to the public, the investment bank provides advice to the firm regarding the type, price, timing, and amount of the security issue. This is particularly important for the first-time issuer of equity, that is, the initial public offering (IPO). The pricing estimate is only tentative, since the investment bank will need to scrutinize the firm's financial and non-financial attributes, and compare the firm with kindred firms that have recently issued similar securities. Volatile market conditions signify that the pricing is confirmed only hours in advance of the commencement of sales.

Documentation

Investment banks have to file documents required by regulatory bodies such as the SEC. In the USA, issuers of the new securities to the general public must file a *registration statement* with the SEC, which contains information about the firm's financial conditions, competition and the industry, and management experience. Registration does not commit the firm to issue securities. Unanticipated deterioration in market conditions may lead the firm to postpone the issue. However, if the firm decides to go ahead with flotation of the issue, it must provide potential investors the *prospectus* containing detailed current information on the issuing firm, before actually offering the security to the public.

Actual underwriting

The investment bank, as the lead manager, forms a syndicate of investment banks, which help to distribute the security at a designated price. The lead manager receives compensation from the issuer by keeping a portion of the proceeds to be received from the sale of the security.

Under the American system, the syndicate agrees to support the price of the security at the designated "floor" for a designated period, say, a day or two. Each syndicate member is assigned a quota, and is paid a commission by the lead manger. Further, each member is responsible for meeting the quota by placing the security at the agreed price, and is expected not to discount the security during this period. The unsold portion may be sold at the lower or discounted price after the support period ends, and losses are allocated to syndicate members.

Under the European system, each member buys the quota at the price that is net of the commission, and is free to sell the security at any price. Thus the European system does not have any price support mechanism.

Private placement

A security issue does not have to be placed with the general public; it may be placed with relatively few investors in a private placement. Private placement obviates the registration and related requirements. The issuer is able to save *time* as a result. Often, a more important consideration in a private placement is the issuer's willingness to share *proprietary information* with a select group of investors that may not be feasible or worthwhile for the public at large. Finally, the debt issuer may obtain greater *flexibility* in debt service payments (e.g., a grace period during which debt service may be reduced or suspended) than would be the case for a publicly placed bond issue.

Private placement avoids expenses related to meeting the registration and sundry requirements of a public placement; however, the net cost for the issuer is generally higher for a privately placed issue. There are mainly three reasons for this:

1   The customized nature of the contract, especially non-standard covenants, may entail expensive legal services.
2   Because the investor clientele is small, the individual investors' contribution will be large. As a result, catering to individual investors' needs (related to specific information or other peripheral services) may entail indirect expenses. Thus the front-end cost charged by the investment bank to the issuer may not be small in comparison to those for the publicly placed issues.
3   Above all, *illiquidity* of the investment (that cannot be routinely traded in the secondary market) carries an additional risk premium. Of course, investors such as insurance companies and pension funds which want to lock in investments for a long period of time may not be concerned about investment liquidity and thus may not require the high liquidity premium demanded by other investors. As a result, insurance companies and pension or retirement funds are important target investors in this segment of the financial market.

The extremity of both the advantages and disadvantages of private placement has been modified by recent changes in the regulatory requirements. For instance, as described later, "shelf registration" permits greater time flexibility for a publicly traded issue; on the other hand, allowing a privately placed issue under s. 415 to trade on the OTC after three years reduces the liquidity premium required by the investor in a privately placed issue.

An access to the ready, willing and able client base allows an investment bank to privately place an issue more expediently than the public offering. Where time is of the essence (e.g., in a takeover bid or leverage buyout), private placement allows the investment bank to reap handsome rewards.

Offshore activities

Large investment banks (as well as commercial banks) have been actively involved in the offshore underwriting and distributing securities as well as related funding activities, such as issues of Euro-CP, NIFs, FRNs, and Eurobonds. These instruments can be found typically in the Eurocurrency market (discussed in Chapter 4).

11.3.2   Trading securities and risk arbitrage

An investment bank serves as a securities broker and dealer in the secondary market. As a broker, it makes arrangements to help buyers and sellers complete a business transaction and it receives commissions/fees for this service. This service may include (a) recommendation of security purchase or disposal to its clientele based on its own research,[4] and (b) helping the client obtain margin credit on the collateral of securities. Related services also include funds placement in the money market mutual funds with instant access to funds through check writing, and credit cards. These services may directly compete with deposit services provided by a commercial bank. Although listed securities are traded on organized exchanges, a broker may find a counterparty off the exchange floor or in a foreign stock exchange where the security is allowed to trade.

Still, profitability from the trading business has been attacked on several fronts in recent years.

- Computer technology has reduced the investor need for research findings from well-established investment banks by lowering barriers to entry in the field.
- As institutional investors have grown in size, they have managed to use their bargaining power in obtaining services at cheaper rates or have their own research staff and in some instances their own traders.
- Acquisitions by commercial banks and/or their entry in investment banking business have not helped the matter.

The investment bank has responded by cross-subsidizing some activities. Bond underwriting has become only marginally profitable at best (partially because of competition from the commercial bank); so bond trading is subsidizing bond-underwriting activities. On the other hand, equity underwriting (M&A-related issues, for instance) generates commissions that subsidize razor-thin commissions on equity trading.

The other response by the investment bank has been to assume additional risk. A broker does not assume risk in a security trade, since the brokerage activity is strictly based on a pure agency relationship. However, as a dealer, the investment bank maintains a position in a security by directly buying and selling on its own account. Since the 1970s, while its profit margins on brokerage and even underwriting might have been whittled down, market volatility has created opportunities for trading securities for profits. In a recent decade, trading in securities on own-account has become a major source of revenue for investment banks. One of the well-known trading strategies is the risk arbitrage (a misnomer!),[5] which involves simultaneous sale of some securities and purchase of other securities in *anticipation* of large gains. This strategy originated from buying and selling shares of companies that are prime candidates for merger or takeover. The significance of the new trading environment has been underscored by the fact that the staff with background and skills in trading have moved to the top echelon of many organizations.

In a cross-border context, the investment bank also manages mutual funds specifically focusing on a country or a geographical region. When a country or region transits from centrally planned to free-market orientation, the potential for value-creation exists because of ill-understood values of enterprises and activities. Further, thin capital markets and the thundering herds, afraid of missing out on the action, often lead to soaring value bubbles. Firms with country funds managers who are physically present in the country and are sufficiently nimble to move funds out earlier rather than later have an advantage over funds that are managed from abroad. A multinational investment or commercial bank has thus a potential advantage over a purely professional mutual fund or institutional investor solely based in the USA or other industrialized nation.

11.3.3   New product development

The current trend in investment banking is innovation or creation of "new products," which can generate profitable opportunities for the organization. These products also change the financial landscape of the industries and firms, which desire to hedge or manage their risks. Basically, innovations are exploitation of financial market imperfections, including taxes, transaction costs, regulations, and ignorance of market participants.

In 1982, Salomon Brothers and Merrill Lynch developed the following concept.

- Strip the Treasury bonds into "tranches" of coupons and the principal (for instance, a five-year, $1 billion with 5 percent coupon payable semi-annually could have nine tranches of $25 million and one tranche of $1.025 billion – comprised of the principal and final interest payment).
- Each tranche with a given maturity can be then traded as a zero-coupon security. (For a five-year maturity of a Treasury bond with semi-annual interest payments, there will be ten tranches.)
- As the yield on the underlying security is a complex average of the pure discount rates of different "zero-coupon securities" corresponding to various maturities, each tranche will be sold on its own pure discount or zero-coupon rate. Some of these rates will be higher and others will be lower than their average, the yield, on the underlying security.
- These strips or tranches can be sold to investors with the following sales pitch:
  - A *guaranteed* reinvestment rate equal to the quoted rate (below the pure discount rate, the difference being the innovator's profit).
  - A rate of return even higher than the return on the government security without increasing the risk (the security is 100 percent backed by the Treasury bond).
  - Potential treatment of the difference between the value at maturity and the initial investment as capital gain rather than interest income, thus lowering or eliminating taxes (as the Japanese tax authorities permitted at the time) and enhancing the after-tax return.
  - Give the product a catchy name like CATS (Certificates of Accrual on Treasury Securities by Salomon) or TIGRS (Treasury Investment Growth Receipts by Merrill Lynch).

It is obvious that this innovation exploited market imperfection of investor and tax authorities' ignorance of the mathematics of finance!

As we saw in Chapters 4–6, the market appetite for risk management products is being satisfied with custom-made derivative products that are essentially combinations of futures (or forwards), put and call options some of which, when not available, can be created by employing the IRPT and/or the put call parity theory.

11.3.4   Advisory services

A major component of the investment banking activity comprises fee-based advisory services for corporate finance transactions. These activities include merger and acquisition transactions, divestiture, leveraged buyouts, infrastructure project financing, and privatization.

As markets become globalized, a company in an industry strives to increase its market share and eventually become the industry leader, which in turn allows it to influence industry behavior. One way to augment the market share is to acquire the competitor. Acquisition in its wake may call for divestiture of some overlapping or redundant activities. The resultant corporate restructuring enables a firm to achieve greater economies of scope and scale. Such restructuring is not confined to operations and activities within the borders of a country but spills over across borders, given the global nature of the market. Firms have sought inputs from the investment banks to

- identify suitable candidates for acquisition that would have a compelling strategic rationale along dimensions such as product mix, management, and organizational structure;
- analyze the financial projections that reflect both divestiture of some activities and transitional costs of integration of other activities;
- identify financing alternatives that meet the parameters of flexibility and control; and
- facilitate financial restructuring in a timely and cost-effective fashion.

In an LBO, a portion or all of a publicly owned company is bought out by a small group (which may include the existing management team) through a transaction financed mostly through debt. The debt will be liquidated over time with funds generated by the acquired company's operations and/or sale of some of its assets. The success of the LBO hinges on

- financing where the interest burden will not cripple the newly formed enterprise;
- financing with a structure of layers where lower layers serve as an "equity cushion" for higher layers, thereby obtaining the higher layers at reasonable cost;
- compensating the lower layers with contingent "growth" participation, that is, in the value creation of the new enterprise; and
- assembling a capable management team which is short on funds (hence disproportionately high debt financing) but long on talent and familiarity with the business of the enterprise that allows it to define the niche, streamline operations and accurately predict operational flows that would comfortably liquidate debt over the foreseeable future without going under.

Privatization and project financing differ from LBOs or takeovers in the magnitude of complexities. For instance, political constraints may reduce managerial flexibility in divesting unprofitable activities; at the same time, governments can be nudged to write options on unprofitable operations or uncollectible obligations, both past and anticipated.

Advisory fees for the investment bank are generally on a sliding scale, percentage basis on the size of the deal. In the latter half of the 1990s, fees in the range of 0.75–1.0 percent on the $100–$500 million deals were not uncommon in the USA. The fees will be larger as one moves to less competitive and more inefficient financial markets. It should be noted that these fees would depend at a given time on the business cycle phase and the number of current and potential deals, as the competition is not just between commercial and investment banks but also among accounting and consulting firms that have jumped into the fray.[6]

Finally, governments have also become more sophisticated in dealing with advisors on infrastructure project financing or privatization of government enterprises.

11.3.5   Complementarities of activities

Theoretically, it makes sense that there is a "synergy" among the major activities pursued by the investment bank. For instance, the advisory service may unearth information that has bearings on not only the brokerage activity but also the underwriting business. In reality, complications may negate this synergy. For instance, Enron enlisted help from Merrill Lynch, involved in underwriting Enron's financing activities, for favorable recommendations for its stock (and went so far as to ask for removal of analysts who had made – or were to make – unfavorable recommendations). Merrill Lynch apparently complied. Subsequently Merrill Lynch had to undertake an intensive advertising campaign in early 2002 to undo the damage from adverse publicity garnered by these activities.

11.4   Scope of Activities by Commercial and Investment Banks

Traditionally, a US commercial bank has provided loans to businesses for varied maturities on a secured or unsecured basis. Over time, it has also helped facilitate their direct access to financial markets. Below are listed some common forms and their variations.

11.4.1   Short-term seasonal loans

A lack of synchronization of sales and production activities creates liquidity needs for a non-financial business. A typical form of this desynchronization is manifest in seasonal loan demands by the business. Two major sources fund this need: suppliers who sell goods and services on credit to the business, and banks. As prospective borrowers are typically a bank's customers, their use of the banking facilities for transactions settlement gives the bank a valuable insight in assessing their ability and willingness to pay, that is, their creditworthiness. Even when an investment bank has customers' money accounts, it does not have the access to their payment habits to the extent the commercial bank does.

When the international dimension is added, as we saw in Chapter 7, export- or import-related financing (either through the letter of credit and banker's acceptance or through collateralized lending) has been the domain of the commercial bank. Thus, commercial banks have traditionally had an upper hand over investment banks with regard to short-term funding needs of the business.

Over time, the large, investment-grade customers have gained a direct access to the money market through issuing unsecured commercial paper for a maturity of less than nine months. Although this paper is a security tradable in the secondary market, it does not require registration or filing of documents with the SEC. As this financing is cheaper than commercial bank loans, large customers (with less perceived information asymmetry) have resorted to this route. Even when the borrowers do not have impeccable credit, they have "borrowed" the name of a creditworthy party (an insurance company or even a bank). This means that the investment bank can arrange such financing, and its ability to place this paper, either directly or through a note issuing facility, has allowed it to compete with the commercial bank.

A third form of meeting business need for the short term has been through securitization of, say, accounts receivable. As we saw in Chapter 6, this form requires predictable payment or cash flow generating behavior of the bundle of underlying assets through actuarial experience. Both commercial and investment banks have shown virtually equal ability to arrange such financing, although commercial banks have had a slight advantage over the investment banks.[7]

A final form is the total return credit derivative (TRCD), where a firm facing illiquidity sells a risky asset to the investor, who agrees to sell it back later to the asset originator, with the proviso that the investor will not bear the default risk of the asset. Although investment banks have the capability to arrange financing through credit derivatives in various forms, commercial banks have an upper edge because of their superior ability to access and evaluate credit information.

Two aspects of TRCD are noteworthy:

1   TRCD is a variation of securitization. Two differences are: (a) investors may bear some predetermined level of risk in the case of securitization, whereas they would not bear any risk in the TRCD; and (b) the cash flows emanating from the securitized assets are untainted by the other flows of the originating firm because of the creation of the special-purpose vehicle.

2   In an aggregated form, large firms are traditionally net lenders (i.e., their direct borrowing is less than their credit extension to their customers) in the USA. Thus, what the banks lost out in terms of direct loans to the large firms has been at least partially offset by their facilitating securitization and credit derivatives for the large firms.

These last two forms, securitization and TRCD, have not reached their potential in the international arena. But as legal and regulatory barriers are being modified, banks in general have a great potential for enhancing their profitability on these fronts.

11.4.2   Medium- and long-term loans and bonds

Commercial banks were the originators of syndicated credits in both medium- and long-term markets. By offering interest and currency swaps as well as options (for instance, on payment amount and currency), they have maintained their stronghold in this area. Nevertheless, investment banks have started making inroads through arranging similar credits such as bridge funds.

Two special forms need a mention here: leveraged lending and infrastructure project financing. They both typically call for restructuring claims. In leveraged loans (typically intended for mergers and acquisitions as well as leveraged buyouts), this is achieved through high-yield, subordinated claims that serve as an equity cushion for the senior lender, that is, the commercial banks. In project financing, as we saw in Chapter 7, risk is unbundled and is apportioned to a party best able to assume it (e.g., a prospective customer providing a loan and in return agreeing to buy a given quantity of the product at an agreed-upon price). Such risk allocation reduces the cost of overall debt financing. Both large commercial banks and investment banks have been formidable competitors in these areas.

Equity-enhanced securities, such as bonds with warrants and convertible bonds, have become popular financing vehicles, partially because of interest and currency volatilities. Earnings volatility induced by volatile interest and currency fluctuations have a positive impact on the equity options attached to the bonds. Investment banks have had a conspicuously strong edge over commercial banks in such financial arrangements.

Over time, simple straightforward debt financing, domestic or offshore, is increasingly giving in to innovative forms of debt financing, whether they are loans, leases, or bonds. These forms have the following common traits:

- They have exploited non-uniform impediments in the financial markets to lower the cost for the borrower without sacrificing the returns for the investors. Typically, these are the transaction cost-, regulation-, and/or tax-driven arbitrage activities.
- These benefits are generated at the expense of one or more governments (and at times some stakeholders in the client firm), sometimes with their blessing, and at other times because of their ignorance, inertia or delay in removing such incentives.
- Scrutiny of legal as well as reporting ramifications requires time and money. When such functions are carried out in-house by the investment or the commercial bank (for obvious competitive reasons), the fixed cost base is enlarged. In turn, such fixed cost, ultimately borne by its clientele, is palatable only when the size of the transaction is large. Hence, large firms are the likely sources of innovations.
- In any case, ways of transferring the cost to the government(s) and thereby generating benefits for the borrower are legal. For instance, a special purpose vehicle (SPV) created (a) to issue preferred stock placed with US corporate investors (who pay lower taxes on preferred dividends than on comparable interest payments), and (b) to transfer the proceeds to the US parent of the SPV in the form of a loan so that interest charges would be tax deductible, is legal provided lawyers have ascertained its bona fide nature. Similarly, accountants can structure the transaction in such a way that the rating agency deems and rates it as a (preferred) equity, and the Financial Statement Accounting Board allows its reporting as a (preferred) equity issue. As a result, the issue will not deteriorate either the earnings coverage or debt-equity ratio!

At the same time, legality today does not ensure future availability or continuity of pursuing a mode of financing. Enron- (and WorldCom-) related business scandals in recent years, for instance, have given a black eye to prominent US commercial and investment banks; prevention of potential re-regulation or legal constraints may make them circumspect in pursuing borderline activities.

The Enron case in instructive in this matter. Enron, an energy trader that was one of the ten largest firms in the USA in early 2000, turned into a basket case by the year end. This spectacular fall may be attributed to the following activities.

1   Enron, an energy wholesaler, booked as revenue not the commission it earned on a transaction but the nominal value of the transaction.
2   Enron reported profits on multi-period contracts immediately instead of reporting them on an accrual basis, that is, in years when profits would be earned.[8]
3   Enron established shell corporations or partnerships to transfer futures transactions it wrote at inflated transfer prices. This not only boosted current revenues and profits, but also allowed Enron to transfer liabilities (and corresponding assets at exaggerated prices). In order to avoid consolidation of financial reports (which would have resulted in a wash), Enron arranged with investment and commercial banks to have 3 percent ownership in these subsidiaries. Of course, these banks were not risking their capital, as Enron compensated them through fees, maintained deposits with them for the money supposedly coming from them, or both!
4   Enron undertook similar profit-enhancing transactions with independent third parties with the mismatched future reversal of transactions to compensate these third parties.[9] (See Box 11.1.) Essentially Enron undertook long-term "repo" transactions in energy trades (and not Treasury obligations) with financial intermediaries that allowed it to enhance profits and disguise loans embedded in these transactions.

Box 11.1   Enron's structured deals

Several structured finance deals, known as the "pre-pay transactions," were executed by Citigroup (and separately by J.P. Morgan Chase) with Enron during 1998–2000. Citigroup structured 14 such transactions, totaling $4.8 billion, and generated $167 million in fee income (while Morgan structured 12 deals, totaling about $3.7 billion for $39 million in fee income).

Under a typical set of transactions the bank would agree to pay Enron the money upfront in return for Enron's promised delivery of energy-related products (e.g., gas, oil, or electricity) in future. Specifically, the following procedure was carried out through two Citigroup-owned conduits.

1   The first conduit, *Yosemite Trust*, would issue notes (at 8.25 percent interest rate) to investors for raising cash.
2   The second conduit, *Delta*, would "buy" energy-based contracts from Enron for future deliveries.

3 Yosemite, in turn, would buy these contracts from Delta with cash obtained from outside investors.

4 Delta would use this cash to pay Enron as prepayment on energy-based contracts.

5 Over time (possibly in the next accounting period), the trade-and-cash cycles would be reversed. Thus Delta, obtaining the trade contracts from Yosemite, would surrender them to Enron, and Enron would compensate Delta for the original amount adjusted for compensation to the investors in notes issued by Yosemite. The cash for compensation would come from a fresh set of "deals."

Taking advantage of a loophole in the financial statement reporting regulation, Enron would report the money received from Delta (for future delivery of energy products) as current revenue, and its obligation for this delivery as trade-related liabilities. Had Enron reported the financing transactions as loans, which would have appeared on Enron's balance sheet, Enron's debt would have risen by 40 percent, and might have signaled investors about Enron's increased vulnerability to bankruptcy.

These maneuvers also allowed Enron to report revenues consistently above 50 percent per annum for the five-year period 1996–2000. It is also remarkable that during this period Enron's reported aggregate pre-tax profits was $1.79 billion and it received net tax rebates of $381 million from the IRS! (In only 1997, Enron had to pay federal tax of $17 million.)

The fifth, or the final transaction, furthermore, raises an important question regarding Enron's financial reports. If such a reversal were premeditated, the transaction would have to be classified as a loan to Enron, and Enron could not report future sales in the current financial statements. That would also be the case, if the transaction were to be reversed in the subsequent accounting period – such a reversal would also require restatement of the previous period's financial reports. Published reports on government investigations reveal that, given Enron's intentions to fudge financial statements, any contemplated reversals were never mentioned in Enron's *written* agreements with Citigroup (and J.P. Morgan Chase).

That Citigroup was aware of and complied with Enron's intentions was reflected in an e-mail in a separate deal called *Roosevelt*: this e-mail clearly ruled out any written agreement for reversals so as to avoid unfavorable financial reporting implications for Enron (a similar e-mail was also circulated earlier at J.P. Morgan Chase). Indeed, employment of two SPVs, Yosemite and Delta, suggests that Delta was intended to legitimize the trade transaction, while Yosemite was intended solely for raising financing. Further, these vehicles were intended to minimize investor and rating agencies' awareness to Enron's devious attempts to hide its precarious financial conditions.

The Enron case raises several interesting issues:

- As Yosemite was financed by outside investors through notes whose risk was linked to Enron's creditworthiness, Citigroup was able to mitigate its own exposure to Enron, while generating attractive fee income. Thus it was a foray of a commercial bank in the investment banking area.
- The transactions per se were not illegal. In our framework, they were arbitrage transactions in a loose sense – profits by Citigroup (and J.P. Morgan Chase) were from exploiting market inefficiency stemming from investor ignorance as well as (reporting) regulatory inconsistency regarding trade deals versus basically "repo" transactions – for energy products rather than government obligations.
- The gray area was where both banks knowingly helped Enron to violate the reporting requirement.
- In spite of handsome compensation, involved banks have incurred heavy, unanticipated costs of litigations by various stakeholders such as Enron's stockholders, lenders, and various government agencies. Further, their reputational capital has taken severe blows. Finally, as Citigroup and J.P. Morgan Chase have painfully realized, these "synergistic" activities not only have created a public relations nightmare, but may also derail their past successful lobbying efforts for deregulation (e.g., repeal of the Glass–Steagall Act). As banks conduct businesses in the gray areas that are deemed undesirable by regulators, the possibility of re-regulation on banking activities will surface again in the future. Thus, banks need to consider the tradeoffs of current profits vis-à-vis future constraints imposed by regulators.

11.4.3 Equity funding

Equity financing is an area where investment banks have a decided advantage over commercial banks. Investment banks have amassed institutional experience for pricing the straight equity issues, timing their flotation, and placing them with the target investors. Commercial banks have had little experience in this area because of the erstwhile Glass–Steagall Act. Although there have been Euro-equity issues in the offshore markets that are simultaneously placed in several offshore financial centers by obviating regulatory requirements such as registration, they have been infrequent.

The US stock markets have been the magnet for very large foreign firms for a variety of reasons such as seeking a diversified investor base, a decrease in reliance on a single domestic market which they dominate because of their sheer size (e.g., Daimler-Chrysler and the German stock market), and the name recognition for facilitating future funding or acquisitions. Major deterrents are: (a) perceived onerous reporting requirements of the SEC; and (b) complications regarding currency risk for investors.

Of course, investors can directly purchase a foreign company's stock in its domicile rather than waiting for it to list the stock in the USA. However, such a direct purchase entails, among other things, larger transaction costs related to foreign exchange and trading in the possibly thin local market, not to mention significant settlement costs. An alternative form that has helped minimize these transaction costs for the US investors has been the American Depository Receipt (ADR). The ADR is a certificate issued by a US bank representing shares of a non-US company, which have been deposited with the bank or its custodian.[10] As a depository bank, the US bank performs various functions, such as receiving and disseminating to the ADR holders financial information as well as information on the shareholder meetings, rights, and exchange offers. The bank also collects and converts dividends in US dollars for the ADR holder.

When a foreign firm seeks to raise funds through an equity issue, it can technically bypass the restatement of financial statements in order to conform to the Financial Accounting Standard Board requirements as well as registration with the SEC through Rule 144A. Essentially this calls for placing the stock with institutional investors (QIBs).[11] Unfortunately, the reporting requirements are not quite avoided by the foreign firm, as it may have trouble locating US underwriters (subject to prohibition by the SEC) and it ultimately remains liable for misrepresenting or omitting pertinent information.[12]

In general, commercial banks are still prevented from direct participation in the day-to-day activities of the securities markets; hence they do not have a "feel" for the market. Further, they have been unable to develop a distribution network for placing securities. However, one emerging trend allows commercial banks to overcome the handicap: merger or acquisition of investment banks.

11.5 Mergers of Commercial and Investment Banks

Acquisitions (or mergers) by US commercial banks of investment banks have gathered momentum, in the wake of the repeal of the Glass–Steagall Act. Similarly, European banks, keenly aware of globalization of financial markets and the huge size of the US securities markets, have focused their sights on the US investment banking business. In turn, decreasing margins on trading in securities, high cost of developing new products, increased self-sufficiency of institutional clientele with regards to investment research and security trading, have all managed to put pressure on investment banks for either consolidation or acquisition by (or of) commercial banks. Commercial banks, in general, have considered or chosen among the following three (non-mutually exclusive) alternatives:

1   In-house investment banking activity development, or foray of foreign banks' own investment banking divisions in the USA; Deutsche Morgan Grenfell (DMG) of the Deutsche Bank of Germany and BZW of Barclays Bank of the UK (now divested by the Barclays Bank) are two such examples.

2   Raiding star employees of successful US investment banks; for instance, in 1996, UBS of Switzerland acquired a team of renowned bond traders from the Credit Suisse unit, CS First Boston.

3   Cross-border acquisition of investment banks; NatWest acquired Gleacher & Co, a specialist in mergers and acquisitions in1995.

So far, no one alternative has emerged as inherently superior to the other two. Development of capability from within (or a direct foray in the foreign market), as BZW painfully learned upon entering the US underwriting market, involves a time delay as well as substantial outlays; hence, the advantage in terms of cost savings over the other two alternatives cannot be taken for granted.

Similarly, acquiring star employees of a rival firm for big money does not automatically translate in enhancing the firm's productivity, nor does it assure their retention if their performance meets or exceeds expectations, both within the firm and outside.

In 1996, DMG acquired a highly regarded group of technology bankers, led by Frank Quattrone, from Morgan Stanley. This team was responsible for flotation of Netscape, a computer-software company. In 1998, Mr Quattrone departed for Credit Suisse First Boston, taking with him most of his 130-strong technology team, reportedly because of Deutsche Bank's indecisiveness that was reflected in several reorganizations.

The acquisition route does not necessarily fare any better.

In 1986, several US banks acquired British investment (or merchant) banks in anticipation of the Big Bang deregulating the securities industry. A US bank paid several million dollars to acquire a firm, with the acquisition price amounting to roughly $1 million per employee.[13] Within six months of the acquisition, all key personnel had left the bank!

Other financial intermediaries hardly fare better than commercial banks.

In August 2002, the largest insurance company in Europe, Allianz, which acquired Dresdner Bank (the second largest commercial bank in Germany) in 2001, reported a second quarter loss of $898 million by Dresdner, and expected to incur further losses for the year 2002.

Similarly, the Credit Suisse Group, a Swiss financial conglomerate, reported a loss of $367 million for the second quarter of 2002. It had to inject $1 billion in cash in its insurance unit Winterthur (acquired in 1997) and that apparently led to suspension of dividends in August 2002, a first-time phenomenon in its 146-year history.

Before a bank considers the acquisition alternative, it should carefully analyze the following issues.

- The investment bank to be acquired has a pulse on the financial market – a trait sometimes viewed more critical than others due to interest rate and currency volatilities.
- Time lag involved in developing such a "pulse" in-house is also regarded undesirable, especially since it would involve significant losses or drain on capital.

- Acquiring a star team either carries too hefty a price tag for a serious consideration or would create severe organizational strains that would be avoided by giving virtual autonomy to an acquired firm (whose management would report directly to the top management of the acquiring firm).
- Acquisition is absolutely essential for preserving or enhancing market share in financing business needs for funds; and
- Market share and profitability are strongly positively correlated.

Some specific caveats should be noted regarding the premises for acquisitions.

1   Competition in the USA has already turned very intense. For instance, Rule 415 for "shelf registration" allows a qualified corporation to issue securities any time within two years of registration of the public offering with the SEC. Nothing can prevent the corporation from employing services of another underwriter, if a previous tranche of offerings resulted in an unsatisfactory experience (e.g., because of underpricing of the issue or overhanging of the issue for an unreasonably long time period) with the initial underwriter.

2   A commercial bank entering in the underwriting activities directly or through acquiring an investment bank, faces potential problems of conflict.

In May 2001, WorldCom, an investment-grade firm at the time, raised almost $12 billion in a bond issue managed by Citigroup. One purpose of the issue was to replace bank loans. A year later, when WorldCom reported an understatement of expenses in prior years (initially roughly $4 billion to be later revised to $7 billion), these bonds were downgraded.

Bondholders are questioning whether underwriters acted in professional manner. A potential fallout may be a spate of lawsuits and, at worst, a revival in some form of the Glass–Steagall Act.

3   The pulse developed by the investment bank regarding the winds in the market place and identifying the right investor group for stock placement is not necessarily institutional as it rests with the key personnel. If the bank is unable to retain these employees after the acquisition, the merger fails to add value to stockholder equity.

In the initial proposal to acquire Bankers Trust for $10.1 billion in December 1998, Deutsche Bank revealed that it is setting aside $400 million to offer incentives to retain key staff over the next few years. (In June 1999, Deutsche Bank integrated Bankers Trust and its affiliates in its own global network.)

When a large bank acquires a small underwriting firm, from the perspective of the employees of the firm being acquired, a large firm is essentially perceived as more bureaucratic and less flexible; hence chances of their remaining with the firm may be slim in spite of lucrative remuneration.

> A difference in compensation schemes for commercial vis-à-vis investment bankers is well known, with the latter garnering substantial bonuses that create significant differences in total compensation. Any efforts made to preserve an erstwhile organization's compensation scheme, while necessary to retain key personnel, are hardly likely to be accepted with equanimity by the employees of the acquiring commercial bank. The resultant jealousy and in-fighting between the two units can be detrimental to the acquiring firm.

4   A successful underwriter would have to (a) correctly assess the market reception to the prospective security offering; (b) price the security with a competitive margin; and (c) have a wide and deep investor network to quickly place the security. A commercial bank acquiring an investment bank during the rising stock market phase may overestimate values for these criteria and end up paying too much during the euphoric market conditions.

11.5.1   Acquisitions for equity underwriting

Certain patterns, however tentative, are discernible in recent acquisitions and mergers.

- Bank purchase of smaller, at times, boutique firms but not the bulge bracket firms (such as Merrill Lynch); for instance, Bankers Trust, virtually an investment bank itself, acquired Alex. Brown specializing in IPOs.
- Purchases have been through a variety of methods, from cash to stock issue; thus, BankAmerica acquired Robertson Stephens for $540 million in cash, whereas Bankers Trust acquired Alex. Brown for $1.9 billion in stock; and Nations Bank acquired Montgomery Securities for 30 percent stock and 70 percent cash, the total amounting to $1.2 billion.
- Purchases reveal a differing focus on complementarity of the two organizations, although they have been to remedy deficiency in equity underwriting.

11.5.2   Acquisitions for other motives

Citigroup

A recent merger of Citicorp and the Travelers Group, to be called Citigroup, differs from the above mentioned acquisitions in several ways.

- This merger represents firms of comparable sizes and not a large firm absorbing a small firm.
- Both firms are well diversified. For instance, the Travelers Group is an insurance company that has turned into a diversified financial services company with Primerica

Financial Services and Commercial Credit and its acquisitions of the brokerage firm Smith Barney and the commodity trader and broker Salomon. Citicorp is the parent company of Citibank, an international banking powerhouse, and is the world's largest issuer of credit cards, with some 60 million bank cards in 1998.

- Cross referral in the consumer group (e.g., insurance sale to credit card holders) represents a great opportunity, and a serious threat to the competition in the financial services industry.
- Initially, Citigroup had up to five years to sell its Travelers insurance business, if Congress were not to repeal restrictions that prevent banks from directly owning insurance companies under the Glass–Steagall Act. At the end of five years, the companies said they would evaluate alternatives in order to comply with whatever laws then apply to bank holding companies. With the recent repeal of the Glass–Steagall Act, this became a moot issue.
- Their goal is to offer globally a range of financial products and services to
  - consumers from cradle to the grave, and
  - corporate and investment bank businesses as well as
  - asset management business for investors.

Each of the businesses before the merger has achieved respectable success. Nevertheless, the issues remain *whether*

- Their redefined one-stop financial product supermarket can pull off when the unprecedented integration of the global financial market has created unanticipated wrinkles throwing well-laid out plans off balance. For instance, the deal that was worth $70 billion in stock value in April 1998 was worth roughly half that amount by October 1998.
- Their operations in 100 countries can be expeditiously melded with regards to co-ordination of overlapping activities as well as the corresponding units' planning and performance evaluation. (It is also instructive to note that Citicorp reported with great fanfare its aim at being the first retail bank in the European Union in the late 1980s; in the 1990s, that goal was not prominently paraded in public.)
- In particular, the two investment banking groups, one Salomon Smith Barney from the Travelers group, and the other from the Citicorp, would be properly integrated to create value for the stockholder.
- Conflicts among management would be easy to resolve: different experience bases, incompatible management styles, and above all egos, among other things, get in the way of arriving at agreement. After many months of damaging vacillation following the merger, Citibank's John Reed, the co-CEO of the merged organization, finally cleared the way for the other co-CEO, Sandy Weil of Travelers, who can now focus on planning his next mega-merger.[14]

Deutsche Bank

As mentioned above, Deutsche Bank integrated Bankers Trust in the June of 1999. Bankers Trust had focused on providing innovative financial products to businesses. However, its legal battles with customers such as Proctor & Gamble (P&G)[15] in 1994 left it bruised and scarred. The resultant top management change shifted the emphasis to leveraged lending, high-yield bonds and M&A advisory service. It rounded out its lack of equity underwriting by acquiring Alex. Brown in 1997. Again, the Russian crisis in August 1998 hit hard its emerging market operations by inflicting losses of around $485 million in the third quarter of 1998.

It is too early to say how this merger will work out. But Deutsche Bank acquired in 1989 the UK investment bank Morgan Grenfell which specialized in M&A transactions. For several years, Morgan Grenfell (DMG) was given autonomy; however, it was prevented from dealing with any M&A transactions in Germany. Subsequent attempts for integrating Morgan Grenfell with the parent's in-house German operations were not perceived successful by market observers. It is not quite clear what returns Deutsche Bank's stockholders have obtained for their overall investment in excess of $4 billion in DMG. Whether that experience will be repeated or Deutsche Bank has learned its lesson well from that experience, only time will be able to tell. At this juncture, what is clear is the Deutsche Bank's strategy for continuous expansion by acquiring and merging other big banks to form a global force in investment banking and money management. Whether this approach means "too big to succeed" or "too big to fail" remains to be seen.

11.5.3 Acquisitions and organizational integration

Although initially a merger looks "picture-perfect" on paper, it fails to deliver the promise over time, and at worst, it unravels. Why? Quite often, the organizational dimension is not carefully considered.

- Very often, additional layers of organization are inserted; they increase the fixed cost, tend to reduce the profitability, and manage to reduce the flexibility of the organization. Also, this action flies in the face of more desirable flatter and leaner organization forms.
- Planning (including budgetary) processes are inconsistent (for instance, the investment bank may focus on revenue-based targets for group-based activities, while the commercial bank is concerned with the target of the cost of running a unit); and prior to the merger, no effort is made to carefully assess whether either approach is suitable for the merged organization, or there is a need for still another approach.
- Bonuses or rewards based on unit-specific targets may foster unnecessary rivalry between two groups who work at cross purposes and whose co-operation would have been in the overall interests of the firm's stockholders (e.g., the commercial loan group does not want to bring in the derivative group due to a fear that it would convince the client to shift from a loan to a security issue).
- No attention is paid to common-purpose information sharing and access. One related aspect is a lack of compatibility of computer hardware as well as software. Top management is often unaware of the huge expenditures required for integrating the information system.
- Finally, a new set of controls may be needed to prevent losses inflicted by a unit on the firm, especially when the management in charge is treading new waters, that is, has no experience or insight in the acquired business.

> In 1997, NatWest Markets, an investment banking arm of the NatWest Bank of the UK, managed to misprice options and lose $124 million. Inadequacy of internal controls was blamed for this loss.

11.6 Capital Adequacy Regulations for Investment Banks

Risks for the investment banking business are inherently different from the commercial banks because of their disparate activities. This is acknowledged by the dissimilar capital requirement proposals put forward by the Bank of International Settlement for the two institutions. Two sets of risks are pertinent for an investment bank: trade-related, and derivative-related.

11.6.1 Trade-related capital

A capital adequacy test for an investment bank needs to address its major risk, that is, position risk. It trades securities or takes short-term positions, hoping to make a profit in the near future. The objective is to run a "trading book." Therefore, it must be in a position to withstand losses whether realized or not. The **position (market) risk**, which stems from falling prices when the bank holds a long position or from rising prices when the bank holds short position, is critical for capital adequacy consideration. An important subset of position risk is identified as **liquidity risk**: it stems from the bank's long (short) position in a security that is disproportionately large in relation to the total market. Naturally, position or liquidity risk must encompass risks related to activities such as foreign currency forward or interest rate swap transactions and other off-balance sheet transactions.

Dimson and Marsh (1995) analyze the three approaches that regulatory authorities have used to examine the position risk for investment banks:

1 *Comprehensive approach.* Used in the USA by the SEC, it specifies the required capital on the basis of the specified proportion of the value of the long plus a proportion of the short position taken;
2 *Building block approach.* Proposed by the International Basel Committee on Banking Supervision, it bases the capital requirement partly on the net and partly on the gross value of the book; and
3 *Portfolio approach.* Used in the UK, it specifies capital that allows for diversification and variability of securities within the portfolio.

Their research suggests that the portfolio approach is the preferred method for setting capital requirements.

11.6.2 Derivative-related capital

On OTC derivatives, the SEC imposes large capital charges, and restricts both credit extension to counterparties and collateralization of a transaction. As a result, investment banks conduct their OTC derivatives business mostly through the holding company's subsidiaries that are not subject to the SEC regulation.

The SEC has finally adopted the Broker-Dealer Lite Proposal containing rules imposing on a broker-dealer firm regulatory requirements that are tailored to the needs of the OTC derivatives market. These requirements also address the issue-related capital adequacy by defining an entity called the OTC derivatives dealer (OTCDD) – affiliation of OTCDD is strictly voluntary.

An OTCDD must hold "tentative net capital"[16] of at least $100 million and "net capital" of at least $20 million. Net capital is computed by subtracting the credit and market risk capital requirements from tentative net capital. With respect to market risk, the rules likely to be applied to commercial banks are also applicable to investment banks: market risk will be assessed by internal VAR models on the basis of 99 percent one-tailed confidence interval over a ten-day period with a multiplier of 3 to 4 (see Chapter 10 for details on the VAR models).

With respect to credit risk, an OTCDD appears to require less capital requirement for investment banks than for commercial banks. The SEC bases its credit risk capital requirement on the replacement value of the assets, which will be multiplied by 8 percent and their corresponding risk counterparty factors. The counterparty factor equals 20 percent for triple-A and double-A counterparties, 50 percent for single-A and triple-B, or 100 percent for junk credits and those in default.

An OTCDD has the option to trade any securities including interest rate derivatives and long-dated forwards. It does not have to be a member of a self-regulatory organization or the Securities Protection Corporation that specifies certain requirements when taking counterparty collateral. However, an OTCDD must obtain authorization to use or modify its VAR model, which has to comply with the SEC's standard of risk management risk control.

11.6.3   A comparison of capital requirements for the two institutions

Our discussion on commercial bank capital in Chapter 10 and the above discussion on investment bank capital make it clear that a commercial bank has stiffer standards imposed by the regulators than an investment bank. Two implications should be noted.

1   A commercial bank has access to a cheaper source of funding in deposits (especially when low-cost deposit insurance is considered), and a broader menu of activities than an investment bank. At the same time, deposits are the major reason why the commercial bank is not subject to voluntary capital standards.
2   Stiffer and more inflexible capital standards may also have contributed to one-way acquisitions, that is, commercial banks acquiring investment banks.

11.7   Challenges and Opportunities

Despite the original intent of the Glass–Steagall Act to compartmentalize investment and commercial banking activities in order to protect depositors, internationalization of banking services and financial market competitiveness have blurred the distinction between these two sets of banking activities. Further, the rationale for protecting the depositor has been weakened by the fact that commercial banks provide short-term loans to securities dealers. Thus these transactions have already forged a link between commercial banks and securities industries; and they have not only generated revenues for commercial banks, but have also managed to increase the bank risk.

In recent years, major commercial banks have started competing with investment banks for the underwriting business from the position of strength due to their size, financial resources, customer list, and far flung geographical presence. An investment bank subsidiary of a bank holding company can underwrite a security, use the bank facilities to distribute the security, and provide bank customers brokerage services. In addition, because of the recent capital adequacy requirements that resulted from the Basel Agreement, the commercial banks have been better equipped with a capital base that allows them to compete with even well-positioned investment banks.[17]

Still, size, financial resources, and an access to an extensive list of potential investors do not assure success. Nor does an acquisition of an investment bank overcome the problem of lack of "feel" of the market. A key issue is whether the commercial bank can hire or retain key personnel and give them sufficient flexibility to make timely decisions. Historically, the rigidity of the organizational structure and rivalry stemming from compensation disparity in the two branches of banking have been the two major stumbling blocks in the path of success for a commercial bank in the investment banking area.

11.8 Conclusion

This chapter discussed major investment banking activities that include four areas: underwriting, fund management, brokerage, and advising. Globalization of financial markets and lowering of legal and regulatory barriers, which have historically compartmentalized commercial and investment banking activities in the USA (and to an extent in Japan and the UK), have created intense competition between these two sets of banking activities. Advances in information technology have added impetus to lowering of barriers, inducing market volatilities – thereby generating demand for risk management products, and devising these products efficiently.

In the process, both branches of banking have felt pressure on the profit margins while their costs have been going up. Their responses have been (a) higher risk assumption; (b) consolidation within their own industry, and (c) "cross-industry" as well as cross-border mergers. Success or effectiveness of a selected alternative is not always clear-cut; however, careful planning and deep pockets help in any adverse situation.

DISCUSSION QUESTIONS

1   Some critics suggest that financial market liberalization over the last two to three decades have significantly contributed to volatilities in the primary securities, interest rates, and foreign exchange rates. They regard the repeal of the Glass–Steagall Act further contributing to market volatility that may end up in market destabilization or even catharsis. Do you agree? Why?

2   In Chapter 1, we saw that both banking forms – commercial and invest-
    ment – owe their existence and survival to information asymmetry. With
    the advent of the Internet and tremendous strides in telecommunications
    technology, information dissemination is no longer a critical consideration
    for financial market participants. Would these continuing developments
    then lead to a demise of these twin forms of banking activities?

3   Discuss the challenges encountered in melding organizations when a
    commercial bank acquires an investment bank. Would these challenges be
    there when an insurance firm acquires an investment bank? Why?

4   a   What are the traditional underwriting activities?
    b   What investment banking activities were performed by US commercial
        banks even prior to the repeal of the Glass–Steagall Act?
    c   Why were they allowed to do so by the regulatory agencies?

5   Compare and contrast stock and bond underwriting activities in the domes-
    tic market. Do they exhibit similar patterns in the Euro-markets? Why?

6   Explain the different types of offshore investment banking activities.

7   What are the distinguishing characteristics of the relationship orientation
    vis-à-vis the transaction orientation? What impact does a particular orien-
    tation have on a multinational bank? Is it the same case for a multinational
    investment bank?

8   Why do non-financial businesses need to rely on banks for short-term sea-
    sonal loans?

9   What are the alternative routes that a commercial bank can take to engage
    in investment banking activities? Compare and contrast these alternatives.

10 What are the capital adequacy requirements for the investment bank?
    How do they differ from those for the commercial bank? Why?

11 Traditionally, investment banking houses were privately owned. Now they
    have started going public. Why?

12 Investigate some of the recent acquisitions that involve both branches of
    banking activities. Do you find any where a commercial bank that has been
    acquired by an independent investment bank? Why?

NOTES

1   Section 20 refers to the Glass–Steagall Act, which prohibited commercial banks from engaging
    in investment banking activities through establishing subsidiaries. The Fed's administrative fiat
    circumvented this prohibition, and initially constrained the subsidiary to generate a maximum
    10 percent of the total revenues from the "prohibited" activities.

2   In 1990, J.P. Morgan introduced a computer-based link between the issuer and institutional
    investors that would allow the issuer to receive direct bids from these investors, thus bypassing
    underwriters (Marr 1995).

3   A subtle difference should be noted: costing of individual products and services (and, hence, the
    bundle offered to the clientele) is now more meticulous and thorough than ever before.

4 As noted in Section 11.1, separation of underwriting and advisory work from research has been a new form of re-regulation in 2002.

5 Nowadays, any large position taken by a dealer is justified on the grounds of risk arbitrage!

6 Political pressures from the Enron–Arthur Anderson episode highlighting conflict of interest have effectively removed accounting firms from the fray.

7 The law of large number underlying the actuarial concept of probabilities may be the reason why the commercial bank has an edge over the investment bank.

8 Reporting requirements provide greater flexibility for "periodic allocation" for commodities than for services. In a contract with Quaker Oats, under which Enron was supposed to provide, among other things, maintenance services, Enron reportedly classified disproportionately large amounts to "commodities" (such as gas) and the small balance to maintenance services so as to obtain this flexibility in frontloading profits: an anticipated profit of about $37 million over a ten-year period (which presumably was inflated in the first place) resulted in $23 million of profits in the year of signing the contract.

9 These repo transactions were reported on a marked-to-market basis. As the maturity of traded contracts in energy "commodity" hardly extends beyond two years, Enron had significant discretion in assigning values for contract legs that matured beyond two years. This flexibility allowed, in turn, Enron to overstate the profit.

10 An ADR program may be sponsored or unsponsored. An unsponsored ADR program is set up by a US bank on its own initiative, without the involvement of the foreign firm. With regards to sponsored issues, regulatory requirements are stiffer for organized exchanges than for the OTC trading; they are also stiffer for new issues than seasoned issues.

11 Although Rule 144A does not allow trading with the general public, the QIBs can trade among themselves, and the resale restriction lifts after three years. Stocks can then trade in the OTC market.

12 Commercial banks placing such issues would not have violated the Glass–Steagall Act. Still, this was advantageous only for large commercial banks, as they and large investment banks were the only ones who had a decided advantage in placing such issues in light of their close contacts with the institutional investors.

13 As if to return the favor, a British bank acquiring a US investment bank paid roughly $3.5 million per employee in the mid-1990s!

14 *The Economist*, March 4, 2000.

15 In 1993, P&G wanted to lower the cost of its commercial paper financing, which it was supposed to achieve from revenues generated by writing options that bet on interest rate stability. Within a short time period, in 1994, the Federal Reserve unexpectedly lifted the discount rate. As a result, P&G lost more than $100 million, and it contended that Bankers Trust did not make it aware of risks involved in writing such derivatives.

16 This is a counterpart of the total Tier I & II capital for commercial banks.

17 Investment banks that have chosen to remain independent have been abandoning the partnership mode in favor of incorporation. The resultant agency issues that manifest in areas such as information disclosure are likely to curtail significantly the flexibility enjoyed by managers under the partnership form.

CHAPTER 12

Bank Strategy

12.1 Introduction

As noted in Chapter 1, competitive *financial* markets, irrespective of competitiveness of *goods* markets but ensuring nonetheless competitive *foreign exchange* markets, make banks' intermediary role less relevant, if not redundant. Due to equal access to relevant information and absence of any roadblocks[1] in entering or exiting financial markets, market participants can engage in a tradeoff between current and future consumption patterns without help from banks. Similarly, it is doubtful whether banks per se are essential to provide an effective conduit for the government in carrying out the monetary policy measures.

Although competitive financial markets in the ideal form are nowhere near reality currently (or, for that matter, in the foreseeable future), imperfections in financial markets are not static in nature. In fact, many of them tend to atrophy over time and are replaced by new ones, as the last quarter of the twentieth century has witnessed in the USA and elsewhere in the world. A gradual birth or removal of and transformation in imperfections in financial markets has thus changed the distance between perfect and imperfect financial markets, affecting thereby the role of banks in these markets. As a result, banks' survival and prosperity will depend on whether they manage to

- accurately forecast changes and assess their impact on (a) the existing product mix, and (b) potential for developing new products or services;
- minimize their vulnerability to unpredictable, adverse changes through maintaining their profitability without increasing their risk; and
- enhance their adaptability by reshaping their role so as to augment their profitability and/or attenuate their risk.

This is the essence of sound strategy formulation and implementation. Students of strategy have debated whether the focus should be on analysis of external environment or core strength of the firm. In the case of a commercial bank, this debate will have to take a back seat since both these aspects are equally crucial for strategy formulation in a global context.

This chapter first considers a review of external environments continually undergoing changes. It then discusses the **life cycle of a product** in the context of the phase of development of an economy so as to highlight the impact of their interrelationship on a bank's strategy. It then investigates strategic implications of transactions versus relationship orientation of an economy. Finally, it examines the issues pertaining to a bank's resources and its ability to augment them on strategy formulation and implementation.

12.2   Changes in External Environments: The International Dimension

It is widely recognized that rapid changes in information technology and a shift in the political ideology toward a free-market approach have managed to change the nature of competition in financial markets. But these changes have not necessarily managed to lower the barriers to competition – often barriers elsewhere have been raised or new ones have been introduced.

- Deregulation (e.g., selective removal or circumventing of regulations, which delay securities flotation, through introduction of shelf-registration and Rule 144a in the USA) has brought in its place new regulations (e.g., higher capital adequacy requirements and more transparency in reporting).
- Repeal of laws that stand in the way of new products (e.g., revision of laws in France and Spain that stood in the way of securitization) has been accompanied by enactment of new laws – or tougher reinforcement of existing laws (e.g., requiring much greater public disclosure of trading activities and derivative position).
- Efforts to lower or harmonize barriers that have stood in the way of capital flows (e.g., lowering or removal of the withholding taxes) that enter or exit national markets have failed to touch promotion of subsidies for exports or export-related activities in both goods and financial markets.
- Break up of old monopolies and public (often quasi-government) enterprises has spurred in its wake emergence of new ones through consolidation both within the traditionally

defined industries and across industries, especially in the service industries (and their size often has allowed them to wield disproportionately high influence on the political processes).

- Creation of demand for new products (especially for risk management) that becomes "commodities" at an unprecedented fast pace is accompanied with a struggle to retain product differentiation through opaqueness even within an organization.
- Extraordinary impetus at micro level to develop new derivative products for managing increased interest and foreign exchange rate volatilities as well as credit risk has added to their aggregated *perceived* potential for systemic failure at the macro level.

From the perspective of the global financial markets, the above changes reflect modifications (raising or lowering) of barriers of taxes, tariffs, regulations, laws as well as non-governmental, structural idiosyncrasies. A useful starting point for analyzing implications of these changes is the juxtaposition of the **life cycle phases of an economy** and the product mix that a bank offers (or can offer).

12.2.1   Economic development and product life cycle

Naturally not all national economies are equally affected by the above changes; some have even managed to remain immune to the sweeping forces of some changes due to structural idiosyncrasies. The process of securitization provides an interesting example. It has taken deep roots in the USA, followed by the UK, France, and Spain.[2] However, it has failed to make a dent in Italy,[3] partly because Italy has not modified the legal structure that impedes securitization.

How economies differ and in what respect cannot be catalogued here, but a classification scheme may serve as a reasonable proxy.

Economic development phase

As financial markets in an economy develop, the economy moves gradually away from traditional products and services offered by banks. (Traditional products and services encompass, but are not limited to, funding short- and medium-term business needs and check collection services for businesses.)

Prior to the 1970s, firms in the USA typically relied on banks for their short-term funding needs. In the early 1970s, tight money market conditions led banks to arrange or facilitate such financing for large firms through their direct access to the money market via commercial paper.[4] Over time, familiarity with such direct access to the financial markets led large companies to bypass banks and tap the markets directly. The ability of the financial market, in both resolving information asymmetry and reducing agency costs between issuers and investors, appears to be critical in the success of the commercial paper issues.

Growth of equity financing can be best understood in a framework that views the equity as an option on the firm's assets, due to the limited liability of the shareholder. Equity (stock) value thus increases as the volatility of the return on the firm's assets increases. Hence, the shareholder will anticipate a higher return on investment in the common stock, when there is substantial uncertainty regarding the future return on the firm's projects. Indeed, these higher return prospects may even prompt the shareholder to shift funds from bank deposits to the firm's equity. Of course, when there is too much noise in the firm's investment opportunities, some investors may prefer to keep their funds in bank deposits to equity investment (Jacklin and Bhattacharya 1988; Hirshleifer 1971). Thus in a well-developed financial market where such noise is muted, investors will seriously consider risky securities for investment, and firms will have the flexibility to raise funds in different forms, instead of primarily relying on banks as the source of financing. In a less-developed financial market with significant noise, on the other hand, bank loans appear to be an overwhelmingly decisive alternative.

Banks, however, do not become redundant[5] in well-developed financial markets, when demand for traditional products falls off. Instead, banks are called upon to provide "new" products and services.

> It has been estimated that commercial banks hold derivative contracts of about $16 trillion in notional value. Of these contracts, 63 percent are in the form of interest rate related derivatives instrument while 35 percent are in currency related instruments (Edwards and Mishkin 1995).

Product life cycle phase

A product or service passes through several distinct phases of a cycle, each with unique or special economic characteristics. These phases may be broadly defined in the following categories.

- *New* (e.g., credit derivatives that distinguish market or interest risk from default risk). These products leave in their wake unresolved problems of information asymmetry and agency issues in the marketplace.
- *Product differentiation* (e.g., reputation for arranging LBO financing quickly, in an innovative way, and at reasonable cost). Customer perception of superior product or services.
- *Mature* (e.g., cash management services in the USA). Product differentiation becomes marginal.
- *Commodity* (e.g., a plain vanilla interest swap). Supplier differentiation does not exist, and what counts is the pricing of the product or service.

Several characteristics of the life cycle of the financial products are noteworthy.

- A "new" product, by its very nature, has structural opaqueness: this allows the innovating bank to earn super-normal profits, provided there is a need for the product.
- As a product's use lowers transaction costs (because of, among other things, the learning curve), the benefit of further use increases.

- As a product moves from the "new" to the ultimate "commodity" phase, opaqueness decreases. This movement is aided by and in turn encourages competition.
- Competition reduces above-average profit margins.

A review of the history of innovative financial products suggests an interesting pattern in which financial products that were originally offered by banks later shifted to the financial market (see Finnerty 1988). For instance, products such as swaps and securitized loans have become standardized and moved from intermediaries to markets (Merton and Bodie 1995). Hence a bank cannot continue to rely on the standardized products for making core business profit in a given financial market. In general, a bank should strive to retain or return to the product differentiation phase. A variety of actions are possible. For instance, a bank may investigate

- bundling of existing products or services;
- unbundling existing products or services giving customers greater choice;
- adding a new product or service either by itself or in a package with the existing bundle;
- guaranteeing product "quality," product availability at lowest cost and/or in a guaranteed small time period; and
- standing ready to customize products or services at a reasonable cost.

Alternatively, a bank may want to investigate the proposition that *a commodity in a more mature economy may be a new product in the emerging economy*. This may be the case even when the opaqueness in the product structure may be well understood and easily duplicable elsewhere; however, structural idiosyncrasies may impart opaqueness to the product. For instance,

- A US bank was approached to issue credit cards to Saudi clientele already having locally issued credit cards. The US bank was offered, among other things, the incentive of interest-free collateral funds worth 80 percent of the credit limit from each prospective cardholder![6] Probably the status conferred by the American credit card and Islamic repugnance toward risk-free interest earning might have been the reasons for this proposition.

Similarly, as an economy orients itself toward a free market, a business will produce in anticipation of demand, and suppliers who provide raw materials to the business will meet only a portion of its funds need. As the products are sold on credit, cash outflows will exceed cash inflows. If one defines the time period between the initial purchase of raw materials and the ultimate collection of accounts receivable as the *cash cycle*, one finds that the cash cycle is generally positive for a business (i.e., the cash outflows come earlier than the cash inflows), and thus it will require short-term loans to meet these short-term needs. This is the need that a bank will be called upon to fulfill in an emerging economy even when such a traditional role may have lost significance in the well-developed economy. (Of course, this does not mean that a bank participating in an emerging economy cannot introduce "new" products.)

- In a financial market with prohibitively high transaction costs, issuing commercial papers to raise funds is not a feasible option. Still, a bank may arrange for a creditworthy local firm to issue Euro-CP at a reasonable cost that still covers satisfactory compensation for its services.

Thus consideration of international dimension in strategy formulation allows a bank from a developed economy to extend the life of the products or services it provides.

Further, it is also conceivable that a well-heeled bank from a less mature economy may offer a product in a more mature economy even when it lacks competitive strength.

- An Italian bank may introduce a product, say, in the USA with a full realization that it will be obsolete before it breaks even in the US market; however, the "learning" or "experience" curve benefits will reap sufficiently handsome rewards later when the bank introduces the product in the European market.

It should be noted that impediments are not always the hallmark of the less mature economies.

- With respect to long-term needs of business firms in the USA, over 50 percent of the external funds are raised by firms through sale of stocks and bonds over the past several decades. Regulatory and legal barriers[7] have hindered commercial banks from fulfilling these needs. However,
  - banks have managed to circumvent these restrictions through Euromarkets;
  - they have also circumvented the loan size restriction through syndicated credits;
  - finally, conduit of another national market may enable a bank to circumvent domestic restrictions.
- In Germany, up until very recently, significant transaction costs[8] dampened demand for equity among individual investors. Businesses routinely relied on banks to provide equity capital, and the practice of universal banking, that is, the combination of commercial and investment banking activities, facilitated equity financing by banks. As a result, banks came to control about 40 percent of the business equity and occupy two-thirds of seats on the corporate boards (Allen and Gale 1995).

In the absence of other impediments, a US bank can circumvent restrictions on undertaking investment banking activities through a German subsidiary.

Naturally, as the differences diminish among various economies along the relevant dimensions, justification on the basis of such reasoning may not remain valid.

Finally, banks may have an inherent advantage over non-bank competitors in introducing new products or sustaining product differentiation. Some products or services, for instance, may require "intermediation" based on realization of actuarial risk. Thus banks have a unique capability to attractively price basket options and credit derivatives that investment banks may lack.

Similarly, catering to small and medium-size businesses entails bureaucracy that an investment bank may be unwilling to create because of fear of inflexibility.

In brief, a bank's target for a cross-border niche requires scrutiny of the bank's existing product mix and anticipated changes in it, as well as each product's life cycle phase vis-à-vis demand and supply characteristics in the existing and potential markets.

12.2.2   Arbitraging structural inefficiencies: Lessons from the Enron case

Given the increasing need for managing risk, a bank creates new products that meet its clients' demand. A structured finance deal in place of a plain-vanilla loan is one such example that has gained increasing currency in the bank business in recent years. Apart from serving its customers more effectively, designing a new financial product either through unbundling or bundling of existing products allows the bank to profit from informational inefficiency that prevents the client or the market from meaningful comparison of competitive products.

An interesting illustration to structured finance deals is the set of transactions carried out by Citigroup (and separately by J.P. Morgan Chase) with Enron, described in detail in Chapter 11. The analysis there showed that underlying transactions were "arbitrage" transactions designed to exploit market inefficiency. In turn, this inefficiency stemmed from investor ignorance as well as regulatory inconsistency with regard to financial reporting. Essentially, reporting these transactions as trade deals (rather than "repo" deals in enery products) allowed Emron to overstate profits and disguise debt. The gray area was where both banks knowingly helped Enron violate the reporting requirement. This fact is likely to trigger adverse regulations that may circumscribe the scope of banks' future business activities. Further, even in the absence of adverse regulatory impact, ill will generated by these actions is likely to affect adversely banks' future cash flows and their market values. Thus the combined negative impact of ill will and added regulatory burden may far outweigh the handsome profits a bank may garner from a dubious transaction.

12.2.3   Phases of economy and relationship versus transaction orientation

A major characteristic that distinguishes a mature from an emerging economy is the transparency in transactions and financial information. In an emerging economy, opaqueness is the rule, whereas such opaqueness is not common in a mature economy.[9] This certainly reinforces the pivotal role of banks in an emerging economy. But additionally, it also underscores the role of *relationship*[10] playing a critical role between a bank and its business customer. To an extent, relationship, reinforced by relatively simple – lacking fine detail – contracts and a longer run viewpoint, obviates the need for an in-depth profitability analysis of a loan transaction. Even when a transaction may have only marginal profit contribution, it may be justified in terms of overall profitability from the customer's business in the long run. The longer-run viewpoint is reinforced by the bank keeping competition at bay in the community or economy. Finally, relationship orientation also allows the bank a privileged access to proprietary information.

In a mature economy, the bank's process of procuring and investing funds turns competitive and complex. As a result, the link between a bank and its business customer is governed by *transaction* orientation. As the business firm is able to procure funds from non-bank investors through issuing varied claims, the bank as a lender faces agency problems of adverse selection and moral hazard, referred to in Chapter 1; and these problems demand inclusion and enforcement of proper covenants in the loan contract. The transition of a bank from one orientation to the other is difficult. In the international arena, the task of transition becomes even more challenging because of the differences in the legal systems. Although the correlation is not perfect, civil law-based societies (e.g., in France, Italy, and Spain) seem to be affiliated with relationship orientation, and common law-based systems (e.g., in the UK and the USA) have transaction orientation.[11]

Some strategic implications of this dichotomy between transactions versus relationship are noteworthy.

- As noted in Chapter 2, the relationship culture promotes P-type (people-skill) managers; and the transaction culture promotes Q-type (quantitative or analytical-skill) managers. The bank will have to assess adequacy or availability of its human resources when it investigates entry in a market with different orientation.
- A joint venture between banks from two different organizational cultures is less likely to survive or succeed than banks with similar orientation.
- Even if an economy has a relationship orientation, the status quo cannot be taken for granted, as illustrated in France and Spain where the legal framework was modified to accommodate securitization. Thus if a bank makes a strategic commitment on the basis of the current status, it may have to reverse or modify its decision later to adapt to the change. This may have costly profitability implications.

In sum, general considerations of both national and product life cycle considerations allow a bank to enhance its profitability, reduce its risk, or both, especially when it manages to convert challenges imposed by barriers into opportunities for itself. Orientation of the legal system provides an interesting example of this prescription especially in terms of its ramifications for the managerial selection, introduction of new products, and joint ventures.

12.3 Changes in External Environments: The Internet

One development with a far-reaching potential is the Internet. Technological developments have shifted emphasis from face-to-face customer transactions to computer-based interactive transactions. Banks are now encouraging customers to use the Internet, Automatic Teller Machines (ATMs), and smart cards that have one element in common: all these transaction modes make conventional physical form of branches superfluous. Below are provided oft-quoted comparative numbers for different modes of transactions during the late 1990s.

- A face-to-face transaction with a teller costs banks $1.07;
- phone banking costs $0.54 per call;
- a visit to the ATM is $0.54;
- A web-based (Internet) transaction, however, costs banks just $0.01.

Validity of these numbers requires scrutiny. Appendix M provides guidelines for such cost analysis. In the final analysis, even when one questions validity of the precise numbers, one conclusion remains inescapable regarding the relative ranking of the alternatives: cost of an Internet transaction to the bank is the lowest, and the face-to-face transaction costs the bank the highest.[12]

12.3.1   Strategic ramifications of Internet banking activities

A typical Internet-based bank has no physical location for branches, and its customers carry out all transactions via ATMs and the Internet. It manages to charge a below-average cost to its customers, pay them above-average interest rates on deposits, and generate a rate of return on investments that is significantly above the rate earned by *conventional*, well-managed banks.

Four significant implications of purely Internet-based banks (PIBB) should be noted.

1   The **economies of scale** applicable to conventional banks is virtually irrelevant. A PIBB, for instance, manages to reach, and exceed, the breakeven volume much earlier in its existence as it requires a much smaller critical mass of the customer base than a conventional bank would have. Thus Internet banking has changed not only the economic parameters but also the benchmarks for assessment.

2   Banks grafting the Internet base are generating profits. However, it is questionable whether they will be able to improve materially their profitability. This is simply because they have added another layer of fixed cost without significantly reducing[13] the existing fixed costs.

3   Perhaps the most significant implication is the impact of the Internet on government-induced international barriers. The Internet makes irrelevant the physical boundaries between countries – and, in the process, makes the question moot regarding removal or harmonization of barriers that impede international banking. Still, structural barriers, such as a desire for face-to-face transactions or personalized attention, could prove to be a challenging barrier for the Internet banking.

4   Finally, with respect to various stakeholders, several pertinent issues are as follows:
    *   The nature of competition altered by Internet is likely to affect favorably investors.
    *   *Customers* will have to weigh benefits of cheaper, faster financial services[14] against the cost from impersonal and at times avoidable complex processes. They may also find it difficult to compare cost of incompatible bundles of services offered by competing banks.
    *   *Employees* will very likely have to adapt to the new demands their jobs will entail, such as computer literacy or competency. At the same time, they may have more flexible work hours and the ability to work from home base.
    *   *Government* revenue from granting charters may change depending on whether it manages to attract or lose banks; however, more significant impact may come from indirect benefits and costs such as increased consumer spending and higher training and unemployment benefits for laid off employees. Still, it appears undeniable that a nation's ability is greatly circumscribed when it comes to controlling offshore banks poaching the territory of domestic banks, regulating, or channeling financial resources toward socially desirable but uneconomic activities.

Box 12.1   Internet offers an alternative for cross-border payment method

It is common to find that banks often charge too much or take too long for sending or receiving payments across borders. New payments networks are now starting to offer a quick, reliable, and more competitively priced service. These services could pose a threat to the traditional bilateral (or corresponding) agreements between individual banks and SWIFT, which is the global network processing most large international payments.

In 1991, Britain's Royal Bank of Scotland and Spain's Banco Santander set up a new entity called the Inter-Bank On-Line System (IBOS) that provided the cross-border payment service. IBOS later joined ING (a Dutch bank) and Chase Manhattan to extend its reach to America and Asia. Now it has 11 member banks from nine countries to form a single virtual bank.

IBOS can complete in just a few seconds what used to take days for conducting transactions in normal correspondent banking and account-to-account payments. It is claimed to be a cost effective alternative to opening an expensive international branch network. Beyond a quick payment service, IBOS wants to develop a platform for all kinds of cash-management products and a global electronic commerce of payment. It should be noted that other Internet networks – other than IBOS – have emerged. These alliances will clearly provide competition that drive banks to offer flexible, price-competitive payments services in the future.

Box 12.1 illustrates the role of the Internet for cross-border payment.

Does this mean that small domestic banks with only peripheral cross-border involvement have little chance for survival? As has been the case with the financial services industry in general, not only will small banks be able to survive, but they will also have improved prospects for prosperity. The critical condition is that they carefully define their niche and follow the precept of the contestable market theory. Customers, both locally and abroad, demanding personalized services – and willing to pay for them – will have, for instance, little use for either the big supermarkets of financial services or the faceless Internet-based banks. The danger, thus, is not so much the squeeze by big banks as it is the small bank management's ambition to play in the big league without requisite wherewithal that will hasten the demise of small banks.

We have considered so far "external" factors such as life cycles, legal system orientation, and the Internet that are likely to have a profound impact on the formulation of a bank's strategy in a global environment through radically altering the economics of the banking activity in terms of not only cost and competition but also of scope and scale of activities.

We discuss below the "internal" considerations in terms of the available financial and organizational resources a bank has (or can augment) for implementing strategies "dictated" by the external considerations discussed so far.

12.4   Strategic Considerations: Activities and Resources

12.4.1   Scope and scale of activities

There are many dimensions that a bank has to consider for examining the scope and scale of its activities globally. Specifically, consideration of the following issues is pertinent.

- Conventional banking activities versus "one-stop" banking that also encompasses traditional activities of other financial institutions.
- Wholesale versus retail banking.
- Acquisition versus internally generated growth.
- Target rate of growth that is feasible, that is, sustainable.
- Divestitures of "non-core" activities.
- Scale of various activities.
- Geographic expansion that focuses on
  - existing and potential competition in the chosen areas
  - core strength of existing management team and the organizational skills.

At times, acquisitions may be undertaken to build skills for penetration in a desirable but highly uncertain arena (with respect to demand) at an opportune later date, when uncertainty is reduced to an acceptable level[15] (Boot et al. 1998).

Consideration of the above factors enables the bank to understand its strength, its limitations, and also the future goals to be achieved before meaningful banking strategies can be formulated and implemented.

12.4.2   Availability and augmentation of resources

A bank exploring business opportunities in a foreign country needs to have a competitive advantage over local banks. Traditionally, a bank would follow its important customers who undertook direct investment in a foreign country to satisfy their banking needs, ranging from intelligence reports, funds transmittal, short-term or seasonal as well as cross-border trade financing needs of the local division or subsidiary, and payroll, etc. The bank would have the comparative advantage of a captive clientele over the local banks.

As MNCs began to pursue global integration strategies in place of a "multi-domestic" network of subsidiaries and opt for direct access to domestic and global financial markets, the traditional rationale for a bank to go abroad has become less relevant.

When changes call for a shift in the bank strategy, the bank should carefully consider the resource constraints. Two basic resources are paramount: financial and human. Each will be discussed in turn.

Financial resources

Banks face financial resources constraints in servicing their clients and expanding their markets. Available financial resources can be augmented by divestiture of existing activities, external funding, or a combination of the two through, say, an acquisition financed with a stock issue followed by a disposal of selected activities. Although augmentation by various external means is more common now than in the past, such financing is still episodic and at times opportunistic (exploiting an ephemeral imperfection in the financial market). For instance, stock issuance in an unusually favorable stock market cannot be planned long in advance. Thus, internally generated funds remain the most important source of funding growth or a shift in the scope or scale of a bank's activities.

Internal generation of funds calls for:

- Activities requiring capital investment with attractive returns. Currently LBO financing and project financing are activities along this line.
- Activities that generate income by creating contingent obligations; these are the "off-balance-sheet" activities such as standby letters of credit and writing derivative instruments.
- Trading activities.
- Activities that generate fee income due to the bank's expertise; trust funds management, and arrangement of financing for a merger, LBO, or an infrastructure project belong to this category.

Although generating fee income sounds very appealing, some caveats should be noted:

- Competition quickly and greatly dissipates extraordinary fees. Project financing in excess of $500 million used to generate fees of $5–10 million around 1992. By 1997, fees on such projects hovered around $1 million.
- Provision of income-generating services requires a critical mass of personnel. Although their compensation is in the form of both salaries and bonuses – and the latter is typically a more significant component, the aggregated fixed cost component for the group may still be sizable, inducing additional earnings volatility.
- Most important, however, is the loss incurred by the client because of the bank's advice.[16] In the short run, there may be potential for losses due to litigation. Any bank victory is likely to be pyrrhic: in the long run, profitability at the expense of the client will not be brushed off by the existing or potential clientele; and the stock price very likely will decline due to heavily discounted future earnings. It is even conceivable that other banks pursuing similar activities may be tarred with the same brush by the market.

Finally, banks, like other businesses, tend to confuse planning for sustainable growth with wishful thinking.

> A major European bank's chief executive officer reportedly set the goal of quadrupling the return on equity from around 6 to 25 percent in a four-year span!

Human resources

As James and Houston (1996) have argued, the recent transformation of products and services offered by a bank has displayed two characteristics:

1. the organizational structure is less rigid than before; and provision of services is both decentralized and more centrally co-ordinated.

2   performance evaluation shifts from return on assets or equity to risk-adjusted return on capital.

Decentralization requires not only delegation of authority for managing a unit of the firm but also performance evaluation in terms of whether this authority is utilized in the best interests of the firm. Performance evaluation in turn requires unambiguous, transparent information signals regarding benchmark standards and performance indices. Higher management can always have access to the information it needs; however, it should know what information is pertinent for evaluation. Transparency desired by outsiders thus differs from internally demanded transparency.

A more critical problem is what the information signal means to higher management.

Higher management, which has risen from one culture (developed familiarity and sensitivity in the process to the signals generated within the organization), faces challenges in interpreting signals generated in the organization from a different culture. For instance,

- A management team that has come up from the traditional commercial bank culture would have difficulties grappling with evaluating the risk dimension of a firm acquired to generate new derivative products. Since the new products with potential for high profitability by definition requires
    - built-in opaqueness (preventing clients from determining what should be a reasonable price for the product, and competition from coming up with a cheaper copycat product),
    - high risk assumption, or
    - a combination of the two,
  the acquiring management should have sufficient familiarity with the risk-return dimensions of similar products. But it was precisely the lack of that skill that led management to acquire the derivative-specialist firm in the first place. Accelerated product obsolescence only hampers the learning process by the higher management, and thereby their ability to demand and interpret accurately relevant information signals.

- Evaluation of risk has become increasingly more difficult due to integration of financial markets. That a crisis in Russia spilling over to Brazil affects the value of a derivative product designed for a Brazilian security illustrates the problem of properly assessing the risk dimension of this product.
- Building capacity from within does not skirt the problem.
- Inability to assess risk of new products, and subsequent losses, may be tolerable if the firm has deep pockets. Large firms are thus better situated than small firms.
- Investor inability to assess properly the risk dimension often translates into impatience. Thus they may not be willing to give management the benefit of the doubt. Deep pockets may be of little solace in this case.

Overall resources

As previous chapters have shown, the bank is arbitraging in terms of dissimilar costs and revenues on the dimensions of transactions, taxes, regulations, and laws as well as structural idiosyncrasies. The bank has to assess (a) its organizational strength in terms of these dimensions and to what extent this strength is internalized; and (b) its access to financial, structural, and human resources and their permanency. This analysis will allow the bank to determine its niche and scope of its activities. To the extent that a shift in focus is desired, the bank has to determine how long it will take to readjust. This may be classified as the time required to break even; and the time required to reach the desirable results. These time periods may be collectively defined as a transitional period.

An important question is whether the bank has or can augment resources to remain afloat during the transition when strategies are being implemented. For the acquisition route, considerations of purchase price, the size relative to existing capacity, cultural fit, and ability to retain competent employees are critical.

Pricing of the product is significant because different premises may lead to conflicting implications. For example, an internally generated growth target may require a bank to ensure consistency of the transitional period with competition constraint. This consideration may necessitate keeping the price of the product low enough to keep the competition at bay while safeguarding its profitability target.[17] At the same time, when product differentiation or opaqueness is not anticipated to last long, the bank may want to cream the market, that is, charge a sufficiently high price that the market will bear.

12.5 Conclusion

This chapter has discussed three interactive areas that bear on a bank's survival and prosperity in a changing global environment: the distinct development phases of an economy; the different phases of a product life cycle; and the ability of a bank to access and augment resources needed to develop products and ensure profitability through entry in or exit from an economy or a product mix.

Naturally the purpose of the discussion has not been to provide a blueprint for strategy formulation – that would be presumptuous any way. Instead, as has been our intention throughout this book, it is to stimulate thinking for devising a sound strategy in the ever-changing global environments that create obsolescence for some banking products while desiring new ones in their place.

DISCUSSION QUESTIONS

1   Do you believe that perfect financial markets are incompatible with the survival of banks? Why?

2   What are the three aspects of bank strategy that are important for a bank's survival and prosperity?

3   What changes in global environments create challenges for a bank? How can a bank turn challenges into opportunities? Give successful as well as unsuccessful examples to illustrate your case.

4 What are the four phases of a product life cycle and their distinctive characteristics?

5 What relationship does a product life cycle have with the "life cycle" of an economy? What is the significance of these two cycles for a bank in formulating its strategy?

6 Explain and discuss how banks can play a critical role in short-term financing in the market.

7 What role do the commercial banks play in terms of the long-term financing of a business?

8 Why is there a difference between financing the long-term need vis-à-vis the short-term need of a non-financial business?

9 Suppose a firm facing long-term financing by its foreign subsidiary approaches a bank. The bank states it will be able to provide funds only on a short-term basis. The firm argues that the bank has provided it the short-term funding for domestic operations and rolled it over, thus effectively making a long-term loan. Why couldn't the bank do the same for its foreign subsidiary? If you were the bank manager approached by the business, what would you do?

10 What paramount considerations should a bank focus on while examining the scope and scale of its activities globally?

11 It is suggested that in an Internet distribution business like Amazon.com, there is a negative cash cycle, that is, cash is generated before the outflow takes place.

   a Is this a harbinger of the future?

   b What implications would such a trend have for banks concentrating on financing short-term needs of non-financial businesses?

12 Discuss the rationale for the current wave of cross-border bank mergers.

APPENDIX M: COST ANALYSIS FOR INTERNET TRANSACTIONS

The cost of a transaction requires consideration from the viewpoints of both the bank and its clientele.

Perspective of the Bank

For the bank, the transaction's profitability requires consideration of its full costing comprised of fixed and variable components. The challenge it faces is in determination of the fixed cost component, which should be ideally arrived at by determining

- the economic life (as against, say, physical or accounting life) estimate of the investment (e.g., the computer or the related programs); this estimate in turn will allow banks to estimate periodic charges based on economic life; and
- the expected transaction volume.

When the periodic charge is spread over the estimated volume, it will yield the proper fixed charge per transaction.

> *Example*: If the discounted cost of the computer and related items[18] is $77,816 today at 10 percent cost of capital, and the computer's useful life is five years, then an annual charge of $20,000 defrayed over an estimated average volume of 50,000 transactions would generate a fixed charge of $20,000/50,000 transactions = $0.40 fixed cost per transaction.
>
> It is obvious that variations in estimates of these items will produce a wide range of the applicable fixed charge.

The fixed cost estimate varies on two dimensions. The first is related to the source: the headquarters versus the branch. The second is related to the timing: front-end charge to be defrayed over the life (e.g., machinery or software purchase cost) versus periodic (e.g., annual repair and maintenance charges).

Alternative transaction modes have a different composition of branch-level versus headquarters-level fixed costs. The branch (subsidiary)-level component will dominate in the face-to-face transaction mode, whereas the headquarter-level component will dominate the Internet-based transaction. A proper treatment of these costs would likely lead to entirely different estimates from those where the fixed cost classification is ignored or lumped together irrespective of the source: a shift of fixed cost from the branch level to the headquarters level has a significant impact on maneuverability.

- In the short run, a shift of the fixed cost from the branch to the headquarter, for instance, allows a branch greater flexibility regarding pricing policy changes. This is because the branch will have to cover branch-based fixed cost (now lowered) and contribute positively to the headquarters-based fixed cost (now raised); hence, the short-run breakeven volume for the branch will be lower than before.
- In the long run, a branch closure keeps the breakeven volume of other surviving units constant with respect to the branch-level fixed cost burden (now avoided), but increases the breakeven volume because of redistribution of the headquarter fixed cost burden (that was previously borne by the closed branch) among other branches.
- The front-end fixed cost (entailed by, for instance, software development) replacing the periodic fixed cost (remuneration, for instance, for the staff that is replaced by the technology) also provides greater pricing flexibility in the short run by lowering the short-run breakeven volume.

Customer Perspective

From the customer's viewpoint, the cost should not just include what the bank charges, but also what the customer's own costs are for transacting the business.[19] For instance, the Internet transaction requires not only computer-based cost but also the incremental costs of a telephone connection and the fees charged by the Internet service provider. Thus, the bank providing Internet access to customers is also shifting a portion of its cost to the customer.

Synthesis

The above two steps allow the bank to determine (a) whether the undertaking will be profitable, and (b) whether it is also advantageous for the customer. The latter acts not only as a constraint but also has strategic implications. Suppose a bank finds that while the undertaking is profitable for itself, advantages of the new offering are only marginal for a majority of its customers. In that case, it may want to target the minority that would benefit from such an offering. It may find in the process that the targeted customer base is inadequate. Again, it may want to consider either abandoning the project or aggressively reaching out the potential customer base. In this sense, the financial analysis has important implications for the entry in a new venture, and on the marketing function in case it chooses to enter the fray.

NOTES

1 More precisely, imperfections would cease to matter if they have a uniform, proportionate impact on all participants. Thus taxes and transaction costs can coexist with competitive markets.
2 Germany has made tremendous progress in securitization since 1998.
3 Practitioners suggest that a major problem in civil-law oriented economies is the ambiguity concerning when a sale is a sale without recourse. A related problem is that the securitizing firm is supposed to notify all parties against whom it holds claims that their obligations are being transferred to an SPV.
4 Financial intermediaries "loaned" their credit through providing the borrowers standby letters of credit.
5 See, for instance, James and Houston (1996) and Rajan (1996) refuting the proposition that banking is a dying industry.
6 The bank could charge interest at regular rates on non-current balances, and was allowed to close the account when the outstanding balance, including interest charges, reached the collateral amount.
7 A constraint on a bank loan of maximum 5 percent bank equity has prevented banks from playing a significant role domestically in providing long-term funding to non-financial businesses.
8 Some observers also attribute investor reluctance to participate in the stock market to the structural impediment in the form of a lingering impact of the hyperinflation of the early 1920s.
9 Recent scandals in the USA involving firms such as Enron and WorldCom are exceptions, one hopes!
10 See Chapter 11 for a discussion on relationship and transaction orientations.
11 In the USA till the mid-1970s and in the UK till the mid-1980s, the relationship was still pivotal in the link between a bank and its customers; however, common law with its focus on the contract (rather than the civil law's focus on the environments or circumstances surrounding the agreement) tremendously facilitated the transition from relationship to transaction orientation.
12 Although the Internet and ownership of a computer have gone hand-in-hand thus far, it may not be so in future, as the current trend of the integration of telephones and televisions for "surfing" on the Internet were to gather momentum.
13 The reduction is constrained by the physical network of branches.
14 For instance, The Wit Capital, a cyberspace investment bank, helps small companies to raise capital without requiring huge fees by a Wall Street underwriting investment banking house such as Merrill Lynch.
15 It is conceivable that initially the acquisitions emanated from an urge to build an empire; and later (ex post) mediocre performance was rationalized by attributing it to the "learning" experience and building the desirable base of necessary skills for future.
16 The suit by Proctor & Gamble against Bankers Trust is an instructive example in this regard.
17 The theory of contestable markets focuses on this issue.
18 This cost is comprised of not just the initial equipment and program acquisition cost but also the present value of periodic operating charges, tax-based depreciation allowances, and repair and maintenance cost. It also encompasses – and is reduced by – the present value of the net salvage at the end of the asset's useful life.
19 A greater accuracy should also consider the savings from the avoided alternative (e.g., cost of physical commuting for transacting the business).

Glossary

Acceptance	A time draft that is accepted by a drawee. The party accepting a draft incurs the obligation to pay at its maturity.
Advised L/C	A letter of credit that has been analyzed by an advisory bank for its content.
Agency	The relationship between the principal and the agent (the party that acts on behalf of the principal).
Agency theory	The theory of the relationship between principals and agents. It involves the nature of the costs of resolving conflicts of interest between principals and agents.
Agent bank	A bank appointed in a syndicated credit to oversee the loan.
Airway bill of lading	Receipt for a shipment by air, which includes freight charges and title to the merchandise.
American option	An option may be exercised anytime up to the expiration date.
Arbitrage	Buying a security or asset in one market at a lower price and simultaneously selling it (security) in another market at a higher price without cost or additional risk.
Arbitrage pricing theory	An equilibrium asset pricing model where the expected return of a risky asset is a linear combination of various fundamental factors (the CAPM is a special case with one factor, the market portfolio).
Asian currency unit	A trading department of a bank in Singapore that has received a license from the monetary authorities in Singapore to deal in external currency deposits. (Also, a concept, corresponding to ECU or European Currency Unit, which would link currencies of member Asian countries to a common currency unit.)
Ask price	The price at which the dealer will sell a currency (also known as the offer price).
At-the-money option	An option whose exercise price is the same as the spot price.

Back-to-back loan	A loan by one business in a currency that allows it to obtain an equivalent loan in another currency; see "parallel loan" below.
Baker plan	A plan by US Treasury Secretary James Baker under which 15 principal middle-income debtor countries would undertake growth-oriented structural reforms in the 1980s.
Balance of payments	The net value of all economic transactions including trade in goods and services, transfer payments, loans, and investments between residents of one country with the rest of the world during a given period.
Balance of trade	The net flow of goods (i.e., export less import) of a country during a given period.
Bank capital adequacy	The minimum level of a bank's equity capital that can withstand various exposures, such as interest rate fluctuations and credit risk, the bank's activities entail without facing bank failure.
Bank holding company	A company which has a controlling influence over the management or policies of a bank or banks.
Bank for International Settlements (BIS)	An organization headquartered in Basel acting as a bank for the central banks. The BIS helps central banks manage and invest their foreign exchange reserves and also holds available reserves of central banks.
Bank syndicate	A group of banks that contribute the necessary financing for a loan.
Banker's acceptance	An agreement by a bank to pay a given sum of money at a future date. It is associated with a letter of credit in an international trade transaction.
Barter	Simultaneous exchange of real goods that avoid money exchange.
Basel Accord	An agreement among central banks in 1988 to establish standardized risk-based capital requirements for banks across countries.
Basket	A bundle of currencies.
Bear and bull spread strategies	Strategies employed to capture the profit potential of the ups or downs of a market.
Bid price	The price at which the dealer will buy a financial asset.
Bill of lading	A contract between a carrier and an exporter in which the former agrees to carry the latter's goods from port of shipment to port of destination. It serves as the export's receipt for the goods.
Black market	An unauthorized or illegal market that often arises when price controls or official rationing lead to price distortion.

Black–Scholes pricing theory	A pricing model for an option such as a call or put, defined in terms of five variables: the risk free rate, the variance of the underlying stock, the exercise price, the price of the underlying stock, and the time to maturity.
Brady bonds	New government securities issued under the Brady Plan whose interest payments were backed with money from the International Monetary Fund.
Branch	A bank unit providing loan and deposit services.
Bretton Woods Agreement	An international agreement signed in 1944 by governments. To maintain fixed exchange rates between their currencies and the US dollar.
Bridge financing	Bank financing for a designated period at the end of which it is replaced by pre-arranged medium- or long-term financing from other sources.
Brokered deposit	Deposit placed with an institution through a broker, who earns a commission or fee on the transaction.
Build-operate-transfer	A barter arrangement in which the investor builds the facility, operates it for a designated period and then transfers it to the local government or private entities.
Buy-back	A barter trade where construction of a manufacturing or processing facility by a company is at least partially paid for in products generated by the facility.
Call option	The right (not obligation) to buy a fixed number of securities (e.g., the number of common shares) at a stated price within a specified time.
Call premium	The price of a call option.
Capital account	The section in the Balance of Payments document depicting capital (both long- and short-term) flows between a country and the rest of the world for a given period.
Capital asset pricing model	An equilibrium asset pricing theory that shows the expected rate of return of a risky asset is a function of their covariance with the market portfolio.
Capital structure	Mix of various debt obligations and equity capital maintained by a firm. It is also called the financial structure.
Cash cycle	The time interval between cash disbursement and cash collection.
Certificate of origin	A document certifying the origin of goods for trade.
Clearing house	An organization that settles trades in a financial market.
Clearing House Interbank Payment Systems (CHIPS)	A bank-owned computerized network for settling business-to-business transactions, lining up about 140 depository institutions that have offices or affiliates in New York city.
Collar	A combination of a (long) cap and a (short) floor that limits the upside and downside of interest rate exposure within a

	defined band. An interest rate collar with both a cap and a floor of the same strike rate is equivalent to an interest rate swap.
Commercial paper	Short-term, unsecured promissory notes issued by a firm with a high credit standing. The maturity ranges up to 270 days in the US but longer in the Eurocurrency market.
Confirmed L/C	A letter of credit guaranteed by a third bank which assumes payment obligation upon default by the bank initiating the original L/C.
Convertible	A bond that can be converted by the holder into stocks
Convexity	Refers to the general shape of the price-yield curve.
Correlation	A standardized statistical measure of the linear relationship of two random variables. It is defined as the covariance divided by the standard deviation of two variables.
Correspondent bank	A bank that holds deposits for and provides services to another bank located in another geographic area on a reciprocal basis.
Counterparty	A party involved in a contractual arrangement.
Counter-purchase	Trading of two separate contracts, each specifying the commodity to be purchased by a party in a designated time.
Countertrade	A foreign trade transaction with at least a portion settled on a non-cash basis.
Country risk	The general level of political and economic uncertainty in a country affecting the value of loans or investments in that country. For a bank, country risk refers to the likelihood of debt default.
Coupon	The stated interest on a debt instrument or preferred stock.
Covariance	A statistical measure of the degree to which random variables move together.
Covered interest arbitrage	Movement of short-term funds between two currencies to take advantage of discrepancies in money and currency markets without taking risk.
Crawling peg	An automatic system for revising the fixed exchange rate at set intervals, according to a formula (such as adjustment due to changes in inflation rate) adopted by the authorities.
Credit scoring	A statistical technique assigning weights to relevant factors in order to determine whether to extend credit (and if so, how much) to a borrower or buyer desiring credit.
Creditor	Entity holding a claim on another entity.
Cross rate	The exchange rate between two foreign currencies, derived from their quotes in a third currency.
Cross-currency interest rate swap	An arrangement where two parties initially exchange principal amounts in two different currencies and agree to

(a) periodically pay interest based on those amounts at designated fixed or floating interest rates in respective currencies, and (b) re-exchange the principal amounts at maturity.

Cumulative probability The probability that a drawing from the standardized normal distribution will be below a particular value.

Currency board A system for maintaining the value of the local currency with respect to some other specified currency such as the US dollar.

Currency swap A transaction involving the exchange of cash flows in one currency for those in another with an agreement to reverse the cash flows at a future date(s) at designated exchange rates.

Current account One of the three sections in the balance of payment. It contains trade in goods and services, compensation related to financial investments, and unilateral transfers..

Cylinder option The payoff profile of a currency collar created through a bundle of a put and a call for different exercise prices. If the cylinder involves a long call (purchase) and a short put (sale), its value increases when the underlying asset's value increases; hence it is a "bull" cylinder. A short call and a long put lead to a "bear" cylinder.

Dealer market A market where traders specializing in a particular financial asset trade in that asset for their own account rather than on behalf of a third party. The interbank market is an example of the dealer market.

Debt-equity swap The sale of sovereign debt for US dollars to investors desiring to make equity investment in the indebted nation.

Default risk The chance that debt service obligation will not be met by the borrower on time or for the designated amount.

Derivative A financial instrument derived from an asset and whose value depends on the value of the underlying asset. Popular derivatives include swaps, forwards, futures, and options.

Devaluation A decrease in the spot value of a currency (in terms of the other currency) by decree of the government issuing that currency.

Direct quote A quote that gives the home currency price of a foreign currency.

Discount yield The yield on the futures contract, which is not the same as yield-to-maturity in bond value.

Down-and-in option An option that comes into existence if and only if the currency value hits a preset barrier.

Down-and-out option An option that expires if and only if the currency value hits a designated barrier. It is thus a knockout option that has a positive payoff to the option holder if the underlying currency strengthens.

Duration	The weighted average time of an asset's cash flows. The weights are determined by present value factors.
Duration analysis	A measurement of the sensitivity of the market value of a bank's assets and liabilities to changes in interest rates.
Economies of scale	A situation in which increasing production leads to a less-than-proportional increase in cost.
Edge Act corporation	A US bank subsidiary which is located in the USA that is permitted to carry on international banking and investment activities.
Eurobank	A bank that makes loans and accept deposits in foreign currencies, which are typically not subject to regulations and taxes.
Eurobond	An international bond sold primarily in countries other than the country in whose currency the issue is denominated.
Euro-commercial paper	Euronotes that are not underwritten.
Eurocurrency	Money deposited in a financial center outside of the country whose currency is involved.
Eurocurrency market	The set of banks that accept deposits and make loans in Eurocurrencies.
Eurodollar	A US dollar deposited in a bank outside the USA.
Euronote	A short-term note issued outside the country of the currency it is denominated in.
European CD	A certificate of deposit denominated in US dollars and issued by a bank not subject to the jurisdiction of US regulatory bodies.
European Monetary System	A monetary system for the member European countries under which the members had agreed to maintain their exchange rates within a specified range. This system was a precursor to the current single-currency Euro adopted by the qualified member countries.
European option	An option contract that may be exercised only on the expiration date.
Exchange controls	Restrictions placed on the transfer of a currency from one nation to another.
Exchange rate	Price of one currency in another currency.
Exchange risk	The volatility in a firm's value due to uncertain exchange rate movements.
Exercise price	The price at which the holder of an option can buy (in the case of a call option) or sell (in the case of a put option) the underlying commodity or financial asset. It is also called the strike price.
Export trade notes	A trade note originally held by the exporter who discounts them without recourse.

Export-Import Bank of the United States (Eximbank)	Chartered in 1945, it is an independent government agency to facilitate and finance US export trade when private financial institutions are unwilling to do so.
Factoring	Sale of a firm's accounts receivable (without recourse) to a financial institution known as a factor.
Financial innovations	The process of unbundling, bundling, transferring, and diversifying risk as well as creating new securities that exploit various tax, transaction and regulatory anomalies in order to lower the cost of financing.
Financial intermediaries	Institutions that provide the market function of matching borrowers and lenders or traders. Financial institutions collect funds from the public and place them in financial assets, such as deposits, loans, and bonds, rather than tangible property.
Financial markets	Markets where savings of lenders are allocated to meet the financial needs of borrowers.
Fisher Effect	The relationship between inflation expectations and the interest rate.
Fixed exchange rate	Exchange rate fixed by the government issuing the currency.
Floating currency	A currency whose value is set by market forces.
Floating rate note (FRN)	A medium-term (with a maturity typically between 2 to 7 years) issued with variable quarterly or semi-annual interest rate, generally tied to the LIBOR.
Foreign Credit Insurance Association (FCIA)	A co-operative effort of the Eximbank and a group of 50 leading marine, casualty, and property insurance companies that administers the US government's export-credit insurance program to protect US exporters against political and commercial risks.
Foreign direct investment	Foreign investment in and operating control of physical assets, such as plant and equipment, by a domestic company.
Foreign exchange market	A market in which arrangements are made today for future exchange of major currencies. It is used to hedge against major swings in foreign exchange rates.
Forfeiting	The discounting at a fixed rate without recourse of medium-term export receivables denominated in fully convertible currencies.
Forward contract	An arrangement calling for future delivery of an asset at an agreed price.
Forward discount	A situation where the forward rate is below the spot rate.
Forward market	A market dealing with transactions for future delivery of a currency at an agreed price.

Forward rate agreement	A cash-settled, over-the-counter forward contract allowing a company to fix an interest rate for a specified future period on a notional principal amount.
Forward transaction	A transaction to settle the trade at a specified future date.
Forward-forward	A set of two forward market transactions to be settled at two different future dates.
Futures contract	A contract that obligates traders to purchase or sell an asset at an agreed price on a specified date. It differs from forward contract in terms of standardization, exchange trading, margin requirement, and marked-to-market.
Gap management	A technique for protecting a financial institution's earnings from losses due to changes in interest rates by manipulating maturities of its interest-sensitive assets and liabilities.
Generalized autoregressive conditional	A time series model in which returns at each instant of time are normally distributed but volatility is a function of recent history of the series.
Glass–Steagall Act	The National Bank Act of 1933 that created the federal deposit insurance system and separated commercial from investment banking. Repealed in 1999.
Globalization	Internationalization or integration of the market.
Gold standard	A monetary system that links its currency with its stock of gold, and allows currency holders to convert the currency into gold or gold into the currency.
Gross domestic product (GDP)	The value of all final goods and services produced in the economy during the course of a year.
Group-5 (G-5)	Organization established in 1985 by five of the world's leading countries (France, Germany, Japan, the UK, and the USA) that meet periodically to co-ordinate economic policies.
Group-7 (G-7)	Organization established in 1985 to foster economic co-operation among countries represented by the G-5 plus Italy and Canada.
Group of 10 (G-10)	Also known as the Paris Club, established in 1962, that includes the wealthiest members of the IMF (G-7 plus Belgium, the Netherlands, and Sweden), who provide most of the money to be loaned and act as the informal steering committee; the name persists in spite of the addition of Switzerland in April 1984.
Hedge fund	A fund, usually for the exclusive clientele of wealthy individuals and institutions, that aims at improved returns through aggressive strategies that are unavailable to mutual

funds, including selling short, leverage, program trading, swaps, arbitrage, and derivatives.

Hedge ratio
The ratio of derivatives contracts to the underlying risk exposure.

Hedging
Taking a set of actions that eliminate a specific source of exposure arising from variability in an economic variable.

Immunized
Immune to interest rate risk.

Incoterms
International commercial terms (incoterms) are a set of benchmark definitions of trade terms extensively utilized by governments, legal authorities, and practitioners worldwide.

Indexed currency option note
A fixed rate issue where the bond holder, in return for a high coupon, will receive a reduced repayment of principal if the currency of denomination falls below a designated value.

Indication pricing schedule
The schedule for interest rate swap arrangement. Helpful for pricing swaps.

Indirect quotation
A quote that states value of a home currency unit in terms of a foreign currency.

Initial margin
Money required to establish a futures or options position so as to meet contract obligations.

Interbank Offer Rate (IBOR)
A benchmark loan rate, an average of the rates at which prime banks loan to other prime banks.

Interest equalization tax (IET)
A tax imposed by the US government on US residents who purchased foreign securities between 1963 and the end of 1973. This measure was undertaken to stem deterioration in the balance of payments due to capital outflows.

Interest rate floor
An option that protects the investor from a falling interest rate by guaranteeing the minimum interest rate.

Interest rate parity
An equilibrium condition that the interest rate differential in two currencies is equal to the forward differential in the two currencies.

Interest rate swap
An agreement between two parties to exchange fixed-for floating interest payments at designated intervals during a specific period on an agreed-upon principal amount.

Interest swap
A transaction involving periodic exchange of interest payments of fixed rate for floating rate in the same currency on an underlying notional principal amount.

International banking facility (IBF)
A bookkeeping entity of a US financial institution permitted to conduct international banking business and is exempt from domestic regulatory constraints.

International Fisher Effect
An equilibrium condition that the interest rate differentialin two currencies is equal to the exchange rate differential (i.e., the difference between the future and spot exchange rates).

International Monetary Fund (IMF)	A multilateral organization created at Bretton Woods, New Hampshire in 1944 to promote exchange rate stability. It, along with the World Bank, have broadened their mission to include rescue packages for national economic/financial crises that pose threats for the international financial system.
In-the-money	Describes an option whose exercise will entail profits.
Invisible trade balance	The net balance for trade in services.
Irrevocable letter of credit	An L/C that cannot be revoked or modified without consent of all parties concerned.
Knockout option	An option that expires if and only if the currency value hits a designated barrier. See also down-and-out option
Lead bank	The bank in charge of organizing a syndicated bank loan or a bond issue flotation.
Letter of credit (L/C)	A letter by a bank, at the initiative of a buyer of merchandise, to a seller, acknowledging to provide eventual payment of a stipulated amount under specified terms and conditions.
Leverage ratio	The ratio of debt to equity.
Leveraged buy-out (LBO)	Takeover of a company financed by significant amount of debt collateralized with the assets of the target company.
Life cycle of the economy	Different phases of an economy signifying growth and maturity as well as efficiency of its markets.
Life cycle of the product	Different phases of a product – from its introduction in the market to growth, maturity, decline and demise – each one with unique or special economic characteristics such as the nature of demand, supply, pricing, costing, and market responsiveness.
Line of credit	An arrangement under which a bank extends a specified amount of unsecured credit to a borrower who makes periodic payments against what has been actually borrowed. (When the credit amount is guaranteed, the borrower periodically pays a commitment fee on the unused credit.)
Liquidation	Selling all assets of a business and using the proceeds to satisfy creditors' claims according to their seniority.
Liquidity risk	The risk facing a bank when the liability holders' demand for cash requires liquidating assets at prices lower than current quotations.
London Interbank Bid Offer Rate (LIBID)	The deposit rate paid by a bank in the Eurocurrency market.
London Interbank Rate (LIBOR)	The loan rate on interbank transactions in the Eurocurrency market.

Long position	More assets than liabilities in a given item.
Maastricht Treaty	The agreement under which the European Community nations established a European Monetary Union with a single central bank having the sole power to issue a single European currency called the euro.
Maintenance margin	Collateral needed to maintain an asset position in a futures contract.
Managed float	An exchange rate system whereby the exchange rate appears to be floating but the government intervenes behind the scene to influence its movements.
Marked–to–market	Daily settlement of obligations on futures positions.
Market completeness	A market is complete if each state of the economy is matched by a security payoff.
Market impediments	Man-made or natural barriers that prevent the market from achieving competitiveness or efficiency.
Market maker	A brokerage or bank that stands ready, willing, and able to buy and sell specific security or financial asset at a publicly revealed bid and ask price for its own account and for its customer accounts.
Market portfolio	A pivotal concept, used in modern portfolio theory, which refers to a hypothetical portfolio containing every security available to investors in a given market in amounts proportional to their market values.
Merchandise account	Records trade in goods only (as against services or "invisible").
Modigliani and Miller's irrelevance proposition (MM)	A proposition that changes in the capital structure of a firm (or, more generally, financial policy changes) do not affect its value under perfect capital markets. An extension of this proposition would be irrelevance of financial intermediaries, given market participants' ability to replicate these intermediaries' functions without incurring significant cost.
Money market	Financial markets for debt securities with maturity less than one year.
Moral hazard	The risk that a change in the behavior of an economic entity in the wake of a contract (alleviating real or perceived potential costs) would lead to undesirable or unacceptable consequences for others.
Mortgage-backed security	A debt obligation that is backed by a bundle or pool of loans secured by mortgages.
Multicurrency clause	An option granted to a Eurocurrency borrower to switch from one currency to another when the loan is rolled over at an interest reset date.
Multi-option facilities	A loan facility granted to the borrower with options as (a) to issue medium-term Euronotes as well as short-term instruments such as bankers' acceptances and (b) to receive or pay in a variety of currencies.

National treatment	Suppose country A permits activities that are not permitted in country B. Then under the national treatment principle, country A will allow banks from country B to undertake activities prohibited in country B, so long as country B does not discriminate against banks from country A.
Note issuance facility (NIF)	A facility provided by a syndicate of banks that agrees to place, over a defined period, short-term notes issued by a borrower at the yield of a designated spread over LIBOR.
Ocean bill of lading	Receipt for a shipment by boat, which includes freight charges and title to the merchandise.
Official reserves	The amount of reserves owned by the central bank of a country in the form of gold, Special Drawing Rights, and foreign cash or marketable securities sometimes as backing for its own currency, but usually only for the purpose of possible future exchange market intervention.
Offset	A form of barter trade where purchase of a big-ticket item by an importing country entails an offset obligation for the supplier that may involve, for instance, hospital construction, technology transfer or licenses. Satisfaction of such obligations is often accomplished by third parties.
Offset clause	A provision under which a swap counterparty is absolved from its obligation when the other counterparty defaults.
Offshore banking center	A financial center where many of the financial institutions have little connection with that country's financial system. Usually established for purposes of tax or transaction cost avoidance.
Option	A right (not obligation) to buy or sell underlying assets at a fixed price at or by a specified date.
Option pricing theory	A theory initially proposed by Black and Scholes for deriving pricing formulae for calls, puts, or other contingent assets.
Out-of-the-money	An option that has no intrinsic value: a call option with a strike price above the current asset price, or a put option with a strike price below the current asset price.
Outright quote	A currency quote that includes all digits after the decimal point.
Overseas Private Investment Corporation (OPIC)	An agency of the US government that provides political risk insurance coverage to US multinationals. Its purpose is to encourage US direct investment in less-developed countries.
Over-the-counter market	An informal network of brokers and dealers for trading securities.
Par value	The stated value of the security such as a bond or stock.
Parallel loan	An arrangement involving two agreements whereby two companies from two different countries borrow each other's currency for a given period of time, in order to avoid currency controls.

Pegged currency	A currency whose value is set by the government.
Performance bond	A bond issued by an insurance company to guarantee satisfactory completion of a project by a contractor.
Peso problem	A situation where data drawn from a period will distort statistical inferences because of investors' anticipation of a catastrophe (generally an event with very low probability) that in fact did not materialize during that period.
Plain-vanilla	A security, especially bond or a swap, issued with standard features.
Position (market) risk	The risk associated with changes in market conditions affecting the asset-liability position held by a bank.
Price Sensitivity Hedge Ratio	The hedge ratio based on the price movement of the futures contract and the duration concept to hedge interest sensitive securities.
Private Export Funding Corporation (PEFCO)	A consortium of commercial banks and industrial companies, that provides, in cooperation with Eximbank, medium- and long-term fixed-rate financing for foreign buyers through the issuance of long-term bonds.
Product cycle theory	A theory suggesting patterns of foreign trade and foreign direct investment flows based on the product life cycle concept. A pivotal role is assigned to R&D for product and process innovations.
Proforma invoice	Document serving as a preliminary invoice, containing – on the whole – the same information as the final invoice, but not actually claiming payment.
Prospectus	The document that must usually be issued, following regulatory guidelines, by a company (or mutual fund) seeking to raise money from the public. It gives details of the financial and management status of the company, and explains the offer, including the terms, objectives (if mutual fund) or planned use of the money (if securities), and other information pertinent for investment decision.
Purchasing power parity (PPP)	A theory that exchange rates move so as to equate purchasing power among currencies.
Put-call forward parity	The relationship between put option, call option, and forward price.
Put call parity	The value of call and put are related according to a pre-specified relation.
Put option	The right to sell specified financial assets at a stated price during a specified time.
Quota	1 A government-imposed restriction on quantity, or sometimes on total value, of the goods. 2 The amount of money that each IMF member country is required to contribute to the institution. Countries have voting power in the IMF in proportion to their IMF quotas.

R^2	Square of the correlation coefficient proportion of the variability explained by the linear model.
Range forward	A contract that provides protection against currency movements outside a defined range.
Reciprocity principle	Suppose country A permits activities that are not permitted in country B. Then under reciprocity principle, country A will not allow banks from country B to undertake activities prohibited in country B, even though country B does not discriminate against banks from country A.
Reference rates	Benchmark rates used in floating interest rate transactions.
Representative office	Facilities established in a distant market by a bank in order to sell the bank's services and help its clients. These offices do not accept deposits or make loans.
Repurchase agreement	Short-term, often overnight, sales of government securities with an agreement to repurchase the securities back at a slightly higher price.
Rule 144A	The rule adopted by the Securities and Exchange Commission (SEC) in 1990 that allows "qualified institutional buyers" (QIBs) to trade in an unregistered private placement, making it a closer substitute for publicly traded issues.
Securitization	The pooling of a group of loans with similar characteristics and the subsequent sale in the resulting pool to investors.
Securitized asset	The bundle of assets of similar kind that is used as collateral for issuing an asset-backed security. The sale of the bundle results in the removal of the underlying loans from the selling institution's balance sheet.
Settlement	Conclusion or termination of an agreement by exchanging predefined commodities or currencies.
Shelf registration	A registration of a new issue which can be prepared up to two years in advance, so that the issue can be offered quickly as soon as funds are needed or market conditions are favorable.
Short hedge	Protecting the value of an asset held by selling a futures contract.
Smithsonian agreement	An agreement by the G-10 countries in December 1971 (a) to devalue the US dollar against gold, and (b) to use widened bands of $+/-2.25$ percent of par values in place of a single par value in an effort to salvage the Bretton Woods fixed exchange rate system.
Society for Worldwide Interbank Financial Telecommunications (SWIFT)	A computer network for facilitating funds transfer messages internationally for more than 900 member banks worldwide.
Special Drawing Rights	An artificial official reserve asset held on the books of the IMF.

Special purpose vehicle (SPV)	An entity created to transfer assets from the parent for obtaining securitized loans.
Speculation	Buy or sell in order to benefit from price movements unanticipated by the market.
Speculative efficient market (SEM) hypothesis	A hypothesis that the forward rate predicts the future spot rate.
Speculative motive	Inventory of cash or goods held in excess of (or below) that required for normal needs due to anticipation of higher acquisition cost or sales price.
Spot exchange rate	The exchange rate between two currencies for immediate delivery.
Spot interest rate	1 The yield on a zero-coupon Treasury obligation. 2 The interest rate on a loan transacted today.
Spot transaction	A transaction agreed upon and settled "today" (currency trades are settled with lags typically of one or two days).
Spreading	Simultaneous buy or sell of the same securities with different maturities.
Standard deviation	The positive square root of the variance.
Standardized normal distribution	A normal distribution with an expected value of 0 and a standard deviation of 1.
Structural impediments	Obstacles that are inherent in the system; e.g., cultural characteristics that discourage entrepreneurial activities; or, inadequate communications networks.
Subsidiary	A foreign-based affiliate that is a separately incorporated entity under the host country's law.
Swap	An exchange between two securities (or currencies). One type of swap involves the sale of a forward contract with a simultaneous agreement to buy another contract with a different maturity. Another type is an interest rate swap, in which one party agrees to pay a fixed interest rate in return for receiving a adjustable rate from another party.
Swap rate	1 The difference between the sale price and the repurchase price in a swap transaction. 2 The "swap rate" is the value of the fixed rate that equates the present value of the fixed payment leg with that of the floating rate leg, where periodic payments are determined by the forward rates (obtained from the zero-coupon yield curve).
Swap (rate) quote	The difference between the forward rate and the spot rate.
Switch	A counter-purchase agreement where the original exporter is allowed to transfer credit to a third party.
Systemic risk	Risk that an event will trigger loss of confidence in a financial system and in turn will induce adverse impact on the other parts of the economy.

Tariff	A tax imposed on imported products and services. It can be used to raise revenue, to discourage purchase of foreign products, or a combination of the two.
Term structure	Relationship between spot interest rates and maturities.
Trade balance	The net difference between export and import of merchandise.
Trade in services	The trade activities in the balance of payment related to services items.
Transaction motive	Inventory of cash or goods held to prevent activity disruption from mismatched inflows and outflows of the relevant asset.
Transferable L/C	A letter of credit that can be transferred to a third party.
Triangular arbitrage	To profit from a situation where the cross rate obtained for two currencies that are quoted in the third currency is not aligned with the corresponding actual spot rate.
Trust receipt	Evidence of transfer of title to goods to the lender bank.
Unbiased predictor of the forward rate	The condition refers to the expected future spot rate for a given day is equal to the corresponding forward rate.
Unilateral transfers	Accounting for government and private gifts and grants in the balance of payment document.
Universal banking	In the broadest sense, it allows a bank to be a conglomerate that offers a complete range of financial services; in a narrower sense, a bank can undertake both the commercial and investment banking activities.
Unsystematic risk	The risk unique to a particular security; risk that can be eliminated through diversification.
Value–at–risk (VAR)	A calculation which allows a financial institution to estimate the maximum amount it might expect to lose in a given time period with a certain probability.
Value date	The date when the value is given for funds deposited in the foreign exchange transaction between banks.
Variation margin	The gains and losses on open futures contracts calculated by marking the contracts to the market price at the end of each trading day. These gains or losses are credited or debited by the clearing house to each clearing member's account, and by members to their respective customer's accounts.
Wild-card option	The right of the seller of a Treasury Bond futures contract to give notice of intent to deliver at or before 8.00 p.m. Chicago time after the closing of the Exchange (3.15 p.m. Chicago time) when the futures settlement price has been fixed.
Wire transfer	An electronic transfer of funds from one bank to another that eliminates the mailing and check-clearing times associated with other cash transfer methods.
Working Capital Guarantee Program	A program conducted by the Eximbank, which encourages commercial banks to extend short-term export financing to eligible exporters. The Eximbank provides a guarantee in the loan's principal and interest.

World Bank	A bank established in 1944 to enhance economic development by providing loans to countries. Initially organized to provide project financing (for infrastructure projects that help alleviate poverty), it now has the broader mission that includes containment of national economic/financial crises with a potential for spillover elsewhere.
Yield to maturity	The interest rate that equates the present value of payments received from a credit market instrument with its value today.
Zero coupon bond	A credit market instrument issued at a price below its face value and promising only one payment at the maturity – no periodic cash flows in the interim.

References and Further Reading

Abuaf, N. and P. Jorion (1990) "Purchasing Power Parity in the Long Run," *Journal of Finance*, March, 157–74.

Adler, M. and B. Lehmann (1983) "Deviations from PPP in the Long Run," *Journal of Finance*, December, 1471–87.

Adler, M. (1983) "Designing Spreads in Forward Exchange Contracts and Foreign Exchange Futures," *Journal of Futures Markets*, 3, 355–68.

Agmon, T. and J.K. Dietrich (1983) "International Lending and Income Redistribution: An Alternative View of Country Risk," Journal of Banking and Finance, 483–95.

Aguilar, L. (1995) "A Current Look at Foreign Banking in the US and Seventh District," *Economic Perspectives*, Federal Reserve Bank of Chicago, January/February, 20–8.

Allen, F. and D. Gale (1995) "A Welfare Comparison of Intermediaries and Financial Markets in Germany and the US," *European Economic Journal*, 39, 179–209.

Barkas, J.M. (1987) "A Bank's Role in Facilitating and Financing Countertrade," in C.M. Korth (ed.), *International Countertrade*, New York: Quorum Books.

Barth, J.R., R.D. Brumbaugh, Jr, L. Ramesh, and G. Yago (1998) "The Role of Governments and Markets in International Banking Crises: The Case of East Asia," working paper, presented at the 73rd Annual Western Economic Association International Conference, Lake Tahoe, June 28–July 2.

Bekfaert, G. and R.J. Hodrick (1993) "On Biases in the Measurement of Foreign Exchange Risk Premiums," *Journal of International Money and Finance*, 12, 115–38.

Benston, G.J. and C.W. Smith (1976) "A Transaction Cost Approach to the Theory of Financial Intermediation," *Journal of Finance*, 31, 215–31.

Berger, A. and D.B. Humphrey (1990) "The Dominance of Inefficiencies Over Scale and Product Mix Economies in Banking," *Journal of Monetary Economics*, 28, 117–48.

Bhagwati, J. (1998) "The Capital Myth: The Difference between Trade in Widgets and Dollars," *Foreign Affairs*, May/June, 7–12.

Biger, N. and J. Hull (1983) "The Valuation of Currency Options," *Financial Management*, Spring, 24–52.

Bilson, J. (1981) "The 'Speculative Efficiency' Hypothesis," *Journal of Business*, July, 54, 435–51.

Bitner, J.W. with R.A. Goddard (1992) *Successful Bank Asset/Liability Management*, New York: John Wiley & Sons.

Black, F. (1975) "Bank Funds Management," *Journal of Financial Economics*, 2, 323–39.

Black, F. (1976) "The Pricing of Commodity Contracts," *Journal of Financial Economics*, 3, 167–79.

Black, F. and M. Scholes (1973) "The Pricing of Options and Corporate Liabilities," *Journal of Political Economy*, 637–59.

Blanden, M. (1993) "No Time for Risks," *Banker*, January, 24–7.

Boot, A., T. Milbourn, and A. Thakor (1998) "Expansion of Banking Scale and Scope: Don't Banks Know the Value of Focus?" Working paper, June, pp. 1–20.

Brainard, L.J. (1990) "Overview of East Europe's Debt: The Evolution of Creditworthiness in the 1980s," *Business Economics*, October, 10–16.

Brealey, R.A., I.A. Cooper, and M.A. Habib (1996) "Using Project Finance to Fund Finance to Fund Infrastructure Investment," *Journal of Applied Corporate Finance*, Fall, 9, 25–38.

Brewer, T. and P. Rivoli (1990) "Politics and Perceived Country Creditworthiness in International Banking," *Journal of Credit, Money and Banking*, 22, 357–69.

Brooks, J. (1987) *The Takeover Game*, New York: Truman Talley Books – E.P. Dutton.

Bussard, W.A. (1987) "An Overview of Countertrade Practices of Corporations and Individual Nations," in C.M Korth (ed.), *International Countertrade*, New York: Quorum Books.

Caesar, C.M. (1992) "Capital-Based Regulation and US Banking Reform," *The Yale Law Journal*, May 1525–49.

Cantor, R. and F. Packer (1995) *Sovereign Credit Ratings, Current Issues in Economics and Finance*, Federal Reserve Bank of New York, June, vol. 1(3).

Cantor, R. and F. Packer (1996) "Determinants and Impact of Sovereign Credit Ratings," *Journal of Fixed Income*, December, 76–91.

Channon, D.F. (1988) *Global Banking Strategies*, New York: John Wiley & Sons.

Cheung, Y.W. (1993) "Exchange Rate Risk Premium," *Journal of International Money and Finance*, April, 182–94.

Cheung, Y.W. and K.S. Lai (1993) "Long-Run Purchasing Power Parity During the Recent Float," *Journal of International Economics*, 34, 181–92.

Cheung, Y.W., H.G. Fung, K.S. Lai, and W.C. Lo (1995) "Purchasing Power Parity under the European Monetary System," *Journal of International Money and Finance*, 14, 179–89.

Chung, R. and H.G. Fung (1998) "The Asian Financial Crisis: A Credit Perspective," *Credit and Financial Management Review*, 3(3), 22–7.

Clifford, M. (1992) "Touch an ATM for the Money," *Banking in Asia, Far Eastern Economic Review*, September 24, 62–4.

Cornell, B. and M. Reinganum (1981) "Forward and Futures Prices: Evidence the Forward Exchange Markets," *Journal of Finance*, December, 1035–45.

Corsetti, G., P. Pesenti, and N. Roubini (1998) "What Caused the Asian Currency and Financial Crisis?" working paper that can be downloaded from www.stern.nyu.edu/~nroubini/asiaHomepgae.html.

Cosset, J.C. and J. Roy (1991) "The Determinants of Country Risk Ratings," *Journal of International Business Studies*, First Quarter, 135–91.

Dil, S. (1987) "Debt and Default: 200 Years of Lending to Developing Countries," *Journal of Commercial Bank Lending*, April, 38–48.

Dimson, E. and P. Marsh (1995) "Capital Requirements for Securities Firms," *Journal of Finance*, July, 821–51.

Documents of the International Organization of Securities Commissions (IOSCO) (1998) "Risk Management and Control Guidance for Securities Firms and their Supervisors," Committee of the Bank of International Settlement.

Donaldson, G. (1961) *Corporate Debt Capacity*, Division of Research, Graduate School of Business Administration, Harvard University, Boston.

Dropsy, V. and R.L. Solberg (1992) "Loan Valuation and the Secondary Market for Developing-Country Debt," in R.S. Solberg, *Country Risk Analysis*, London: Routledge.

Dufey, G. and I.H. Giddy (1994) *International Money Market*, Englewood Cliffs, NJ: Prentice Hall.

Edwards, F. and F.S. Mishkin (1995) "The Decline of Traditional Banking: Implications for Financial Stability and Regulatory Policy," *Federal Reserve Bank, New England, Economic Review*, July, 27–45.

Eun, C. and B. Resnick (1988) "Exchange Rate Uncertainty, Forward Contracts and International Portfolio Selection," *Journal of Finance*, March, 197–215.

Evans, J.S. (1992) *International Finance*, New York: Dryden Press.

Eyssell, T. and A. Nasser (1990) "The Wealth Effects of the Risk-Based Capital Requirement in Banking: The Evidence from the Capital Market," *Journal of Banking and Finance*, 14, 179–97.

Finnerty, J.D. (1988) "Financial Engineering in Corporate Finance: An Overview," *Financial Management*, winter, 14–33.

Forrester, J.P. (1995) "Role of Commercial Banks in Project Finance," *The Financier*, May, 2(2), 59–63.

Frankel, J.A. (1979) "On the Mark: A Theory of Floating Exchange Rates Based on Real Interest Rate Differentials," *American Economic Review*, September, 610–22.

French, K. (1983) "A Comparison of Futures and Forward Prices," *Journal of Financial Economics*, November, 311–42.

Fung, H.G. and S. Isberg, "The International Transmission of Eurodollar and U.S. Interest Rates," *Journal of Banking and Finance*, August 1992, 757–69.

Fung, H.G., S. Isberg, and W.K. Leung (1992) "A Cointegration of the Asian Dollar and Eurodollar Interest Rate Transmission Mechanism," *Asian Pacific Journal of Management*, October, 167–77.

Fung, H.G., W. Lee, and H. Jang (1997) "International Interest Rate Transmission and Volatility Spillover," *International Review of Economics and Finance*, 6, 67–75.

Fung, H.G. and W.K. Leung (1991) "The Use of Forward Contracts for Hedging Currency Risk," *Journal of International Financial Management and Accounting*, 3, 78–92.

Fung, H.G. and W.C. Lo (1992) "Deviations from Purchasing Power Parity," *Financial Review*, November, 553–70.

Fung, H.G. and W.C. Lo (1995) "An Empirical Examination of the Ex Ante International Interest Rate Transmission," *Financial Review*, February, 175–92.

Fung, H.G., W. Lee, and D.R. Mehta (1996) "Business Conditions, Expected Returns and Volatility of Bonds," working paper, Georgia State University.

Furlong, F.T. and M.C. Keeley (1991) "Capital Regulation and Bank Risk-Taking: A Note," *Economic Review (Federal Reserve Bank of San Francisco)*, Summer, 34–8.

Garman, M. and S.W. Kohlhagen (1983) "Foreign Currency Option Values," *Journal of International Money and Finance*, 2, 231–7.

Gartner, M. (1993) *Macroeconomics under Flexible Exchange Rates*, Hertfordshire: Harvester Wheatsheaf.

Geisst, C.R. (1995) *Investment Banking in the Financial System*, New Jersey: Prentice Hall.

Giddy, I., G. Dufey, and S. Min (1979) "Interest Rates in the US and Eurodollar Markets," *Weltwirtschaftliches Archiv*, 115(1), 51–67.

Goodman, L. (1998) "CBOs/CLOs: An Introduction," *Derivatives Quarterly*, Fall, 21–7.

Grabbe, J.O. (1991) *International Financial Markets*, New York: Elsevier Science Publishers.

Greenbaum, S.I. and Thakor, A.V. (1995) *Contemporary Financial Intermediation*, New York: Dryden.

Hakkio, C.S. (1992) "Is Purchasing Power a Useful Guide to the Dollar," Federal Reserve Bank of Kansas City, Third Quarter, 37–51.

Hanweck, G.A. and B. Shull (1993) "Interest Rate Risk and Capital Adequacy," *The Bankers Magazine*, September/October, 41–8.

Hartman, D.G. (1984) "The International Financial Market and US Interest Rates," *Journal of International Money and Finance*, April, 91–103.

Haubrich, J.G. and P. Wachtel (1993) "Capital Requirements and Shifts in Commercial Bank Portfolios," *Economic Review, Federal Reserve Bank of Cleveland*, 29, 2–15.

Hector, G. (1983) "The Bank's Latest Game: Loan Swapping," *Fortune*, December 12, 111–12.

Hempel, G.H., A.B. Coleman, and D.G. Simnson (1986) *Bank Management*, New York: John Wiley & Sons.

Hendershott, P.H. (1967) "The Structure of International Interest Rates: The US Treasury Bill Rate and the Eurodollar Deposit Rate," *Journal of Finance*, September, 455–65.

Hirshleifer, J. (1971) "The Private and Social Value of Information and the Reward to Inventive Activity," *American Economic Review*, 61, 561–74.

Hoshi, T. and A. Kashyap (1999) "The Japanese Banking Crisis: Where Did it Come From and How Will it End?" Social Science Research Network #171645 working paper.

Huang, R.D. (1989) "An Analysis of Intertemporal Pricing for Forward Exchange Contracts," *Journal of Finance*, March, 183–94.

Huang, R.D. (1990) "Risk and Parity in Purchasing Power," *Journal of Money, Credit and Banking*, August, 338–56.

Hull, J.C. (1993) *Options, Futures and other Derivative Securities*, New Jersey: Prentice Hall.

Jacklin, C. and S. Bhattacharya (1988) "Distinguishing Panics and Information-based Bank Runs: Welfare and Policy Economy," *Journal of Political Economy*, 96, 568–92.

Jackson, P., D.J. Maude, and W. Perraudin (1998) "Bank Capital and Value at Risk," Working Paper, Bank of England.

James, C. and J. Houston (1996) "Evolution or Extinction: Where Banks are Headed?" *Journal of Applied Corporate Finance*, Summer, 8–23.

Jarrow, R.J. and S.M. Turnbull (1995) "Pricing Derivatives on Financial Securities Subject to Credit Risk," *Journal of Finance*, March, 53–85.

Jensen, M. and W.H. Meckling (1976) "Theory of the Firm: Managerial Behavior, Agency Cost and Ownership Structure," *Journal of Financial Economics*, 3, 31–7.

Kaminsky, G. (1993) "Is There a Peso Problem? Evidence from the Dollar/Pound Exchange Rate," *American Economic Review*, June, 450–72.

Kaufman, G.G. (1985) "The Securities Activities of Commercial Banks," in R.C. Aspinwall and R.A. Eisenbeis (eds.), *Handbook for Banking Strategy*, New York: John Wiley and Sons.

Keeley, M.C. and F.T. Furlong (1991) "A Reexamination of Mean-Variance Analysis of Bank Capital Regulation," *Economic Review, Federal Reserve Bank of San Francisco*, Summer, 40–6.

Key, Sydney, J. (1985) "The Internationalization of US Banking," in R.C. Aspinwall and R.A. Eisenbeis (eds.), *Handbook for Banking Strategy*, New York: John Wiley and Sons.

Kim, D. and A.M. Santomero (1988) "Risk in Banking and Capital Regulation," *Journal of Finance*, December, 1219–31.

Kim, T. (1993) *International Money and Banking*, New York: Routledge.

Kim, Y. (1990) "Purchasing Power Parity in the Long Run: A Cointegration Approach," *Journal of Money, Credit and Banking*, November, 491–503.

Koch, T.W. (1992) *Bank Management*, Orlando, FL: The Dryden Press.

Kolb, R.W. (1991) *Understanding Futures Markets*, Florida: Kolb Publishing Company.

Kroner, K.F. and J. Sultan (1993) "Time-Varying Distributions and Dynamic Hedging with Foreign Currency Futures," *Journal of Financial and Quantitative Analysis*, December, 535–51.

Kwack, S.Y. (1971) "The Structure of International Interest Rates: An Extension of Hendershott's Tests," *Journal of Finance*, September, 897–900.

Leung, W.K. and H.G. Fung (1991) "A Pricing of Foreign Currency Investments," *Global Finance Journal*, 2, 99–118.

Levin, J.H. (1974) "The Eurodollar Market and the International Transmission of Interest Rates," *Canadian Journal of Economics*, May, 205–24.

Lintner, J. (1965) "The Valuation of Risk Assets and the Selection of Risky Investments in Stock Portfolios and Capital Budgets," *Review of Economics and Statistics*, February, 13–47.

Little, J. (1990) "Capital Adequacy: The Benchmark of the 1990s," *The Bankers Magazine*, January/February, 14–18.

Lo, W.C., H.G. Fung, and J. Morse (1995) "A Note to Euroyen and Domestic Yen Interest Rates," *Journal of Banking and Finance*, October, 1309–21.

Mahajan, A. and D.R. Mehta (1991) "Exchange Exposure Management and Efficiency of the Markets: Insights and Implications," *Managerial Finance*, 26, 36–44.

Mark, N.C. (1988) "Time-Varying Betas and Risk Premium in the Pricing of Foreign Exchange Contracts," *Journal of Financial Economics*, December, 335–54.

Markowitz, H. (1952) "Portfolio Selection," *Journal of Finance*, March, 77–91.

Marr, W. (1995) "The SEC and the Institutional Investor: Rule 415 and Rule 144a," *Journal of Investing*, Spring, 74–7.

Marshall, D. (1998) "Understanding the Asian Crisis: Systemic Risk as Coordination Failure," *Economic Perspectives, Federal Reserve Bank of Chicago*, Third Quarter, 13–28.

McCauley, R.N. and L.A. Hargraves (1987) "Eurocommerical Paper and US Commercial Paper: Converging Money Markets?" *Federal Reserve Bank of New York Quarterly Review*, autumn, 24–35.

Merton, R.C. (1973) "Theory of Rational Option Pricing," *Bell Journal of Economics and Management Science*, 141–83.

Merton, R.C. (1974) "On the Pricing of Corporate Debt: The Risk Structure of Interest Rates," *Journal of Finance*, 29, 449–70.

Merton, R.C. and Z. Bodie (1995) "A Conceptual Framework for Analyzing the Financial Environment," Working paper #95–062, Division of Research, Harvard Business School.

Mester, L. (1987) "Efficient Product of Financial Services: Scale and Scope Economies," *Federal Reserve Bank of Philadelphia, Business Review*, January/February, 15–25.

Mihaljek, D., A. Husain, and V. Cerra (1998) "People's Republic of China-Hong Kong Special Administrative Region: Recent Economic Developments," *IMF Staff Country Report* No. 98/41, April.

Millon-Cornett, M. (1988) "Undeterred Theft as a Social Hazard: The Role of Financial Institutions in the Choice of Protection Mechanisms," *Journal of Risk and Insurance*, December, 88(4), 723–33.

Modigliani, F. and Miller, M. (1958) "The Cost of Capital, Corporation finance and the Theory of Investment," *American Economic Review*, June, 261–97.

Nusbaum, D. (1997) "Seeing is Believing," *Risk*, 10, #9, September, 26–8.

Ozler, S. (1993) "Have Commercial Banks Ignored History?" *American Economic Review*, June, 608–20.

Perry, G. and L. Serven (2002) "The Anatomy of a Multiple Crisis: Why Was Argentina Special and What Can We Learn From It," working paper at World Bank, May (http://pages.stern.nyu.edu/~nroubini/asia/).

Radelet, S. and J. Sachs (1998) "The East Asian Financial Crisis: Diagnosis, Remedies, Prospects," working paper at Harvard Institute for International Development, April.

Rajan, R.G. "Why Banks Have a Future: A New Theory of Commercial Banking," *Journal of Applied Corporate Finance*, Summer, 114–28.

Rajan, R. and L. Zingales (1998) "Which Capitalism? Lessons from the East Asian Crisis," *Journal of Applied Corporate Finance*, Fall, 11, 40–8.

Rhee, S.G. and R.P. Chang (1992) "Intra-Day Arbitrage Opportunities in Foreign Exchange and Eurocurrency Markets," *Journal of Finance*, March, 363–79.

Robock, S.H. (1971) "Political Risk: Identification and Assessment," *Columbia Journal of World Business*, July/August, 6–20.

Roll, R. (1979) "Violations of Purchasing Power Parity and Their Implications for Efficient International Commodity Markets," in M. Sarnat and G.P. Szego (eds.), *International Finance and Trade*, 1, Cambridge, MA: Ballinger Publishing Company.

Saunders, A. (1988) "The Eurocurrency Interbank Market: Potential for International Crises?" *Federal Reserve Bank of Philadelphia, Business Review*, January/February, 17–27.

Saunders, A. (1997) *Financial Institutions Management*, Boston: Irwin.

Semones, C.A. and R.L. Solberg (1992) "Managing Non-performing Sovereign Assets," in R.L. Solberg (ed.), *Country Risk Analysis*, London: Routledge.

Shah, S. and A. Thakor (1987) "Optimal Capital Structure and Project Financing," *Journal of Economic Theory*, August, 42, 209–43.

Shapiro, A.C. (1992) *Multinational Financial Management*, Boston: Allyn and Bacon.

Shapiro, A.C. (1999) *Multinational Financial Management*, Boston: Allyn and Bacon.

Sharpe, W. (1964) "Capital Asset Prices: A Theory of Market Equilibrium Under Conditions of Risk," *Journal of Finance*, 19(3), 425–42.

Simon, J.D. (1992) "Political-Risk Analysis for International Banks and Multinational Enterprises," in R.L. Solberg (ed.), *Country Risk Analysis*, London: Routledge.

Smith, R.C. and I. Walter (1990) *Global Financial Services*, New York: Harper Business.

Stevens, E. (2000) "Evolution in Banking Supervision," *Federal Reserve Bank of Cleveland*, March 1.

Stiglitz, J. and A. Weiss (1981) "Credit Rationing in Markets with Imperfect Information," *American Economic Review*, 393–410.

Stoneham, P. (1996) "Whatever Happened at Barings? Part 2: Unauthorized Tradings and the failure of controls," *European Management Journal*, June, 269–78.

Swanson, P.E. (1988) "The International Transmission of Interest Rates: A Note on Causal Relationship between Short-term External and Domestic US Dollar Returns," *Journal of Banking and Finance*, 563–73.

Swanson, P. and S.C. Caples (1987) "Hedging Foreign Exchange Risk using Forward markets: An Extension," *Journal of International Business Studies*, Spring, 75–82.

Swoboda, A.K. (1982) "International Banking: Current Issues and Perspective," *Journal of Banking and Finance*, 6(3), 323–48.

Thapa, S.B. and D.R. Mehta (1991) "An Empirical Investigation of the Determinants of the Supply of Bank Loans to Less Developed Countries," *Journal of Banking and Finance*, 15, 535–57.

Thomson, J.B. (1989) "Bank Lending to LBOs: Risks and Supervisory Response," *Federal Reserve Bank of Cleveland, Economic Commentary*, February 15, 1–4.

Venedikian, H.M. and G.A. Warfield (1992) *Export-Import Financing*, New York: John Wiley & Sons, Third Edition.

Wagster, J. (1996) "Impact of the 1988 Basle Accord on International Banks," *Journal of Finance*, 1321–46.

Walter, I. and R.C. Smith (1990) *Investment Banking in Europe*, Cambridge: Blackwell.

Wolff, C.C.P. (1987) "Forward Foreign Exchange Rates, Expected Spot Rates, and Premia: A Signal-Extraction Approach," *Journal of Finance*, June, 395–406.

Zagorski, D. and J. McPartland (1999) "Multicurrency Regulatory Encumbrances Affecting US Futures Industry," *Derivative Quarterly*, Summer, 11–20.

Zamora, A.J. (1990) *Bank Contingency Financing: Risks, Rewards, and Opportunities*, New York: John Wiley & Sons.

Index